Houghton Mifflin Science

DISCOVERYWORKS

 HOUGHTON MIFFLIN

Boston • Atlanta • Dallas • Denver • Geneva, Illinois • Palo Alto • Princeton

Authors

William Badders
Elementary Science Teacher
Cleveland Public Schools
Cleveland, OH

Lowell J. Bethel
Professor of Science Education
The University of Texas at Austin
Austin, TX

Victoria Fu
Professor of Child Development
and Early Childhood Education
Virginia Polytechnic Institute and
State University
Blacksburg, VA

Donald Peck
Director (retired)
The Center for Elementary Science
Fairleigh Dickinson University
Madison, NJ

Carolyn Sumners
Director of Astronomy and Physical Sciences
Houston Museum of Natural Science
Houston, TX

Catherine Valentino
Author-in-Residence, Houghton Mifflin
West Kingston, RI

Acknowledgements appear on page H46, which
constitutes an extension of this copyright page.

Printed in the U. S. A.

ISBN 0-395-98681-8

4 5 6 7 8 9 10 RRD 08 07 06 05 04 03 02 01 00

CONTENTS

THINK LIKE A SCIENTIST

UNIT A — Systems in Living Things

THINK LIKE A SCIENTIST

CHAPTER 1 — Life Processes   A4

CHAPTER 4   Living in Space   B74

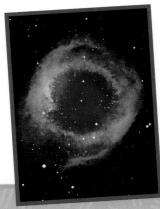

Matter and Energy

UNIT D   Populations and Ecosystems

THINK LIKE A SCIENTIST
BLOOMING DESERT

CHAPTER 1   Living Things and Environments   **D4**

The Solid Earth

THINK LIKE A SCIENTIST

CHAPTER 3

Earth's Structures   E64

UNIT F Light and Sound

THINK LIKE A SCIENTIST
BRILLIANT SOUND F2

CHAPTER 1 Properties of Light F4

Light, Lenses, and Color   F28

SCIENCE and MATH TOOLBOX

THINK LIKE A SCIENTIST

HOW TO THINK LIKE A SCIENTIST

Make Observations

To think like a scientist, learn as much as you can by observing things around you. Everything you hear, smell, taste, touch, and see is a clue about how the world works. As you test your ideas, you'll continue to make careful observations.

Make Observations

Ask a Question

Look for patterns. You'll get ideas. For example, you notice that you get static electric shocks on certain days but not on others. Ask questions such as this.

What conditions change from day to day that would affect static electric shock?

Make a Hypothesis

Make Observations

If you have an idea about why something happens, make an educated guess, or hypothesis, that you can test. For example, suppose your hypothesis is that static electric shock is more likely to occur on dry days than on humid ones.

Plan and Do a Test

Plan how to test your hypothesis. Your plan would need to consider some of these problems.

How will you measure daily humidity?

How will you test for the presence of static electric shock?

Then test your hypothesis.

Record and Analyze

When you test your idea, you need to observe carefully and record, or write down, everything that happens. When you finish collecting data, you may need to do some calculations with it. For example, you may need to compare the frequency of static electric shock to daily humidity.

Make Observations

Draw Conclusions

Whatever happens in a test, think about all the reasons for your results. Sometimes this thinking leads to a new hypothesis. For example, besides humidity, might other weather conditions affect the frequency of static electric shock? If the frequency of static shocks increases as humidity decreases, what other weather conditions might affect static shocks?

Make Observations

Now read "Mmmmm, Smells Good . . ." to see scientific thinking in action.

THINK LIKE A SCIENTIST

PRACTICE THINKING LIKE A SCIENTIST

Mmmmm, Smells Good...

Make Observations

Carmen and Lou were on their way to lunch. As they walked into the school cafeteria, Carmen inhaled.

"Mmmmm, smells good, like freshly-made pizza. Just what I'm in the mood for," Carmen said. Lou sniffed and shook his head. "I can't smell anything. I have a cold."

The students sat and began eating their pizza. After a few bites, Lou told Carmen that he couldn't taste a thing—not the cheese, nor the onions and peppers, nor even the tomato sauce.

To learn about the world, you observe it. **Observations** can be made with any of the senses—sight, hearing, touch, taste, or smell.

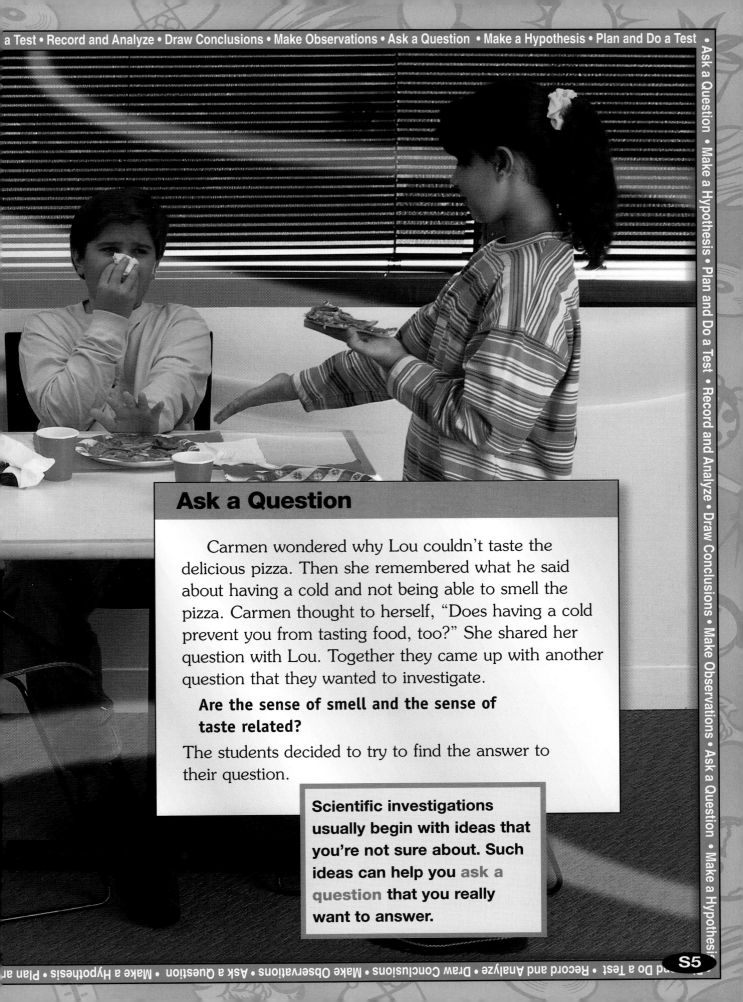

Ask a Question

Carmen wondered why Lou couldn't taste the delicious pizza. Then she remembered what he said about having a cold and not being able to smell the pizza. Carmen thought to herself, "Does having a cold prevent you from tasting food, too?" She shared her question with Lou. Together they came up with another question that they wanted to investigate.

Are the sense of smell and the sense of taste related?

The students decided to try to find the answer to their question.

Scientific investigations usually begin with ideas that you're not sure about. Such ideas can help you ask a question that you really want to answer.

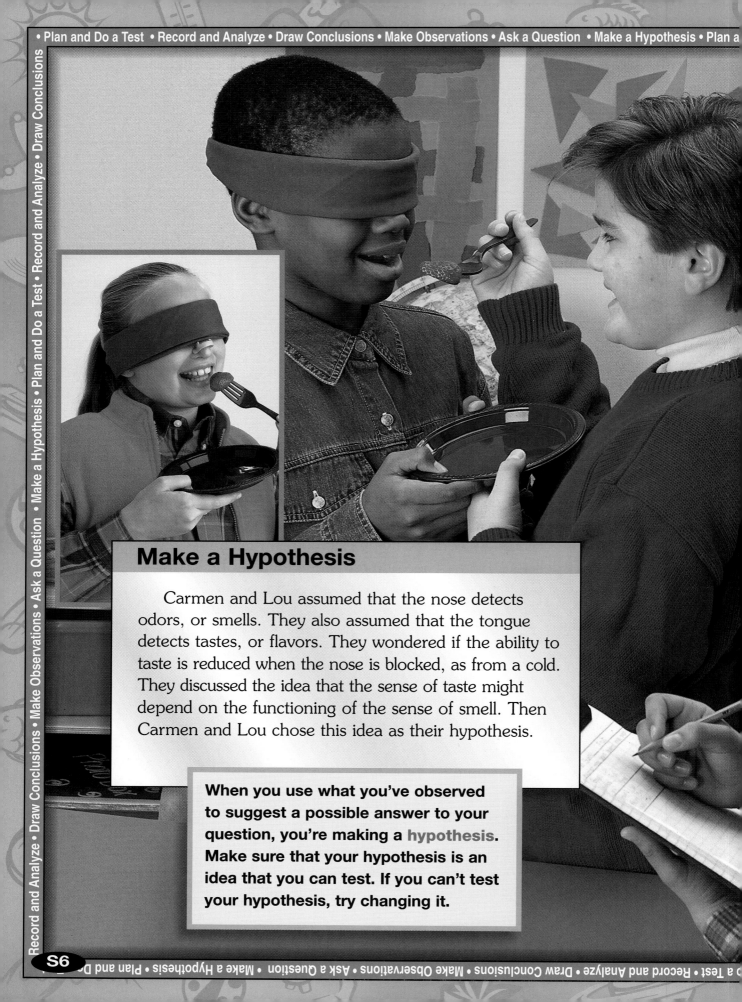

Make a Hypothesis

Carmen and Lou assumed that the nose detects odors, or smells. They also assumed that the tongue detects tastes, or flavors. They wondered if the ability to taste is reduced when the nose is blocked, as from a cold. They discussed the idea that the sense of taste might depend on the functioning of the sense of smell. Then Carmen and Lou chose this idea as their hypothesis.

When you use what you've observed to suggest a possible answer to your question, you're making a hypothesis. Make sure that your hypothesis is an idea that you can test. If you can't test your hypothesis, try changing it.

Plan and Do a Test

Carmen and Lou designed an experiment to test their hypothesis. They cut up four different fruits—banana, strawberry, orange, and peach—into small, equal-sized samples. They set up two groups of three students each.

Students in Group 1 were blindfolded and asked to taste and identify a sample of each fruit. As each group member tasted the samples, only Carmen and Lou were present. This kept the other group members from hearing the responses.

Students in Group 2 were also blindfolded. In addition these students wore a nose clip, the kind used by swimmers. The nose clip blocked their sense of smell as they tasted and tried to identify the fruit samples. Again, only Carmen and Lou were present for this part of the test.

One way to try out your hypothesis is to use a test called a controlled experiment. The setups in this kind of experiment are identical in all ways except one. The one difference is the variable. In Carmen and Lou's experiment the variable is the use of the nose clip.

Record and Analyze

As each blindfolded student tried to identify a fruit, Carmen and Lou recorded their responses. They used a chart like the one shown to keep track of the data from the experiment.

Next, Carmen and Lou carried out their experiment two more times with different groups. When they analyzed all the data they noticed that the results each time were similar.

When you do an experiment, you make observations so that you can obtain information called data. You need to write down, or record, this data and then organize it. Graphs and tables are ways to organize data. Analyze the information that you collect by looking for patterns. To see if your results are reliable, repeat the experiment several times.

Taste Test

✔ = correct
✗ = incorrect

	Students tested	Fruit			
		banana	strawberry	orange	peach
Group 1 (blindfold only)	Jill	✔	✔	✔	✔
	Rick	✔	✔	✗	✗
	Marna	✔	✗	✔	✔
Group 2 (blindfold and nose clip)	Sal	✗	✗	✗	✔
	Erin	✔	✗	✗	✗
	Toni	✗	✗	✗	✗

Draw Conclusions

From the information that they collected, Carmen and Lou concluded that the results of their experiment supported their hypothesis. When a person's nose is blocked, as from a cold, the sense of taste and the sense of smell are affected.

After you have analyzed your data, you should use what you learned to draw a conclusion. A **conclusion** is a statement that sums up what you learned. The conclusion should be about the hypothesis you made. A hypothesis supported by a lot of evidence may be called a **theory**.

USING SCIENCE PROCESS SKILLS

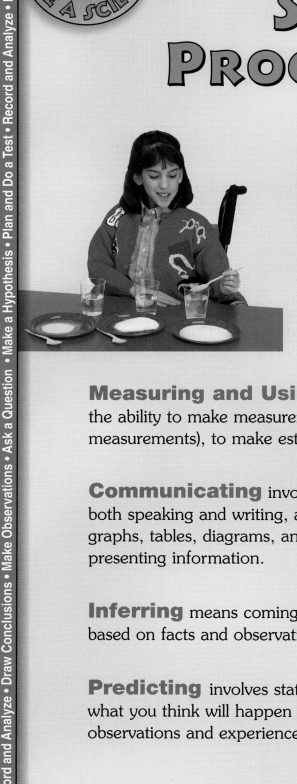

Observing involves gathering information about the environment through your five senses—seeing, hearing, smelling, touching, and tasting.

Classifying is grouping objects or events according to common properties or characteristics. Often you can classify in more than one way.

Measuring and Using Numbers involves the ability to make measurements (including time measurements), to make estimates, and to record data.

Communicating involves using words, both speaking and writing, and using actions, graphs, tables, diagrams, and other ways of presenting information.

Inferring means coming to a conclusion based on facts and observations you've made.

Predicting involves stating in advance what you think will happen based on observations and experiences.

Collecting, recording, and interpreting data

all involve gathering and understanding information. This skill includes organizing data in tables, graphs, and in other ways. Interpretation includes finding patterns and relationships that lead to new questions and new ideas.

Identifying and controlling variables

involves determining the effect of a changing factor, called the variable, in an experiment. To do this, you keep all other factors constant, or unchanging.

Defining operationally

means to describe an object, an event, or an idea based on personal observations. An operational definition of a plant might be that it is a green living thing that is attached to soil and that does not move around.

Making a hypothesis

is suggesting a possible answer to a question or making an educated guess about why something happens. Your hypothesis should be based on observations and experiences.

Experimenting

is testing your hypothesis to collect evidence that supports the hypothesis or shows that it is false.

Making and using models

includes designing and making physical models of processes and objects, or making mental models to represent objects and ideas.

READING TO LEARN

RESOURCE

Before You Read

1. **Scan** each page.
   - titles
   - subheads
   - highlighted words
   - photos and illustrations
   - captions

2. **Identify** the main topic.

3. **Ask** yourself what you know about the topic.

4. **Predict** what you will learn by turning subheads into questions.

Wanderers in the Night Sky

Reading Focus What is the difference between a star and a planet?

Other than the Sun and the Moon, most of the objects in the night sky look about the same to the unaided eye. They all seem to be just tiny points of light. Are all of those shiny objects stars? If not, what are they? And how can you tell which ones are which?

You can begin to answer these questions yourself by simply looking a little bit longer and a little more closely at those points of light in the sky. If you do, you'll soon realize that they are *not* all exactly alike.

A Different Sort of "Star"

Have you ever seen the "morning star"? This is an object that seems to be a very bright star. It can be seen at certain times on the eastern horizon (hə-rī'zən), just before the Sun rises. The

horizon is the line formed where the Earth and sky seem to meet. If you look closely at this bright object, it seems to shine with a steady light. Almost all the other "stars" seem to twinkle.

If you observe the morning star through a telescope, it will no longer look like a tiny point of light. Instead you'll see a small round disk. This object, in fact, has phases like the Moon does, so you might see either a fairly full disk or a thin crescent.

If you use a more powerful telescope to observe the morning star, you'll see a larger disk. But no matter how powerful your telescope is, most of the other stars in the sky will still appear to be just tiny points of light.

If you look for the morning star several days in a row, you'll notice something else. It's moving! And it's moving not just *along with* all the other stars, but *in relation to* the other stars, including the Sun.

Over a period of weeks, you'll see the morning star move closer and closer to the Sun until it disappears in the Sun's glare. Then something even more interesting happens. The same object reappears in the west just after sundown as the evening star!

▲ The "morning star"

B16

Scientists use scientific methods when they do experiments. They also use special methods when they read to learn. You can read like a scientist, too. Just follow the steps below.

▲ The Sun, Moon, and planets appear to move in the same narrow band across the sky.

Of all the starlike objects easily seen by the unaided eye, only five are like the morning star. That is, they shine steadily rather than twinkle, appear in a telescope as disks rather than points of light, and move against the backdrop of the other stars.

These five objects share one other trait with the morning star. They can only be seen in a certain part of the sky. Although they all move, these "stars" appear only in a narrow band. That band is roughly the same as the path of the Sun and the Moon across the sky.

The Wandering Planets

The ancient Greeks called these five special objects "wandering stars." In English, we call them *planets*—a name that comes from the Greek word for

"wanderer." These five objects—and a few others like them that are not easily seen by the unaided eye—are really in a different class from stars. They are planets.

A **star** is a huge globe of hot gases that shines by its own light. The Sun is a star. It just appears bigger because it's much closer to Earth than are other stars. A **planet** is a large object that circles a star and does *not* produce light of its own. We can see planets only because they reflect sunlight.

The morning and evening star is really Venus, one of nine known planets that revolve around our Sun. Until very recently, scientists thought there were only nine planets in the universe. By 1998, however, astronomers had discovered 13 planets circling other nearby stars. ■

INVESTIGATION 1 WRAP-UP

REVIEW

1. How do a star and a planet differ?

2. What motion of the Earth causes the Sun to seem to rise and set each day?

CRITICAL THINKING

3. The constellation Leo is visible in the east on a January evening but in the west on a July evening. Explain why.

4. Explain why the Earth has seasons.

B17

SAFETY

The best way to be safe in the classroom and outdoors is to use common sense. Prepare for each activity before you start it. Get help from your teacher when there is a problem. Always pay attention.

Stay Safe From Stains

- Wear protective clothing or an old shirt when you work with messy materials.
- If anything spills, wipe it up or ask your teacher to help you clean it up.

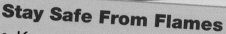

Stay Safe From Flames

- Keep your clothes away from open flames. If you have long or baggy sleeves, roll them up.
- Don't let your hair get close to a flame. If you have long hair, tie it back.

Make Wise Choices About Materials

- Use only the amount of material you need.
- Recycle materials so they can be reused.
- Take care when using valuable tools so they can be used again.

Stay Safe From Injuries

- Protect your eyes by wearing safety goggles when you are told that you need them.
- Keep your hands dry around electricity. Water is a good conductor of electricity, so you can get a shock more easily if your hands are wet.
- Be careful with sharp objects. If you have to press on them, keep the sharp side away from you.
- Cover any cuts you have that are exposed. If you spill something on a cut, be sure to wash it off immediately.
- Don't eat or drink anything unless your teacher tells you that it's okay.

Stay Safe During Cleanup

- Wash up after you finish working.
- Dispose of things in the way that your teacher tells you to.

HAIR Keep it out of the way of a flame.

EYES Wear safety goggles when you are told to.

MOUTH Don't eat or drink ANYTHING unless your teacher tells you it's okay.

HANDS Keep your hands dry around electricity. Cover any cuts. Wear gloves when told to. Wash up after you finish.

DON'T MAKE A MESS If you spill something, clean it up right away. When finished with an activity, clean up your work area. Dispose of things in the way your teacher tells you to.

CLOTHES Keep long sleeves rolled up. Protect yourself from stains. Stay away from open flames.

MOST IMPORTANTLY

If you ever hurt yourself, or one of your group members gets hurt, tell your teacher right away.

UNIT
A

Systems in Living Things

Theme: Systems

THINK LIKE A SCIENTIST

BREATHING SPACE

You are looking inside the gas-exchange organ of the human body—the lung. In this magnified image, you can see some of the many tiny sacs (the dark spaces) that fill with air each time you breathe. The orange-colored spheres are red blood cells, which pick up oxygen from the lungs. The lungs are just one of the many kinds of organs that work together in the body to keep you alive and healthy.

THINK LIKE A SCIENTIST

Questioning In this unit you'll study the life processes and systems of plants and animals. You'll investigate questions such as these.

- What Is a Living Thing?
- How Does the Respiratory System Work?

Observing, Testing, Hypothesizing In the Activity "Lung Power," you'll observe a working model of a lung. You'll also hypothesize what happens in your body when you breathe.

Researching In the Resource "Breathing Basics," you'll gather more information about the parts of the respiratory system and how the parts work together.

Drawing Conclusions After you've completed your investigations, you'll draw conclusions about what you've learned— and get new ideas.

CHAPTER 1

LIFE PROCESSES

How can you tell the difference between a living thing and a nonliving thing? What are the parts of a plant? of an animal? Which systems of living things allow them to eat, grow, and repair injured parts? In this chapter you'll explore the answers to these questions.

Connecting to Science
ARTS

Topiary Artist Linda Rodriguez has an unusual job. She creates animals from plants! The animals that Linda Rodriguez creates are sculptures called topiaries (tō′pē er ēz). She is a topiary artist for the San Diego Zoo. Her job is to make sculptures of lions, tigers, bears, and other zoo animals. She makes her sculptures in two different ways. Sometimes she allows bushes to grow. Then she snips the bushes into different animal shapes. Other times she begins with a hollow mesh frame. She packs the frame tightly with moss and then roots ivy in the moss. As the ivy grows, Linda Rodriguez cuts and trains the growing plants to the shape of the frame. Her knowledge of living things— both plants and animals—helps make her creations realistic as well as fun!

Coming Up

◄ Linda Rodriguez sculpts an ivy-covered animal.

WHAT IS A LIVING THING?

Can you tell whether something is alive just by looking at it? Seeds appear lifeless, but they can grow into giant trees. Some silk flowers look very much alive. Yet, when you touch them, you know they are fakes. In this investigation you'll explore the main features that make living things different from nonliving things.

Activity

Alive or Not?

What information do you need to determine if something is alive or not? In this activity you'll become a detective. Your job will be to ask the right questions to learn if something is a genuine living thing or if it is a clever fake.

MATERIALS
• *Science Notebook*

Procedure

1. Look at the pairs of photos on this page and on A7. You'll need to decide which photo in each pair shows something that is alive.

B2

B1

A1

A2

2. **Observe** each pair of photos carefully. In your *Science Notebook,* **record** a general description of the objects in each pair. Be sure to identify both the letter and number of the object you are describing.

C2

3. For each pair of objects, look for clues that suggest which of the pair is alive. **Talk with your group** and together **brainstorm** a list of questions about each pair of objects. The questions should help you decide whether each object is alive or not.

4. Make a list of tests you could carry out to find out whether the objects are alive or not. **Describe** the tests you would carry out for each pair of objects.

C1

Analyze and Conclude

1. In your *Science Notebook,* make a chart that lists the tests your group came up with for step 4. In the chart, explain how each test would help you know which object in each pair was alive and which was not.

 *See* SCIENCE *and* MATH TOOLBOX *page H11 if you need to review **Making a Chart to Organize Data.***

2. Have one member of your group list six things, some of which are living and some of which are nonliving. Decide whether your tests could help identify each thing as living or nonliving.

3. Based on the results of this activity, **make a generalization** about what characteristics, or traits, distinguish living things from nonliving things.

D2

D1

E1

E2

Activity

Observing Plant Cells

The part of the onion you eat is actually a ball of leaves called a bulb. Onions, like all plants, are made up of basic units called cells. Look at an onion through a microscope to see what plant cells look like.

- -

Procedure

1. Take a section of an onion and snap it in half. A thin piece of skin should separate from the section. Peel this piece off with tweezers, as shown below.

2. Place the onion skin on a microscope slide. Add one drop of iodine solution. Use a toothpick to smooth out the wrinkles. Cover the onion skin with a cover slip.

See **SCIENCE** and **MATH TOOLBOX** page H2 if you need to review *Using a Microscope.*

MATERIALS

- goggles
- onion
- tweezers
- microscope slide
- iodine solution
- toothpick
- cover slip
- microscope
- *Science Notebook*

SAFETY

Wear goggles during this activity. Be careful when handling glass slides. Iodine will stain clothing and is poisonous if swallowed.

Step 1

Step 2

3. Observe the onion skin under a microscope at low power and draw what you see in your *Science Notebook*. Then observe the skin under high power and draw what you see.

4. The small circular structure that turned deep red inside the onion cell is called a nucleus (noō′klē əs). Label the nucleus in your drawings.

5. The boundary of the cell is called the cell wall. Label the cell wall in your drawing.

Step 3

Analyze and Conclude

1. Like all living things, plants are made of cells. Describe the appearance of the cells that you observed.

2. A cell wall is found only in plant cells, not in animal cells. Hypothesize what job the cell wall has.

3. Suppose you looked through a microscope at cells from an unknown living thing. How could you tell whether you were looking at plant cells or animal cells?

INVESTIGATE FURTHER!

EXPERIMENT

Use a dropper to add two drops of water to a microscope slide. Place a single *Elodea* leaf in the water and cover it with a cover slip. Observe the leaf under a microscope's low power. Then study the leaf under high power and make a sketch of what you see. Describe any structures that you see in the leaf cell that you did not see in the onion cell in the activity. Infer what the functions of such structures are, based on the leaf's role in a plant.

It's Alive!

Living things are all around you. Every tree, every blade of grass, and *every* insect is alive. Scientists have found life on the highest mountains and in the deepest oceans. They have discovered life on bare rocks and in snowbanks.

Alive—Or Not?

As the activity on pages A6 and A7 shows, it can be difficult to tell whether an object is living or nonliving. Montana moss agate (ag'it), for example, has fooled many people. This rock contains green streaks that "grow" and are often mistaken for moss or roots. The streaks are actually mineral crystals. The crystals grow, but not the way that living things grow.

▲ **Moss agate, a kind of rock. Moss agate as seen through a microscope (*inset*) .**

Look closely at the objects in the ocean beach scene below. Which ones do you think are alive?

Many of the seemingly lifeless objects in this scene are really alive. ▼

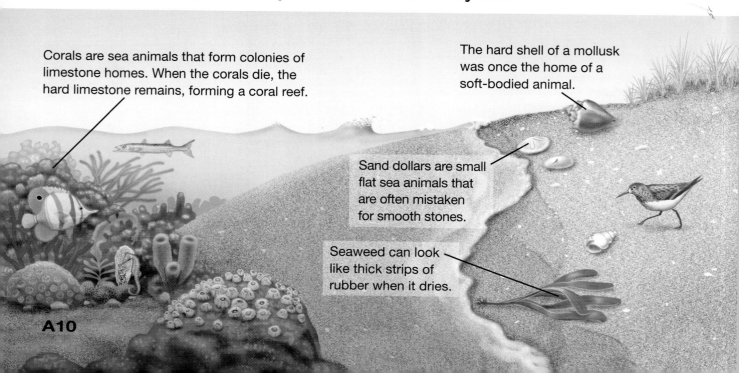

Corals are sea animals that form colonies of limestone homes. When the corals die, the hard limestone remains, forming a coral reef.

The hard shell of a mollusk was once the home of a soft-bodied animal.

Sand dollars are small flat sea animals that are often mistaken for smooth stones.

Seaweed can look like thick strips of rubber when it dries.

Life Processes

A **cell** is the basic unit of living things. Some simple organisms consist of only one cell. Most living things are composed of many cells. These cells work together to carry out the life processes of that organism. **Life processes** are the functions that a living thing must carry out in order to stay alive and produce more of its own kind.

Living things, as you have seen, can sometimes look like they are nonliving. What trait separates living from non-living things? A living thing carries out basic life processes. For example, all living things must take in **nutrients** (noo'trē ənts), which are substances that are needed for an organism to live and grow. Living things also increase in size and change in other ways during their life cycle.

The basic life processes are listed in the table that follows. Examples are given of how plants and animals carry out these processes. Look for ways that the life processes are alike and different in plants and animals.

Comparing Life Processes

Life Process	Plants	Animals
Taking in materials, such as nutrients and gases	Take in carbon dioxide from air and take in water and minerals from soil	Take in oxygen from the air and nutrients from the food they eat
Releasing energy in food to carry out life processes	Release energy from the food they make	Release energy from the food they eat
Giving off wastes	Give off oxygen as a waste product of food making; also give off carbon dioxide and water as waste products	Give off carbon dioxide and other waste products
Reacting to surroundings	Stems grow toward a source of light; roots grow toward a source of water.	Move to find food, water, and suitable temperatures
Growing and developing	Increase in size and undergo change during their life cycle	Increase in size and undergo change during their life cycle
Reproducing	Most form seeds that result from the union of male and female reproductive cells	Produce offspring that result from the union of male and female reproductive cells

Cells—The Building Blocks of Life

Reading Focus How do plant and animal cells differ from each other?

Recall that the cell is the basic unit that makes up living things. It is the building block of both plants and animals. Each cell contains various parts, each with its own unique role in keeping the cell alive.

Comparing Plant and Animal Cells

The activity on pages A8 and A9 shows plant cells. Plant and animal cells have certain parts in common. There are also some cell parts that are unique to, or occur only in, plant cells. Other cell parts are unique to animal cells.

The drawings on page A13 show a typical plant cell and a typical animal cell. Notice the colored numbers pointing to the cell parts. You'll see that some parts are found in both kinds of cells. Some parts are found only in plant cells; others are found only in animal cells.

Cells Work Together

How do cells work together to form a living thing? Similar cells working together form a **tissue** (tish'o͞o). Muscle cells, for example, work with many other muscle cells to form muscle tissue. Different types of tissues work together to form an **organ**, such as the liver, heart, stomach, and small intestine.

In plants, as in animals, there are tissues and organs. For example, cells containing green pigment work together to form leaf tissue. Groups of tissues together form plant organs, such as the leaf, stem, and root. Each organ performs a certain function that helps the plant, or animal, maintain life.

Groups of organs work together to form an **organ system**, such as the circulatory system. The circulatory system brings oxygen to each cell of the body and removes waste products in animals. Together, groups of organ systems form a living thing, such as a pine tree, a cat, or a person.

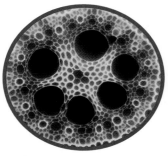

◀ Plant cells— a cross section of a root

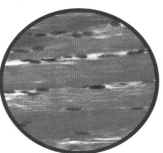

◀ Animal cells— skeletal muscle

Comparing Plant and Animal Cells

Plant Cell

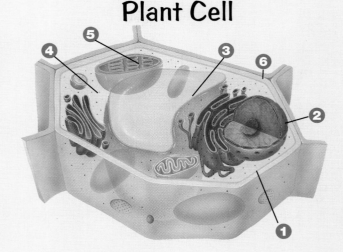

1. **CELL MEMBRANE** A thin layer that surrounds all cells, the **cell membrane** allows water and dissolved materials to pass into and out of the cell.

2. **NUCLEUS** (noo'klē əs) The **nucleus** controls all the cell's activities and is very important in cell reproduction.

3. **VACUOLE** (vak'yoo ōl) A **vacuole** is a large storage area filled with a liquid that contains various substances.

4. **CYTOPLASM** (sīt'ō plaz əm) The jellylike substance that fills much of the cell; other cell structures are found in the **cytoplasm.**

5. **CHLOROPLAST** (klôr'ə plast) The structure in which food making occurs, the **chloroplast** contains the green-colored pigment chlorophyll.

6. **CELL WALL** The **cell wall** is the tough outer covering of a plant cell that gives it a rigid shape; it is made of cellulose.

Animal Cell

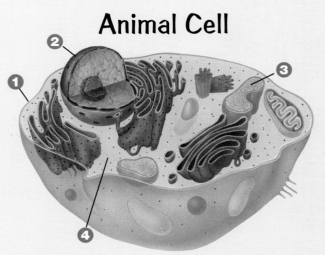

INVESTIGATION 1 WRAP-UP

REVIEW

1. List at least three basic life processes. Give examples of how plants and animals carry out these processes.

2. Draw and label a picture of a typical plant cell.

CRITICAL THINKING

3. How can a nonliving thing be mistaken for a living thing? How can a living thing be mistaken for a nonliving thing? Give examples of each.

4. Make a table that compares a typical plant cell with a typical animal cell.

HOW DO THE PARTS OF A PLANT HELP IT MEET ITS NEEDS?

How do you obtain nutrients? Your body needs food to function. You have breakfast, lunch, and dinner. Sometimes you munch a snack in between. How does a plant, such as a geranium, get nutrients? You will investigate the parts of a plant and find out which ones help a plant get what it needs.

Activity

Take It Apart

Seed plants, such as a geranium and a maple tree, have the same basic parts—roots, stems, and leaves. As they mature, these plants develop flowers, fruits, and seeds. Examine a seed plant and get to know its parts.

MATERIALS

- goggles
- potted plant
- hand lens
- metric ruler
- newspaper
- plastic knife
- cut flower
- *Science Notebook*

SAFETY /////

Wear goggles during this activity.

Procedure

1. With other members of your group, **observe** a potted plant. In your *Science Notebook*, **list** all the plant parts you can see. **Infer** what parts might be hidden from view.

2. **Examine** the leaves. **Describe** and **record** their shape. Compare the width of a leaf to its length. Describe the thickness, texture, and color of a leaf. Describe how the leaves are attached. **Record** your observations. **Draw** a leaf.

3. **Observe** the stem. **Record** whether the stem has branches. Note whether the main stem is stiff or flexible. **Record** your observations.

Step 2

4. Carefully hold the pot upside down over a newspaper. Tap the bottom of the pot gently until the plant and soil come out. If the soil is stuck to the pot, use a plastic knife to loosen it. You may remove some of the soil so that you can observe plant parts that were hidden. **Record** your observations.

5. Note whether your plant has a flower. If your plant doesn't have a flower, **examine** a cut flower. Use a hand lens to **observe** the structures in the center of the flower. **Record** your observations. **Draw** the flower, showing all of its structures.

Analyze and Conclude

1. What are the main parts of a flowering plant?

2. On your drawings of a leaf and a flower, **label** any parts that you can identify.

3. In what ways is your plant similar to a tree? On what do you base your conclusions?

4. If you have ever examined other plants, **compare** ways in which these plants were different from the plant you observed in this activity. How were they the same?

Technology Link CD-ROM

INVESTIGATE FURTHER!

Use the **Science Processor CD-ROM**, *Plants* (Investigation 1, Inside Plants) to find out more about the parts of plants. View a magnified stem and leaf and learn about the inner workings of these plant parts.

Step 4

Roots and Stems

Reading Focus How are roots and stems alike and different?

Roots

Did you know that when you sit under a shady tree on a hot summer day, you are seeing half the tree or less? For all of the tree that you see above ground, there is an equal or even greater part below ground—the roots.

The **roots** are the underground foundation of a plant. Roots anchor the plant and absorb water and minerals. Roots also help transport these materials to other parts of the plant. Some roots, such as those of a carrot and a beet, also store food.

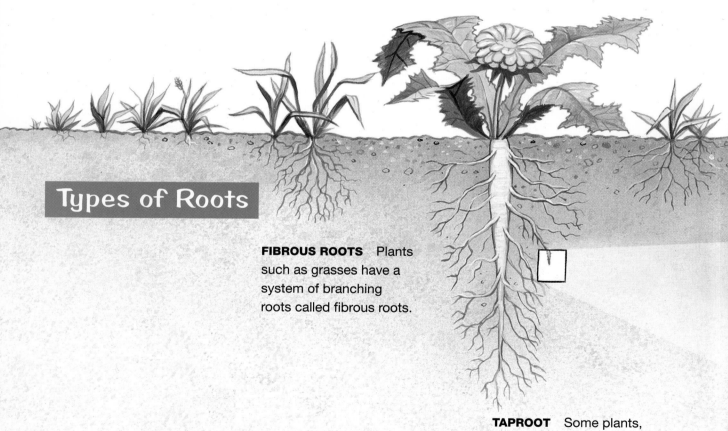

Types of Roots

FIBROUS ROOTS Plants such as grasses have a system of branching roots called fibrous roots.

TAPROOT Some plants, such as a carrot or a dandelion, have one main root, or taproot, that stores food.

Some plants have one main root, called a taproot. Other plants have many, branching roots, called fibrous roots. Compare these two types of roots in the drawing on page A16.

Study the drawing that shows the inside of a root. What type of tissue carries water toward the stem? What type of tissue carries nutrients from the leaves and stem into the root? What other kinds of tissue are found in a root? The root hairs near the tip of a root are very important. Water and minerals enter the root through these tiny structures. The drawing at the right shows how water and minerals move from the root hairs into the root's main transport system. Roots are observed in the activity on pages A14 and A15.

TRANSPORT IN A ROOT The arrows show the paths of water and minerals into a root. ▼

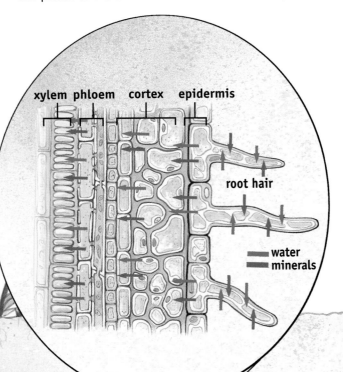

xylem phloem cortex epidermis

root hair

water
minerals

Inside a Root

CORTEX This layer connects the epidermis with the inner core.

XYLEM TISSUE This tissue is made of tubes that carry water and minerals from the soil upward.

EPIDERMIS This layer of cells covers the root.

PHLOEM TISSUE This tissue is made of tubes that carry sugars and other nutrients from the leaves through the stem and down to the root.

ROOT HAIRS These are tiny extensions that take in water and minerals.

ROOT CAP The tip of the root, called the root cap, pushes the root through the soil.

Stems

The root is connected to the next main part of the plant—the stem. The **stem** is the part of a plant that connects the roots and the leaves. The stem supports the other above-ground parts of the plant, the leaves and flowers. The transport tissues that you saw in the roots on page A17 continue through the stem and into the leaves and flowers. Water and minerals move through the xylem tissue toward the leaves.

Sugar, the food made by the plant, moves through the phloem tissue toward the roots.

Stems vary in structure. Small flowering plants, such as buttercups and daisies, have short, thin, somewhat soft stems. The trunks of large trees, such as oaks and maples, are hard, sturdy, and may be more than 30 m (100 ft) in height! Compare the nonwoody and woody stems in the drawings on this page. ■

CUTAWAY VIEW OF NONWOODY PLANT STEM This stem has thick walls and fibers running through it. The fibers give the stem its strength. This view shows the xylem and phloem cells that make up the transport system of the stem. Daisies and dandelions have nonwoody stems.

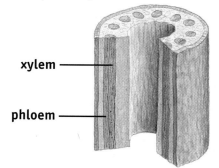

xylem

phloem

CUTAWAY VIEW OF WOODY PLANT STEM This trunk, which is actually a woody stem, is formed of many layers of cells. These layers have an outside protective covering called bark. This view shows the transport system of xylem and phloem. Each year the xylem cells form new layers of growth called annual rings.

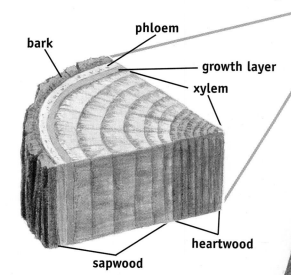

phloem

bark

growth layer

xylem

heartwood

sapwood

Using Math *A count of the number of annual rings can be used to estimate the age of a tree. About how old would you estimate this tree to be?*

Leaves

Reading Focus What are the parts of a leaf, and what is the function of each?

In autumn in some parts of the country, you will find great numbers of fallen red, yellow, and brown leaves. Why do plants have so many leaves? What do leaves do?

Look at the picture below of two kinds of leaves. A **leaf** is a plant part that grows out of the stem and is the food-making factory of a plant. The thin flat part of a leaf is called the blade. The blades of broad-leaved plants are often shaped so that the greatest amount of leaf is exposed to the Sun. Sunlight is an essential part of **photosynthesis** (fōt ō sin'thə sis), the food-making process in plants. The leaves of

Types of Leaves

NEEDLE LEAVES Plants such as a pine, a spruce, and a fir have needle leaves. The shape of these leaves helps reduce water loss.

BROAD LEAF Plants such as a maple and an oak are called broad-leaved trees and have broad flat leaves.

VEINS Along with the petiole, the veins form the transport system of the leaf. Water enters the leaf through the veins.

BLADE The blade is the broad flat part of a leaf.

PETIOLE The petiole is an extension of the xylem and phloem tubes of the stem.

A19

Structure of a Leaf

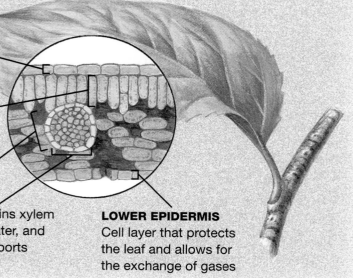

UPPER EPIDERMIS Cell layer that protects the leaf from drying out

PALISADE LAYER Columnlike cells where food making occurs

SPONGY LAYER Loosely-packed cells where food making occurs and where veins are located

VEIN Structure that contains xylem tissue, which transports water, and phloem tissue, which transports sugar and other nutrients

LOWER EPIDERMIS Cell layer that protects the leaf and allows for the exchange of gases

both broad-leaved plants and needle-leaved plants, such as a pine and a spruce, carry on this process.

Inside a Leaf

A typical leaf may be very thin, but it contains many cells, as shown above. If you cut across a leaf, producing a cross section, you'll find several layers of cells. The leaf's main function is to pro-duce food for the plant. The structure of a leaf is well suited to that purpose.

Photosynthesis takes place in the two middle layers of cells. The top and bottom layers protect the leaf and keep it from drying out. Openings in the bottom layer allow for the exchange of gases with the environment. A leaf also contains many veins, which help transport water and manufactured food. ■

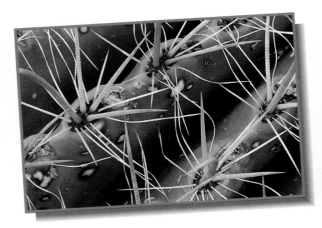

▲ The pointy spines of a cactus do not make food. They protect the stem from animal intruders. Cactus spines are modified leaves.

▲ In pea plants some leaves function as tendrils. They twist around objects and support the plant.

Energy Traps

Reading Focus What is needed for photosynthesis to occur, and what does this process produce?

Imagine that you're walking home from school and you begin to feel hungry. It would be great if you could manufacture a tasty snack on the spot. But you can't, of course. Your body can't produce its own food. But plants can.

Making Food

Plants produce their own food by using light energy, carbon dioxide, and water. Plants can't move around to find these things. But they can trap light energy and collect the substances they need to make their own food.

Plants trap energy in their leaves. Some leaf cells contain hundreds of disklike parts called chloroplasts. Recall that chloroplasts are tiny cell structures that contain a green pigment called chlorophyll. This pigment collects light energy from the Sun. Chlorophyll works much like a solar panel, absorbing light energy, which is then stored as food energy.

Chlorophyll uses the Sun's light energy to change two substances, carbon dioxide and water, into food. Carbon dioxide is a gas found in air. It enters the plant through tiny holes usually found on the underside of the leaves. Water enters the plant through the roots. Recall that transport tissue carries water from the roots to the stems to the leaves.

The food produced by a plant is called glucose (glo͞o′kōs), a form of sugar. The process of using light energy to combine carbon dioxide and water to produce glucose is called photosynthesis. *Photo-* means "light," and *synthesis* means "joining together."

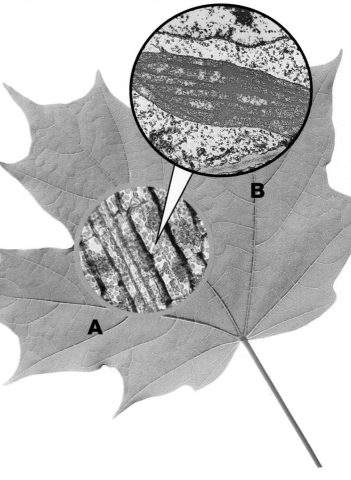

**Chloroplasts are tiny green disklike cell parts that trap energy during photosynthesis.
(A) Groups of chloroplasts
(B) one enlarged chloroplast**

Photosynthesis

Sun

| carbon dioxide + water | light energy → | glucose + oxygen |

Plants trap light energy from the Sun during photosynthesis.

sunlight

■ Carbon dioxide enters the leaf through holes in its surface.

■ Oxygen, a waste product of photosynthesis, is released.

Glucose is produced in the leaf cells.

Water enters roots through root hairs at the tips of roots.

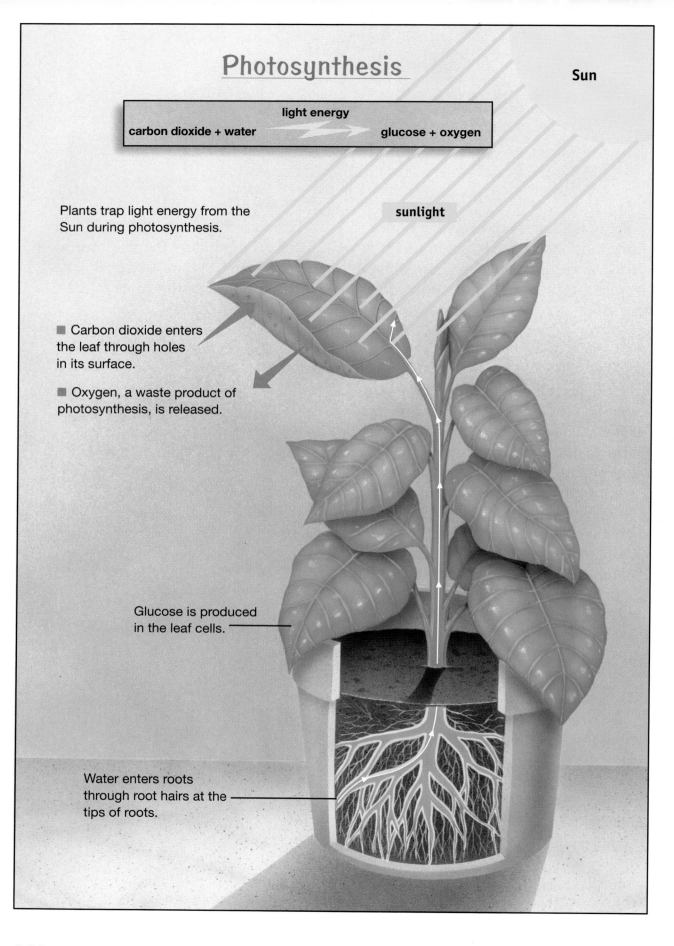

▲ **Radishes store starch in the roots.**

The drawing on page A22 shows the process by which plant cells produce glucose. In addition to glucose, photosynthesis produces a "waste" product. This waste product, oxygen, is one that humans and other animals need to survive. Oxygen and any leftover water leave the plant by way of the same tiny openings in the leaves through which carbon dioxide enters.

Storing and Using Food

Plants do not produce food all the time. Because photosynthesis requires sunlight, the process of trapping sunlight can't take place at night or on very

▼ **Lettuce stores starch in its leaves.**

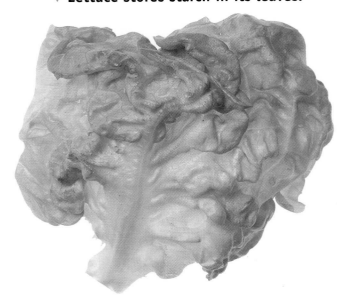

cloudy days. Although carbon dioxide is always available, water may be scarce at times. To survive, a plant must produce food when light energy, carbon dioxide, and water are all available. Many plants can store the food they make. Plants usually store food in the leaves, but sometimes they store it in the roots, stems, or other plant parts.

▲ **Celery stores starch in its leafstalks.**

Most plants store extra glucose in the form of starch, a chemical that is made up of a chain of simple sugars. This starch might be stored in the plant leaves (lettuce), in leafstalks (celery), in roots (carrots), or in underground stems (white potatoes).

Plants use the energy in glucose to grow, to produce seeds, and to carry out all their life functions. They use the energy from glucose in much the same way that you use the energy in the foods you eat. Both plant cells and animal cells use oxygen to release the energy in food. This process is called **cell respiration** (res pə rā′shən). ■

Internet Field Trip

Visit **www.eduplace.com** to find out more about the life processes of plants.

Plant Responses

> **Reading Focus** What are some ways a plant responds to its environment?

Have you ever seen someone grow a sweet potato plant in a glass of water? If so, you probably noticed that the roots grow down into the glass. The stems grow up, usually toward a light source. The sweet potato plant is reacting, or responding, to its environment. A plant response to conditions in the environment is called a **tropism** (trō′piz əm).

Growth Toward Gravity

Roots respond to Earth's gravity by growing toward the center of Earth. Growing toward the center of Earth is a geotropic response. The word *tropism* comes from a Greek word that means "a turning." The word part *geo-* means "Earth." So *geotropism* is a turning (of the roots) toward Earth. This growth response ensures that the roots will grow down into the soil, the plant's source of water and nutrients. Leaves and stems have the opposite response to gravity. They grow away from Earth's center. This response helps ensure that leaves and stems will be exposed to sunlight, which the plant needs to make its food.

Growth Toward Light

Leaves and stems grow toward a source of light. Growing toward light is a phototropic response. *Photo-* means "light." You have probably seen the leaves of houseplants turned toward a bright light source. Stems may also bend toward that light source. The bending of stems occurs because they are actually growing toward light. Such growth allows the leaves to capture the greatest amount of light, which is needed for the process of photosynthesis. What can you do with a houseplant to keep the stems and leaves from bending in one direction?

Growth Toward Water

When plant roots are in soil that has lots of water in one area, they grow toward the wet area. This kind of growth is a hydrotropic response. (*Hydro-* means "water.") However, roots do not "know" where the moisture is. They do not "try" to find the water. Instead, when roots come into contact with moist soil, they continue to grow toward the moisture. Roots touching only very dry soil may grow very slowly or not at all.

Hanging On

Some plants have threadlike parts called tendrils that wrap around objects to support the plant. This response is another kind of tropism called thigmotropism, or response to touch. (*Thigmo-* means "touch.") Picture 4 on page A25 shows the thigmotropic response of a pea plant.

① Roots showing a geotropic response. ② Leaves showing a phototropic response. ③ Two plants showing a hydrotropic response. ④ Tendrils curling around garden stakes, showing a thigmotropic response.

INVESTIGATION 2 WRAP-UP

REVIEW

1. Draw a leaf, such as a maple leaf, and label the veins, blade, and petiole.

2. Describe the roles of xylem tissue and phloem tissue in stems.

CRITICAL THINKING

3. Explain why the parts of the word *photosynthesis (photo-* and *synthesis)* help explain the process of photosynthesis.

4. What do you think would happen to the roots of a plant if you turned the plant upside down for two weeks? Explain.

INVESTIGATION 3

HOW DO THE PARTS OF AN ANIMAL HELP IT MEET ITS NEEDS?

Roots, stems, and leaves help a plant meet its needs. Animals have body parts, too. These parts appear very different from those found in plants. But surprisingly, an animal's body parts have the same basic job as a plant's parts—to help the organism meet its needs.

Activity

Come and Get It

You know that a plant's roots absorb water. And you've learned that carbon dioxide is taken in through its leaves. A plant uses these materials to make food. Unlike plants, animals must obtain food from their environment. Find out what body parts help a snail do this.

MATERIALS
- goggles
- plastic gloves
- garden snail
- plastic container
- hand lens
- snail food
- *Science Notebook*

SAFETY
Wear goggles and plastic gloves while doing this activity.

Procedure

1. Obtain a garden snail from your teacher. Place the snail on the inside wall of a plastic container.

2. Use a hand lens to observe the snail. In your *Science Notebook*, make a sketch of the snail. Label any body parts that you can identify.

Step 2

3. **List** each body part that you labeled. **Infer** the job done by each part listed. **Record** your inferences.

4. Add food to the plastic container and place the snail near the food. **Observe** the snail's behavior. **Record** your observations.

5. **Identify** any body parts that you think help the snail obtain food. **Describe** these body parts.

6. **Compare** your observations with those of another group of students in your class.

Analyze and Conclude

1. **Make a chart** that compares the basic needs of a snail with those of a plant. List any similarities.

2. **Compare** the way that a snail obtains food with the way a plant obtains food.

3. Both a snail and a plant use food. **Hypothesize** whether the food is used for the same purpose in both organisms. Explain your reasoning.

UNIT PROJECT LINK

For this Unit Project you will create a museum display comparing systems in a plant, an invertebrate, and a vertebrate. Research where each organism lives and what it eats. Write a brief report as part of your display.

Technology Link

For more help with your Unit Project, go to **www.eduplace.com**.

Science in Literature

STOP THE DISAPPEARING ACT

"Follow the trunks of the trees as they rise straight up from the forest floor. You'll see them open like umbrellas, branching out to form the rooflike canopy of the rain forest. In this dense layer of green, leaves bathed in full sunlight absorb energy and use it to make food."

Why Save the Rain Forest?
by Donald Silver
Illustrated by Patricia J. Wynne
Julian Messner, 1993

Read about the role of rain forest trees in keeping carbon dioxide from building up in the air. In *Why Save the Rain Forest?* Donald Silver describes the importance of photosynthesis in balancing the life-support systems of Earth.

A27

Staying Alive!

Reading Focus What life processes do all living things carry out?

A Look Back

You've compared the structure of plant cells and animal cells. You learned that plants obtain and use materials from their environment. You also learned that through the process of photosynthesis, plants are able to produce their own food.

You've seen how plant organs—roots, stems, and leaves — help plants meet their needs. Animals must also meet their needs. Like plants, they have organs and systems that help meet those needs. Let's take a look at the organ systems of two animals—the frog and the human.

Frogs and Plants—Alike or Not?

Like a plant, a frog carries out basic life processes. The frog obtains and digests food. Digestion is the process of breaking down food into nutrients that cells can absorb. The digested food provides the frog with the energy needed to carry out its life processes. The nutrients in food are also used to build new cells and to repair damaged cells. A plant uses food in these same ways.

As it carries out its life processes, a frog produces waste products, which are removed from the body. Plants also produce and release waste products as they carry out their life processes.

Organ Systems of a Frog

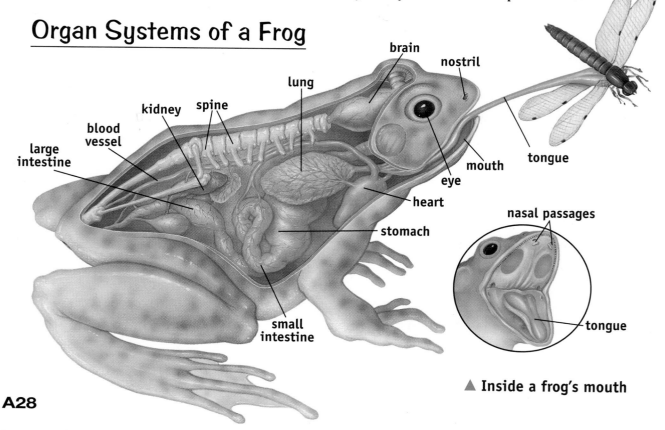

brain

nostril

lung

kidney   spine

blood
vessel

large
intestine

mouth

tongue

eye

heart

stomach

small
intestine

nasal passages

tongue

▲ Inside a frog's mouth

A28

Food Getting and Digesting

A major difference between a frog and a plant involves the way each obtains food. In the presence of light, plants take in water and carbon dioxide and make sugar, which is their food. They give off oxygen as a waste product of the food-making process. All animals, including frogs, must obtain their food from their surroundings. They must then digest, or break down, the food to release the energy it contains.

A frog has a group of organs, the digestive system, that work together to digest food. As you read, find parts of the frog's digestive system in the drawing on page A28.

A frog's digestive system begins at its mouth. A frog uses its tongue to obtain food. Notice from the drawing that a frog's tongue is attached to the front of its mouth. By flicking out its sticky tongue, a frog can catch passing insects.

Next, the frog swallows the insect whole, without chewing. Frogs have very tiny teeth that are good for gripping, not biting or chewing! The food is pushed down the frog's throat in an interesting way. As the frog blinks, its large eyeballs push the insect down its throat!

The mouth connects to a short tube, the esophagus (i säf′ə gəs), that connects to the stomach. Partly digested food remains a short time in the stomach and then moves on to the coiled small intestine. Digestion continues in this organ.

Digested food containing nutrients is absorbed from the small intestine into the bloodstream. The bloodstream carries the nutrients to all the frog's cells. The small intestine joins to a large intestine, which narrows to a rectum. Undigested food leaves the body through an opening at the end of the rectum.

Gas Exchange

The cells of a frog's body use oxygen to break down sugar obtained from food. Oxygen is brought into a frog's body by its respiratory system. Air, which contains oxygen, passes through a frog's mouth and down a tube to the lungs. Here, oxygen is picked up by the frog's transport system. At the same time, the transport system picks up carbon dioxide, a waste gas. The carbon dioxide is carried from the blood to the lungs and is then exhaled, or breathed out.

Transporting and Excreting

The circulatory system is the frog's transport system. A frog's circulatory system includes a heart that pumps the blood through blood vessels to all parts of the frog's body. Blood carries oxygen and digested food to the body's cells.

As the frog carries on its life processes, its cells produce waste products. If allowed to build up, these wastes become harmful. Wastes are removed, or excreted, from the frog's body by the excretory (eks′krə tôr ē) and digestive systems.

Blood traveling through the body carries carbon dioxide and other wastes from cells. Blood passes through the kidneys, which are organs of the excretory system that filter the blood. The kidneys remove wastes, minerals, and excess water from the frog's blood. The liquid wastes are stored in a bladder and then passed out of the body.

Human Body Systems

You've just learned about what's inside a frog. What would you find inside a human body? The same life processes that keep a frog alive also keep a human being alive. People must digest food and get rid of the waste products of digestion. They must breathe in air and release the waste products of respiration. They must also circulate the nutrients that are made available during digestion.

The drawings on this page show four human body systems. On the left is a drawing of the digestive and excretory systems. On the right is a drawing of the circulatory and respiratory systems. You can probably recognize some of the organs in these four systems. For example, find the stomach, kidneys, lungs, and heart.

In the next two chapters, you'll learn in more detail how human body systems work to keep the body alive and well.

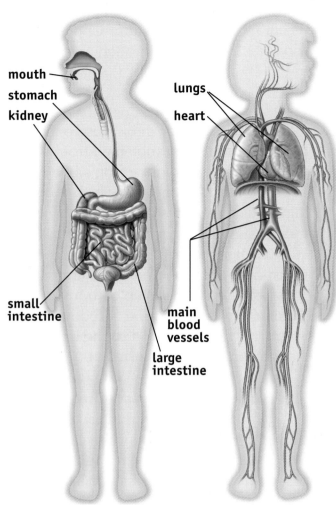

▲ The digestive and excretory systems

▲ The circulatory and respiratory systems

mouth
stomach
kidney
small intestine

lungs
heart
main blood vessels
large intestine

INVESTIGATION 3 WRAP-UP

REVIEW

1. Describe the major difference in food-getting between plants and animals.

2. Why is it vital for living things such as frogs to digest food?

CRITICAL THINKING

3. How is the transport system of a plant similar to the transport system of a frog? How do the systems differ?

4. Explain how the digestive and circulatory systems work together to supply nutrients and energy to the body's cells. Use information about the frog to support your answer.

REFLECT & EVALUATE

Word Power

Write the letter of the term that best matches the definition. *Not all terms will be used.*

1. Cell structure that controls all the cell's activities
2. Plant responses to conditions in the environment
3. Functions that a living thing must carry out to stay alive
4. Jellylike substance that fills most of a cell
5. Food-making process in plants
6. Chlorophyll-containing structure in a plant cell

a. chloroplast
b. cytoplasm
c. life processes
d. nucleus
e. organ
f. photosynthesis
g. tropisms
h. vacuole

Check What You Know

Write the word in each pair that correctly completes each sentence.

1. Tubes that carry nutrients from the leaves through the stem and down to the roots are (xylem, phloem) tissue.
2. The process by which animal cells and plant cells use oxygen to release energy in foods is (photosynthesis, cell respiration).
3. The outermost layer of an animal cell is the (cell membrane, cell wall).

Problem Solving

1. A potted plant is growing on a windowsill in bright light. The plant is rotated one-half turn each morning. How would this turning affect the way the plant's stems grow?
2. In your own words, explain why a leaf can be called an "energy trap."
3. Explain the function of digestion; use digestion in a frog to support your explanation.

Make a sketch of this plant cell. Label the parts. In a short paragraph describe how the parts in a drawing of an animal cell would be different from the parts in a drawing of a plant cell.

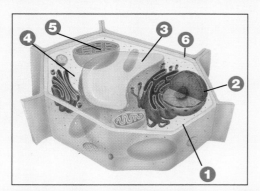

DIGESTION AND RESPIRATION

Human body systems consist of many organs working together. What happens to the food that we eat? What is the purpose of breathing? In this chapter you'll explore the workings of two important body systems—the digestive system and the respiratory system.

● ●

Connecting to Science
CULTURE

Ancient Remedies Treatment for problems of the digestive system dates back to ancient times. As long ago as 2500 B.C. the Chinese treated various digestive disorders with acupuncture. Acupuncture is a treatment in which very thin needles are placed into the body at key points. This treatment has been proven to control appetite and to reduce stomach upset.

The ancient Chinese also used plants to treat digestive disorders. Plants used in this way are called herbs. The yellow underground stem of Chinese rhubarb has been used for more than 2,000 years to regulate digestion. Another herb used as medicine since ancient times is garlic. The Chinese, Babylonians, Greeks, Romans, Hindus, and Egyptians all used garlic to treat various intestinal disorders. Read on to learn more about the human digestive system.

Coming Up

◀ Dr. Malcolm Johnson in front of a chart of acupuncture points

HOW DOES THE DIGESTIVE SYSTEM WORK?

Did you ever swallow a large piece of food without properly chewing it? How did that feel? For food to be used by your body, it must be broken down by the digestive system. The breakdown begins in the mouth.

Activity

Sink Your Teeth Into This

Have you ever looked very carefully at your teeth? Are they all the same size and shape? Are the edges of your teeth smooth or ragged? Find out in this activity.

MATERIALS
- mirror
- celery stick
- *Science Notebook*

SAFETY
During this activity, eat foods only with your teacher's permission.

Procedure

1. Use a mirror to **observe** your teeth. Count the number of teeth in your lower jaw. Then count the number of teeth in your upper jaw. **Record** these numbers in your *Science Notebook*. **Compare** the numbers with those of other students in your class.

2. Look for four main kinds of teeth in your mouth. Look at the drawing to the right, which shows the teeth in a person's mouth. In your *Science Notebook*, **list** the four kinds and describe how they are alike and how they are different.

Step 2

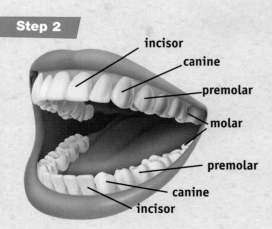

incisor
canine
premolar
molar
premolar
canine
incisor

3. **Talk with group members** about how the four kinds of teeth differ. **Infer** why these teeth are different.

4. Close your teeth and **observe** how the upper teeth and lower teeth meet. In your *Science Notebook,* **describe** how your teeth meet. Note whether the way the teeth meet affects how you chew your food.

5. Eat a celery stick. Note which teeth you use to bite the celery. Note which teeth you use to chew the celery. **Record** this information in your *Science Notebook.*

Analyze and Conclude

1. How many teeth do most students have in their lower jaw? in their upper jaw? Is there a difference between the kinds of teeth in the upper jaw and the lower jaw?

2. In what ways do you use your front teeth? In what ways do you use your back teeth? How do the shapes of the front teeth and the back teeth differ? **Describe** how the shape of your teeth is related to how you use them.

INVESTIGATE FURTHER!

RESEARCH

Find pictures of the teeth of different animals such as a squirrel, a deer, a bear, an alligator, and a wolf. Compare the shapes and sizes of the teeth. Find out the diet of each animal. Hypothesize whether diet and tooth shape are related.

Science in Literature

WHEN FOOD GOES DOWN THE "WRONG WAY"

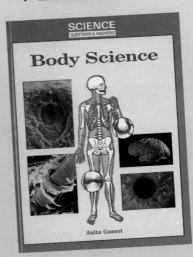

Body Science
by Anita Ganeri
Dillon Press, 1992

"When you swallow a piece of food, a flap called the epiglottis covers the top of your windpipe, and the food goes down your esophagus and into your digestive system. But this process can go wrong. If you accidentally breathe in as you swallow the food, the epiglottis opens up. Then the food gets into your windpipe. You may choke on it. . . ."

Does your food ever go down the "wrong way"? Does your stomach ever rumble? Find out about your digestive system and many other parts of the human body as you read *Body Science* by Anita Ganeri.

Activity

How Sweet It Is

Some foods contain sugar. You'll use a glucose test strip to find out if glucose, a kind of sugar, is present in certain foods. You'll also find out how a chemical called an enzyme (en'zīm) *can change a sugar from one form to another.*

MATERIALS

- goggles
- marker
- four paper cups (3 oz)
- dropper
- apple juice
- orange juice
- cranberry juice
- milk
- glucose test strips
- lactase drops
- *Science Notebook*

SAFETY //////

Wear goggles while doing this activity.

Procedure

1. Use a marker to label four paper cups *apple juice*, *orange juice*, *cranberry juice*, and *milk*.

2. Use a dropper to add ten drops of apple juice to the first paper cup. Wash the dropper thoroughly. Then add ten drops of orange juice to the second paper cup.

3. Wash the dropper. Add ten drops of cranberry juice to the third cup. Wash the dropper again. Add ten drops of milk to the fourth cup.

4. You will use a glucose test strip to find out if the liquid in each cup contains the sugar glucose. A glucose test strip changes from light green to dark green or brown when it contacts glucose. In your *Science Notebook*, **make a chart** like the one shown below. **Predict** what will happen to the test strip when each liquid is tested. **Record** your predictions in your chart.

Glucose Present?		
Food	**Prediction**	**Result**
apple juice		

See **SCIENCE** and **MATH TOOLBOX** page H11 if you need to review **Making a Chart to Organize Data.**

5. Test each liquid by dipping a dry glucose test strip into each cup. **Record** your results in your chart.

6. Lactose is a kind of sugar found in milk. Lactase is a chemical, called an enzyme, made by the body. Lactase breaks down lactose to simple sugars, such as glucose. Put one drop of lactase into the cup of milk. Now dip a dry glucose test strip into the milk. **Record** your observations.

Analyze and Conclude

1. What happened to the glucose test strip in the apple juice, orange juice, cranberry juice, and milk? Which liquid contained glucose? How do you know?

2. Compare the two glucose test strips you used in the milk both before and after you added the lactase. How were they alike or different? **Infer** what could have caused a difference in the results.

3. Recall that lactase breaks down lactose, the sugar in milk. Some people do not make enough lactase. If such people drink milk or milk products, they can become ill. **Hypothesize** how these people might be able to drink milk without becoming ill.

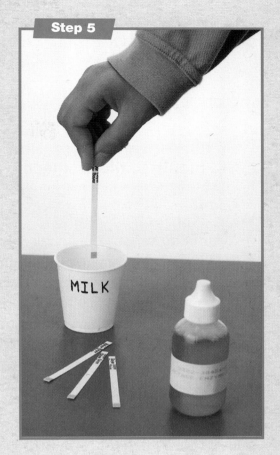

Step 5

MILK

UNIT PROJECT LINK

For the plant that you selected for your museum display, research the plant system that allows for gas exchange. For the two animals you chose, research the respiratory system of each. Create a display that compares all three systems. Your display might include posters, models, or another medium of your choice.

Technology Link

For more help with your Unit Project, go to **www.eduplace.com**.

How Digestion Starts

Reading Focus How is food digested as it moves from the mouth to the stomach?

Your Stomach "Speaks"

Your body sends you signals when it is time to eat. Many people feel tired, weak, or even grouchy when they're hungry. Yet it isn't really food the body needs. The body's cells need chemicals called nutrients (noo′trē ənts) for energy, to build new cells, to repair damaged cells, and to control body processes.

Foods provide tasty packaging for nutrients. After you take a bite, food travels through about 9 m (30 ft) of digestive organs. These organs make up the human **digestive system**, in which food is broken down into a form that body cells can use.

From Your Plate to a Cell

The digestive organs grind, mash, and churn food into smaller and smaller particles. They also release chemicals that soften food and change it from one form to another. Once food has been changed to a form that cells can use, it passes out of the digestive system. The nutrients from food pass into the bloodstream and then to the body's cells.

Digestion in the Mouth

Think about your last meal. The digestive process probably began before you took your first bite. At just the sight and smell of the food, your salivary (sal′ə ver ē) glands went to work.

The drawing at the bottom of page A39 shows your salivary glands, which are located under your tongue and near your ears. The glands produce **saliva** (sə lī′və), the watery liquid that moistens the mouth and food. Each day as much as $1\frac{1}{2}$ L (about 6 c) of saliva flow into your mouth. Saliva begins the chemical breakdown of the food.

The Role of the Teeth

When you eat solid food, you bite off pieces with your front teeth, the incisors (in sī′zərz). The incisors are cutting teeth as the activity on pages A34 and A35 shows. The teeth on either side of them are canines, which tear food. To help the digestive process, you chew your food well with your back grinding teeth, the premolars and molars.

From about 6 months to 26 months of age, your baby teeth grow in. Then those teeth fall out and are replaced by permanent teeth. All your permanent teeth will appear by age 20. Look at the drawing of teeth on page A39 and find the four main kinds of teeth. The cutting, tearing, and grinding action of the teeth physically breaks food into smaller pieces, helping digestion.

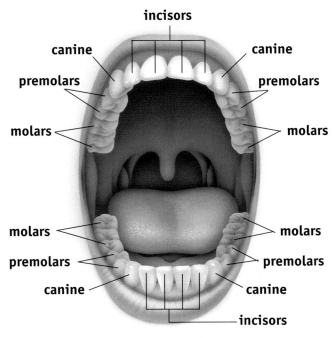

incisors
canine — canine
premolars — premolars
molars — molars
molars — molars
premolars — premolars
canine — canine
incisors

▲ **Teeth in an adult's mouth**

Your teeth would not work very well without your tongue. The tongue is the muscular organ that helps you swallow and pushes food against your teeth. After you bite, slice, and tear food, your tongue pushes it to the grinding surfaces of the back teeth.

As you chew, your salivary glands produce chemicals called **enzymes** (en'zīmz), which help break down food. Ptyalin (tī'ə lin) is an enzyme in saliva that breaks starch into simple sugars. After food is ground and mixed with saliva, it becomes a soft, wet mass. This mass of food is ready to be swallowed.

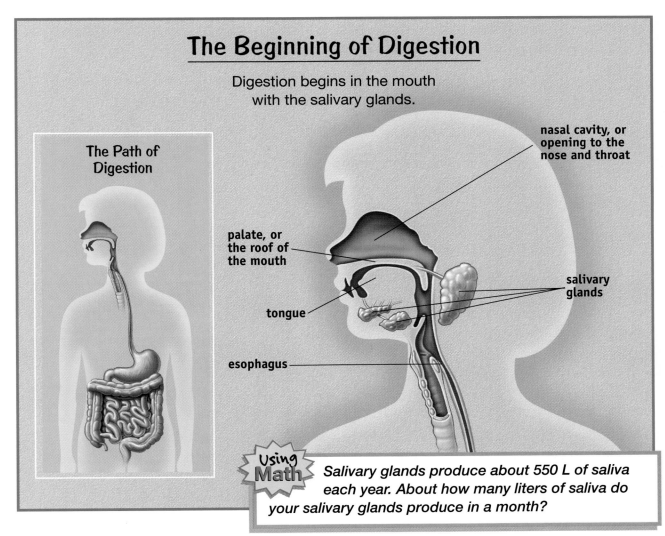

The Beginning of Digestion

Digestion begins in the mouth with the salivary glands.

The Path of Digestion

nasal cavity, or opening to the nose and throat

palate, or the roof of the mouth

salivary glands

tongue

esophagus

Using Math *Salivary glands produce about 550 L of saliva each year. About how many liters of saliva do your salivary glands produce in a month?*

A39

Swallowing

You control the start of a swallow. When the food is moist and soft, your tongue pushes it to the back of the throat. Once food reaches the back of the throat, automatic processes take over. Then the food cannot go down the "wrong pipe"—the trachea, or windpipe.

Look at the numbers in the drawings below to see what happens during the automatic part of swallowing.

Choking

Sometimes the automatic processes of digestion fail. Suppose you talk and laugh while eating. The food in your mouth can enter the nose or the windpipe. You can even choke. A person trained in giving the Heimlich maneuver (hīm′lik mə nōō′vər) can help to dislodge the stuck food. First, the trained person wraps his arms around the choking person under that person's ribs.

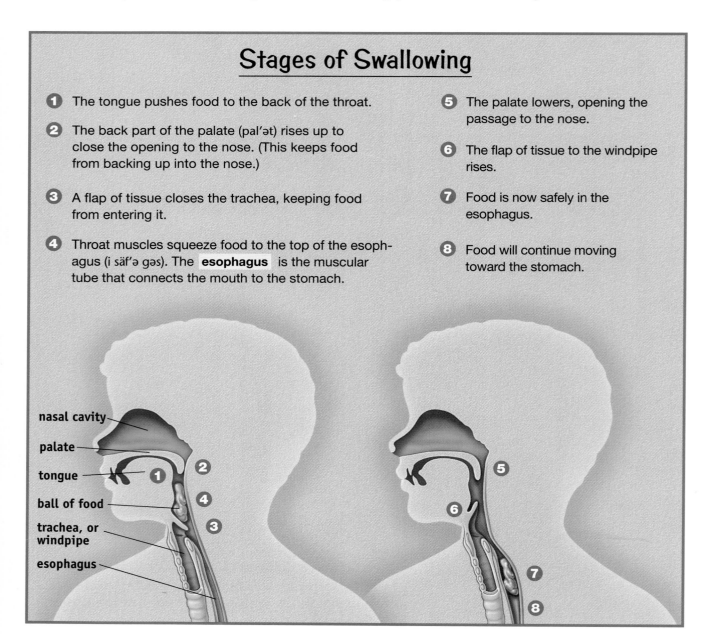

Stages of Swallowing

❶ The tongue pushes food to the back of the throat.

❷ The back part of the palate (pal′ət) rises up to close the opening to the nose. (This keeps food from backing up into the nose.)

❸ A flap of tissue closes the trachea, keeping food from entering it.

❹ Throat muscles squeeze food to the top of the esophagus (i säf′ə gəs). The **esophagus** is the muscular tube that connects the mouth to the stomach.

❺ The palate lowers, opening the passage to the nose.

❻ The flap of tissue to the windpipe rises.

❼ Food is now safely in the esophagus.

❽ Food will continue moving toward the stomach.

nasal cavity

palate

tongue

ball of food

trachea, or windpipe

esophagus

Then he presses strongly in and up under the breastbone. This action can help to force the stuck food up and out of the windpipe.

Down to the Stomach

The esophagus moves food along, using a wavelike motion known as **peristalsis** (per ə stal'sis). Rings of muscles contract, or tighten, above the mass of food. At the same time, rings of muscles below the food relax. This contracting and relaxing of muscles pushes the food down to the stomach.

The esophagus ends at the **stomach**, a muscular organ that stores food and helps digest it. Between the esophagus and the stomach is a round muscle that acts as a gatekeeper. This muscle opens, allowing the swallowed food into the stomach. Once the food is in the stomach, the muscle closes, preventing the food from moving back into the esophagus.

In the Stomach

An adult's stomach can hold about 1 L (1 qt) of food. The food stays in the stomach two to six hours, where it is further broken down.

Even before food reaches the stomach, glands in the stomach lining begin to produce digestive juices. One juice, hydrochloric acid, is strong enough to make a hole in a carpet or dissolve metal. Why, then, isn't the stomach digested by its own acid? The walls of the stomach and other digestive organs are protected. They produce mucus (myōō'kəs), a slippery material that forms a thick, protective coating inside digestive organs.

The stomach also makes digestive enzymes. Some stomach enzymes begin to break down the proteins found in meat, eggs, dairy products, and beans. Like the esophagus, the stomach undergoes peristalsis. Waves of muscle action mash and churn the food and digestive juices. The food soon becomes a thick, soupy liquid called chyme (kīm). Then it is ready to leave the stomach.

Two to six hours after food is swallowed, chyme begins to leave the stomach. Sugars and starches leave first, then proteins. Fats remain in the stomach longest. A few simple chemicals, such as sugar, alcohol, and some medicines, pass directly from the stomach to the bloodstream. But most nutrients are passed along for further digestion. ■

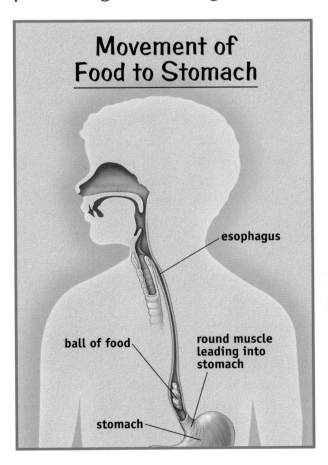

Movement of Food to Stomach

esophagus

ball of food

round muscle leading into stomach

stomach

How Digestion Ends

Reading Focus What happens to food after it leaves the stomach?

Digestion in the Small Intestine

Did you know that a person can live without a stomach? How can this be? Look at the drawing. Recall that the main role of the stomach is to store food, not digest it. Most nutrients are absorbed into the bloodstream in the next part of the digestive system—the small intestine. The **small intestine** is the long, coiled organ where most digestion takes place.

The "small" intestine is not really small. About 6 m (20 ft) long, it can be three times as long as the body it occupies. You can see that it is coiled, allowing it to fit inside the body. It is called the *small* intestine because it is narrower than the *large* intestine.

Recall that in the stomach, food becomes a soupy liquid called chyme. Chyme from the stomach enters the first part of the small intestine. Then, over the next five hours, the digestive process is completed. The small intestine produces digestive juices and enzymes, such as the enzyme lactase. As the activity on pages A36 and A37 shows, lactase changes lactose, a sugar found in milk, to glucose, a simpler form of sugar.

Other organs work with the small intestine. Find the liver in the drawing. The liver is an organ that performs more than 500 functions in several body systems. One function in digestion is to produce bile, which breaks fats into smaller pieces.

Made in the liver, bile is stored in the gallbladder, a small pear-shaped organ. The gallbladder supplies bile to the small intestine as it is needed. Another organ, the pancreas, lies behind the stomach and is connected to the small intestine.

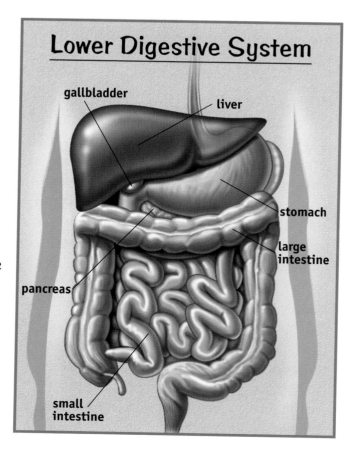

Lower Digestive System

gallbladder

liver

stomach

large intestine

pancreas

small intestine

The pancreas produces pancreatic juices. These juices are a mixture of digestive enzymes and other substances that aid in digestion.

Absorption in the Small Intestine

Most carbohydrates, proteins, and water are absorbed in the second part of the small intestine. Vitamins and minerals that dissolve in water are also absorbed there.

In the wall of the small intestine are **villi** (vil′ī), shown below. Villi are like the loops on a terry-cloth towel. In the villi is a network of blood vessels. Dissolved nutrients pass from the small intestine through these vessels into the blood. The blood then carries the nutrients to every cell in the body.

Waste Removal

After food passes through the small intestine, some material, such as fiber, still remains undigested. Fiber is important to digestion. It helps in the movement of food through the digestive system. But humans cannot digest fiber. It must be passed out of the body.

Peristalsis moves undigested matter into the large intestine. The **large intestine** is the organ that absorbs water and salts from undigested material. It returns much of the water through its walls to the bloodstream. The large intestine also moves undigested material out of the body. About 24 to 48 hours after a meal is eaten, the undigested materials pass out of the body through an opening called the anus (ā′nəs). ■

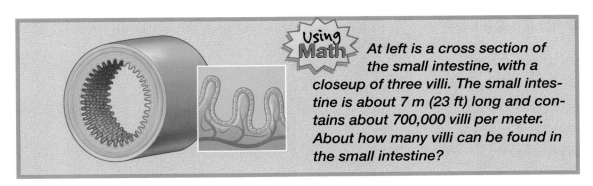

Using Math

At left is a cross section of the small intestine, with a closeup of three villi. The small intestine is about 7 m (23 ft) long and contains about 700,000 villi per meter. About how many villi can be found in the small intestine?

INVESTIGATION 1 WRAP-UP

THINK IT
WRITE IT

REVIEW

1. What is the function of the digestive system? Describe digestion in the mouth and the stomach.

2. Explain why a person can live without a stomach.

CRITICAL THINKING

3. As food moves through the digestive system, it is changed in two main ways. Identify these two changes. Explain the role of the mouth, stomach, small intestine, and large intestine in these changes.

4. Describe the structure of the small intestine. How does this structure aid in the absorption of nutrients?

HOW DOES THE RESPIRATORY SYSTEM WORK?

Breathe in. Hold that air. Then breathe out. What is going on inside your body when you inhale and exhale? In this investigation you'll learn what is happening to air as it moves through your respiratory system.

Activity
Breathing Rates

Your breathing rate is how often you inhale in one minute. Find out what things affect this rate.

MATERIALS
- chair
- timer
- *Science Notebook*

Procedure

Sit in a chair in a relaxed position. Have a group member **count** the number of times you breathe in during one minute. Have another member use a timer to keep track of the time. **Record** the number in your *Science Notebook*.

Predict how exercise will affect your breathing rate. **Record** your prediction. Run in place for one minute. Then **count** and **record** how many times you breathe in during one minute.

Analyze and Conclude

1. How did exercise affect your breathing rate? **Infer** why exercise had this effect.

2. **Hypothesize** about other things that could affect your breathing rate. Explain your ideas.

Activity

Lung Power

Without special devices you can't look inside your chest to observe how your lungs work. But you can make a working model of a lung in this activity.

MATERIALS

- 2 balloons (1 small, 1 large)
- drinking straw
- tape
- scissors
- small clear plastic bottle with bottom cut off
- modeling clay
- *Science Notebook*

Procedure

1. Work with your group to **build a model** of a lung. Pull the opening of a small balloon over one end of a drinking straw. Use tape to attach the balloon to the straw.

2. Cut the neck off a large balloon. Have a group member hold a plastic bottle from which the bottom has been cut off. Stretch the balloon over the cut end of the bottle. Secure the balloon with tape.

3. Push the end of the straw with the small balloon into the mouth of the bottle. Then use modeling clay to seal the mouth of the bottle and to hold the straw in place.

4. **Predict** what will happen to the small balloon when you pull down and push up on the large balloon. **Record** your prediction in your *Science Notebook*.

5. **Observe** what happens when you pull down and then push up on the large balloon. **Make drawings** of your observations.

Analyze and Conclude

1. What happened to the small balloon when you pulled down on the large balloon? What happened when you pushed up?

2. Based on observations of your model, **hypothesize** what happens in your body when you breathe.

3. You have just made a model of the way the lungs work. **Describe** at least one way in which this model differs from a real lung.

Step 3

Breathing Basics

Reading Focus What happens when you breathe in and breathe out?

Breathing is the process by which the body takes in "fresh" air containing oxygen and pushes out "used" air containing waste gases. The parts of the body that work together to take air into the body and push it back out form the **respiratory system**. The drawing below illustrates the parts of this system.

Air Enters

What happens when you take in a breath of air, or inhale? Air can enter through either the mouth or nose.

Your nose both warms and moistens the air you breathe. Small hairs inside the nose trap dust and other particles in the air. If tiny particles slip past the hairs, they are trapped by mucus. On page A41 you read about mucus in the digestive system. The respiratory system is also lined with a sticky layer of mucus.

From your mouth or nose, the inhaled air moves to the back of your throat. There it enters the trachea (trā′kē ə), or windpipe. The **trachea** is the air tube that connects the throat to the lungs. Find the trachea below.

To feel your trachea, gently move your hand up and down the front of your neck. You will feel bumpy rings of cartilage (kärt′'l ij), a tough but bendable material. Cartilage helps the trachea keep its shape. Without cartilage, the trachea would collapse when you inhale.

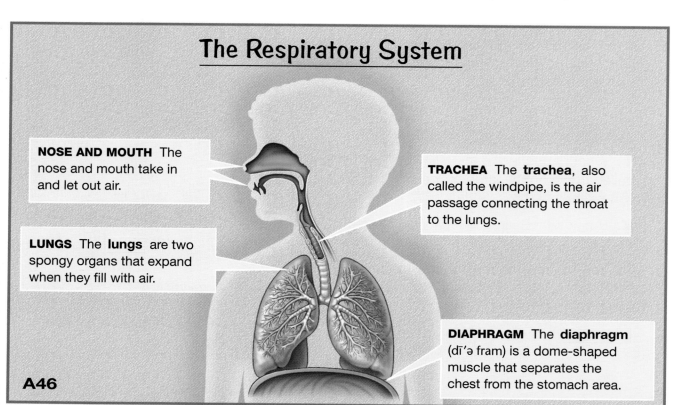

The Respiratory System

NOSE AND MOUTH The nose and mouth take in and let out air.

LUNGS The **lungs** are two spongy organs that expand when they fill with air.

TRACHEA The **trachea**, also called the windpipe, is the air passage connecting the throat to the lungs.

DIAPHRAGM The **diaphragm** (dī′ə fram) is a dome-shaped muscle that separates the chest from the stomach area.

Muscles Do the Work

The activity on page A45 shows that the breathing process starts in your chest. The process depends on the diaphragm and the muscles between your ribs. Follow the numbered steps in the drawing to see what happens during breathing.

Inhaling

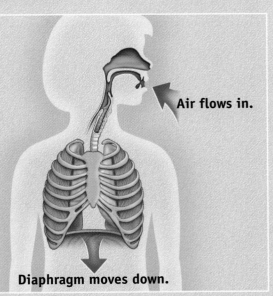

1. When you begin to inhale, the rib muscles tighten and get shorter, pulling the chest out and up.

2. The diaphragm tightens and moves down, further increasing the space inside the chest.

3. When the space inside the chest increases, the lungs expand and air rushes in.

Air flows in.

Diaphragm moves down.

Exhaling

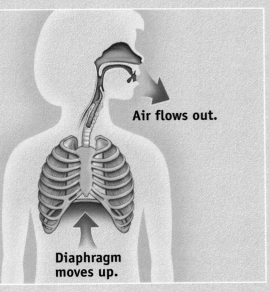

1. When you begin to exhale, the rib muscles relax and get longer and the chest gets smaller.

2. The diaphragm relaxes and moves up, making less space inside the chest.

3. Air is forced out of the lungs as the space in the chest gets smaller.

Air flows out.

Diaphragm moves up.

Breathless!

Your breathing rate is the number of times you inhale each minute. When you're sleeping or sitting quietly, your rate is slow. If you're walking, the rate increases, since your body needs a greater amount of oxygen supplied to the lungs. If you're exercising heavily, your breathing rate increases still more. The only way to get more oxygen into the body is to breathe more quickly and deeply. The activity on page A44 shows how a person's breathing rate increases during exercise. ■

Exchanging Gases

Reading Focus Which gases are exchanged inside the lungs?

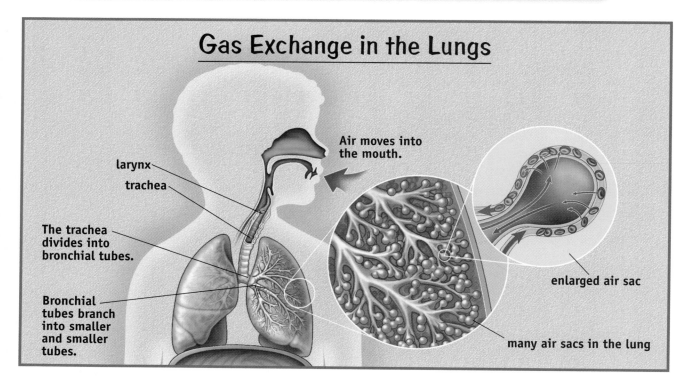

Gas Exchange in the Lungs

Air moves into the mouth.

larynx

trachea

The trachea divides into bronchial tubes.

Bronchial tubes branch into smaller and smaller tubes.

enlarged air sac

many air sacs in the lung

Imagine that you're going to dive into a deep pool. Inhale and hold your breath for as long as you can. At some point, probably within a minute, you have no choice—the muscles in your chest force you to breathe. This is your body's response to the fact that cells could soon be in danger of injury. They need oxygen for energy. And they must get rid of waste gases that are building up. Breathing meets both these needs.

The Bronchial Network

How does the oxygen you inhale get to the cells that need it? After passing through the nose or mouth, air enters the larynx (lar'iŋks), or voice box. The **larynx** is the part of the throat that is used in speaking.

Look at the drawing and find the parts described here. Below the larynx is the trachea. In the middle of the chest, the trachea splits to form two **bronchial tubes**. The bronchial tubes carry air from the trachea to the lungs. One tube enters each lung. Inside the lungs the bronchial tubes branch out into smaller and smaller tubes, much as tree branches do. The branches get smaller until they are like the tiniest twigs. Each twig ends in a tiny air sac.

Through the Wall

The spongy tissue of the lungs has millions of tiny air sacs. These **air sacs** are thin-walled chambers through which oxygen moves into the blood. Around the thin wall of each air sac is a network of tiny blood vessels. Oxygen from inhaled air passes into the air sacs, through the thin walls, and into blood vessels. Here the oxygen is picked up by the blood. Once oxygen passes into the blood, it is carried to the cells where it is needed.

For the air sacs to do their jobs, their walls must be kept clean. For example, when the walls become coated with tobacco smoke, they cannot take in enough oxygen. These delicate air sacs can also be injured by particles in air, called air pollutants, that are breathed in.

An Even Exchange

To release the energy in digested nutrients, cells need oxygen. In releasing this energy, the cells produce a waste product, the gas carbon dioxide. This gas can be dangerous to the cells. In fact, too much of it can poison them. When the blood delivers oxygen to the cells, it takes back the carbon dioxide that is given off. The carbon dioxide is carried by the blood back to the air sacs in the lung.

An exchange of gases takes place in the air sacs. The inhaled air brings oxygen to the air sacs in the lung. As oxygen passes from the air sacs to the blood, carbon dioxide passes from the blood to the air that fills the air sacs.

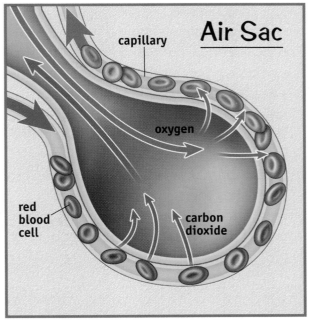

▲ **Gas exchange in an air sac**

Out With the Old

Next, the carbon dioxide in the air sacs must be pushed out of the body. When you hold your breath, the buildup of carbon dioxide signals your body to breathe. From the air sacs, the air passes through the bronchial tubes. After passing through the trachea, it travels through the larynx and out through the mouth or nose.

Exhaled air contains less oxygen than inhaled air and more carbon dioxide than inhaled air. If you breathe on a mirror, you'll notice that the exhaled air also picks up water vapor inside the body. Breathe on a mirror and see for yourself!

Internet Field Trip

Visit **www.eduplace.com** to learn more about the human body.

How You Say It

Moving air allows you to speak. Air flowing through the larynx helps you produce speech sounds. Notice your breathing as you speak. Are you inhaling or exhaling? You need exhaled air to speak.

In the larynx are bands of tissue called vocal cords, shown below. If they are stretched tightly, air flowing between them makes them vibrate. When they vibrate, they produce sounds. Find the larynx in the drawing. Then find your own larynx and place your hand over it. Make a sound. When the sound begins, you'll feel a vibration in the larynx.

When you speak, the muscles in your larynx stretch the vocal cords. Stretched tightly, they are close together. Exhaled air passing through the larynx makes the vocal cords vibrate, producing sound.

Both the respiratory and digestive systems need a way to transport substances to the cells. In the next chapter you'll learn about this transport system.

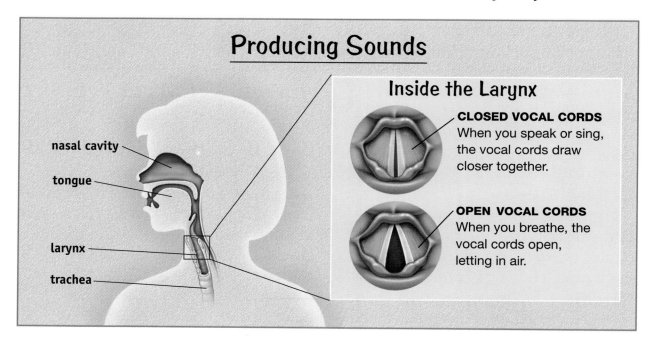

Producing Sounds

Inside the Larynx

CLOSED VOCAL CORDS
When you speak or sing, the vocal cords draw closer together.

OPEN VOCAL CORDS
When you breathe, the vocal cords open, letting in air.

nasal cavity

tongue

larynx

trachea

INVESTIGATION 2 WRAP-UP

REVIEW

1. Starting with the nose, list the main parts of the respiratory system.

2. Describe gas exchange in the air sacs.

CRITICAL THINKING

3. Describe the movement of the lungs and diaphragm when you exhale and when you inhale. Relate this to air flow into and out of the body.

4. During exercise, breathing rate increases. How would you expect an increase in the breathing rate to affect the heart rate? Give reasons for your answer.

REFLECT & EVALUATE

Word Power

Write the letter of the term that best matches the definition. *Not all terms will be used.*

1. The long, coiled organ where most digestion takes place
2. A watery liquid that moistens the mouth and food
3. The air passage connecting the throat to the lungs
4. The muscular tube that connects the mouth to the stomach
5. Looplike structures through which dissolved nutrients pass into the blood

a. bronchial tubes
b. esophagus
c. large intestine
d. peristalsis
e. saliva
f. small intestine
g. trachea
h. villi

Check What You Know

Write the term in each pair that best completes each sentence.

1. When you exhale, you release (oxygen, carbon dioxide).
2. The teeth used mainly for grinding are the (incisors, molars).
3. A tough, but bendable, body material is (mucus, cartilage).
4. When you inhale, the diaphragm moves (up, down).

Problem Solving

1. Imagine that you've just taken a bite out of an apple. Describe what happens to this apple as it moves from your mouth through your digestive system.

2. Pneumonia causes liquids to build up in the air sacs. Based on what you've learned, describe how pneumonia can affect gas exchange. Explain how this might affect the entire body.

Copy this drawing of an air sac in the lungs. Explain what the disklike objects are and why they are in different colors. Then explain what the arrows show about gas exchange in the air sac.

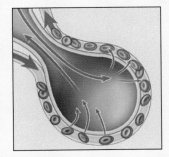

CHAPTER 3

CIRCULATION
AND EXCRETION

Your body has a network of connecting tubes that are part of a transport system. These tubes carry materials vital to your body's cells. In this chapter you will explore the transport system's role in supplying needed materials to cells and in removing waste products from those cells.

PEOPLE
USING SCIENCE

Medical Illustrator You can see the work of Richard LaRocco on many pages in Chapters 2 and 3 of this unit. He is a medical illustrator, an artist who specializes in drawings of the human body systems. By the age of 16, Richard LaRocco had decided to pursue art as a career. His art teacher, Mrs. Brosch, encouraged him to take art seriously and to develop his skills. His college studies at the Rochester Institute of Technology included human anatomy, medical illustration, and graphic design.

In his work, Richard LaRocco often begins with a paper-and-pencil sketch. Then he goes "high-tech." He scans the art into a computer and completes the work with an "electronic pen." Thinking about art as a career? Richard LaRocco's advice: Learn to draw very well and draw all the time!

Coming Up

◀ Richard LaRocco at work on a drawing of the upper digestive system

HOW DOES THE CIRCULATORY SYSTEM WORK?

The circulatory system, the body's transport system, has three main parts—the heart, the blood vessels, and the blood. In this investigation you'll explore how these three parts work together to transport nutrients and remove wastes.

Activity

Squeeze Play!

How hard does a human heart work to pump blood? Try this activity and find out!

MATERIALS
- rubber ball
- timer
- *Science Notebook*

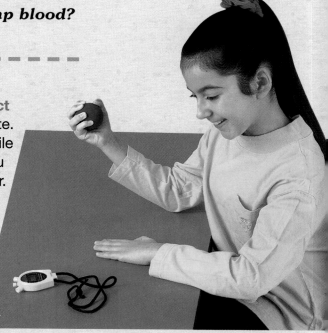

Procedure

Squeeze a rubber ball hard and then release it. **Predict** how many times you can squeeze the ball in one minute. **Record** your prediction in your *Science Notebook*. While a group member times you, count how many times you can squeeze the ball in one minute. **Record** the number. Repeat this two more times. Next, try to squeeze the ball 70 times in one minute. See how long you can continue at that rate. **Record** your results. **Compare** your results with those of other groups.

Analyze and Conclude

1. On average, the heart beats about 70 times per minute. How long could you squeeze the ball at the rate of 70 squeezes per minute without stopping?

2. What does this activity tell you about the heart?

Activity

In a Heartbeat

You've learned that the average person's heart beats about 70 times each minute. Find out how hard your own heart is working and what factors affect it.

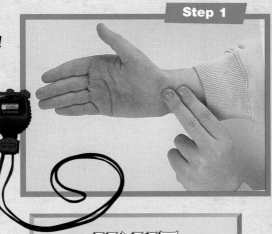

Step 1

Procedure

1. Find your pulse in your wrist, as shown. The **pulse** is the throbbing you can feel in a blood vessel caused by the beating of your heart.

2. Count how many times your heart beats in one minute. This is your heartbeat rate. **Record** this number in your *Science Notebook*.

3. Repeat step 2 two more times. Find the average of the three rates. **Record** the average heartbeat rate.

 See **SCIENCE** *and* **MATH TOOLBOX** page H5 if you need to review *Finding an Average.*

4. **Predict** whether your heartbeat rate will change if you exercise. **Record** what you think the rate for one minute will be after exercising.

5. Run in place for one minute. Immediately afterward, find your heartbeat rate as you did in step 2. Then rest for five minutes.

6. Repeat step 5 two more times. Find and **record** the average of the three heartbeat rates.

Analyze and Conclude

1. **Compare** your average heartbeat rate before and after exercising.

2. **Infer** why exercise would cause changes in your heartbeat rate.

UNIT PROJECT LINK

For your chosen plant, research the system that allows for transport of water, minerals, and sugars. Then research the circulatory system in the two animals chosen. Compare these three systems. How are they alike? How are they different? Add materials, such as models or posters, to your display that show how these systems compare.

Technology Link

For more help with your Unit Project, go to **www.eduplace.com**.

The Circulatory System

Reading Focus What is the job of the circulatory system?

The **circulatory system** is the transport system of the human body. It carries oxygen and nutrients to all cells and then removes carbon dioxide and other wastes. There are three main parts to this system—the heart, the blood vessels, and the blood. The **heart** is the pump that pushes the blood throughout the entire system. A vast network of tubes, called blood vessels, carries the blood. **Blood** is a tissue made up of a liquid called plasma and several types of cells. Blood carries materials to and from the body's cells.

Look at the drawing below to find the main organs of the circulatory system. Then follow the steps to see how blood circulates throughout the body.

The Circulatory System

vein

artery

capillaries

1 The left side of the heart pumps oxygen-rich blood through arteries, which carry the blood to all parts of the body.

2 Blood from the arteries enters tiny capillaries. In the capillaries, oxygen and nutrients move to the cells. Wastes, including the waste gas carbon dioxide, move from the cells into the capillaries.

3 Veins carry blood with wastes and carbon dioxide to the right side of the heart. The right side of the heart pumps blood to the lungs.

4 In the lungs, carbon dioxide is exchanged for inhaled oxygen. The oxygen-rich blood moves from the lungs to the heart. From there it is again pumped to the arteries.

- ARTERIES carry blood away from heart.
- VEINS carry blood to the heart.
- CAPILLARIES connect arteries to veins.

Circulation in the Heart

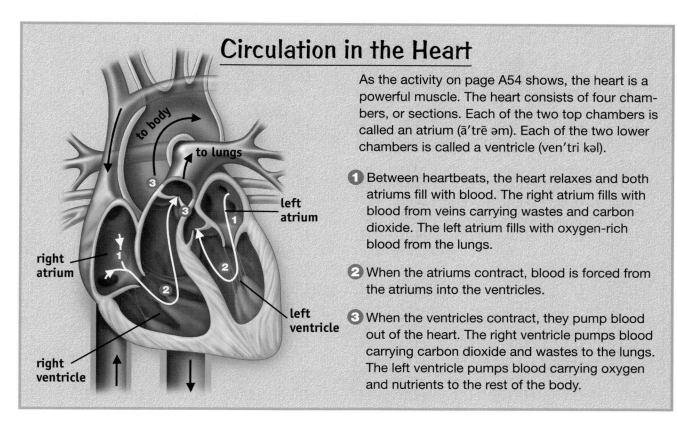

to body

to lungs

left atrium

right atrium

left ventricle

right ventricle

As the activity on page A54 shows, the heart is a powerful muscle. The heart consists of four chambers, or sections. Each of the two top chambers is called an atrium (ā′trē əm). Each of the two lower chambers is called a ventricle (ven′tri kəl).

1 Between heartbeats, the heart relaxes and both atriums fill with blood. The right atrium fills with blood from veins carrying wastes and carbon dioxide. The left atrium fills with oxygen-rich blood from the lungs.

2 When the atriums contract, blood is forced from the atriums into the ventricles.

3 When the ventricles contract, they pump blood out of the heart. The right ventricle pumps blood carrying carbon dioxide and wastes to the lungs. The left ventricle pumps blood carrying oxygen and nutrients to the rest of the body.

The Blood-Vessel Network

The blood vessels form a network through which the heart pumps blood. There are three kinds of blood vessels—arteries, capillaries, and veins.

Arteries are blood vessels that carry blood away from the heart. Most arteries carry oxygen-rich blood, which is bright red. The thick, muscular walls of the arteries stretch when the heart pumps blood into them. Large arteries branch many times into smaller arteries.

The smallest arteries lead into tiny blood vessels called **capillaries**. The capillaries connect the smallest arteries with the smallest veins. Look at the capillaries in the inset drawing on page A56. What happens inside the capillaries?

Veins carry blood from the capillaries to the heart. As blood travels to the heart, the many small veins join to form large veins, much like streams join to form rivers.

Blood and Its Parts

Blood is a fluid made up of blood cells and platelets in a pale yellow liquid called plasma. Plasma contains water, nutrients, wastes, and salts. Red blood cells give blood its color. They carry oxygen from the lungs to the body's cells. They carry carbon dioxide back to the lungs. White blood cells fight germs and break down dead cells. The number of white cells increases when the body is fighting infection. Platelets are tiny discs in plasma that help the blood clot, or thicken.

The Pulse

Your arteries expand and contract as blood pushes through them. You can feel a throbbing where arteries are close to the skin. The throbbing caused by blood rushing into the arteries when the lower chambers of the heart contract is called a **pulse**. Pulse rate is measured in the activity on page A55. ■

Ancient Blood Transfusions

Reading Focus Why could the Incas safely receive blood more than 500 years ago?

Why would a medical treatment work well in one part of the world and have mixed results in another? This medical mystery stumped scientists until they learned more about blood.

Early Transfusions

The mystery begins more than 500 years ago with the Incas. The Incas were a group of people who lived along the western coast of South America. Inca doctors learned how to give blood transfusions to injured people who had lost a lot of blood. A blood transfusion is the transfer of blood from one person to another person. Inca doctors let the

▲ Machu Picchu, the site of ancient Inca ruins

blood pass from a blood vessel of a healthy person, through a tube, to a blood vessel of an injured person. This was often a lifesaving measure.

When blood transfusions were tried in Europe in the 1600s, many patients died. In 1818 an English doctor, James Blundell, saved 11 of 15 patients by giving them blood. He noticed that when transfusions failed, the blood cells in the patient were stuck together.

Blood Types

In 1901 the mystery began to unfold. Karl Landsteiner, an Austrian-born doctor working in the United States, found that there are several types of human blood. He named these blood types A, B, AB, and O. He also learned that a **recipient** (ri sip'ē ənt), a person who receives blood, can only safely be given blood of a certain type. Blood from the **donor**, the person who gives blood, must be matched to the recipient's blood. If the blood types don't match, the blood cells clump, or stick together. This clumping of cells causes illness or death.

Look at the table on page A59 to see which recipients can receive blood from which donors. What clues does the table give for solving the mystery?

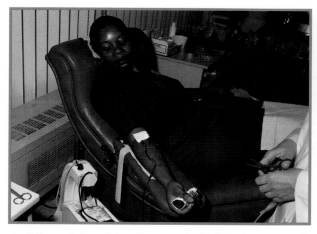

▲ When blood is donated, it is also typed.

▲ Blood cells clumped in mismatched blood

Scientists now think the reason the Incas were successful in blood transfusions was that most of them had type O blood. In western Europe the most common blood types were A and O. It's likely that many early blood transfusions in western Europe failed because of mismatched blood, which caused the blood cells to stick together.

Today, blood is typed when it's drawn. That means it's tested to find out what type it is. Then each unit of blood is labeled by type. As a safety

Blood Types	
Recipient (receives blood)	**Donor** (gives blood)
A	A or O
B	B or O
AB	A, B, AB, or O
O	O

measure, some donor red blood cells are mixed in a tube with some of the patient's plasma. If these mixed cells clump, the blood isn't used. ■

───── **INVESTIGATION 1 WRAP-UP** ─────

THINK IT WRITE IT

REVIEW

1. What are the main parts of blood? Briefly describe each part.

2. Name and describe the three types of blood vessels.

CRITICAL THINKING

3. How does the blood entering the right atrium differ from the blood entering the left atrium? Account for the difference.

4. One blood type is called the "universal donor." From the table above, tell which blood type is the universal donor and explain what is meant by that term.

INVESTIGATION 2

HOW DOES THE EXCRETORY SYSTEM WORK?

Your body gets energy when it "burns" nutrients. Just as burning wood produces ash, "burning" nutrients produces wastes in your body. In this investigation you'll find out about a body system that gets rid of body wastes, such as water and salts.

Activity

MATERIALS
- hand lens
- *Science Notebook*

Peering at Pores

Skin is the largest body part. How does it help you get rid of wastes? Find out.

Procedure

Observe the skin on your arms and hands with a hand lens. In your *Science Notebook*, **record** all the features you observe. **Make a sketch** of what you see through the hand lens. Then **compare** observations with your group members. As a group, **list** the things the skin does for the body. **Record** your group's list. Give reasons for each item you put on the list. **Compare** your list with those of other groups.

Analyze and Conclude

1. What are some of the features you saw on your skin? What do you think these features do for the body?

2. How do you think the skin helps the body get rid of wastes?

Activity

Your Watery Body

Your body needs water to help it get rid of wastes. You take in much of this water in the liquids that you drink. In this activity you'll measure how much liquid you drink in one day.

MATERIALS
- metric measuring cup
- plastic cup
- marker
- *Science Notebook*

Procedure

1. **Predict** how much liquid you'll drink in one day. Include all liquids. **Record** your prediction in your *Science Notebook*.

2. **Make a chart** like the one shown below.

Drinks in a Day		
Time	Type of Liquid	mL of Liquid

3. Make a plastic cup into a liquids measurer. Use a measuring cup to add 50 mL of water to the plastic cup. Use a marker to mark the water line. Label this mark *50 mL*. Add another 50 mL and mark the new water line. Label this mark *100 mL*. Continue marking the cup in this way to its top. Use your liquids measurer as your drinking glass for one day.

 *See* **SCIENCE** *and* **MATH TOOLBOX** *page H7 if you need to review* **Measuring Volume.**

4. In your chart, **record** all the liquids you drink during one day. **Record** the time you drink the liquid, the type of liquid, and the amount. Rinse out the measurer each time you use it.

5. **Compare** your results with those of other students.

Analyze and Conclude

1. How much liquid did you drink during the day?

2. Was your intake of liquid about the same as, more than, or less than that of other students?

INVESTIGATE FURTHER!

RESEARCH

Find out how much liquid doctors think a person should drink each day. Research what effect a person's age, weight, health, and activity have on the amount of liquid suggested. Find out the percentage of water in common foods and research the percentage of water in a human body.

The Excretory System

Reading Focus How does the body get rid of wastes?

Your body is constantly busy—even while you are asleep. It is building and replacing cells, releasing energy from food, and maintaining parts that keep the body running smoothly.

All this activity creates body wastes. The human body has a system for ridding itself of harmful wastes produced by the cells. This system is called the **excretory** (eks′krə tôr ē) **system**. The picture below shows the main parts of the excretory system.

Notice that the excretory system includes organs that are part of other body systems. The lungs are part of the respiratory system. But they also

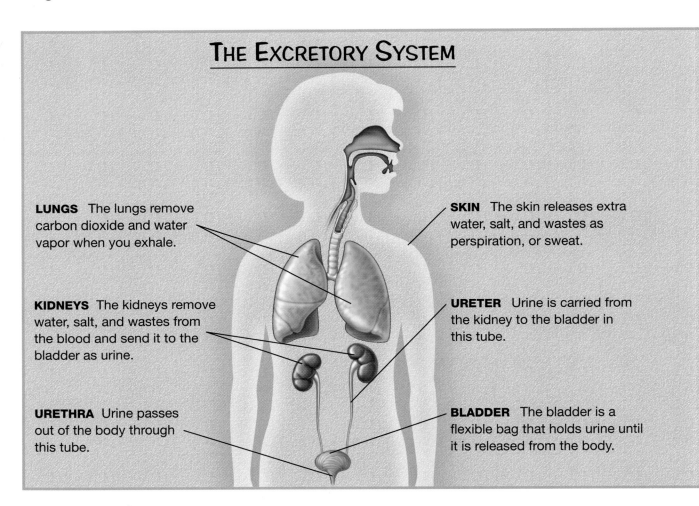

THE EXCRETORY SYSTEM

LUNGS The lungs remove carbon dioxide and water vapor when you exhale.

KIDNEYS The kidneys remove water, salt, and wastes from the blood and send it to the bladder as urine.

URETHRA Urine passes out of the body through this tube.

SKIN The skin releases extra water, salt, and wastes as perspiration, or sweat.

URETER Urine is carried from the kidney to the bladder in this tube.

BLADDER The bladder is a flexible bag that holds urine until it is released from the body.

remove many wastes in exhaled air. For example, the lungs remove excess water. It leaves the body as water vapor, or water in the form of a gas.

But the major waste-removal job of the lungs is to release the wastes formed when carbohydrates and fats are broken down in the cells of the body. Carbohydrates and fats are broken down by oxygen, releasing energy. The carbon in these materials combines with the oxygen to produce carbon dioxide, a waste gas. The carbon dioxide passes into the blood. Then the blood carries this waste gas to the lungs. From the lungs the carbon dioxide is exhaled.

How the Kidneys Work

The **kidneys** are two organs that clean and filter the blood. The filtering of the blood results in the yellowish liquid called **urine** (yo͝or′ in). Kidneys remove excess water and salts. They also remove the wastes that are produced when proteins are broken down into smaller molecules.

From the drawing on page A62 you can see the location of the kidneys. They lie on either side of the spine. Each kidney weighs less than 0.225 kg (about 0.5 lb) and is about the size of a fist.

The drawing on this page shows a closeup of one of millions of tiny filtering units in the kidney. These units, or nephrons (nef′ränz), are found in the outer layer of the kidney. Each unit has a cup-shaped end packed with a tightly coiled ball of capillaries.

Blood passes through the nephron and is filtered under pressure, removing wastes and water. The filtering of blood by the nephron produces urine. The urine drains out of the filtering units into tubes in the middle part of the kidney. From there the urine drains through larger tubes into the bladder, where it collects. Small round muscles keep the urine in the bladder until it is ready to be emptied. When about 250 mL (1 c) of urine has collected, a person has an urge to empty the bladder.

On average, an adult passes about 1.5 L (1.6 qt) of urine per day. Only a small fraction of the water filtered by the kidneys passes into the urine. To help keep a healthy balance of fluids, the kidneys send most of the water and some salt and nutrients back to the blood.

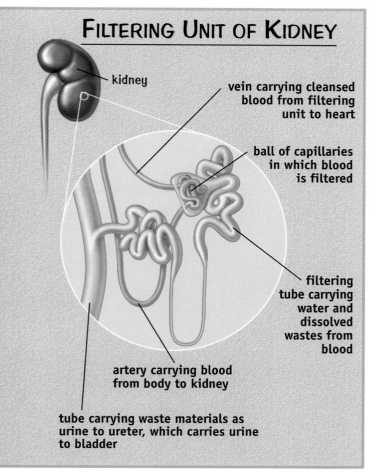

FILTERING UNIT OF KIDNEY

kidney

vein carrying cleansed blood from filtering unit to heart

ball of capillaries in which blood is filtered

filtering tube carrying water and dissolved wastes from blood

artery carrying blood from body to kidney

tube carrying waste materials as urine to ureter, which carries urine to bladder

The Skin

A person also loses water and wastes through the skin. Weighing about 4 kg to 7 kg (9 lb to 15 lb) in an adult, the skin is the largest organ in the body.

The skin removes wastes and water by perspiring, or sweating. Sweating is the release of water, salts, and wastes through pores in the skin. Look at the drawing below. Notice the **sweat glands**, which are small coiled tubes that end at pores on the skin's surface. These pores can be observed in the activity on page A60.

The main function of sweating is to cool the body. When the body produces extra heat, such as during exercise, the circulatory system delivers more blood to the capillaries near the skin. Water, carrying heat, passes into the skin tissues and moves to the sweat glands. This water then reaches the skin surface as perspiration, or sweat. As water evaporates from the skin, it removes some of the heat from the body.

Sometimes a person can lose too much water, salt, and minerals through sweating. Working hard in hot weather, a person can lose as much as 3 L (3 qt) of water! The kidneys can adjust the level of water in the body. But a person needs to drink extra water on a hot day or after exercise to replace the lost water. ■

Internet Field Trip
Visit **www.eduplace.com** to learn more about human body systems.

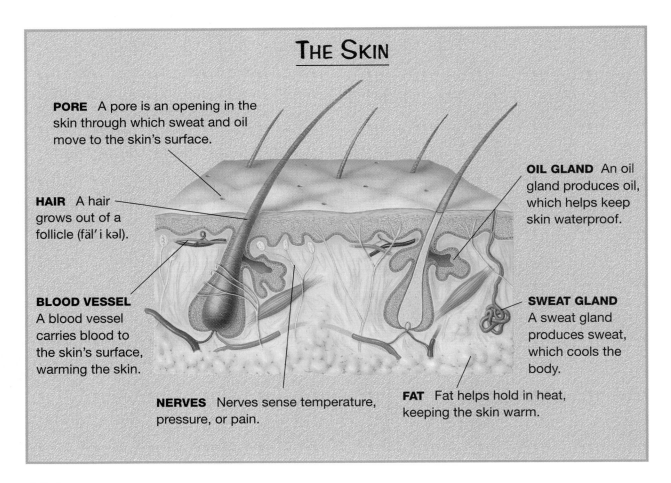

THE SKIN

PORE A pore is an opening in the skin through which sweat and oil move to the skin's surface.

HAIR A hair grows out of a follicle (fäl' i kəl).

BLOOD VESSEL A blood vessel carries blood to the skin's surface, warming the skin.

OIL GLAND An oil gland produces oil, which helps keep skin waterproof.

SWEAT GLAND A sweat gland produces sweat, which cools the body.

NERVES Nerves sense temperature, pressure, or pain.

FAT Fat helps hold in heat, keeping the skin warm.

Goose Bumps

Reading Focus What causes goose bumps, and how are they helpful?

Does your skin get covered with little bumps when you are cold or frightened? You probably call these bumps "goose bumps" or "goose pimples." Are goose bumps helpful? Look at the pictures on page A66 to see what causes them. These pictures show two sections of skin. On the left is warm skin. On the right is cold skin.

When you are cold, several things occur. Nerves in the skin signal the brain that it's cold. Small muscles at the bottom of each hair contract, pulling each hair straight up. At the same time, blood vessels near the skin's surface become narrower. Blood flows through blood vessels that are deep within the skin. This process helps to keep the skin warm.

When all the hairs on the skin stand on end, they trap air close to the skin's surface. This layer of trapped air helps to keep the skin warm. As the hair stands straight up, it pulls on the skin

Science in Literature

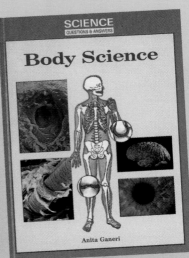

Body Science
by Anita Ganeri
Dillon Press, 1992

WHY IS BLOOD RED?

"Your red blood cells contain a special substance called hemoglobin, which carries oxygen around your body and also gives blood its red color. As your blood flows through your lungs, the hemoglobin takes in oxygen and carries it throughout your body. When the hemoglobin is filled with fresh oxygen, it looks red."

Do you have more questions about your blood and your heart? Many of your questions will be answered by this colorful and informative book. Check out *Body Science* by Anita Ganeri.

around it, forming a bump. This bump is the goose bump!

Do other animals besides humans get goose bumps? Yes! Animals with fur or hair also get cold. When this happens, the hair or fur stands straight up, trapping air that helps to keep the animal warm. Now think about a frightened animal, such as a cat. The fur on a fright-ened cat fluffs out. This makes the cat look bigger to its enemies. The cat's enemies may stay away if the cat looks scary.

Since humans don't have a thick coat of fur or hair, goose bumps don't do a lot to keep them warm. But goose bumps can let you know when it's time to put on a sweater or to stop watching a scary movie! ■

 Using Math

What Celsius temperatures might cause the reactions shown? What Fahrenheit temperatures might do the same?

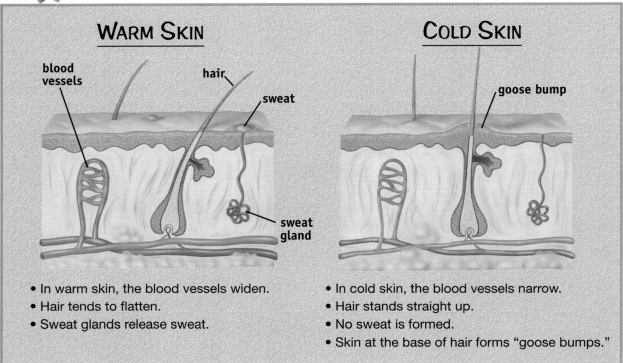

WARM SKIN

blood vessels
hair
sweat
sweat gland

• In warm skin, the blood vessels widen.
• Hair tends to flatten.
• Sweat glands release sweat.

COLD SKIN

goose bump

• In cold skin, the blood vessels narrow.
• Hair stands straight up.
• No sweat is formed.
• Skin at the base of hair forms "goose bumps."

INVESTIGATION 2 WRAP-UP

 **THINK IT WRITE IT**

REVIEW

1. List and describe the three main parts of the excretory system. Explain the function of each part.

2. Describe what happens in a filtering unit of the kidney.

CRITICAL THINKING

3. Explain why the skin can be thought of as part of the excretory system.

4. How is a bird with fluffed-up feathers like a person with goose bumps?

REFLECT & EVALUATE

Word Power

Write the letter of the term that best matches the definition. *Not all terms will be used.*

a. arteries
b. blood
c. capillaries
d. donor
e. heart
f. kidneys
g. recipient
h. veins

1. A tissue that carries materials to and from the body's cells
2. Blood vessels that carry blood from the capillaries to the heart
3. Blood vessels that carry blood away from the heart
4. A pair of organs that clean and filter the blood
5. A person who gives blood for transfusions
6. Blood vessels that connect the smallest arteries with the smallest veins

Check What You Know

Write the term in each pair that best completes each statement.

1. Urine passes out of the body through the (ureter, urethra).
2. Tiny discs that help blood to clot are called (platelets, pores).
3. The two lower chambers of the heart are the (atriums, ventricles).

Problem Solving

1. Explain how the filtering units of the kidneys are somewhat like the air sacs in the lungs.

2. While fixing his bicycle, a boy cut a large blood vessel in his hand. Every few seconds, the blood would spurt out. What would this tell you about the kind of blood vessel that was cut? Explain your answer.

BUILD YOUR PORTFOLIO

Copy this drawing of the excretory system. Identify parts *a–e*. Briefly describe the function of each part. Which of these parts also belongs to another body system? Name that system.

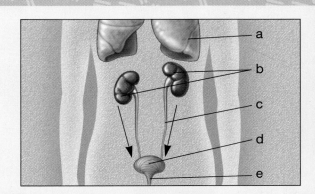

a
b
c
d
e

CHAPTER 4

LIFE CYCLES

All living things pass through a life cycle. They might crack out of an eggshell or sprout from a seed. Some live only a few days; others live more than one hundred years. In this chapter you'll explore the life cycle of several different animals and plants.

PEOPLE USING SCIENCE

Animal Nutritionist Dr. Diane A. Hirakawa is a specialist in the field of animal nutrition. She develops tasty, nutritious pet food suited to the age, activity, and health of pets. "Animals always greet you with a wag of a tail or a lick on the face," writes Dr. Hirakawa, who chose her career because she loves animals.

Dr. Hirakawa is Senior Vice President of Research and Development at The Iams Company, producers of pet foods. To prepare for her career, Dr. Hirakawa studied companion animal biology in college. Then she earned a Ph.D. in nutritional biochemistry. In 1995 she coauthored a book on animal nutrition. Her book deals with dietary needs of animals at different stages in their life cycle.

▲ These dogs are eating food suited to the life cycle stage they are in.

INVESTIGATION 1

WHAT ARE THE STAGES IN AN ANIMAL'S LIFE CYCLE?

Are there any babies in your family? Are there any people older than 80? All living things pass through stages. In this investigation you'll explore the life cycle of several different animals.

Activity

Life Cycle of a Brine Shrimp

Do animals change as they age? What is the importance of change in the life of an animal? By observing changes in the life of a tiny animal, the brine shrimp, you'll discover answers to some of these questions.

Procedure

1. Obtain some brine shrimp eggs from your teacher. Use a hand lens and microscope to examine the eggs. Note their size, color, and texture. **Record** your observations in your *Science Notebook*.

 See **SCIENCE** and **MATH TOOLBOX** page H2 if you need to review **Using a Microscope.**

2. With your group, **brainstorm** questions about how the brine shrimp grow and develop. **Record** your questions.

MATERIALS

- brine shrimp eggs
- hand lens
- microscope
- plastic cup
- salt water
- measuring cup
- red marker
- dried powdered yeast
- dropper
- plastic teaspoon
- microscope slides
- cover slip
- *Science Notebook*

SAFETY ///////

Wash your hands before and after working with brine shrimp. Clean up spills immediately.

3. Prepare an egg hatchery. Obtain room-temperature salt water from your teacher. Add 250 mL of this water to a plastic cup. With a red marker, mark the level of water on the outside of the cup.

4. Sprinkle one fourth of a teaspoon of brine shrimp eggs into the cup. Check with your teacher. You may need to add a pinch of yeast to the water as food for the brine shrimp. Stir the mixture. Place the hatchery in a warm place, where it will not be disturbed.

5. Make a chart like the one shown below. Leave enough space to record three weeks of observations.

Step 7

Date	Observations	Drawing

6. Observe the egg hatchery the next day. Record your observations.

7. Each day for three weeks, use a dropper to carefully remove a few eggs. Observe them with a hand lens and through a microscope. Record any changes you notice. Draw what you see when you observe the brine shrimp with the hand lens and the microscope. Return the brine shrimp you observe to the plastic cup. As water evaporates from the cup, add salt water up to the red line.

8. Compare your observations with those of other members of your class.

Analyze and Conclude

1. What stages of development did you observe in the brine shrimp?

2. Were your questions about the brine shrimp's growth answered by the activity? Explain.

3. What changes occurred in the brine shrimp at each stage?

4. What stage was reached by about the twentieth day? Infer why this stage is important.

INVESTIGATE FURTHER!

EXPERIMENT

Can you speed up the life cycle of a brine shrimp? Plan and carry out an experiment that would decrease the number of days needed for eggs to hatch and grow into adults. You may wish to use a computer, including CD-ROM programs, to plan your experiment and to record and analyze your results.

The Human Life Cycle

Reading Focus What are the main stages in the human life cycle?

Where are you in your life cycle? You've changed a lot since you were a tiny baby. Now you're just a couple of years from being a teenager. Find out about the stages that humans pass through from infancy to old age.

Infancy

Infancy is a stage that lasts from birth to about age 1. At birth an infant is almost completely dependent on its parents for survival. Through the first year, the baby gains control of its muscles and other systems. As a baby develops, it can sit up, creep, then crawl, stand, and walk. During this period the infant is growing at a tremendous rate.

An infant shows traits that are inherited, or passed down, from its parents. For example, the infant might have inherited straight black hair from its father and dimples from its mother.

Childhood

Childhood is a stage that lasts from about age 1 to about age 12. This stage begins with the ability to walk. Most children learn to walk from 9 months to about 15 months. Through the first year of childhood, the growth spurt of infancy continues. The growth rate is fairly steady from age 4 until age 11 or 12.

▲ The human life cycle

A72

During childhood a person learns many skills that will be used for the rest of life. A child learns how to speak his or her parents' language by imitating what the parents say. A lot is learned from the child's environment. A child may learn about the pain of touching a hot stove. Through such a painful experience, the child learns to stay away from a hot stove.

Adolescence

Adolescence lasts from about age 11 to about age 18 to 20. It is during this stage that a person grows into adulthood. A second growth spurt occurs, and the adult body takes shape. During this stage a person becomes able to reproduce.

Adulthood

Adulthood is the stage that begins at the end of the teenage years and lasts the rest of a person's life. Early in this stage, the body is at the peak of its physical abilities. This is usually when the person has the greatest strength and greatest physical endurance. Responsibilities during this stage may include raising a family and earning a living. Physical ability declines in later adulthood.

In the United States, a male born in 1993 can expect to live an average of 72.2 years. A female born in 1993 can expect to live an average of 78.8 years. As medical science advances, people are able to live longer and more healthfully. ■

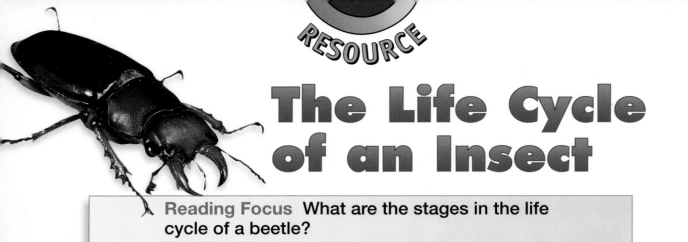

The Life Cycle of an Insect

Reading Focus What are the stages in the life cycle of a beetle?

You've learned about the stages in the life cycle of a human. You know that a baby looks somewhat like an adult human being—just much smaller! With some kinds of animals, each stage in the life cycle is very different. The animal looks very different at each stage. It also lives in different places and eats different kinds of food. The beetle, which is an insect, is such an animal.

How a Beetle Changes

A beetle goes through four distinct stages in its life cycle. Animals that go through these four stages are said to pass through **complete metamorphosis** (kəm plēt′ met ə môr′fə sis). Refer to the table on page A75 to see what happens at each stage.

The **egg** is the first stage in the beetle's life cycle. An adult beetle lays her eggs in the openings of wet decaying wood or in soil. The **larva**, also called a grub, is the wormlike stage that follows the egg stage. A beetle larva eats wet decaying wood or other rotting material in soil. As the grub eats and develops, it gets larger. Once it reaches a certain size, it molts, or sheds its outer skin. After it molts, the larva comes out, a bit larger than before.

The **pupa** (pyōō′pə) is the stage between the larva and the adult. During this stage, the beetle might look like it's at rest. Actually the insect is going through many changes. It changes color and develops a hard outer case. Adult organs form, and the beetle develops wings. The insect may stay in this stage for a few days or several weeks, depending on the kind of beetle it is. The photograph on this page shows the inside of the pupa case.

The **adult** is the final stage in the beetle's life cycle. The adult beetle comes out of the pupa fully grown. It now has six legs, two pairs of wings, complex mouth parts, and adult organs.

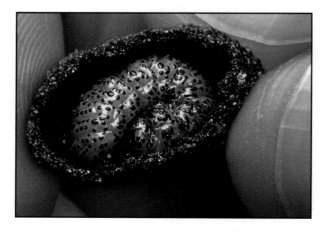

▲ Lengthwise section of a beetle pupa, showing the developing insect

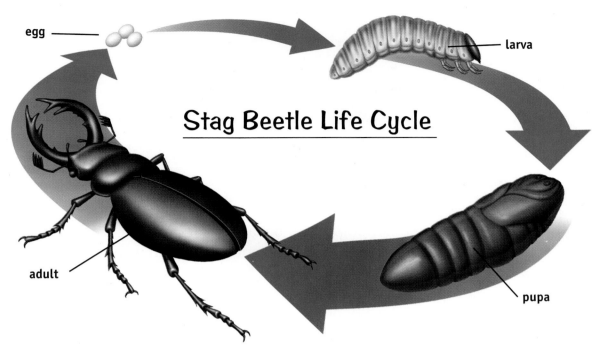

Stag Beetle Life Cycle

egg — larva

pupa

adult

The adult male and adult female beetle mate. Then the female lays her eggs in wet decaying wood. The entire cycle begins again.

The Moth and the Butterfly

Like beetles, moths and butterflies go through complete metamorphosis. They pass through the same four stages—egg, larva, pupa, and adult.

There are a few differences between the life cycles of beetles, moths, and butterflies. The table below shows you these differences and the names given to each of the stages. You are probably most familiar with the terms *cocoon* and *caterpillar*. Notice that the pupa stage of a moth is called a cocoon. The pupa stage of a butterfly is called a chrysalis (kris′ə lis). ■

Life Cycles of Three Insects

Beetle	Moth	Butterfly
egg	egg	egg
larva (grub)	larva (caterpillar)	larva (caterpillar)
pupa	pupa (cocoon)	pupa (chrysalis)
adult (beetle)	adult (moth)	adult (butterfly)

Vertebrate Life Cycles

Reading Focus What are the stages in the life cycles of some vertebrates?

Fish and humans share an important characteristic. A fish, like a human, is a **vertebrate** (vʉr′tə brit), an animal with a backbone. Vertebrates have a series of bones that make up their backbone.

A Fishy Story

Some kinds of fish live in fresh water and some live in salt water. Some kinds live in both fresh water and salt water at different times in their life cycle. The drawings on page A77 show the life cycle of a fish that you might eat for dinner—the salmon.

Adult salmon live in the ocean. When it's time to reproduce, these fish return to the same freshwater stream where they hatched. Salmon may swim as far as 3,220 km (2,000 mi) to where they hatched.

This behavior—returning to the freshwater stream—is instinctive (in stiŋk′tiv)

behavior. It is behavior that the salmon inherits, or is born with. A salmon does not have to learn to do this.

As she prepares to lay her eggs, the adult female salmon forms several nests in the gravel at the bottom of the stream. She lays 2,000 to 17,000 sticky eggs. The adult male salmon releases male sex cells over the eggs.

When a male sex cell joins with an egg, or female sex cell, the result is called a fertilized egg. A young salmon develops from a fertilized egg. Each fertilized egg forms a yolk sac, which is food for the tiny fish.

At the next stage, the salmon looks like a tiny spotted fish. By the time a young salmon is two years old, it takes on the silvery color of the adult fish. It begins the long journey from its freshwater home to the ocean.

After swimming great distances to the ocean, the adult male and female salmon remain in the ocean until they are ready to reproduce. When the females are ready to lay eggs, all adults swim upstream, against the flow of water, to the same freshwater river where they hatched. After the female lays her eggs and the male releases male sex cells over the eggs, the adult salmon die. Then the cycle continues.

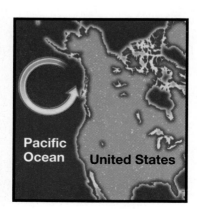

Pacific Ocean United States

◀ The yellow arrow on this map shows the great distance the salmon swims from its hatching place to the ocean and back again.

Salmon Life Cycle

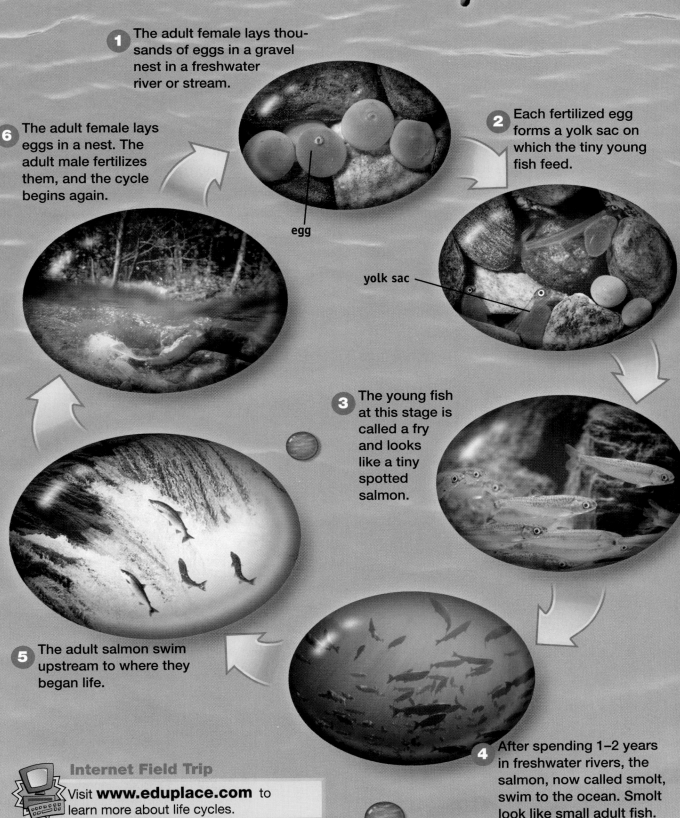

1 The adult female lays thousands of eggs in a gravel nest in a freshwater river or stream.

egg

2 Each fertilized egg forms a yolk sac on which the tiny young fish feed.

yolk sac

6 The adult female lays eggs in a nest. The adult male fertilizes them, and the cycle begins again.

3 The young fish at this stage is called a fry and looks like a tiny spotted salmon.

5 The adult salmon swim upstream to where they began life.

4 After spending 1–2 years in freshwater rivers, the salmon, now called smolt, swim to the ocean. Smolt look like small adult fish.

Internet Field Trip
Visit **www.eduplace.com** to learn more about life cycles.

It's for the Birds

Woodpeckers use their pointed beaks to hunt for insects in bark. They sleep in larger holes that they drill in the sides of trees. Hunting for insects and drilling holes is instinctive. That is, a woodpecker is born with the ability to drill holes. This bird inherits from its parents the ability to drill holes in wood.

Woodpeckers mate for life. After a courtship dance in the spring, a pair of birds mate. Then the female lays up to fourteen eggs in a hole drilled in a tree. Male and female birds take turns sitting on the eggs to warm them. Inside each egg, a tiny woodpecker is developing.

In about 12 days, the young bird pecks open the shell. It comes out with wrinkly pink skin and no feathers. Its eyes don't open for 8 days. The young birds remain in the hole in the tree, and the parent birds bring caterpillars for their young to eat. The parents defend the young birds from enemies. This behavior by the adults is also instinctive. In a couple of weeks, the baby birds have grown feathers. By four weeks of age they are ready to learn to fly and hunt for themselves.

The family remains together throughout the summer. By November the birds are ready to live on their own. Each young woodpecker drills a hole in a tree for shelter and seeks a mate. Next spring the young woodpeckers will reproduce, and the cycle will continue.

Science in Literature

SECRETS OF SURVIVAL

"When it is time for the butterflies to lay their yellow eggs, the passionflower leaves provide the perfect spot. Once the eggs hatch, the emerging caterpillars chomp into the vine's leaves without being harmed by the poison. Why? The caterpillars are able to store the poison inside their bodies. They use it as a weapon against birds that eat caterpillars. . . ."

Why Save the Rain Forest?
by Donald Silver
Illustrated by Patricia J. Wynne
Julian Messner, 1993

Find out about the amazing ways that butterflies survive in the rain forest. Read these stories of survival in *Why Save the Rain Forest?* by Donald Silver.

These eggs will hatch in about twelve days.

Newly hatched birds are blind and helpless.

Woodpecker
Life Cycle

Very young birds are fed by their parents.

An adult woodpecker drills a hole for a nest.

These birds search for insects in a tree trunk.

INVESTIGATION 1 WRAP-UP

REVIEW

'1. Describe the four main stages in the life cycle of an insect that goes through complete metamorphosis.

2. Name and describe four stages in the human life cycle. Name a learned and an inherited trait.

CRITICAL THINKING

3. Compare the human life cycle with the bird life cycle. Consider such things as how an infant and a young bird obtain food.

4. Compare the life cycle of a butterfly with that of a beetle. How are they alike? How are they different?

INVESTIGATION 2

WHAT ARE THE STAGES IN A PLANT'S LIFE CYCLE?

Which came first—the acorn or the oak tree? The answer may always be a matter of opinion. In this investigation you'll explore how plants change during their life cycle.

Activity

The Secret of a Seed

You put a seed in soil and keep it moist. In a few days a tiny new plant with roots, a stem, and leaves appears. How can a new living plant come from a seed that seems lifeless? Find out what secrets a seed holds!

MATERIALS
- soaked lima bean seeds
- soaked corn kernels
- plastic knife
- hand lens
- toothpicks
- *Science Notebook*

SAFETY
Use care in handling the knife.

Procedure

1. Examine and compare a lima bean seed and a corn kernel, which is actually a corn seed. Record your observations in your *Science Notebook*. Make drawings of the seeds.

2. Carefully peel off the thin outer coverings of a lima bean and a corn kernel. Observe each covering with a hand lens. Record the differences and similarities you see.

Step 3

3. Gently split open the bean seed with either your fingernail or a plastic knife. Spread open the two halves of the bean seed and **examine** each half with a hand lens. **Draw** what you observe. **Record** your osbservations.

Math Hint *As you examine each half of the seed, note any symmetric shapes or structures.*

4. **Predict** what you will find inside the corn kernel. Then use the knife to carefully cut the corn kernel in half lengthwise through the side. Lay the halves flat.

5. **Examine** each half with the hand lens. **Compare** the inside of the corn kernel with the inside of the bean seed. **Draw** the inside of the corn kernel. **Discuss** what you have observed with other members of your group.

6. Use a toothpick to scrape off a bit of the material that fills up each seed. **Examine** the material with the hand lens. **Compare** the material from the bean seed with that from the corn seed.

Analyze and Conclude

1. How was the covering of the lima bean seed different from the covering of the corn kernel? How was it similar? **Infer** the purpose that each covering serves.

2. What structures did you find inside each seed?

3. **Hypothesize** the function of the material that fills up each seed.

4. What can you **infer** about seeds from this activity?

UNIT PROJECT LINK

Research the life cycles of the same three organisms you have been using in your museum display. Use posters or models to show how their life cycles compare. Point out how their life cycles are alike and how they are different. Add these materials to your display. Invite other classes to view the completed display.

 **Technology Link**

For more help with your Unit Project, go to **www.eduplace.com**.

Activity

It's Just a Stage

Infant, child, adolescent, adult are the stages of the human life cycle. In this activity you'll use fast-growing radish seeds to find out if plants have similar life-cycle stages.

MATERIALS

- small flowerpot
- fast-growing radish seeds
- soil
- water
- liquid houseplant fertilizer
- dropper
- good source of artificial light
- metric ruler
- red marker
- cotton swab
- *Science Notebook*

SAFETY

Do not eat any seeds or soil!

Procedure

1. Fill a small flowerpot with soil. Place 4 fast-growing radish seeds in the pot, spaced evenly apart near the rim. Cover them lightly with soil. Water the seeds. Using a dropper, add liquid houseplant fertilizer to the soil according to the package directions.

2. Place the flowerpot under a good source of artificial light. Keep the light on 24 hours a day. Check the soil each day, making sure to keep it moist, not wet, at all times. When the seeds sprout, assign each tiny plant a different number to help you keep track of its growth. Write the number on the pot, near each plant.

3. In your *Science Notebook*, **make a chart** for recording height as the plants grow. **Measure** and **record** each plant's height each day. Then **make a line graph** that shows the growth of each plant. As the plants grow, **record** your observations and **draw** the plants.

Plant #	Height (cm)				
	Day 1	Day 2	Day 3	Day 4	Day 5
1					

 See **SCIENCE** *and* **MATH TOOLBOX** page H13 if you need to review **Making a Line Graph.**

Step 4

4. When the stems are 5 cm tall, use a red marker to make a dot on the stem just below the leaves. Each day **measure** and **record** the distance between the soil and the dot.

 Measure and record the distance at the same time each day.

5. If your plants form flowers, follow your teacher's instructions for using cotton swabs to transfer pollen from the flower of one plant to the flower of another plant. **Record** your method of pollination.

6. Continue to **observe** your plants. If fruits are produced, open several when they are ripe and **examine** the contents.

Analyze and Conclude

1. Seedlings are the tiny plants that first appear above the soil. How many days after planting seeds did most seedlings appear? If you saw flower buds, how many days after planting did they appear? If your plants formed fruits, how many days did it take for them to form fruits with seeds?

2. What can you **infer** about stem growth from the measurements you made each day?

3. What stages in the life cycle of a plant did you observe?

4. What stage in the plant's life cycle is similar to the life-cycle stage you are in? Explain your answer.

From Flower to Fruit

Reading Focus How do fruits and seeds form from a flower?

How would you encourage someone to visit you? You might prepare some food, put on your best clothes, and make sure you smell good. That's just what many flowers do to attract insects. When an insect visits a flower, however, the visit begins the process that ends with seed production.

The flower is the reproductive organ of a flowering plant. Some kinds of plants have flowers that produce both male and female sex cells. Other kinds have flowers that produce either male or female sex cells. When an insect visits a flower, it transfers the male sex cells from one flower to another. This transfer is part of the process of sexual reproduction in the flower. During **sexual reproduction** a male sex cell joins with a female sex cell to produce a fertilized (furt″l īzd) egg. In flowering plants, this fertilized egg develops into a tiny plant enclosed in a seed. Through sexual reproduction, the tiny plant inherits traits, such as petal color and leaf shape, from each parent plant.

How a Fruit Forms

STAMEN The **stamen** is the male part of the flower. It produces pollen.

Anther The anther holds pollen grains, which contain male sex cells.

PISTIL The **pistil** is the female part of a flower.

Stigma The stigma is the sticky part on the top of the pistil to which pollen grains stick.

Ovary The ovary becomes the fruit.

Ovule The ovule produces the female sex cells. If fertilized, the ovule develops into a seed.

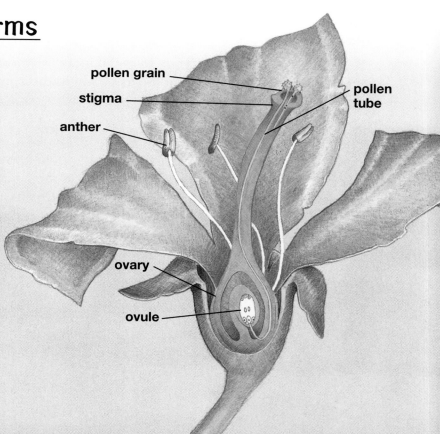

pollen grain

stigma

anther

pollen tube

ovary

ovule

Producing Seeds and Fruits

Look at the pictures on pages A84 and A85 to see how seeds and fruits are formed. The first step in producing seeds is the transfer of pollen grains from the male part of a flower (the stamen) to the female part of another flower (the pistil). The **pollen grain** contains the male sex cell. When an insect, a bird, or a bat brushes against an anther, which contains the pollen grains, some of the pollen sticks to the animal's body. As the animal moves to the next flower, some pollen brushes off its body onto the stigma, which is at the tip of the pistil. This transfer of pollen grains is called **pollination** (päl ə nā'shən).

Some flowers are pollinated when wind or rain carries pollen to them from another flower. These flowers usually are not scented or brightly colored. They do not attract animals for pollination.

Pollination can take place only between plants of the same kind. For example, if pollen from an apple blossom lands on a tulip, no pollination occurs. A tulip must be pollinated by pollen grains from another tulip.

Inside the ovule, the fertilized egg forms an **embryo** (em'brē ō), a tiny new plant. Other cells in the ovule produce a food supply for the embryo. The ovule then forms a protective seed coat around the embryo and its food supply, forming a seed. In the activity on pages A80–A81, bean seeds and corn seeds are opened to reveal a tiny embryo and its food supply. Every seed contains these basic parts. The activity on pages A82 and A83 shows the germination of a seed and its growth into a flowering plant. As growth continues, the flower forms a fruit and seeds.

The ovary surrounding the seed or seeds enlarges and develops into a **fruit**. The fruit protects the seeds as they grow. Some fruits, such as cherries, have only one seed; others, such as oranges, have many seeds. ■

1 Pollen grain lands on the stigma of the pistil.

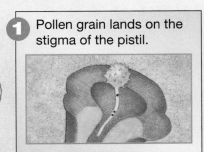

2 A pollen tube grows down into the ovary. **Fertilization** (fʉrt 'l i zā'shən) takes place when a male sex cell from the pollen grain joins with the female sex cell inside the ovary.

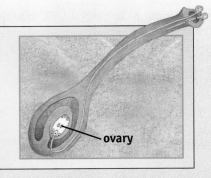

ovary

3 Following fertilization, the ovary enlarges and begins to form a fruit.

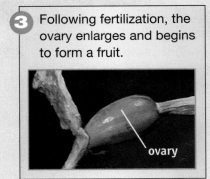

ovary

4 The ovary continues to enlarge, and seeds begin to form.

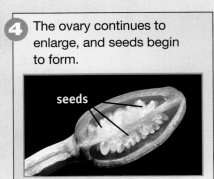

seeds

5 The fruit has ripened and has split open, releasing the seeds.

The Story of a Flowering Tree

Reading Focus What are the main stages in the life cycle of a flowering tree?

The Story of a Flowering Tree

In late spring, red maple seeds ripen and fall off the tree. The seeds are inside the fruit, connected in pairs. A thin "wing" allows the wind to carry the seeds away from the parent tree.

As they fall to the ground, many seeds are eaten or hidden, to be eaten at a later time by insects and small animals, such as squirrels. Some fruits lie on the ground long enough to open and release the seeds.

1 **GERMINATION** Water in the soil softens the seed coat of a maple seed. **Germination**, or sprouting, occurs. Inside the seed, the embryo grows. This tiny embryo has inherited traits, such as leaf shape, from two parent plants. As the root grows into the soil, it absorbs nutrients and water, and the rest of the embryo sprouts. The tiny plant uses food stored in the seed leaves that surround it.

2 **SEEDLING** As its stem appears above the ground, the plant becomes a seedling. True leaves develop in the familiar shape of the red maple. Then, with the cooler days of fall, the seedling stops growing. Chlorophyll in its leaves disappears, leaving behind the bright colors that were there all along.

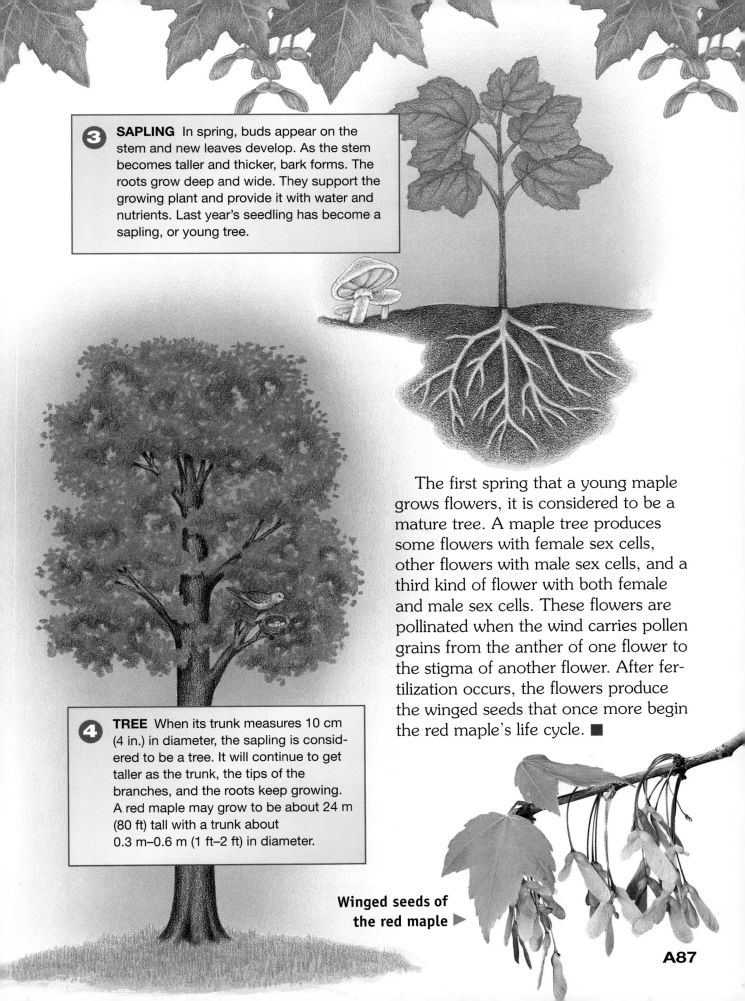

3 **SAPLING** In spring, buds appear on the stem and new leaves develop. As the stem becomes taller and thicker, bark forms. The roots grow deep and wide. They support the growing plant and provide it with water and nutrients. Last year's seedling has become a sapling, or young tree.

The first spring that a young maple grows flowers, it is considered to be a mature tree. A maple tree produces some flowers with female sex cells, other flowers with male sex cells, and a third kind of flower with both female and male sex cells. These flowers are pollinated when the wind carries pollen grains from the anther of one flower to the stigma of another flower. After fertilization occurs, the flowers produce the winged seeds that once more begin the red maple's life cycle. ■

4 **TREE** When its trunk measures 10 cm (4 in.) in diameter, the sapling is considered to be a tree. It will continue to get taller as the trunk, the tips of the branches, and the roots keep growing. A red maple may grow to be about 24 m (80 ft) tall with a trunk about 0.3 m–0.6 m (1 ft–2 ft) in diameter.

Winged seeds of the red maple ▶

The Life of a Bristlecone Pine

Reading Focus How long has this bristlecone pine been growing?

One of the oldest living things on Earth is a bristlecone pine named Methuselah. Methuselah has been growing in Great Basin National Park in California's White Mountains for about 4,600 years!

Today only a small portion of Methuselah is still alive. We know how old Methuselah is because scientists used a tiny hollow drill to bore into the tree. They removed a thin core of wood. From this core, they counted the annual rings, which tell the tree's age.

If the twisted, wind-battered tree called Methuselah could talk, what might it tell us about the important events that have occurred during its lifetime? The time line shows some of the events during Methuselah's long life.

"Methuselah" is now a mature 200-year-old tree.

2500 B.C.

A bristlecone pine seed germinates on land that later becomes known as California.

2700 B.C.

2500 B.C.
Egyptian workers begin to build the pyramids, where they will bury the bodies and possessions of their kings.

2700 B.C.
Egyptian kings rule over the fertile valley of the Nile River.

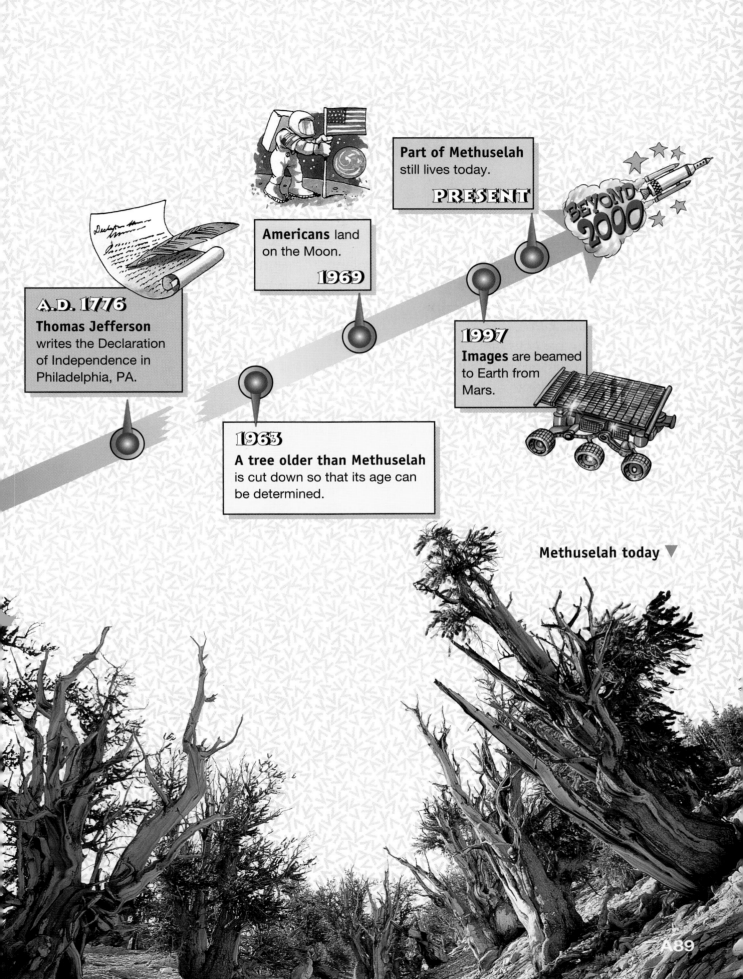

A.D. 1776
Thomas Jefferson writes the Declaration of Independence in Philadelphia, PA.

Americans land on the Moon.
1969

Part of Methuselah still lives today.
PRESENT

BEYOND 2000

1963
A tree older than Methuselah is cut down so that its age can be determined.

1997
Images are beamed to Earth from Mars.

Methuselah today ▼

Growing Plants Without Seeds

Reading Focus What are two ways that new plants can grow without seeds?

SCIENCE TECHNOLOGY & SOCIETY

When you plant seeds, you are planting the result of sexual reproduction—the joining of male and female sex cells from the parent plants. However, you can also grow new plants without using seeds. Such plants are produced by asexual reproduction. In asexual reproduction, offspring are produced from one or more cells of a single parent.

Cuttings

One way to produce new plants without planting seeds is by using cuttings. For example, with some kinds of plants you can cut a length of stem that has one or more leaves. The stem will grow roots when placed in water for a few days or weeks. The rooted stem can then be planted in soil and will grow into an entire new plant. This is a type of asexual reproduction. The new plants grown this way are clones, or exact copies of the parent plants.

Tissue Culture

Another type of asexual reproduction is tissue culture. A group of cells that works together is called a *tissue.* *Culture* is another word for "growing." Tissue culture is growing new plants in the laboratory from the cells of other

plants. The growth is done in test tubes or in culture plates.

When might a plant be grown through tissue culture instead of from a seed? Suppose most plants in a crop are affected by a disease. Then one of the plants is found to have a trait making it resistant to disease. Tissue from this healthy plant is grown by means of tissue culture. Since the new plant tissue is exactly like that of the parent plant, the new plants grown are also resistant to disease. Tissue culture can lead to a disease-resistant crop.

A leaf cutting (*left*) and plants grown from tissue culture in test tubes (*right*). ▼

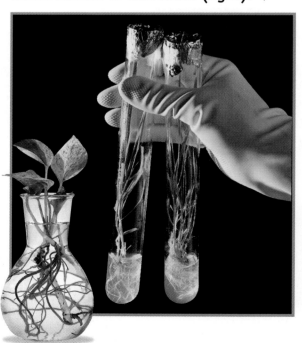

Life Cycle of a Cone Plant

Reading Focus What are the stages in the life cycle of a cone plant?

You've probably seen pine cones lying on the ground beneath a tall pine tree. Have you ever wondered what pine cones are?

Trees that produce cones are called **conifers**. The word *conifer* means "cone-bearing." Conifers have a life cycle that is similar to that of flowering plants. But instead of producing flowers and fruits, they produce cones. Seeds form inside the cones.

A pine is a type of conifer, or cone-producing tree. Both male and female cones grow on a pine tree. Compare the male and female cones in the photograph on this page.

What's in a Cone?

During winter the male cone produces pollen grains. Recall that the pollen grains contain the male sex cells. As the male cones grow in the spring, they open, releasing the pollen grains. Wind carries the pollen grains to the female cone.

In the spring, female cones are soft and green. Like flowers, the female cones contain ovules from which the seeds grow. The female cone produces a sticky material that traps the pollen grains. The process by which pollen grains from the male cone are transferred to the female cone is pollination.

After the pollen becomes trapped in the female cone, a pollen tube grows from the pollen into the ovule. Male sex cells from the pollen travel to the egg inside the ovule. Fertilization occurs when the male sex cell and the female sex cell, or egg, unite. From these two parts, the seed will grow. After fertilization, the female cone grows

Female cone of white pine (*left*); male cones (*right*)

seed ▶

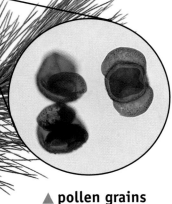

▲ **pollen grains**

A91

larger, becomes woody, and the spaces between the scales close.

What's in a Seed?

Like a seed in a flowering plant, the seed in a cone plant contains three main parts. It contains an embryo, a layer of food used by the very young plant, and a seed coat that protects the seed.

In the fall the female cone opens and the seeds are released and carried by the wind. Many will be eaten by animals. Those that remain will not germinate until spring. A young tree grows for several years before it is mature and produces cones. When it produces male and female cones, the life cycle begins again. ■

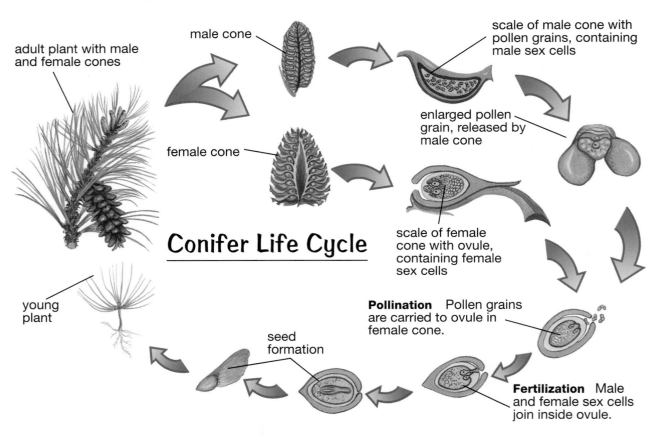

male cone

scale of male cone with pollen grains, containing male sex cells

adult plant with male and female cones

enlarged pollen grain, released by male cone

female cone

Conifer Life Cycle

scale of female cone with ovule, containing female sex cells

young plant

Pollination Pollen grains are carried to ovule in female cone.

seed formation

Fertilization Male and female sex cells join inside ovule.

INVESTIGATION 2 WRAP-UP

THINK IT WRITE IT

REVIEW

1. Describe the four main stages in the growth of a maple seed into an adult tree.

2. Describe how seeds and fruit form in a flower. Identify some inherited traits in plants.

CRITICAL THINKING

3. List two ways in which a female cone is like a flower. List two ways in which it is different.

4. Compare the life cycle of a flowering plant to that of a cone plant.

REFLECT & EVALUATE

Word Power

Write the letter of the term that best completes each sentence. *Not all terms will be used.*

1. The ovary surrounding the seed or seeds develops into a _____.

2. The wormlike stage in the life cycle of an insect is called a _____.

3. A tree that bears cones is a _____.

4. The process that takes place when a male sex cell from a pollen grain joins with a female sex cell inside an ovary is _____.

a. cone
b. conifer
c. fertilization
d. fruit
e. invertebrate
f. larva
g. pollination
h. pupa
i. vertebrate

Check What You Know

Write the term in each pair that best completes each sentence.

1. The stage of metamorphosis at which an insect appears to be at rest but is actually changing is the (larva, pupa) stage.

2. In a human life cycle a person is most likely to have a growth spurt during (adulthood, adolescence).

3. The reproductive organ of a maple tree is the (leaf, flower).

Problem Solving

1. Drawings showing an insect's life cycle are often in the shape of a circle. Explain why.

2. Seeds of flowering plants usually have a hard seed coat and a supply of food. How does this structure help a plant?

3. Make a table that shows how the life cycles of a salmon and a woodpecker are alike and different.

BUILD YOUR PORTFOLIO

Make a sketch of this flower. On your sketch, label all the numbered parts. Show which part of the flower will grow into the fruit.

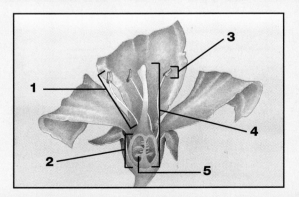

Main Idea and Details

When you read science, it's important to recognize which facts and details support or explain the main idea. First identify the main idea by looking for clues such as a title, or a topic sentence that states the main idea. Then look for statements that support that idea.

> Look for clues to find the main idea.
>
> Look for statements, facts, and details that support the main idea.

Read the paragraph below. Then complete the exercises.

From Flower to Fruit

The flower is the reproductive organ of a flowering plant. Some kinds of plants have flowers that produce both male and female sex cells. Other kinds have flowers that produce either male or female sex cells. When an insect visits a flower, it transfers the male sex cell from one flower to another. This transfer is part of the process of **sexual reproduction** in the flower. During sexual reproduction a male sex cell joins with a female sex cell to produce a fertilized egg. In flowering plants, this fertilized egg develops into a tiny plant enclosed in a seed. Through sexual reproduction, the tiny plant inherits traits, such as petal color and fruit shape, from each parent plant.

1. Write the letter of the sentence that states the main idea of the paragraph.

   a. The flower is the reproductive organ of a flowering plant.

   b. Tiny plants inherit traits, such as petal color and fruit shape, from each parent plant.

   c. Some plants produce both male and female sex cells.

   d. The fertilized egg develops into a tiny plant.

2. What clue helped you find the main idea?

3. List the most important facts and details that support the main idea.

Using Math Line Graph

Bamboo is a fast-growing giant grass. The 24-hour growth of a shoot of one species of bamboo is shown on the line graph below.

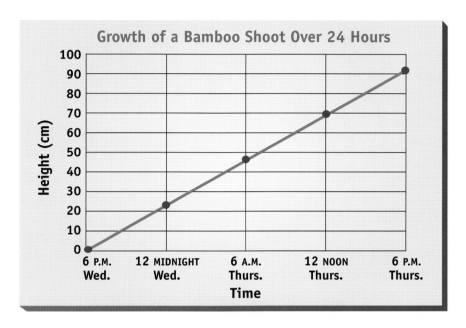

Growth of a Bamboo Shoot Over 24 Hours

Use the information in the graph to complete the exercises that follow.

1. What does the line on the graph represent? Estimate how much the bamboo shoot grows in one hour. Explain.

2. In the line graph above, the line is a straight line. Is the line of every line graph a straight line? Explain.

You may want to use a calculator for Exercises 3 and 4.

3. Some bamboo species can grow to a height of 37 m. If the bamboo shoot shown continued growing at the rate shown, how long would it take to reach a height of 37 m? Round your answer to the nearest whole number.

4. Suppose another species of bamboo grows at one half the rate of the bamboo species shown on the graph. How long would it take a shoot of that species to grow to a height of 10 m? Round your answer to the nearest whole number.

WRAP-UP!

On your own, use scientific methods to investigate a question about systems in living things.

THINK LIKE A SCIENTIST

Ask a Question

Pose a question about plants or animals that you would like to investigate. For example, ask, "How does turning a seedling upside down affect the direction in which its roots grow?"

Make a Hypothesis

Suggest a hypothesis that is a possible answer to the question. One hypothesis is that the roots of a seedling that is turned upside down will curve downward and grow toward the ground.

Plan and Do a Test

Plan a controlled experiment to find the effect that turning a seedling upside down has on the direction in which roots grow. You could start a number of seedlings growing on wet paper towels placed inside sealed clear plastic bags. Develop a procedure that uses these materials to test the hypothesis. With permission, carry out your experiment. Follow the safety guidelines on pages S14–S15.

Record and Analyze

Observe carefully and record your data accurately. Make repeated observations.

Draw Conclusions

Look for evidence to support the hypothesis or to show that it is false. Draw conclusions about the hypothesis. Repeat the experiment to verify the results.

WRITING IN SCIENCE
Letter of Request

Write a letter to request information about lung diseases and their prevention. Use these guidelines to write your letter of request.

- Find the Internet addresses of helpful Web sites that have reliable information.
- Use the parts of a formal letter: heading, inside address, greeting, and closing.
- Clearly state your request.
- Include a self-addressed, stamped envelope.

UNIT B

The Solar System and Beyond

Theme: Scale

THINK LIKE A SCIENTIST

A COMET'S TALE

Comet Hale-Bopp was discovered on June 23, 1995. Astronomers, scientists who study the sky, anxiously waited to see clear views of this new visitor to the sky. On March 30, 1997, this photo of the comet was taken in Finland. Hale-Bopp is seen here above the greenish glow of the aurora borealis. Through their study of comets, astronomers have learned such things as what a comet is made of and how to predict when a comet will make a return visit. Astronomers look forward to uncovering many more secrets of the sky.

THINK LIKE A SCIENTIST

Questioning In this unit you'll learn about the solar system, stars, and living in space. You'll investigate questions such as these.

- What Is the Life Cycle of a Star?
- What Is It Like to Travel in Space?

Observing, Testing, Hypothesizing In the Activity "Making a Telescopic Camera," you'll compare the image you see through the camera you make with the real image. You'll hypothesize what astronomers might do to make their images of stars brighter.

Researching In the Resource "Telescopes," you'll gather more information about the tools that astronomers use.

Drawing Conclusions After you've completed your investigations, you'll draw conclusions about what you've learned—and get new ideas.

1

EXPLORING THE NIGHT SKY

In the daytime sky the Moon, when visible, is a pale ghost. Seen on a clear night, it's round and full at times. At other times it's a curved sliver that looks like a comma. And what about the stars? On a dark, clear night you'll see hundreds and hundreds of them twinkling. Many, many objects are visible in the night sky. What could you see with a telescope?

PEOPLE USING SCIENCE

Astronomer From a hilltop Carolyn and Eugene Shoemaker scan the sky with a telescope. Carolyn Shoemaker is an astronomer, a scientist who studies bodies in space through a telescope. Eugene is a geologist and amateur astronomer, who worked until 1993 for the U.S. Geological Survey. Carolyn and Eugene are among the leading comet discoverers in the world.

In March 1993, the Shoemakers and David Levy, another comet hunter, discovered a comet on a collision course with Jupiter. Sixteen months later, this comet slammed into Jupiter, producing one of the greatest collisions ever observed. This comet was named Shoemaker-Levy 9, in honor of its discoverers.

Coming Up

From left to right, David Levy, Carolyn Shoemaker, and Eugene Shoemaker (*inset*).

WHAT CAN YOU SEE IN THE NIGHT SKY?

Star light, star bright,
First star I see tonight,
I wish I may, I wish I might
Have the wish I wish tonight.

Have you ever looked for the "first star" in this nursery rhyme? What do astronomers see when they look at the night sky?

Activity

Constellation in a Can

Individual stars are much easier to identify once you've learned to recognize star patterns called constellations. Learn a few of them now!

Procedure

1. Place the bottom of a 35-mm film canister on a piece of tracing paper. Trace a circle around the canister.

2. Select one of the constellation patterns your teacher will provide. Use a black marker to trace that pattern inside the circle you drew on the tracing paper.

MATERIALS

- goggles
- black plastic 35-mm film canister
- tracing paper
- constellation patterns
- black marker
- scissors
- tape
- pushpin
- *Science Notebook*

SAFETY ///////

Wear goggles when punching holes.

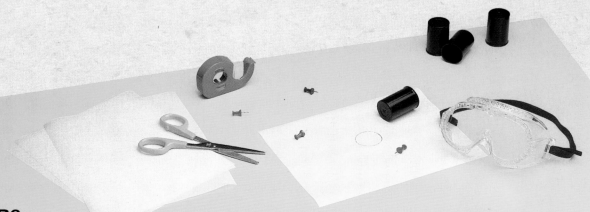

3. Cut out the circle, leaving about 3 cm of paper all the way around it.

4. Place the circle of tracing paper over the outside bottom of the film canister, with the drawing to the inside. Tape the paper to the canister.

5. With a pushpin, punch a small hole through the paper and the canister bottom for each star in the pattern. Remove the paper and tape from the canister.

6. Hold the film canister up to the light and look through it. Turn the canister counterclockwise and **observe** the constellation pattern inside.

7. Trade canisters with your classmates. Try to **identify** the other students' constellations. **Compare** what you see inside their canisters to the star pattern your teacher gave you.

Analyze and Conclude

1. In your *Science Notebook,* **make a list** of the patterns that you could identify and another list of the ones you could not.

2. **Analyze** how turning the canisters affects the way the constellations appear. **Draw** four pictures that show four different views of your own constellation as you turn your canister around.

3. **Hypothesize** why constellations might look different at different times of the night.

Technology *Link* **CD-ROM**

INVESTIGATE FURTHER!

Use the **Science Processor CD-ROM**, *The Solar System & Beyond* (Investigation 1, Starry Night) to find out more about constellations. You can see the movement of constellations at different times of the night and different seasons of the year.

Activity

Making a Planisphere

Do the constellations always appear in the same positions in the sky? How can you predict when and where a particular constellation will be visible? Here's one way.

MATERIALS
- scissors
- horizon mask
- star wheel
- paper fastener
- cardboard
- glue
- *Science Notebook*

Procedure

1. Cut along the dashed lines on the horizon mask provided by your teacher. Be sure to cut out the large oval and the small slits.

2. Cut along the outer edge of the star wheel provided by your teacher.

3. With a paper fastener, punch a small hole in the center of the star wheel where the star Polaris is. Then use the fastener to attach the star wheel to the middle of a piece of cardboard, as shown.

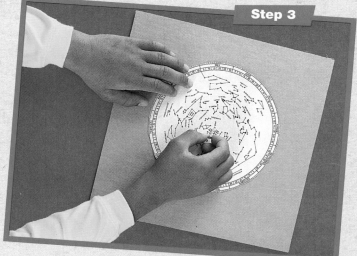
Step 3

4. Attach the corners of the horizon mask to the cardboard with glue, as shown, so that the outer portion of the star wheel is visible around the outer circular edge of the horizon mask. The wheel should turn freely behind the mask.

5. You have now made a planisphere, a map of the sky that can show the positions of the stars at different times. To use it, find the time of year you're interested in on the star wheel. Then turn the wheel until that date lines up with the hour you're interested in on the horizon mask. The stars in the sky at that time will have the same pattern as they do in the oval window of your planisphere.

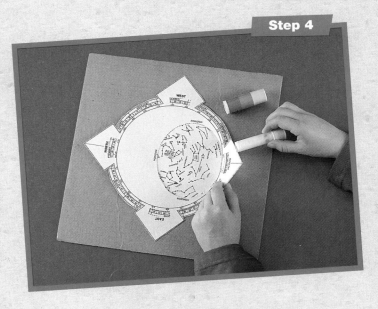
Step 4

6. Use your planisphere to see how the Big Dipper and the Little Dipper will look at 8:00 P.M. tonight. **Draw** these star patterns in your *Science Notebook* and mark the compass directions to match those on the horizon mask. **Label** your drawing with today's date and the time 8:00 P.M.

7. **Predict** how the Big Dipper and Little Dipper will look at 11:00 P.M. tonight. Use the planisphere to check your prediction. **Draw** these star groups again with their compass directions, the date, and the new time. How will these two star groups change during the three hours from 8:00 P.M. to 11:00 P.M.?

8. **Predict** how the Big Dipper and Little Dipper will look at 11:00 P.M. three months from now. Check your prediction. Then **draw** these star groups with their compass directions, the date, and the time. How will these two star groups change during the next three months?

Analyze and Conclude

1. Based on what you learned in steps 6 and 7, **infer** how the appearance of the Big Dipper and the Little Dipper will change throughout the entire night tonight.

2. Based on what you learned in steps 7 and 8, **infer** how the appearance of these two star groups would change throughout an entire year if you looked at them at the same time every night.

3. **Hypothesize** what might cause these changes. Do you think the stars are really moving in the way they appear to move in the sky? If not, what else might explain their apparent motion? Do you think the changes you see occurring nightly and the changes you see throughout the year are caused by the same thing? Explain your reasoning.

Internet Field Trip

Visit **www.eduplace.com** to learn more about the constellations.

INVESTIGATE FURTHER!

EXPERIMENT

Go outside on the next clear night. Set your planisphere for the correct date and time. Hold it overhead, with the compass directions oriented correctly. Then identify the brighter constellations in the sky.

EAST
MARCH

HORIZON

FEBRUARY

JANUARY

SOUTH
DECEMBER

HORIZON

CAPRICORNUS
SAGITTARIUS
AQUILA
Altair
SERPENS CAUDA
OPHIUCHUS
Antares
SCORPIUS
SERPENS CAPUT
Arcturus
CORONA BOREALIS
HERCULES
LYRA
Vega
Northern Cross
CYGNUS
Deneb
CEPHEUS
DRACO
URSA MINOR
Polaris
Little Dipper
Big Dipper
URSA MAJOR
BOOTES
ANDROMEDA
CASSIOPEIA
PEGASUS
Great Square

B9

Star Patterns in the Sky

Reading Focus What are constellations, and what are some well-known examples?

Have you ever been out on a clear night and just looked up to see what you could see in the sky? Even if you live in a city with lots of bright lights, you can still spot dozens of stars. If you live in or visit the country, you can see thousands of beautiful, sparkling objects in the night sky.

How do you find your way around the sky? It's easy to learn! The activities on pages B6 to B9 help with recognizing star patterns and in knowing what might be seen on a certain night.

Identifying Groups of Stars

The activities show pictures of constellations (kän stə lā′shəns). A **constellation** is a group of stars that forms a pattern in the night sky.

Throughout history, different cultures have identified and named such star patterns. Today's astronomers recognize a total of 88 constellations.

The constellations that can be seen from Earth's Northern Hemisphere received their names from Greek and Roman mythology. Leo, Pisces (pī′sēz), and Taurus, for example, were named for a lion, two fish, and a bull. Orion (ō rī′ən) and Cassiopeia (kas ē ō pē′ə) are the names of a hunter and a queen in Greek and Roman myths.

The Southern Hemisphere's constellations probably aren't very familiar to you. These star patterns were named between the 1400s and the 1700s, when explorers from Europe first sailed south of the equator. The constellations they sighted were named for tools they used and for objects and animals they saw. Telescopium, for instance, was named for the telescope, and Tucana was named for the South American bird called a toucan.

Using Math *The constellation Taurus is shown at the left. If line segments are used to show Taurus, what geometric shapes can you find?*

When you think of constellations, which ones come to mind first? The most widely recognized star patterns are probably the Big Dipper and the Little Dipper. These two are not really constellations by themselves, however, but are portions of two larger constellations. The Big Dipper is part of the constellation called Ursa Major, the Great Bear. The Little Dipper belongs to Ursa Minor, the Little Bear.

▲ **The constellation Orion**

The Big Dipper and the Little Dipper are so well known not just because of their recognizable shapes, but also for where they are in the sky. What's most important is that these two patterns can always be found in the same area of the northern sky. Polaris, the star at the tip of the Little Dipper's "handle," is known as the North Star because it always appears almost exactly above the North Pole. You'll learn why Polaris does this—and why other stars don't—as you go through this investigation.

A Map of the Sky

Today's constellations no doubt started out as pictures in the minds of our ancestors, much as you might see castles or dragons in clouds during the daytime. But constellations also serve an important practical purpose. They provide us with a map of the sky.

Since the sky is so huge, it can be difficult to tell someone where to find a certain object in it. But constellations divide the sky into 88 imaginary sections, just as a map of the United States divides the country into 50 states. Astronomers use constellations to identify the "address" of a certain sky object, just as you use your state to identify where you live. We say that the bright reddish star Betelgeuse (bet''l j$\overline{oo}$z), for example, is located within the constellation called Orion. Rigel (rī'jəl), a bright bluish star, is also part of Orion. It marks Orion's heel.

Now that you have a map, won't it be easier to find your way around the sky? One clear night, look up and see how many of the constellations you find! ■

▲ **The constellations Ursa Minor and Ursa Major**

Why the Stars Appear to Move

Reading Focus How do Earth's movements affect what you see in the sky?

Look at the picture at the right. What are all those rings? They're the tracks of stars as they move throughout the night!

The tiny circle in the center is the track of Polaris, the North Star. This object hardly seems to move at all, while most of the other objects in the sky appear to revolve around it. If you point a camera at Polaris and leave the shutter open, you will take a picture like this one.

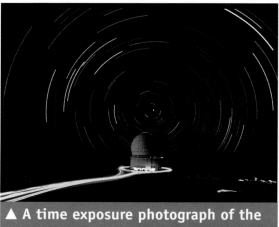

▲ A time exposure photograph of the northern night sky

While you can watch the northern constellations circle Polaris every night, other changes in the sky take place over many months. Both types of changes are modeled in the planisphere activity on pages B8 and B9.

Orion is a good example of a constellation whose position shifts slowly with the seasons. On a late autumn evening, it can be seen low in the eastern sky. If you look for Orion on future autumn evenings, you'll find that it appears to move higher and higher in the sky. It reaches its highest position in the sky in mid-December. Then, on winter evenings the constellation is found in the western sky. By early spring, it can only be seen on the western horizon. By late spring, Orion has completely disappeared from the sky for the summer.

Two Kinds of Movement at Once

How can you explain the apparent daily and yearly movements of the constellations? To better understand what you're seeing, try this exercise.

Imagine you're a pitcher on the mound in a baseball game. You wind up and throw a curveball—a ball that spins as it flies through the air. Suppose that a housefly lands on your baseball and hangs onto its stitches as it races toward home plate. What will that insect see as the ball flies through the air?

Let's suppose you released the ball so that it spins from side to side, instead of from top to bottom. As the baseball rotates, the fly will see the player at third base appear to race by several times. But the girl playing third base hasn't really moved. She has only appeared to move, from the fly's point of view, because the ball on which the fly sits is spinning.

But the ball isn't just spinning. It's also traveling from the pitcher's mound toward home plate. As it does, the fly's view of the girl at third base changes. At first, the fly sees her from the side. But as the ball nears the plate, the fly is able to see the girl from the front.

The third-base player hasn't really moved. Instead, it's the fly who has moved. And yet, to that insect on the baseball, the girl has appeared to turn toward the fly and move backward. The girl appears to move farther and farther away as the fly's viewing angle and the distance between the ball and third base have changed.

Earth Rotates and Revolves

If you can imagine a fly on a baseball, you can imagine yourself standing on a planet. The planet is Earth, and just like the baseball, it moves in two ways at once.

First, Earth spins. To be more precise, it rotates on its **axis**, an imaginary rod stretching through the planet between the North and South Poles. Earth takes 24 hours, or one day, to turn completely around on its axis and finish one **rotation**, even though it is spinning at a great speed.

Second, as Earth rotates, it also moves from one part of space to another. Rather than following a straight line, Earth follows a roughly circular orbit

A curveball spinning and moving toward home plate in a baseball game (*above*) may be compared to Earth rotating and revolving in space (*below*).

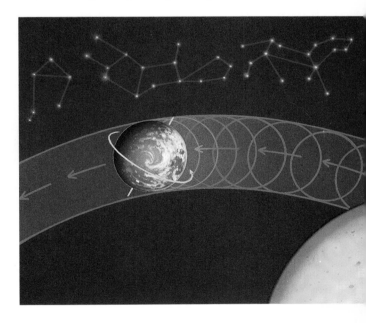

around the Sun. The distance Earth travels in its orbit around the Sun is so great that each round trip—one **revolution** —takes about 365 days, or one year.

B13

Earth is so huge and its gravity is so strong that you cannot feel the planet rotate or move through space in its orbit. But evidence for both kinds of motion is all around you.

Earth's rotation, for example, makes the Sun appear to rise in the east and set in the west. When a spot on Earth rotates away from the Sun, it's night for that location.

Earth's revolution around the Sun and the tilt of Earth's axis cause seasons. The tilt of the axis causes the angle at which the Sun's rays strike Earth and the number of hours of daylight at any location to change in a regular pattern. Summer and winter in the Northern and Southern Hemispheres are opposite. When one hemisphere is tilted toward the Sun, the other is tilted away from the Sun. For example, when it is summer in the United States, it is winter in Argentina.

The Stars' Apparent Motion

Can you now see why the stars appear to move? Think back to the fly on the baseball. Do you remember the third-base player who seemed to be moving but was actually standing still?

▲ Earth's rotation makes the stars appear to circle Polaris.

The stars are like the player, and Earth is like the baseball. It's our planet's rotation that makes the stars appear to move each night from east to west.

It's worth noting here that the stars are *not* in fact standing still. They're just so far away that they'd *seem* to be motionless if Earth itself weren't moving. But that's a story for Chapter 3!

To people viewing the sky from Earth, only the North Star appears almost motionless. That's because the North Star lies directly above the North Pole—the northern tip of Earth's axis. This makes Polaris seem like the center of the sky, with all the other stars revolving around it.

Earth's revolution around the Sun means that different stars appear in the sky at different times of the year. The viewing "window" that we look through—the direction in space that the night side of Earth faces—keeps changing as Earth moves in its orbit. Each month we see about 30° of new star groups in the east and lose sight of 30° of old star groups in the west. Different constellations wait to greet us as we sail along through space. ■

Moving Bears of the Native Americans

Reading Focus What does the Micmacs' story about the Celestial Bear help to explain?

Scientists call it Ursa Major. Most people know it as the Big Dipper. To the Micmac Native Americans of eastern Canada, this pattern of stars is known as the Celestial Bear.

When the Micmacs look at the night sky, they see a bear in the four stars that we think of as the "dipper." Earth's daily rotation and yearly revolution make it appear that the bear is moving. The Micmacs have created a story about why the position of the bear keeps changing.

They say that in early May the bear climbs out of her "den"—a circle of stars higher up in the sky—and is pursued by seven hunters. The three stars behind her that form the "handle" of the dipper are hunters named Robin, Chickadee, and Moose Bird. Following close by are hunter stars called Pigeon, Blue Jay, Hoot Owl, and Saw-whet.

In midsummer the bear runs across the northern sky trying to get away from her pursuers. In mid-autumn she "stands up" to defend herself. At this time of year, the four stars near the Big Dipper set below the horizon. So only three hunters remain to pursue the bear. In late autumn the bear falls on her back and the three hunters catch her. The bear's blood falls to Earth and turns the autumn leaves bright red.

This story is the Micmacs' way of describing what they observed about the movement of the stars and the changing of the seasons. The story is based on activities in their everyday lives. The Micmac story can help you remember how the stars appear to change position. ■

The Big Dipper as seen by the Micmacs ▼

Wanderers in the Night Sky

Reading Focus What is the difference between a star and a planet?

Other than the Sun and the Moon, most of the objects in the night sky look about the same to the unaided eye. They all seem to be just tiny points of light. Are all of those shiny objects stars? If not, what are they? And how can you tell which ones are which?

You can begin to answer these questions yourself by simply looking a little bit longer and a little more closely at those points of light in the sky. If you do, you'll soon realize that they are *not* all exactly alike.

A Different Sort of "Star"

Have you ever seen the "morning star"? This is an object that seems to be a very bright star. It can be seen at certain times on the eastern horizon (hə-rī′zən), just before the Sun rises. The

horizon is the line formed where the Earth and sky seem to meet. If you look closely at this bright object, it seems to shine with a steady light. Almost all the other "stars" seem to twinkle.

If you observe the morning star through a telescope, it will no longer look like a tiny point of light. Instead you'll see a small round disk. This object, in fact, has phases like the Moon does, so you might see either a fairly full disk or a thin crescent.

If you use a more powerful telescope to observe the morning star, you'll see a larger disk. But no matter how powerful your telescope is, most of the other stars in the sky will still appear to be just tiny points of light.

If you look for the morning star several days in a row, you'll notice something else. It's moving! And it's moving not just *along with* all the other stars, but *in relation to* the other stars, including the Sun.

Over a period of weeks, you'll see the morning star move closer and closer to the Sun until it disappears in the Sun's glare. Then something even more interesting happens. The same object reappears in the west just after sundown as the evening star!

▲ The "morning star"

▲ **The Sun, Moon, and planets appear to move in the same narrow band across the sky.**

Of all the starlike objects easily seen by the unaided eye, only five are like the morning star. That is, they shine steadily rather than twinkle, appear in a telescope as disks rather than points of light, and move against the backdrop of the other stars.

These five objects share one other trait with the morning star. They can only be seen in a certain part of the sky. Although they all move, these "stars" appear only in a narrow band. That band is roughly the same as the path of the Sun and the Moon across the sky.

The Wandering Planets

The ancient Greeks called these five special objects "wandering stars." In English, we call them *planets*—a name that comes from the Greek word for "wanderer." These five objects—and a few others like them that are not easily seen by the unaided eye—are really in a different class from stars. They are planets.

A **star** is a huge globe of hot gases that shines by its own light. The Sun is a star. It just appears bigger because it's much closer to Earth than are other stars. A **planet** is a large object that circles a star and does *not* produce light of its own. We can see planets only because they reflect sunlight.

The morning and evening star is really Venus, one of nine known planets that revolve around our Sun. Until very recently, scientists thought there were only nine planets in the universe. By 1998, however, astronomers had discovered 13 planets circling other nearby stars. ■

─────── **INVESTIGATION 1 WRAP-UP** ───────

REVIEW

1. How do a star and a planet differ?

2. What motion of the Earth causes the Sun to seem to rise and set each day?

CRITICAL THINKING

3. The constellation Leo is visible in the east on a January evening but in the west on a July evening. Explain why.

4. Explain why Earth has seasons.

HOW DO ASTRONOMERS LEARN ABOUT SPACE?

How can you learn about objects that are as far away as stars and planets? This is a problem that has puzzled scientists for centuries. Two solutions to this problem are to use telescopes and to collect material that has fallen to Earth from space. You can do these things, too!

Activity

Making a Telescopic Camera

Astronomers use many tools to help them study the sky. In this activity you'll build a simple version of one of those tools.

MATERIALS
- convex lens
- metric ruler
- 2 cardboard tubes
- scissors
- tape
- wax paper
- *Science Notebook*

SAFETY
Never look at the Sun through a lens. Your eyes could be injured. Do not use the lens to focus sunlight.

Procedure

1. Hold a convex lens above a table and directly below a ceiling light. Adjust the height of the lens above the table until an image of the ceiling light appears on the table.

2. **Measure** the distance between the lens and the table. Then cut a cardboard tube so that it's about three fourths of this length.

See **SCIENCE** and **MATH TOOLBOX** page H6 if you need to review *Using a Tape Measure or Ruler.*

Step 3

3. Cut a second cardboard tube of the same length. Then cut this second tube lengthwise. Overlap the edges and tape them so that this tube is slightly narrower in diameter than the first tube. This narrower tube should slide smoothly inside the first tube.

4. Using tape, attach the lens to the open end of the wider tube.

5. Cut a square of wax paper to cover the open end of the smaller tube. Tape the wax paper in place. You have now made a simple type of telescopic camera—a device that projects a magnified image of distant objects onto film (or, in this case, wax paper).

Step 6

6. Aim the lens of your camera toward a bright area—perhaps out a window. Look at the wax paper at the other end of the camera. Slide the tubes until you get a clearly focused image on the wax paper.

Analyze and Conclude

1. **Compare** the image on the wax paper with the real scene. In your *Science Notebook,* **make a list** of the ways in which the image is different from the real thing.

2. In a real camera on a telescope, film is used instead of wax paper. **Make a list** of other ways in which your cardboard-tube camera differs from a real camera on a telescope.

3. Is your image on the wax paper brighter than the real object? **Hypothesize** what astronomers might do to make their images of faint stars brighter.

UNIT PROJECT LINK

For this Unit Project you will turn your classroom into a simulated space station. On large sheets of paper, draw windows for your space station. Within the windows, draw the stars of several constellations that are near each other in the sky. Then use your telescopic camera to take sightings on certain stars.

TechnologyLink

For more help with your Unit Project, go to **www.eduplace.com**.

Activity

Mining for Meteorites

Have you ever seen a "falling star"? Do you know what one looks like up close? Find out!

- -

Procedure

1. Place a magnet inside a clear plastic bag. Then run the bag-covered magnet through the rainwater your teacher has collected.

Step 1

2. Use a hand lens to look carefully at the outside of the bag. If you find any small spheres, or round objects, use a craft stick to scrape them onto a microscope slide.

3. Observe the objects through a microscope. If they still look like round objects, what you probably have are meteorites—pieces of space dust that came to Earth as falling stars!

See **SCIENCE** *and* **MATH TOOLBOX** *page H2 if you need to review* ***Using a Microscope.***

Analyze and Conclude

1. Infer what material your meteorites contain. What part of the activity provided you with this information?

2. Hypothesize what might cause most meteorites to be rounded in shape.

Step 2

3. Hypothesize how small meteorites could end up in rainwater. In your *Science Notebook*, **draw** a picture of Earth that shows where you think your meteorites were before they fell to the ground during a rain shower.

Telescopes

Reading Focus How does a refracting telescope differ from a reflecting telescope?

Imagine that you're living hundreds of years ago. All that you know about the stars and planets is based on what you can see with your unaided eyes. Then you learn of a new device called a telescope—a viewing instrument that can magnify distant objects.

You aim your telescope at the speck of light called Jupiter. Until now, Jupiter looked to you like a very bright star. But today, instead of appearing as a tiny point of light, Jupiter can be clearly seen as a round disk. Not only that, but four smaller points of light—previously invisible to you—can now be seen close to Jupiter. As you watch through the telescope each night, it becomes obvious that the four smaller objects are moons. They circle Jupiter, just as our own Moon orbits Earth. What an amazing discovery this is!

The person who actually made this discovery in the seventeenth century was the great Italian scientist Galileo Galilei. What he found changed people's views of the universe. He made his observations by using one of the most useful devices ever developed by human beings—the telescope.

The two main types of telescopes are pictured on the next page. A **refracting** (ri frakt'iŋ) **telescope** is an instrument for viewing distant objects that uses two lenses to gather light and produce an image. The telescope looks like a long, narrow tube, such as a sea captain might use. You look directly through the tube. Light from a distant object is focused by a large lens and then magnified by a smaller lens before it reaches your eye. The camera in the activity on pages B18 and B19 uses a simple single-lens refracting system.

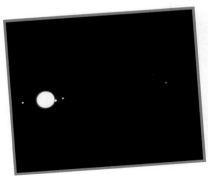 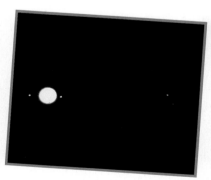 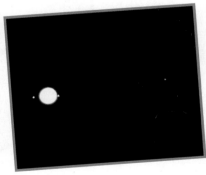

▲ Galileo discovered four moons of Jupiter by viewing scenes like these through his telescope.

A refracting telescope ▼

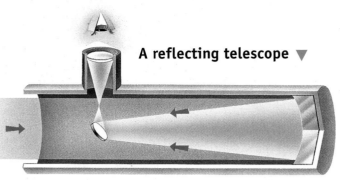

A reflecting telescope ▼

A **reflecting telescope** gathers light in a curved mirror at the back of its tube. It then reflects and focuses the light on a smaller mirror near the front. The small mirror is often angled to send the image out through an *eyepiece* on the side of the tube. The eyepiece contains lenses that can be changed to give you different magnifications.

Because it's easier to build large mirrors than large lenses, the largest telescopes in the world are reflectors. A mirror has only one surface that must be precisely made. A lens must be shaped perfectly from top to bottom! Since a mirror reflects light, a mirror's bottom surface can rest on a supporting struc-

ture. Light must pass through a lens, so a lens has to be supported around the edge. The world's largest reflecting telescope, at McDonald Observatory, in Texas, has mirrors with a combined diameter of 11 m (436 in.). The lens of the world's largest refracting telescope, at Yerkes Observatory, in Wisconsin, is only about 1 m (40 in.) in diameter.

Wonders in the Heavens

No one is sure who made the first telescope, although many historians believe it was a Dutch spectacle-maker named Hans Lippershey. It is known, however, that by the early 1600s the Dutch had learned how to line up two curved lenses

◄ The observatory at Palomar Mountain, California, contains a 5-m (200-in.) reflecting telescope.

▲ The Hubble Space Telescope (HST) is shown here about to be released from an orbiting space shuttle. HST is about 13 m (43 ft) long and 4 m (13 ft) wide.

in a tube and look through them to make faraway objects appear closer.

As soon as Galileo heard about the Dutch invention, he set out to make his own telescope. Soon he had built several, each one more refined and more powerful than the last. Then he did something no one else had ever done. He took his most powerful telescope outside and looked up.

Galileo's telescope could bring the heavens only 30 times closer, yet what he saw astounded him! The Moon became an alien wonderland covered by deep craters and towering mountains. And there were many more stars than he had ever imagined, some gleaming with newly visible colors.

An important advance over Galileo's telescope came from the English scientist Sir Isaac Newton. The simple lenses of his day distorted color, but a mirror did not. So Newton designed a reflecting telescope that would collect light in a mirror before passing it through a lens.

Since Newton's time, astronomers have learned new ways to use telescopes to see things the human eye cannot see. For example, astronomers can capture pictures of very faint objects. They used to do this by attaching a camera to a telescope's eyepiece and exposing the film for long periods of time. Today, most astronomers use equipment to send telescope images directly to computers.

Putting Telescopes in Space

Today there is a large telescope in orbit around Earth. The Hubble Space Telescope (HST) is positioned beyond our planet's atmosphere, so it avoids distortions caused by looking through the air. Even though the mirror in the HST is smaller than that of many telescopes on Earth, it can see more clearly and see objects that are fainter and farther away than telescopes on the ground can see. Space telescopes can even see wavelengths of light that aren't visible from Earth's surface. ■

Comets and Meteors

Pretend that you're a giant. Build yourself a huge snowball, about 5 km (3 mi) wide. Stuff some dirt and rocks in with the snow. Let the whole thing freeze rock-hard. Then send it hurtling through space at about 250,000 km/h (150,000 mph).

Aim your snowball so that it will swing in toward the Sun, go completely around it, and then head out into the most distant regions of the solar system before it returns. The snowball's path should look like a long thin oval. Congratulations! You have now made and launched your own **comet**, an icy ball that contains dust and rock and travels in an elliptical (ē lip′ti kəl) orbit around the Sun.

Snowballs That Melt in the Sun

From Earth a comet can look like a ball of fire. Yet real comets begin just as your imaginary one did, as giant chunks of ice. At the core, comets are mostly frozen water, ammonia, and methane,

mixed with enough dust and debris to create what you might call a "dirty snowball."

A comet spends most of its life drifting through the cold outer reaches of the solar system. But when its orbit brings it closer to the Sun, that's when the show begins!

Because the main body of a comet is made of frozen material, it is doomed to slow destruction by the Sun's heat. But the fiery look of a comet is not because the comet is burning up in the heat of the Sun. Instead, as the comet approaches the Sun, its body begins to melt, releasing its frozen gases into space. These gases spread out to form a huge misty head around the comet's front end.

A comet's tail is made of gases and grains of dust—the "dirt" streaming off the dirty snowball. A stream of charged particles given off by the Sun, called the solar wind, causes a comet's tail to point

Using Math *Halley's comet—shown at the top of this page as a telescope on Earth would see it—follows a 76-year orbit. It was last seen from Earth in 1986. How old will you be when it can be seen again?*

away from the Sun. No matter in which direction the comet is moving, its tail always points away from the Sun.

Some comets with very long orbits have only appeared once during re-corded history. Others have reappeared regularly many times. The most famous one, Halley's comet, revolves around the Sun once every 76 years.

Comets: The Meteor Makers

The dirt particles left behind by the comet can drift toward Earth as Earth orbits the Sun. These particles then speed up into Earth's atmosphere and burn up there as "shooting stars," or **meteors** (mē'tē ərz).

Not all meteors come from comets, but comets do appear to cause many

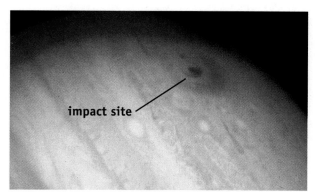

▲ **One of the impact sites of comet Shoemaker-Levy 9 on the planet Jupiter**

large meteor showers. The meteors that do not come from comets come from rocky material called asteroids. Most meteors burn up before they reach the ground. Sometimes meteors from aster-oids can fall to Earth. The material that lands is called a **meteorite** (mē'tē ər īt).

Science in Literature

OBSERVING THE NIGHT SKIES

"Amateur astronomers . . . discover most of the new comets that pass through the inner Solar System. Comets, which are mountain-sized chunks of frozen gases, ice, and rock, are of great scientific inter-est because they can tell us more about how the Solar System formed. Each year, one or two new ones are found."

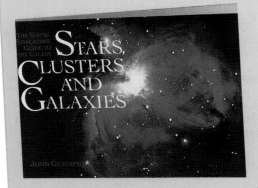

Stars, Clusters and Galaxies
by John Gustafson
Julian Messner, 1992

This information about the discovery of new comets comes from *Stars, Clusters and Galaxies* by John Gustafson. In this book you will find a wealth of information and tips for observing the galaxies in the night sky, as well as directions for making your own telescope.

Using Math
The Barringer meteor crater in Arizona has a diameter of about 1,200 m (4,000 ft). Estimate the distance around the crater.

Collisions between comets and planets are rare, but when they do occur, the results can be spectacular! In July 1994, a comet called Shoemaker-Levy 9 struck the planet Jupiter. The photograph at the top of page B25 shows where the comet struck the planet. After the collision, the scars on Jupiter were two to three times the size of Earth!

Most scientists believe that Earth's dinosaurs became extinct because a comet or an asteroid struck our planet 65 million years ago. But the chances of something like that happening today are very, very small. When material from space does reach Earth—in the form of a meteorite—scientists can then examine and study it.

Meteorites are made of either metal or rock. The tiniest ones—like those in the activity on page B20—are so light that they often remain suspended in the atmosphere until a rain shower brings them to Earth.

Astronomers think that material from comets may date back more than 4 billion years, to the time of Earth's beginnings. By studying meteorites, scientists can learn about comets and the origins of the solar system. ■

INVESTIGATION 2 WRAP-UP

REVIEW

1. What are the two main kinds of telescopes?

2. What is the name of the telescope that orbits Earth?

CRITICAL THINKING

3. Suppose you could build a telescope anywhere on Earth. Where would you build it, and what kind of telescope would it be? Explain the reasons for your choices.

4. How does studying meteorites help scientists learn about comets?

REFLECT & EVALUATE

Word Power

Write the letter of the term that best matches the definition. *Not all terms will be used.*

1. Device that has two lenses and is used for seeing distant objects
2. Huge globe of hot gases that shines by its own light
3. Group of stars that forms a pattern in the night sky
4. Yearly movement of Earth around the Sun
5. Imaginary rod stretching between Earth's North and South Poles.

a. axis
b. constellation
c. planet
d. reflecting telescope
e. refracting telescope
f. revolution
g. rotation
h. star

Check What You Know

Write the term in each pair that best completes each sentence.

1. The seasons of the year are caused by Earth's (rotation, revolution).
2. The "morning star" is actually (Venus, Polaris).
3. The powerful telescope that orbits Earth is named after (Galileo, Hubble).

Problem Solving

1. Use what you have learned about the apparent motion of the stars to explain how stars might be used as a navigational tool.

2. With your unaided eye you see an object in the night sky. It looks like a bright point of light. How would you go about identifying this object?

BUILD YOUR PORTFOLIO

Copy this drawing of the Little Dipper as it appears at 7:00 P.M. in the February sky. Then redraw the picture to show how it will appear at 1:00 A.M. the same night. Label Polaris in each drawing. Add an arrow to show the direction in which the constellation appears to be moving. Then explain why the constellation appears to move.

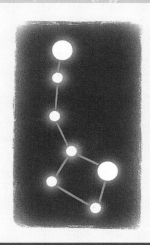

CHAPTER 2

THE SOLAR SYSTEM

When you look out into the vast reaches of the sky, do you wonder
about the planets? To those who live upon it, Earth seems enormous.
Actually, Earth is a medium-sized planet among the nine planets
that orbit the Sun. How Earth compares to the other planets has
fascinated people for ages.

PEOPLE
USING SCIENCE

Aerospace Engineer Dr. Aprille Ericsson-Jackson
is an aerospace engineer at the NASA Goddard Space
Flight Center. As part of her work, she conducts simulations
for spacecraft designs. A simulation is an attempt to
duplicate on Earth a situation found in space. From the
simulation, Dr. Ericsson-Jackson suggests changes in the
spacecraft's design.

In junior high school, she realized she had an aptitude for
mathematics and science. Dr. Ericsson-Jackson is the first
African American woman with a Ph.D. in Engineering to
work at the NASA Goddard Space Flight Center. By serving
as a career advisor, mentor, and friend, Dr. Ericsson-Jackson
encourages students to enter careers in science, math,
and engineering.

Coming Up

◄ Dr. Aprille Ericsson-Jackson at
NASA Goddard Space Flight Center

WHAT IS THE SOLAR SYSTEM MADE OF?

Our solar system's diameter is about 11.8 billion km. Can you picture that? Start walking at a rate of 5 kilometers per hour. Don't stop! You will walk a distance equal to the solar system's diameter in about 275,000 years. Now learn about the objects that make up our solar system and how they came to be.

Activity

When to Go Planet Watching

You've learned that the planets in our solar system seem to move across a narrow band in the sky. In this activity you'll discover how the planet Mars really moves in space. And you'll see how that motion affects the way Mars looks in Earth's night sky.

Step 1

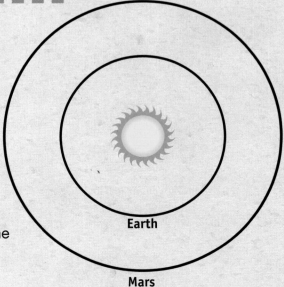

Earth

Mars

Procedure

1. Use a colored pencil to **make a drawing** in your *Science Notebook* like the one on this page, but larger. Your drawing should show the Sun, Earth's orbit around the Sun, and the larger orbit of the planet Mars around the Sun.

2. Choose two small round objects to represent Earth and Mars. Place each object on your drawing at any location along each planet's orbit.

3. Use another colored pencil to trace around each object and show its position in your drawing. **Label** the two traced objects *Earth* and *Mars*.

MATERIALS

- 2 small round objects to use as planet models
- pencils of different colors
- metric ruler
- *Science Notebook*

4. With a ruler, **measure** how far apart the two planets are in your drawing. **Record** that measurement.

See **SCIENCE** and **MATH TOOLBOX** page H6 if you need to review *Using a Tape Measure or Ruler.*

5. Move both planet models along their orbits until you have them as close together as they can be. **Draw** these positions, using a third color. Then **measure** and **record** the new distance between the two objects.

6. Move both planet models along their orbits until you have them as far apart as they can be. **Draw** these positions, using a fourth color. **Measure** and **record** the distance between the objects.

Analyze and Conclude

1. Look at the locations of the Sun, Earth, and Mars when Mars is as close to Earth as it can be. **Predict** what time of day you'd see Mars in Earth's sky when the real planets are positioned this way. **Infer** whether Mars would be visible from the daytime or nighttime side of Earth.

2. **Observe** the locations of the Sun, Earth, and Mars when Mars is as far from Earth as it can be. **Predict** what time of day you would see Mars when the real planets are positioned this way. **Infer** whether the daytime or night-time side of Earth would be facing Mars. Where would Mars appear to be in Earth's sky in relation to the Sun? Would you be able to see Mars from Earth at this time?

3. Look at the first positions you chose for the Earth and Mars objects. **Predict** whether you'd be able to see Mars from Earth if the planets were positioned in this way.

Technology
Link
CD-ROM

INVESTIGATE FURTHER!

Use the **Science Processor CD-ROM**, *The Solar System & Beyond* (Investigation 2, Planet Explorer) to find out more about the solar system and to take an imaginary trip to a planet.

Step 4

Activity

Comparing Planetary Distances

MATERIALS
- 10 index cards
- 400-sheet roll of toilet paper
- calculator
- *Science Notebook*

How far from Earth and from the Sun are the other eight planets? How can you better understand such large distances in the solar system? Here's one way to do it.

- -

Procedure

1. To **create a model** of planetary distances, go with nine other students to a large open area. One student represents the Sun while the others represent the nine planets.

2. Each student should label an index card with the name of the body he or she represents.

3. The Sun student should sit on the floor with one hand holding down the end of a roll of toilet paper. The planet students should unroll the toilet paper and count the sheets. As each student comes to the sheet number that's listed on the table for his or her planet, that student should sit. The student should then place the index card on the sheet representing his or her planet's average distance from the Sun.

Step 3

Planet	Sheet Number
Mercury	3
Venus	between 5 and 6
Earth	between 7 and 8
Mars	between 11 and 12
Jupiter	40
Saturn	74
Uranus	149
Neptune	233
Pluto	305

4. Back in the classroom, use a calculator to find the distance between each two neighboring planets in terms of toilet paper sheets. Make calculations for the distances between Mercury and Venus, Venus and Earth, Earth and Mars, and so on. Record the results in your *Science Notebook*.

 See **SCIENCE** *and* **MATH TOOLBOX** page H4 if you need to review *Using a Calculator.*

5. Calculate and record the distance in sheets between each planet and Earth.

Analyze and Conclude

1. Compare the distances between neighboring planets. Which two are closest together? Which two are farthest apart? As a group, which set of planets is closest together—those nearest the Sun or those farther out?

2. With other students, hypothesize about the effects of a planet's distance from the Sun. Which planets would be hottest? Which would be coldest? What would the Sun look like from each one? How long would a year be on each planet? Compare your ideas with those of your classmates.

3. Suppose you want to send a radio signal from Earth to each of the other planets at the time when each planet is closest to Earth. Which planet would receive a signal most quickly? Which would take the longest to get a signal? Use the results of step 5 to make a list of the planets according to their distance from Earth.

Step 4

UNIT PROJECT LINK

Future trips to other planets may begin from an Earth-orbiting space station. Create a docking port for your simulated space station. Begin to collect information so that you can decorate the docking port area with travel posters of different planets and moons. Which ones would you and your classmates like to visit most?

 Technology *Link*

For more help with your Unit Project, go to **www.eduplace.com**.

Earth's Neighborhood— The Solar System

Reading Focus Starting with the Sun, what is the order of planets in the solar system?

On pages B10 and B11, the way the sky is divided up into 88 constellations is compared to the way the United States is divided up into 50 states. In the same way, you can consider a solar system to be a "neighborhood" in the sky.

A **solar system** consists of a star and the objects that revolve around it. A model of our own solar system is shown here. In addition to the Sun, our solar system includes nine known planets and the moons that orbit those planets. It also includes many smaller objects, such as comets and the small rocky bodies known as asteroids. The force of gravity keeps planets in orbit around the Sun.

The activity on pages B32 and B33 shows the relative distances between planets. The planets are tiny compared to those distances. To show the planets clearly, on pages B34 and B35 they are drawn much larger than they should be, compared to the size of their orbits. ■

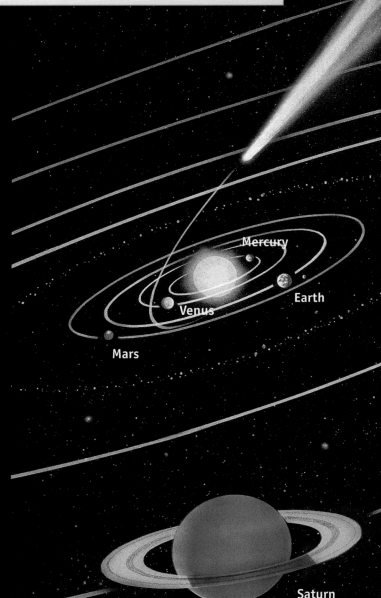

Mercury

Earth

Venus

Mars

Saturn

Neptune

Uranus

Pluto

asteroid belt

Jupiter

Planet	Average Distance From the Sun (in millions of km)	Period of Revolution (in Earth years)	Number of Known Moons
Mercury	58	0.24	0
Venus	108	0.62	0
Earth	150	1.00	1
Mars	228	1.88	2
Jupiter	778	11.86	16
Saturn	1,429	29.46	18
Uranus	2,875	84.01	15
Neptune	4,504	164.79	8
Pluto	5,900	248.60	1

Using Math

In Earth days, how long is one year on Mercury? Round your answer to the nearest whole day.

Ptolemy Was Right—and Wrong

Reading Focus What is the heliocentric model of the solar system, and what other model came before it?

"Pygmies placed on the shoulders of giants see more than the giants themselves." It may seem to you that this saying has little to do with science. But it applies to two giants in the world of astronomy. One of these men was totally wrong about a major principle. Yet his work prepared the way for later astronomers to arrive at a better understanding of the universe. That man's name was Ptolemy (tăl'ə mē).

Ptolemy lived in Egypt in the second century A.D. He tried to understand why the planets seem to wander across the sky. After charting their movements, he worked out a model that seemed to explain what he was seeing.

The Maya in Central America use astronomical observations to create the most accurate calendar in the world. **300**

Greek philosopher Aristarchus proposes that Earth and the other planets are spheres that revolve around the Sun.

260 B.C.

A.D. 145 Ptolemy, an astronomer studying in Egypt, popularizes the theory that the Sun, Moon, and planets all revolve around a motionless Earth.

Sun

Earth

3000 B.C. The Chinese begin recording and predicting the apparent movements of the Sun, Moon, and planets.

▲ **Ptolemy's model of the solar system**

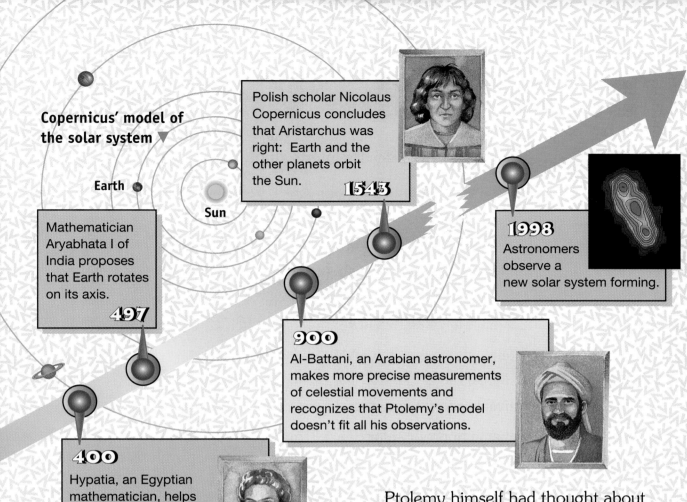

Copernicus' model of the solar system ▼

Earth

Sun

Polish scholar Nicolaus Copernicus concludes that Aristarchus was right: Earth and the other planets orbit the Sun.
1543

1998
Astronomers observe a new solar system forming.

Mathematician Aryabhata I of India proposes that Earth rotates on its axis.
497

900
Al-Battani, an Arabian astronomer, makes more precise measurements of celestial movements and recognizes that Ptolemy's model doesn't fit all his observations.

400
Hypatia, an Egyptian mathematician, helps develop instruments to measure an object's apparent position in the sky.

Ptolemy's model was an Earth-centered, or **geocentric** (jē ō sen′trik), **model**. To him that seemed perfectly logical, since Earth appeared to Ptolemy to be steady and unmoving. To explain the motions of the Sun, Moon, and planets, he reasoned that they all must revolve around Earth.

Ptolemy's model was used for more than 1,000 years. But in 1543 a Polish clergyman, Nicolaus Copernicus, put forth a different idea. He placed the Sun at the center of the universe and suggested that all the planets, including Earth, revolve around it.

Ptolemy himself had thought about such a Sun-centered, or **heliocentric** (hē lē ō sen′trik), **model**, but he had rejected the idea. That's because Ptolemy's model explained the solar system based on the best data available to him at the time. It's a basic principle in science that you can't get the right answer if you don't have all the necessary information. But you can't wait for everything to be discovered before you try to use what you know, either.

That's where "standing on the shoulders of giants" comes in. When Copernicus came along, he had a head start because he was able to build on Ptolemy's work. By adding his own observations to Ptolemy's, Copernicus could create a more accurate theory. That theory formed the basis for all of modern astronomy. ■

Birth of the Universe

Reading Focus How do scientists think that the universe was formed?

▲ **Formation of the universe according to the big-bang theory**

Where did the universe and our solar system come from? This is one of the biggest questions that human beings have ever asked. The answer may never be completely discovered or proved to everyone's satisfaction. But based on all the evidence people have uncovered over the centuries, this is what most scientists consider the best explanation they have so far.

The Big Bang

All the matter and energy that exist make up the **universe**. At one time, all of this matter and energy was concentrated in an incredibly tiny, extremely hot, unbelievably dense ball. (The word *dense* in this case means "very closely packed.")

Then all at once, at least 14 billion years ago, this ball of matter and energy exploded. The explosion sent a vast cloud of matter swirling out in all directions into space.

Time passed—*lots* of time. As it did, little by little, concentrations of matter began to form within the massive, expanding cloud. Each separate concentration was huge beyond anything we can imagine. Together these concentrations must have been millions of times bigger than Earth and all the planets combined in order to have contained enough material to condense into all the objects that now exist.

But condense they did, due to gravity. Gravity is the force that causes bodies to be attracted to each other. Very slowly, each clump of matter began to contract. Different clumps joined together, forming bigger clumps. And as these bigger clumps contracted, they began to spin. At the same time, each clump continued to move outward, away from all the other clumps.

These huge spinning collections of matter would eventually become galaxies, which are giant clusters of stars.

The story you've just read is commonly known as the **big-bang theory** of the origin of the universe.

The Sun and Planets Form

More time went by—billions of years. Then, within one of the galaxies, one particular collection of gas and dust began to condense. This was an event of special importance to us, for this material would eventually form our solar system! Refer to the drawings as you read about this event.

As the cloud of gas and dust rotated and flattened, most of the material collected in the center, where it would become our Sun. At the same time, in the swirling clouds around this future Sun, separate spinning clouds of matter began condensing to form the planets, including Earth. By about 4.6 billion years ago, the major objects in our solar system were in place.

What was happening in our own neighborhood was just one tiny chapter in a much larger story. For throughout the billions of kilometers of outer space, other collections of matter were also condensing. These collections formed other galaxies, other stars, and even—scientists think—other planets around those stars.

How Do We Know It's All True?

How do scientists know that the big bang happened this way? Well, they don't, not for certain. But the evidence continues to mount as we gather more and more data about the universe. Piecing together the cosmic puzzle of our origins is a tremendous job. ■

Formation of the Solar System

❶ Gas and dust cloud spins in space.

❷ Material condenses and the Sun and planets begin to form.

❸ The solar system forms.

INVESTIGATE FURTHER!

RESEARCH

Research other scientific theories on the birth of the universe. Compare these theories as to their strengths and weaknesses.

Mission to Mars!

Reading Focus What can rocks on Mars tell about the planet?

▲ The Mars landscape, as seen during the Mars Pathfinder mission at the Jet Propulsion Center in Pasadena, California

STS SCIENCE TECHNOLOGY & SOCIETY

In July 1997 the eyes of everyone in the mission control room in Houston, Texas, were glued to the TV screen. What were they watching? Their attention was on Shark, Half Dome, and Moe —three of the rocks named by mission scientists on the surface of Mars. The scientists were awed by the sight of the detailed images beamed back by Mars Pathfinder from the surface of Mars!

The Mission

Pathfinder was the first successful United States Mars mission since 1976. Its lander was equipped with a camera to take detailed pictures of the planet's rocks. It carried devices to measure and record daily Mars weather. To cushion the landing, the Pathfinder carried airbags. These airbags, looking like a huge white skirt, are shown on page B41.

Mars and the Internet

The Mars Pathfinder mission got world-wide interest. Images were shown on a NASA Web site for the whole world to see. Anyone on the Internet— from school students to senior citizens—could view what the scientists were seeing. On one single day, July 8, 1997, the Web site was visited about 47 million times!

What's the cost of sending an unpiloted spacecraft to Mars? It's about the same as making a major motion picture. Unpiloted flights cost much less than flights with people onboard. Even without a crew, a mission can gather a lot of information. Robots such as Pathfinder's Mars rover, Sojourner, collect data from the surface of the planet. Sojourner gathered information about the Martian rocks and sent the information back to Earth.

What Rocks Tell

Why study rocks? Every rock has a story to tell about where it came from and what it's made of. Here's what Martian rocks suggest to scientists about Mars. Billions of years ago, Mars

▲ This photograph, taken with the aid of a microscope, shows possible traces of microorganisms in a Mars meteorite.

▲ Sojourner, the Mars rover (*left*) and Mars Pathfinder, the lander (*right*). Airbags are under the lander.

was more Earthlike. Rounded pebbles on the surface have led scientists to believe that a long time ago there was water on Mars. That time was about 1.8 to 3.5 billion years ago. Since then, Mars has been dry and very cold.

Could the presence of water mean that life once existed on Mars? Scientists aren't sure about what other conditions were needed to spark life. Some doubt that Mars ever had an environment that could support life forms. Others think it is possible that life existed on the red planet.

Scientists have found 13 meteorites on Earth thought to be from Mars. At least one of these meteorites has features that are thought by some to be once-living microbes. Scientists do not have other strong evidence that there has been life on Mars. Future missions, however, will build on the evidence gathered by Mars Pathfinder. ■

INVESTIGATION 1 WRAP-UP

REVIEW

1. Name the nine planets in our solar system in order. Start with the planet closest to the Sun.

2. Describe the big-bang theory of the origin of the universe.

CRITICAL THINKING

3. You have read about and probably made models of the solar system. Explain how a model can help you understand the solar system. How does a model differ from the real thing?

4. Compare the heliocentric model of the Sun and planets with the geocentric model.

INVESTIGATION 2

HOW DO THE PLANETS DIFFER?

My Very Elegant Mother Just Served Us Nine Pickles. This sentence is a tool that will help you remember the names of the planets in order of their distance from the Sun. The first letter of each word is the same as the first letter of a planet. Now learn what distance from the Sun has to do with the characteristics of each planet.

Activity

MATERIALS
- sheet of paper
- *Science Notebook*

Measuring Planet Sizes

Which planets are the biggest? Which are the smallest? How large is the difference between them? Find out!

Step 2

Procedure

1. Make an Earth ruler like the one pictured on the facing page. Place the edge of a sheet of paper just below the picture. **Draw** lines on the paper's edge at exactly the same places as the lines in the picture. Number the spaces on your ruler as shown.

Pluto   Neptune   Uranus   Saturn

2. Place your Earth ruler over the picture of each planet on these two pages. Use the ruler to **measure** the distance across the middle of each planet in terms of Earth diameters. **Record** each measurement.

3. **Rank** the planets from smallest to largest.

4. Using graph paper, **make a bar graph** showing the diameters of the nine planets. **List** the planets' names on one side of the graph and the number of Earth diameters on the other.

 See **SCIENCE** and **MATH TOOLBOX** page H3 if you need to review **Making a Bar Graph.**

Analyze and Conclude

1. With classmates, **hypothesize** about the differences between the larger planets and the smaller ones. For example, how strong might each planet's gravity be compared to Earth's gravity? **Hypothesize** how gravity might affect whether or not a planet has an atmosphere. **Discuss** and **compare** your ideas.

2. Imagine that you live on a moon of each planet. Assume that each moon is about the same distance from its planet as Earth's Moon is from Earth. **Predict** how much of the sky each of the planets would fill.

3. **Compare** the pictures of large planets with those of small planets. **Make a list** of the differences you observe.

INVESTIGATE FURTHER!

RESEARCH

Look at the order of the planets. Are the biggest planets close to the Sun or far away? Hypothesize why those giant planets are located where they are. Look in an astronomy book that tells about the origins of the solar system to find out scientists' theories about this.

EARTH RULER *(Earth diameters)*

| 1 | 2 | 3 | 4 | 5 | 6 | 7 | 8 | 9 | 10 | 11 | 12 | 13 | 14 | 15 | 16 | 17 | 18 | 19 | 20 |

Jupiter

Mars

Earth

Venus

Mercury

Sun

The Inner Planets

Reading Focus What are some characteristics of the four planets closest to the Sun?

The inner planets of our solar system are Mercury, Venus, Earth, and Mars. All four planets are close to the Sun and are like Earth in size, in density, and in their mostly rocky makeup. Because of these likenesses they are known as **terrestrial** (tə res′trē əl) **planets**, meaning those that are Earthlike.

Two of the inner planets and all of the outer ones have satellites. Astronomers use the terms *moon* and *satellite* when they refer to natural objects that revolve around a planet. (The word *satellite* can also mean an orbiting object built by people.) Now find out about each of the inner planets.

☿ MERCURY

MERCURY is the closest planet to the Sun and the second smallest of the nine planets. It looks a lot like Earth's Moon, with a rocky surface covered by craters. Mercury has almost no atmosphere, just faint traces of helium and one or two other gases that it probably "captured" from the Sun. Surface temperatures on Mercury get hot enough to melt lead. This speedy planet takes about three months (measured in Earth time) to revolve around the Sun.

♀ VENUS

VENUS is the second planet from the Sun. Although it's named after the Roman goddess of beauty, it's not a very pleasant place. The Venusian (vi noo′-shən) atmosphere consists mainly of carbon dioxide with sulfuric acid clouds. It's so dense that the atmospheric pressure on the planet's surface is tremendous. Temperatures there reach about 500°C (900°F).

Venus' clouds appear featureless in normal light, but certain cameras reveal swirling patterns *(above right)*. Radar provided this computer-generated view of the surface *(right)*. ▶

⊕ EARTH

EARTH is the only planet in the solar system on which life is known to exist. It's the third planet from the Sun and the largest of the four inner planets. Earth has a vast core of molten metal and rock, with a thin crust of solid rock. Our planet's atmosphere is about 78 percent nitrogen and 21 percent oxygen, plus traces of other gases. As seen from space, Earth is one of the most beautiful planets, with bright blues indicating the abundant water and swirling whites, its scattered clouds.

☾ MOON

The Moon is Earth's only natural satellite. It has no atmosphere and is one of the largest satellites in the solar system. The force of gravity keeps the Moon in orbit around Earth. The Moon is the brightest object in Earth's night sky. This brightness is caused by the reflection of the Sun's light off the Moon's surface. The Moon rotates on its axis and moves around Earth once each month. During this cycle, the Moon passes through phases, so from night to night the lighted part of the Moon appears to change shape when seen from Earth.

♂ MARS

MARS, the fourth planet from the Sun, resembles Earth more than any other planet. Mars is smaller and less dense than Earth, which gives it less gravity and a thinner atmosphere. But the Martian day is only 41 minutes longer than the Earth day, and the planet has four seasons similar to those on Earth. Surface temperatures on Mars dip down to −90°C (−130°F) and seldom rise above 0°C (32°F). Iron oxide gives Martian soil the reddish color of rust. There are also white polar caps that grow and shrink with the seasons, and dark patches that were once mistaken for canals or vegetation. We now know that these dark areas come and go as dust storms cover and uncover darker rock.

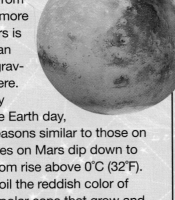

▲ **The features on Venus** range from smooth plains to volcanic mountain ranges. A computer created this false-color ground view from radar data.

▲ **Venus' surface** was photographed by a probe that landed on the planet.

MARS continued

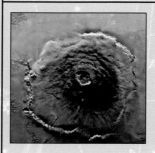

◀ **Olympus Mons** (ō lim′pəs mänz) is a huge extinct volcano on Mars, nearly three times the height of the tallest mountain on Earth.

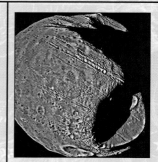

◀ **Phobos** (fō′bəs) is a Martian satellite just 27 km (16 mi) long. Its companion moon Deimos (dī′məs) is even smaller. Many scientists think these rough-shaped objects are asteroids that were captured by Mars' gravity.

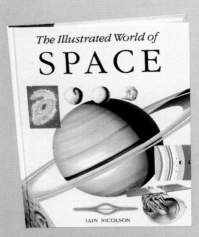

◀ Sojourner, the Mars rover, scooped up soil and rock samples.

Science in Literature

THE FACES OF VENUS

"Venus is very nearly as large as the Earth but is a very hostile place. Its surface is hidden beneath deadly clouds of sulphuric acid droplets. The atmosphere consists mainly of carbon dioxide and is so heavy that any astronaut on the planet's surface would be crushed. The atmosphere retains so much heat that the surface temperature is about 880°F, hot enough to melt lead."

The Illustrated World of Space
by Iain Nicolson
Simon & Schuster
Books for Young Readers, 1991

There are lots of beautiful pictures and interesting facts in *The Illustrated World of Space* by Iain Nicolson. Read it to find out what might happen to the Earth and the Sun in 5 or 6 billion years.

The Outer Planets

Reading Focus What are some characteristics of the five planets farthest from the Sun?

Four of the five planets farthest from the Sun are very much alike. They're quite large in comparison to the inner planets, and they have ring systems. They're also made up mostly of substances that would be gases on Earth. For this reason, Jupiter, Saturn, Uranus, and Neptune are often referred to as the **gas giants**. The outermost known planet, Pluto, seems to be more like the inner terrestrial planets in size and composition. Take a closer look at this planet and its neighbors.

♃ JUPITER

JUPITER is the fifth planet from the Sun and the largest planet in our solar system. When the solar system was forming, Jupiter almost became a star. But the nuclear reactions that keep the Sun burning could not occur, and so Jupiter cooled and became a planet instead. It's composed mainly of gaseous and liquid hydrogen and helium. The gases probably surround a small rocky core. The planet's upper atmosphere features swirling cloud bands and the Great Red Spot, a huge circular storm that's lasted for centuries. Jupiter has a set of rings, but they're so thin and dark that they're practically invisible.

Io (ī′ō), a satellite of Jupiter, is the most volcanically active object we know of in the solar system. This rocky moon's volcanoes regularly coat the satellite's surface with lava. ▶

Io's volcanoes send up towering plumes of gas, visible in this false-color view. ▶

♄ SATURN

SATURN is the sixth planet from the Sun and the last planet you can easily see with your unaided eye from Earth. It's almost as big as Jupiter, with a very similar composition and banded atmosphere. Strong winds sweep across Saturn almost constantly, reaching speeds of 1,800 km/h (1,100 mph). The planet's spectacular rings are its most distinctive feature.

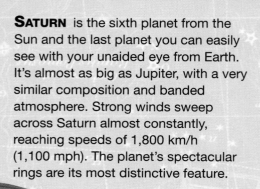

▲ **Saturn and some of its moons** are shown in this composite photo. Saturn has the most known satellites of any planet. Some have rocky surfaces and others are ice-covered.

▲ **Saturn's rings** are shown in a false-color view that brings out their details. The planet's ring system is made up of countless ice and rock fragments. These fragments orbit so closely together that the rings look solid from a distance.

▲ **Titan**, the largest of Saturn's satellites, is the only moon in the solar system with a dense atmosphere. Its haze is shown clearly in this false-color photo. Titan's atmosphere may resemble that of early Earth.

♅ URANUS

URANUS (yŏŏr'ə nəs), blue-green in color, is the seventh planet from the Sun. Like Jupiter, it has thin, dark rings that are too faint to be easily photographed. Since this planet can't readily be seen from Earth without a telescope, its existence wasn't recognized until the 1700s. Because of its distance from the Sun, Uranus is very cold, with temperatures near -215°C (-355°F) in the cloud tops.

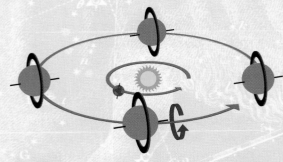

▲ **The tilt of Uranus' axis** is the most unique feature of this planet. In contrast to Earth's axis, Uranus' axis is tilted way over on its side. As Uranus revolves around the Sun, its poles take turns pointing toward the Sun.

◄ **Uranus and its moon Miranda** (mə ran'də) are seen in this computer-generated photo. The picture shows what Uranus' faint rings might look like from nearby. Miranda has been called the most bizarre object in the solar system. Scientists think the patchwork appearance of its surface resulted when the moon was torn apart by collisions and then was reassembled by its own gravity.

♆ NEPTUNE

NEPTUNE was discovered in the 1800s. It's a planet very similar to Uranus, but it doesn't have a severely tilted axis. Neptune's rings, like those of Jupiter and Uranus, are too faint to be seen from a distance. While Uranus' cloud tops present a pretty bland face, Neptune's atmosphere has swirling blue and white features.

Triton is a rocky, ice-covered moon of Neptune that seems to be active despite being very cold. It has geyserlike features that send up plumes of material into Triton's thin atmosphere. ▼

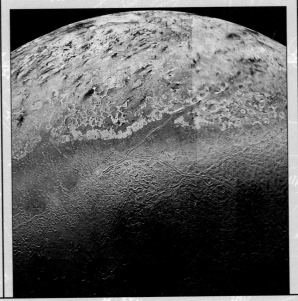

♇ PLUTO

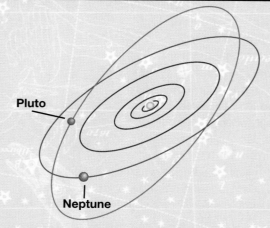

PLUTO is the most remote planet in the solar system— at least, it usually is! It's also the smallest planet, about the same size as Earth's Moon. Not much is known for sure about Pluto, since no space probe has ever visited it. Indeed, Pluto is so small and so far away that only Earth's most powerful telescopes can see it at all. The Hubble Space Telescope took this photo (*above*), which shows the planet and its one known moon, Charon (ker'ən). It's cold beyond imagination on Pluto, probably never warmer than −223°C (−370°F).

Pluto

Neptune

▲ **Pluto's unusual orbit** makes it the ninth planet most of the time but sometimes brings it inside the orbit of Neptune. When that happens, Pluto becomes the eighth planet and Neptune is the ninth! Pluto was closer to the Sun from 1979 to 1999.

◀ **Pluto's surface** may look something like this artist's view. Scientists think that Pluto's rocky ground is covered with a frost of frozen gases, under a very light atmosphere of methane and nitrogen. The artist has pictured the moon Charon and the tiny-looking Sun in Pluto's sky.

Internet Field Trip

Visit **www.eduplace.com** to learn more about the solar system.

INVESTIGATION 2 WRAP-UP

THINK IT WRITE IT

REVIEW

1. Compare Earth and the Moon.

2. Name and describe the sixth planet from the Sun.

CRITICAL THINKING

3. Describe some ways that the inner planets and the outer planets are alike and different.

4. Suppose you could set up a scientific outpost on any planet. Where would you build it? Explain your choice.

REFLECT & EVALUATE

Word Power

Write the letter of the term that best completes each sentence. *Not all terms will be used.*

1. Other than Pluto, the outer planets are called ——.
2. The idea that the Sun, Moon, and planets revolve around a motionless Earth is the ——.
3. How the universe began is described by the ——.
4. A star with objects revolving around it is a ——.
5. Earthlike planets are also called ——.

a. big-bang theory
b. gas giants
c. geocentric model
d. heliocentric model
e. satellite
f. solar system
g. terrestrial planets

Check What You Know

Write the term in each pair that best completes each sentence.

1. Scientists have a theory that our solar system formed about (10,000 years, 4.6 billion years) ago.
2. Mercury, Venus, Earth, and Mars are all (outer planets, inner planets).
3. The planet with the Great Red Spot is (Uranus, Jupiter).

Problem Solving

1. A friend tells you that Mars is the planet most like Earth. Explain why you agree or disagree.
2. Use sketches to illustrate some scientists' theories on how the solar system formed.

BUILD YOUR PORTFOLIO

Use the information given here to help you arrange the planets in order of increasing distance from the Sun. Use the information from the chapter to make a labeled drawing of the solar system showing the relative sizes of the planets.

Planet	Period of Revolution (in Earth years)
Saturn	29.46
Mars	1.88
Pluto	248.60
Venus	0.62
Uranus	84.01

Planet	Period of Revolution (in Earth years)
Jupiter	11.86
Earth	1.00
Mercury	0.24
Neptune	164.79

3

STARS AND GALAXIES

The main entrance to an ancient ceremonial hall in New Mexico was built to face the North Star. The ceilings of some caves in Arizona are covered with ancient drawings of stars. Native Americans identified and located stars and planets thousands of years ago. Why did they do it? How accurate were they?

Connecting to Science
CULTURE

Ancient Astronomer Two thousand years ago in Mexico, a large city was laid out according to knowledge of the Sun, Moon, planets, and stars. Pyramids dedicated to the Sun and Moon were constructed in the city. A hall was built so that on the first day of spring it would align a distant point on Earth with the Sun.

Carved rocks found throughout the Americas were used to mark the rising and setting of stars. Early Native Americans designed a 365-day calendar and determined the four compass directions from their knowledge of the night sky.

Coming Up

◀ An ancient Native American rock carving of stars in New Mexico

WHAT ARE STARS, AND HOW DO THEY DIFFER?

When you look at the stars at night, do they all look the same? The next chance you get, look carefully at the night sky. You might be surprised at some of the differences you can observe among the stars.

Activity

Capturing Colors

Stars come in many colors. Find out how astronomers observe the colors in starlight.

Procedure

In a dark room, view a glowing light bulb. **Describe** what you see in your *Science Notebook*. **Observe** the bulb through a red filter, then through a green filter. **Describe** what you see through each. **Observe** the bulb through a spectroscope. **Draw** a color picture of the band of light, or spectrum, that you see. Place the red filter over the opening of the spectroscope, view the bulb, and **draw** a color picture of what you see. Do the same with the green filter.

Analyze and Conclude

1. How did the filters and the spectroscope affect the appearance of the bulb? Based on your observations, what can you **infer** about white light?

2. **Hypothesize** how astronomers might use spectroscopes and filters to help them obtain information about the stars.

Activity

How Big Is Betelgeuse?

Stars come in many sizes. Betelgeuse is a giant red star. Our Sun is a medium-sized yellow star. What would our solar system be like if Betelgeuse were our star? Find out!

Step 2

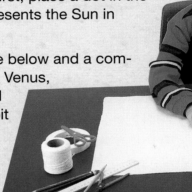

Procedure

1. On a large sheet of paper, **draw a model** of the solar system from the Sun to Jupiter. First, place a dot in the center of the paper. This dot represents the Sun in your model.

2. Using the data from the table below and a compass, **draw** the orbits of Mercury, Venus, Earth, and Mars. Use a string and pencil, as shown, to draw the orbit of Jupiter. Label each orbit.

3. Finally, **draw** a circle 12 cm in diameter (a radius of 6 cm) around the Sun in your model. Shade everything inside this circle red. This circle represents the giant red star Betelgeuse.

 Math Hint *Remember, a diameter is a line segment that connects two points on a circle and passes through the center of the circle.*

Analyze and Conclude

1. Based on your model, **compare** the relative sizes of the Sun and Betelgeuse.

2. In your *Science Notebook*, **hypothesize** what would happen to Earth if our Sun were to grow to the size of Betelgeuse. Use your model to support your hypothesis.

Planet	Distance From the Sun
Mercury	1.2 cm
Venus	2.2 cm
Earth	3.0 cm
Mars	4.6 cm
Jupiter	15.6 cm

How Stars Differ

Reading Focus How are stars classified?

When Galileo first looked through his telescope at the night sky, he noticed differences among the stars. Some were extremely bright, but others seemed dim and plain. Scientists now know that stars differ from one another in many ways. Four of the obvious differences involve brightness, size, temperature, and color.

The Characteristics of Stars

You don't need a telescope to know that some stars are brighter than others. Stars also range in size from dwarfs to supergiants. The largest body in our solar system, the Sun, is an average-sized star with a diameter of about 1.4 million km (865,000 mi). A supergiant can have a diameter 1,000 times that of the Sun. Some dwarf stars have diameters less than half that of Earth.

The temperature and color of a star are closely linked. In fact, temperature determines a star's color, as it sometimes determines the color of heated materials on Earth. For example, melted iron that glows with a white light is hotter than heated iron that glows with an orange light.

Stars show a wide range of colors, indicating different temperatures. Astronomers use spectroscopes to study the light given off by stars, in much the same way as one is used to study light in the activity on page B54.

The surface temperatures of the hottest stars may be as high as 50,000°C (90,000°F). These stars shine with a bluish light, while the coolest stars shine with a red light. The table below shows the relationship between star color and temperature.

Star Color and Temperature		
Star Color	**Surface Temperature**	**Examples**
Blue	11,000°–50,000°C	Regulus, Rigel
Blue-white	7,500°–11,000°C	Deneb, Sirius
White	6,000°–7,500°C	Canopus, Procyon
Yellow	5,000°–6,000°C	The Sun, Alpha Centauri
Orange-red	3,500°–5,000°C	Aldebaran, Arcturus
Red	2,000°–3,500°C	Betelgeuse, Proxima Centauri

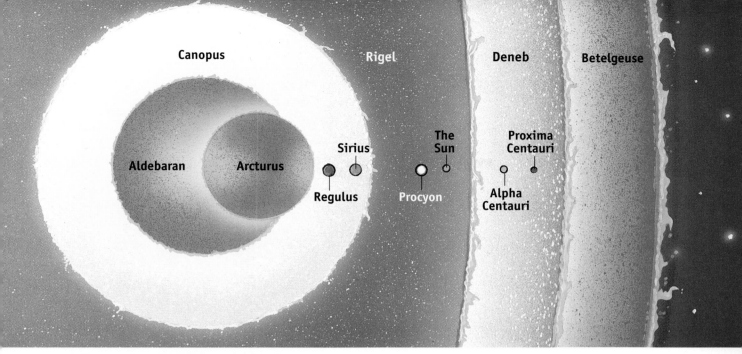

▲ Stars of various sizes and colors

The picture above shows the relative sizes of the stars in the table. Find the red star Betelgeuse, which is modeled in the activity on page B55. Now find the red star called Proxima Centauri. These two stars are the same color and so have similar surface temperatures. But, as you can see, stars of the same color can vary greatly in size.

How a Star Gets Its Energy

Although stars have different visible features, they all have one thing in common: the way they produce energy. A star is a huge ball of hot glowing gases. In the center of the star, energy comes from nuclear reactions that change hydrogen into helium. It's as if millions of hydrogen bombs were going off every second inside the star.

Unlike a hydrogen bomb, a star doesn't explode and fly apart. Its mass is so great that it is held together by its own gravity. So the energy released by the nuclear reactions moves throughout the star, generating heat and light. ■

INVESTIGATION 1 WRAP-UP

REVIEW

1. What are four ways in which stars differ from one another?

2. What is the temperature range of a "cool" star? of a "hot" star?

CRITICAL THINKING

3. How does our Sun differ in size and temperature from the star Rigel?

4. When viewed from Earth, a red star and a blue star appear to be equally bright. What could you infer about these two stars?

HOW FAR AWAY ARE THE STARS?

If you traveled beyond our solar system at the speed of light, you could reach the closest one of these objects in about four years. What are these objects? They are stars.

Activity

Star Light, Star Bright

As you look up at the twinkling stars, some seem very bright. Others seem dim and almost disappear into the blackness of night. In this activity, find out why all stars don't shine with the same brightness.

MATERIALS

• grease pencil
• 2 flashlights of the same size
• transparent tape
• large sheet of white paper (poster size)
• metric ruler
• metric tape measure
• *Science Notebook*

Procedure

1. Use a grease pencil to **label** one flashlight *A* and another flashlight *B*. In your *Science Notebook*, **make a chart** like the one shown below.

Flashlight	Distance From Wall	Diameter of Circle of Light	Brightness
A			
B			

2. Attach a large sheet of white paper to a wall at about shoulder height. Darken the room.

3. Have one student stand at least 1 meter from the white paper. Ask this student to shine flashlight *A* on the paper.

4. Have a second student stand at least twice the distance from the paper as the first student is standing. Ask this student to shine flashlight *B* on the same paper, to the right of the light from flashlight *A*.

5. Have a third student use a metric ruler to **measure** the diameters of the central spots of light from flashlight *A* and flashlight *B*.

See SCIENCE *and* MATH TOOLBOX
page H6 if you need to review **Using a Tape Measure or Ruler.**

6. With a measuring tape, **measure** the distance from the wall to flashlight *A*. Then **measure** the distance from the wall to flashlight *B*. **Record** this information in your *Science Notebook*.

7. **Compare** the brightness of the circles of light from each flashlight. **Record** which circle is brighter and which is dimmer.

8. **Compare** your results with those of other groups in your class.

Analyze and Conclude

1. What is the relationship between the distance of the flashlight from the paper and the diameter of the circle of light formed? **Hypothesize** why this relationship exists.

2. What is the relationship between the distance of the flashlight from the wall and the brightness of the circle of light?

3. From this activity, what can you **infer** about the apparent brightness of two identical stars at different distances from the Earth?

Step 4

INVESTIGATE FURTHER!

EXPERIMENT

Write a hypothesis on the appearance from Earth of a large star and a small star that are the same distance from Earth. Plan an experiment that would model how two stars of different sizes but the same distance from Earth would look from Earth. Tell what equipment you would use. Write the steps of the experiment. After you discuss the experiment with your teacher, actually do it.

Measuring Distances in Space

Reading Focus How do you measure a star's distance from Earth?

Incredibly large distances separate stars from Earth. Scientists can't run a tape measure across space to measure these distances. Instead, they measure something called parallax (par'ə laks).

To understand parallax, try this exercise. Close one eye. Hold up one finger at arm's length. Line up your finger with a reference point, such as a mark on a chalkboard. Keeping your finger and head still, open your closed eye, and close the eye that was open. Observe how your finger *appears* to move in relation to your reference point.

In this exercise, nothing actually moved. But your finger appeared to shift position because you were viewing it from a slightly different location with your other eye. Such an apparent shift in position is called parallax.

Astronomers use parallax to figure out distances to nearby stars. As shown below, they view a star from two different places in Earth's orbit. Then they measure how far the star appeared to move in relation to other, more distant stars. They use this information to calculate the distance to the star.

Distance and Brightness

The measure of a star's brightness is called magnitude (mag'nə tōōd). Astronomers use a device called a photometer to measure how bright a star *appears* to be. That is the star's **apparent magnitude**, and it depends

  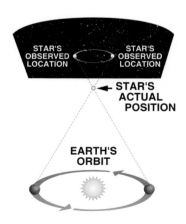

STAR'S OBSERVED LOCATION

STAR'S OBSERVED LOCATION

STAR'S ACTUAL POSITION

EARTH'S ORBIT

▲ A student's finger appears to shift due to parallax, just as a star's position against more distant stars appears to shift.

on two things: (1) how far away the star is, and (2) the star's absolute magnitude. **Absolute magnitude** is a measure of how bright the star really is.

Imagine looking at a bonfire and a match. If these two sources of light are the same distance from you, the bonfire will seem brighter. However, if the bonfire is a kilometer away and the match is at arm's length, the match will appear brighter. The "absolute magnitudes" of the two light sources won't have changed—but their apparent magnitudes will vary with distance.

Astronomers can find the absolute magnitude of a star if they know the star's apparent magnitude (which can be measured) and its distance from Earth (using the parallax method). They can also use apparent magnitude to estimate the distance to faraway stars, where parallax cannot be used.

Because distances between stars are so great, astronomers measure these distances using units called light-years. A **light-year** is the distance that light travels in one year. The speed of light is about 300,000 km (186,000 mi) per second. So a light-year is about 9.5 trillion km (5.9 trillion mi). Imagine having to write out numbers this great. ■

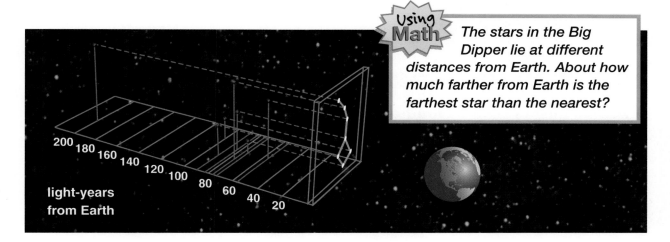

Using Math *The stars in the Big Dipper lie at different distances from Earth. About how much farther from Earth is the farthest star than the nearest?*

light-years from Earth

200 180 160 140 120 100 80 60 40 20

INVESTIGATION 2 WRAP-UP

REVIEW

1. What is a star's absolute magnitude?

2. On what two things does a star's apparent magnitude depend?

CRITICAL THINKING

3. The star Sirius (sir′ē əs) appears to be about ten times brighter than the star Deneb. Yet scientists have found that Deneb gives off much more light than Sirius does. How can you explain this puzzling situation?

4. Why is the light-year a useful unit for measuring distances to stars?

INVESTIGATION 3

WHAT IS THE LIFE CYCLE OF A STAR?

The stars that you see today are the same ones that ancient astronomers viewed thousands of years ago. But stars do change over very long periods of time. In this investigation you'll discover the different stages a star can go through.

Activity

MATERIALS

• *Science Notebook*

Studying Nebulas

*A **nebula** (neb'yə lə) is a cloud of gases and dust in space. In this activity you'll learn about the role nebulas play in the life cycle of stars.*

- -

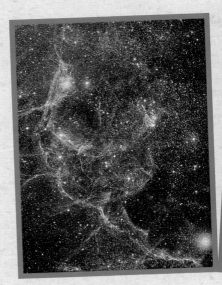

▲ **A nebula in Vela**

▲ **The Orion Nebula**

▲ **The Horsehead Nebula**

Procedure

1. Each of the six photographs on these two pages shows a nebula. Study the photos carefully and **describe** each one in your *Science Notebook*.

2. Astronomers think that stars form from the gases and dust that make up nebulas. **Identify** the photo or photos that show evidence that stars may have recently formed or may be forming now. **Describe your reasons** for choosing these photos.

3. It is thought that the gases and dust in nebulas come from old stars that have exploded. **Identify** the photo or photos that support this hypothesis. **Describe the evidence** you see in those photographs.

4. Under certain conditions, stars may form in groups or clusters. **Identify** the photo or photos that provide such evidence. **Explain the evidence** you see.

Analyze and Conclude

1. **Compare** the nebulas in the photographs. What characteristics do they have in common? How are they different?

2. Explain why you think astronomers study nebulas to learn about the life cycle of stars.

Technology Link CD-ROM

INVESTIGATE FURTHER!

Use the **Science Processor CD-ROM**, *The Solar System & Beyond* (Investigation 3, A Star Is Born!) to view the life cycle of a star.

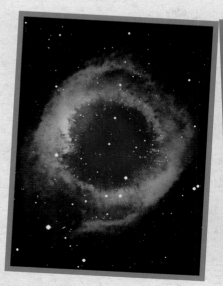

▲ **The Helix Nebula**

▲ **The Lagoon Nebula**

▲ **The Pleiades**

The Life Cycle of a Star

Reading Focus What are the stages in the life cycle of a star?

Although a star is not a living thing, it has a "life cycle." Like a living thing, a star passes through several stages as it ages. These stages include birth, growth and development, middle age, old age, and death.

The life cycle of a star covers a huge span of time. For example, our Sun is a middle-aged yellow star of average size and temperature. It has been shining for about 4.6 billion years. It should continue to shine for another 4.6 billion years before it begins to change very much.

The Birth of a Star

Huge clouds of gases and dust, called **nebulas**, are scattered through many regions of space. Nebulas provide the raw materials from which stars form. Under certain conditions, portions of a nebula begin to contract, forming clumps of spinning gases. Over millions of years, gravity causes these clumps to shrink, or condense, into dense pockets of matter within the nebula. These pockets of matter form the beginnings of stars and are called **protostars** (prō′tō stärz).

Stages in the life cycle of stars. Each star's fate depends on its mass. ▼

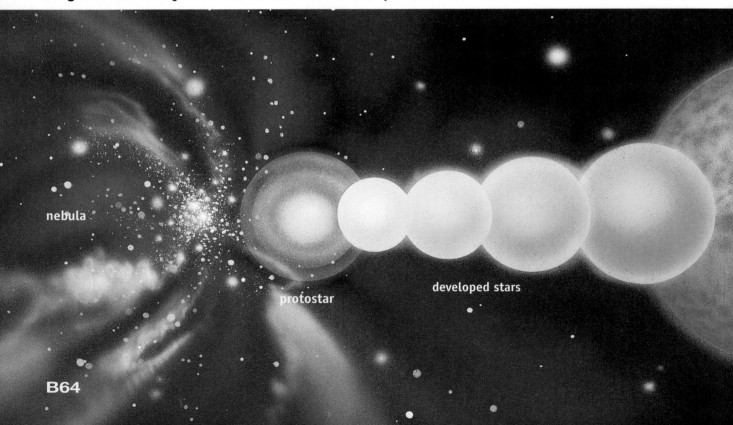

nebula

protostar

developed stars

As a protostar condenses, its particles are squeezed closer together, creating great pressure at the center. This pressure causes the core of the protostar to become very hot. When the core's temperature reaches about 10,000,000°C, nuclear reactions begin, releasing tremendous amounts of energy. At this point the protostar stops shrinking and begins to shine. It is now a star.

The Life of an Average Star

How long does a star "live"? The main factor that determines a star's life span—and the kind of death it will have—is the star's mass. A star of medium mass, like our Sun, shines for billions of years by changing its hydrogen into helium.

Eventually, though, the star's hydrogen fuel begins to run out. The star's core, now made up mostly of helium, shrinks and releases energy as it collapses. This energy, when added to the energy of the remaining nuclear reactions, causes the outer layers of the star to expand far out into space. The star swells to many times its original size.

As the outer layers expand, they move farther from the star's hot core. The outer layers cool, the light reddens, and the star becomes a **red giant**. This is what will happen to our Sun, though not for billions of years.

After a long period as a red giant, the last traces of fuel will run out. Then the Sun will collapse again. It will become a **white dwarf**, not much larger than Earth is now. At this stage, the Sun will still be shining, but only dimly. The particles of matter in the Sun will be packed tightly together at a density a million times greater than that of water. Finally the Sun will die completely and become a cool, darkened **black dwarf**.

red giant or supergiant

massive star

supernova

very high mass

black hole

high mass

neutron star

low-mass star

white dwarf

black dwarf
(dead star)

How Massive Stars Die

Stars that begin with much greater mass than our Sun live shorter lives. They also end their life in a much more spectacular fashion.

When a massive star forms, enormous pressure is created as it condenses. Although the early part of the life of a massive star is much like that of an average star, the larger star reaches the red-giant stage much sooner.

After that, the star's life is a constant battle between two opposing forces. The outward pressure caused by ever-increasing core temperatures opposes the inward push of gravity. As this battle is waged, the massive star may expand and contract several times before its "death."

When the star's fuel is finally used up, the outer layers of the star fall into the core at tremendous speeds. The great pressure created by the star's rapid contraction can result in a gigantic explosion known as a **supernova**. This is one of the most dazzling events in the universe. A supernova can appear as a bright "new" star in Earth's sky. It can produce as much light as an entire galaxy. The material released by a supernova includes elements from which future stars may be created. The Crab Nebula, shown on page B67, is the remains of a supernova.

Science in Literature

BLACK HOLES— FACT OR FICTION?

"The pull of a black hole's gravity increases dramatically near its edge. The nose of an approaching spacecraft would be dragged toward the black hole, causing it to stretch. This stretching force (called a 'tidal force') would become so strong that the spacecraft would quickly be torn to shreds."

Black holes are one of the amazing features of space that you can read about in *The Illustrated World of Space* by Iain Nicolson. The book has some beautiful pictures that help you appreciate the incredible size of the universe.

The Illustrated World of Space
by Iain Nicolson
Simon & Schuster Books
for Young Readers, 1991

The Illustrated World of
SPACE

IAIN NICOLSON

▲ The Crab Nebula is what remains of a supernova observed by Chinese astronomers nearly 1,000 years ago.

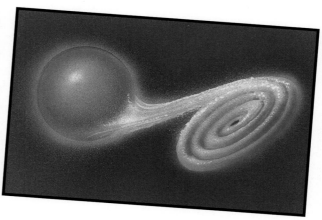

▲ A black hole—normally invisible—might be detected if material from a nearby star is pulled into it.

Neutron Stars and Black Holes

The life of a massive star doesn't end with a supernova. Some matter remains after the explosion. This material may become one of two space features. The surviving shrunken core of the star can become either a neutron star or a black hole.

In a **neutron star**, the collapse of the core is so powerful that it crushes the star's remaining matter. A typical neutron star is less than 20 km (12 mi) in diameter. Its material is so tightly packed that only a spoonful would weigh as much as a billion tons on Earth!

The collapse of the core of a massive star may be so powerful that it does not stop at the stage of a neutron star. The star may keep shrinking until it has collapsed to a tiny region, or point, with a very strong gravitational field. This region or point is called a **black hole**. The gravitational attraction of a black hole is so strong that absolutely nothing can escape it—not even light! ■

Internet Field Trip
Visit **www.eduplace.com** to learn more about the life cycle of a star.

INVESTIGATION 3 WRAP-UP

REVIEW

1. What is meant by the phrase "a star's life cycle"?

2. How long does a medium-sized star, such as our Sun, "live"? What fuel does it use?

CRITICAL THINKING

3. Compare the life cycle of an average-sized star with the life cycle of a very massive star.

4. The matter that makes up a star today may have been part of another star that died billions of years ago. How can this be?

WHAT ARE GALAXIES, AND HOW DO THEY DIFFER?

Sometimes a point of light in the night sky looks like a single star. Actually it is a huge group of stars so far away that their light seems to come from a single source. Learn about these star collections, or galaxies.

Activity

MATERIALS
• *Science Notebook*

Classifying Galaxies

Each night, astronomers study distant galaxies. In this activity you can observe and compare some, too.

- -

Procedure

1. The photographs on these pages show several different galaxies. Study each galaxy carefully and **describe** it in your *Science Notebook*.

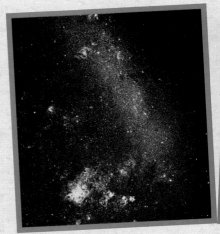

▲ **The Large Magellanic Cloud**

▲ **Galaxy NGC 7217**

▲ **The Whirlpool Galaxy**

▲ **Galaxy NGC 1365**   ▲ **The Centaurus A Galaxy**   ▲ **The Small Magellanic Cloud**

2. Different galaxies may have characteristics in common. These characteristics can be used to classify galaxies into groups. Study the photos on these pages again. Then **classify** the galaxies into two or more groups.

Analyze and Conclude

1. Based on your observations, **identify** one or more characteristics that all the galaxies have in common.

2. Identify the characteristics you used to classify the galaxies. How many different groups did you have?

3. Astronomers recognize three general classes of galaxies: spiral, elliptical, and irregular. Use these terms to **classify** each of the galaxies on these pages.

4. Before galaxies were properly identified, astronomers thought that such objects were nebulas. Recall that nebulas are huge clouds of gases and dust. **Compare** the characteristics of galaxies with those of nebulas. Why might astronomers have confused nebulas with galaxies?

The Milky Way and Other Galaxies

Reading Focus What is the Milky Way Galaxy like?

If a visitor from outer space asked you your address, what would you say? You'd probably mention a house or an apartment number, a street, a city or a town, and a state. You could then add a country and even a planet—Earth. But how could you tell the visitor the location of your planet?

Earth and eight other planets are members of a solar system, all revolving around a star we call the Sun. The solar system belongs to a gigantic cluster of stars known as the **Milky Way Galaxy**.

Our Sun is just one of more than 100 billion stars that make up the Milky Way.

Is there anything bigger than a galaxy? Yes, there is! You, your planet, your solar system, and your galaxy are all part of the universe. Recall that the universe includes absolutely everything that exists.

Building Blocks of the Universe

A **galaxy** is a huge collection of stars. A typical galaxy may contain hundreds of billions of stars, all revolving

---

Using Math *The drawing shows the Milky Way Galaxy as it might look from another galaxy. Using a fraction, estimate the distance our solar system is from the center of the galaxy and its outer edges.*

location of our solar system

▲ An elliptical galaxy   ▲ A spiral galaxy   ▲ An irregular galaxy

around a central core. Galaxies can be thought of as building blocks of the universe. The reason is that they're the largest single structures that astronomers have identified so far. There may be as many as 100 billion galaxies in the universe.

Edwin Hubble (1889–1953) is the man for whom the Hubble Space Telescope is named. Hubble was a well-known American astronomer who spent many years studying galaxies. He found that they can be classified into three basic groups, based on their shapes. Galaxies are classified in the activity on pages B68 and B69.

The most common type of galaxy is an elliptical galaxy that is shaped like a slightly flattened sphere, with no clear features. The second most common type is a spiral galaxy, with arms that make it resemble a pinwheel spinning in space. The third type of galaxy is irregular, having no definite shape.

The Milky Way Galaxy

The Milky Way is not a "special" galaxy in any way—except, of course, that you and everyone you know live inside it! The Milky Way is a spiral galaxy with at least two arms that

extend out from a central bulge. This bulge is some 3,000 light-years in diameter. The solar system is in one of the spiral arms, about 26,000 light-years from the center. A trip from one side of our galaxy to the other, traveling at the speed of light, would take about 100,000 years.

From our location in one of the galaxy's arms, the Milky Way appears as a broad band of light stretching across Earth's night sky. You can see this band for yourself if you're out in

INVESTIGATE FURTHER!

RESEARCH

Learn more about how Edwin Hubble discovered that all galaxies are moving away from each other. Look up the term *Doppler effect* in a dictionary. Find out how the Doppler effect operates in everyday life—for example, when you hear a sound produced by a moving object, such as the whistle of a passing train. Then learn how Hubble applied this principle when he studied the colors of light produced by distant galaxies.

the country, away from bright city lights, on a clear, moonless night. The stars and dust clouds of our galaxy seem to form a milky-white path across the sky, giving the galaxy its name.

How Do Galaxies Move?

Every galaxy, in addition to rotating around its own imaginary axis, is also moving in another way. It was Edwin Hubble, in 1929, who discovered the second way that galaxies move.

While studying the light given off by distant galaxies, Hubble came to an amazing conclusion. He found that most galaxies seemed to be moving away from planet Earth. What would explain such an observation?

Hubble was smart enough to realize that his findings didn't mean that Earth lay at the center of the universe. He wasn't about to become another Ptolemy! Instead, Hubble realized that *all* galaxies, including our own Milky Way, are moving rapidly *away* from one another.

For help in visualizing this expanding universe, imagine a deflated balloon with many dots on its surface. What happens to the dots as you inflate the balloon? They all move away from one another. This is similar to what's going on in the universe. Pretend you're looking out from a dot that represents the Milky Way Galaxy. All the other dots on the balloon will appear to be moving away from you—even though you too are moving!

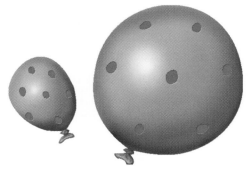

▲ **The expanding universe can be compared to a balloon that's being inflated.**

Hubble's discovery of the expanding universe later became an important part of the big-bang theory, which you learned about in Chapter 2. Hubble helped astronomers realize that the universe, a big place right now, is getting bigger and bigger all the time! ■

INVESTIGATION 4 WRAP-UP

REVIEW

1. What is the difference between a galaxy and the universe? Which is larger?

2. Name and describe three types of galaxies.

CRITICAL THINKING

3. In the past, many astronomers thought that the universe was steady and unchanging. How did Edwin Hubble's discovery and conclusions contradict that view of the universe?

4. Describe a simple model that explains Edwin Hubble's theory of the universe.

REFLECT & EVALUATE

Word Power

Write the letter of the term that best matches the definition. *Not all terms will be used.*

1. Unit used to measure distances between stars
2. Huge cloud of gases and dust that can be found in many regions of space
3. Pockets of matter that form stars
4. Gigantic collection of stars
5. How bright a star appears to be

a. absolute magnitude
b. apparent magnitude
c. galaxy
d. light-year
e. nebula
f. protostars
g. supernova
h. white dwarf

Check What You Know

Write the term in each pair that best completes each sentence.

1. Edwin Hubble discovered that galaxies are moving (toward, away from) each other.
2. When a star collapses into a tiny region, it is called a (protostar, black hole).
3. The final stage in the life cycle of a star like our Sun is a (nebula, black dwarf).
4. The general shape of the Milky Way Galaxy is (spiral, elliptical).

Problem Solving

1. Two stars have the same absolute magnitude, yet one seems very bright and the other very dim. Explain how this could happen.
2. Make a list showing the relative size of each of the following, from the smallest to the largest: planet, galaxy, universe, solar system, black dwarf.
3. Describe the movement of the Milky Way Galaxy as seen from another galaxy.

BUILD YOUR PORTFOLIO

Identify each type of galaxy. Explain which is most like the Milky Way Galaxy. Make a drawing of the Milky Way Galaxy and indicate the position of our solar system.

1   2   3

4

LIVING IN
SPACE

"Houston? We have just received a signal that
may have been sent by alien beings! Request advice."
Will the International Space Station send this kind of message some
day? What should we be doing to prepare for such an event?

PEOPLE
USING SCIENCE

Astronaut Dr. Ellen Ochoa once said,
"Only *you* put limitations on yourself about what
you can achieve, so don't be afraid to reach for
the stars." She took her own advice quite literally, becoming the first Latina astronaut to fly in
space. She flew in space shuttle missions in
1993 and 1994 and has logged almost 500
hours in space.

She grew up in California and earned her doctorate in
electrical engineering at Stanford University. She has won
several honors, including the Women in Aerospace
Outstanding Achievement Award. In addition to her accom-
plishments in the space program she holds patents for optical
technologies and is both a classical flutist and a private pilot.

Coming Up

◄ Dr. Ellen Ochoa in orbit aboard the space shuttle

INVESTIGATION ①

WHAT IS IT LIKE TO TRAVEL IN SPACE?

Imagine floating as if you had no weight at all. This is what you would experience if you were in orbit on a space shuttle. In this investigation you'll learn what causes the experience of "weightlessness" and how it can make many everyday activities unique.

Activity

Free Falling

What does the term free fall *mean? How does it affect astronauts? Find out!*

MATERIALS

- goggles
- paper cup
- string
- scissors
- metal washer
- *Science Notebook*

SAFETY /////

Wear goggles during this activity.

Procedure

1. Punch small holes on opposite sides of a paper cup, below the rim. Make a handle by pushing each end of a string through one of the holes. Then tie a knot in each end.

2. Next put a shorter length of string through a washer. Tie both ends of this string to the handle. The washer should hang about even with the top of the cup, as shown.

3. Hold the cup with one hand. Hold the handle of the cup with the other hand. Release only the handle as you continue to hold the cup. **Observe** what happens. **Record** the results in your *Science Notebook*.

4. Hold the cup by the handle at waist height. Then release both the cup and handle. With members of your group, watch the objects fall. Listen for the sound of the cup hitting the floor and the sound of the washer hitting the bottom of the cup. **Record** when you hear each sound.

Step 2

Step 3

5. Repeat step 4 at least three times. Make sure the objects fall straight to the floor without hitting each other on the way. Make sure you can tell when the two sounds occur. **Observe** whether each sound always occurs at about the same time.

6. **Draw** four pictures showing step 4. Show what the cup setup looks like (a) just before you let it drop, as you hold it up by the strings; (b) when it's falling in midair; (c) at the moment the cup touches the floor; and (d) at the moment the washer touches the bottom of the cup.

Analyze and Conclude

1. **Compare** how the washer fell in step 3 with the way the washer and cup fell in step 4. **Suggest a hypothesis** to explain the differences you observed.

2. Pretend you are a tiny bug sitting on the washer. How would you feel when the washer is released? How would the cup below you look as both objects fall toward the ground in step 4? Would the cup appear to stay the same distance away from you or not? At what point would you start to move closer to the cup?

3. An astronaut in a spaceship orbiting Earth is said to be in "free fall," with both the astronaut and the space-ship "falling" around Earth. **Infer** how this activity might relate to astronauts feeling weightless in orbit. If the imaginary bug on the washer represents an astronaut, what does the cup represent?

4. **Infer** some ways that free fall would affect an astro-naut. **Discuss** your inferences with your group.

INVESTIGATE FURTHER!

EXPERIMENT

Punch a small hole in the side of a plastic-foam cup, near the cup's bottom. Fill the cup with water and hold it over a sink. What happens? Refill the cup with your finger over the hole. With your teacher's supervision, observe the hole as you drop the cup into the sink from as great a height as possi-ble. What happens? Suggest a hypothesis that would explain your observations.

B77

Activity

Eating and Drinking in Space

Can you swallow in space if you are in free fall? Try this activity and see.

Procedure

1. Pour water into a sealable plastic bag until the bag is about half full. Insert a plastic straw into the top of the bag.

2. Seal the bag around the straw. Wrap tape around the straw where it enters the bag to keep water from escaping.

3. Prop up one end of a bench by placing books under the legs, so that this end is 7 or 8 cm higher than the other. Lie on your stomach on the bench, with your feet at the high end and your head extending out over the low end.

4. Have a group member hold the plastic bag so that it is several centimeters below your head. Try to suck water into your mouth through the straw.

Step 2

Analyze and Conclude

1. In your *Science Notebook*, **describe** the path of the water from the bag to your stomach. Is it going uphill or downhill?

2. **Hypothesize** whether gravity is necessary when you eat. Does gravity move food from your mouth to your stomach? How do you know?

3. Based on your experiment, **infer** whether astronauts can drink from a squeeze bottle in space.

Step 4

Living in Free Fall

Reading Focus What is it like to be inside a spacecraft orbiting Earth?

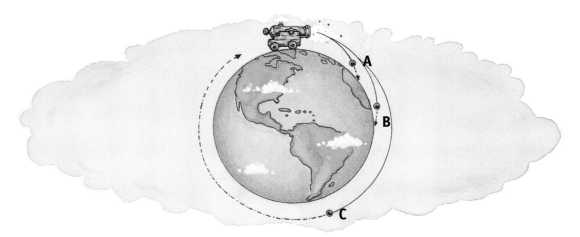

▲ **An imaginary cannonball goes into orbit.**

Imagine that you had a huge cannon, like the one in the picture above. If you shot a cannonball, like ball *A*, as shown, it would arc down toward the ground because of Earth's gravity. If you shot a second ball, ball *B*, with more speed, it would go farther before it fell. If you could shoot a third cannonball, ball *C*, with so much speed that the arc of its fall matched the curve of Earth, the ball would go into orbit.

The third cannonball would still be falling because of Earth's gravity, but Earth's gravitational pull would also keep the cannonball from flying off into space. All other things being equal, the imaginary ball would keep falling forever around and around Earth. That's what it's like to be in orbit and experience **free fall**, the motion of a freely falling object.

Coasting "Weightless" in Space

People often refer to free fall as "weightlessness" or "zero gravity." Although these terms describe the way objects appear to behave in free fall, they are not completely accurate.

Astronauts are not really totally weightless in space. They just feel that way because they and their spacecraft are falling. Have you ever gone high up on a swing and felt weightless for a split second at the top? You weren't *really* weightless—but you *were* in free fall for an instant!

There's still plenty of gravity present in an orbiting spacecraft. You'd have to be millions of kilometers farther away

Internet Field Trip

Visit **www.eduplace.com** to find out more about living in space.

B79

to escape the effects of Earth's gravity. It's just that you don't feel the effects of gravity in free fall, because there's nothing resisting your fall.

Most of the time, an orbiting spacecraft coasts with its engines off, literally just falling around planet Earth. Astronauts inside the craft are falling along with it, just as the washer falls along with the cup in the activity on pages B76 and B77. Like an imaginary bug on a washer, the astronauts feel weightless as they fall.

On Board the Space Shuttle

For a space shuttle crew, weightlessness is both enjoyable and challenging. Imagine being able to float all over the shuttle's cabin, with hardly any effort! All you need to get around is a little push.

Most astronauts experience a little motion sickness at the beginning of a space flight, but then they adjust to weightlessness. Soon they can eat, drink, sleep, and do just about anything else they might do on Earth.

Food and drink must be kept in sealed packages and consumed carefully so that pieces and droplets don't float around the cabin. Each crew member has a sleeping bag that can be tied to the wall, floor, or ceiling. If the bag weren't tied down, the dozing astronaut would float around the space shuttle.

Taking showers or baths in space is difficult, so shuttle astronauts wash by wetting a cloth with a water gun. Instead of plumbing that relies on gravity, the shuttle toilet uses suction to draw the waste away like a vacuum cleaner.

The human body is suited to function where the pull of gravity is resisted by Earth's surface. In free fall the body undergoes many changes, which are described on page B81.

When astronauts return to Earth, it takes just a short time for their muscles to adjust to gravity again. But weightlessness for long periods could have permanent effects on the human body. Many questions must be answered before humans can take extended trips in space.

An orbiting space shuttle and the astronauts inside it are in free fall. ▼

Technology Link CD-ROM

INVESTIGATE FURTHER!

Use the **Science Processor CD-ROM**, *The Solar System and Beyond* (Investigation 4, Shuttle Ride) to take a journey on a space shuttle and learn how it feels to be in space.

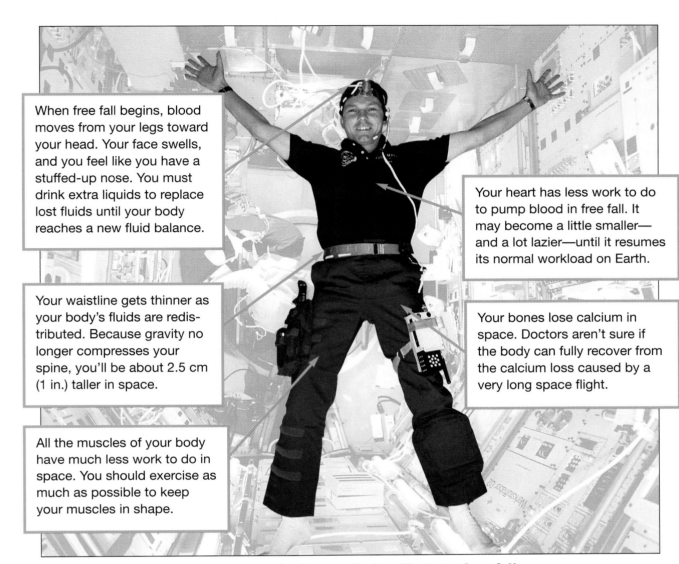

When free fall begins, blood moves from your legs toward your head. Your face swells, and you feel like you have a stuffed-up nose. You must drink extra liquids to replace lost fluids until your body reaches a new fluid balance.

Your heart has less work to do to pump blood in free fall. It may become a little smaller—and a lot lazier—until it resumes its normal workload on Earth.

Your waistline gets thinner as your body's fluids are redistributed. Because gravity no longer compresses your spine, you'll be about 2.5 cm (1 in.) taller in space.

Your bones lose calcium in space. Doctors aren't sure if the body can fully recover from the calcium loss caused by a very long space flight.

All the muscles of your body have much less work to do in space. You should exercise as much as possible to keep your muscles in shape.

▲ **How the human body adjusts to free fall**

INVESTIGATION 1 WRAP-UP

REVIEW

1. Describe some of the challenges faced by astronauts living in a space shuttle.

2. Describe three changes that take place in the body during free fall.

CRITICAL THINKING

3. Explain why the term *zero gravity* is not completely accurate in describing conditions in an orbiting spacecraft.

4. Astronauts train for weightlessness by riding in a plane that goes into a steep dive. How is the dive like being in orbit?

INVESTIGATION 2

HOW DO HUMANS SURVIVE IN SPACE?

What would you pack for a trip to another planet? You'd need more than just a change of clothing! What would you eat and drink? What would you breathe? What would you use for shelter? In this investigation you'll think about what humans need to survive and then explore some answers to these questions.

Activity

Survival on the Moon

What are the most important supplies you'd need to survive on the Moon? Pretend you're a stranded astronaut and figure out the answer.

Procedure

1. Imagine that your spacecraft has just crash-landed in daylight on the Moon. You were scheduled to meet the command ship 320 km (about 200 mi) away on the lighted surface of the Moon, but the rough landing has destroyed all the equipment on board. All that is left are the 15 items listed at the right. Your crew's survival depends on reaching the mother ship. Some supplies will be critical for the long trip to meet the command ship. But you don't want to carry the extra weight of items you cannot use.

first-aid kit containing bandages, medicines, injection needles, and related items

packages of food concentrate

solar-powered portable heating unit

self-inflating life raft

magnetic compass

map of the stars

box of matches

2 large tanks of oxygen

parachute silk

2 pistols

packages of powdered milk

solar-powered radio receiver and transmitter

nylon rope

signal flares

5 containers of water

2. In your *Science Notebook*, make a list of the 15 items. Number the items in order of importance, with the number 1 indicating the most important item for survival. **Discuss** your choices with your group before assigning each number. Keep in mind that you might wish to use some items for purposes other than those originally intended.

Analyze and Conclude

1. Identify the objects that are most critical to your survival. Why are they so important?

2. Identify the objects that are useless. Why?

3. Identify any objects you could use in ways for which they were not originally intended. How would you use them?

4. Compare your group's rankings with the rankings provided by your teacher, which come from NASA—the U.S. space agency. Subtract to find the difference between each item's NASA ranking and your own group's ranking for it. Add up all the differences to find your total score.

5. Compare your score to the figures below to see how well your group did.

UNIT PROJECT LINK

For your space-station simulator, create a life-support storage area and a kitchen. In the life-support storage area, use large sheets of paper as the fronts of storage lockers for water and oxygen tanks. Decide what foods you would store in the kitchen and how much water and oxygen you'd need for one month. Plan a space meal, using only foods that astronauts can store and eat easily in free fall.

Technology
Link

For more help with your Unit Project, go to **www.eduplace.com**.

0–25	*Excellent*
26–32	*Good*
33–45	*Average*
46–55	*Fair*
56–70	*Poor*
71–112	*Stay home!*

International Space Station

Reading Focus Why build a city in space?

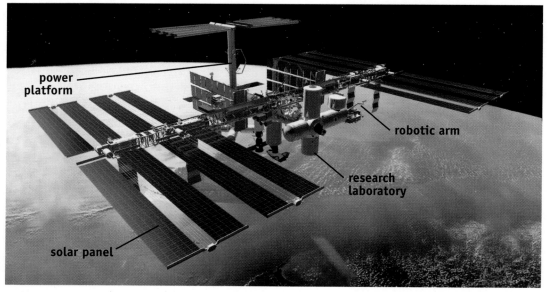

power platform

robotic arm

research laboratory

solar panel

▲**The completed ISS will be longer than a football field. With its solar panels it will be 108.6 m (358.4 ft) long and 79.9 m (263.7 ft) wide.**

An international space project is underway. Scientists and engineers from 16 countries are designing and building the International Space Station (ISS). The first four crews to live and work on the ISS come from the United States and Russia. These crews are constructing the ISS in space.

Spacewalks

From 1998 to 2004, more than 90 spacewalks have been scheduled. Astronauts will spend hundreds of hours building the ISS. When finished, it will be home for up to seven astronauts.

Why build a space station? First, it's a great adventure to be able to live and work in space. Second, the ISS is a permanent space laboratory with people working in it for as long as a year.

The ISS provides a unique environment that is nearly free of the effects of gravity. This condition of very low gravity is called **microgravity**. Many experiments in medical science are planned for the ISS under microgravity. The results of these experiments may help fight diseases such as the flu, diabetes, cancer, and AIDS.

Living in Space

All the living and nonliving things on Earth together form a self-contained system. The food, water, carbon dioxide, oxygen, and nitrogen that are needed for life are here on Earth.

When astronauts go out into space on short trips, they don't need to worry about recycling resources. They just carry enough food, water, and oxygen to last the length of the trip. But for longer voyages, such as on the International Space Station, they need to recycle water, carbon dioxide, and other materials.

On the ISS the astronauts will grow wheat, rice, soybeans, and peanuts in space gardens. By growing their own food, ISS crews will be less dependent on shipments from Earth. They'll also be investigating how well plants grow in microgravity.

The food the astronauts eat on the ISS is "out of this world." Cooks in the best kitchens on Earth are working hard to give the ISS crews tasty and nutritious foods. The astronauts have a microwave oven, rice cooker, bread machine, and machine for making tofu and soy milk.

Space Tools

New tools assist the astronauts in their work. One is a 16.5 m (55 ft) long robotic "arm" that can move along the outside of the ISS and pick up large, heavy objects. This robotic arm, called the "Canadian Hand," helps astronauts assemble and maintain the space station. Another tool is a robotic "eye" that can fly around and inspect the outer surface of the ISS for trouble spots. ■

The robotic arm, known as the "Canadian Hand" ▼

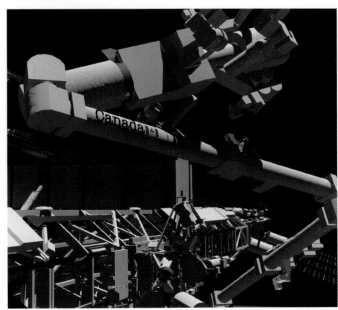

INVESTIGATION 2 WRAP-UP

REVIEW

1. What is microgravity?

2. Give an example of how the ISS could help people on Earth.

CRITICAL THINKING

3. Why do you think it's a good idea to make the space station an *international* project?

4. Suppose you could live for a year on the ISS. Give reasons why you would or would not want to go on this mission.

IS THERE OTHER LIFE IN THE UNIVERSE?

Have you ever watched a science fiction movie about aliens from outer space? How did the movie director imagine they looked? In this investigation you'll learn what astronomers think the possibilities are for finding life beyond planet Earth.

Activity

A Postcard From Earth

If intelligent life exists beyond Earth, that life could be very different from intelligent life as we know it. How would you communicate with a being from another planet? Give it a try!

- -

Procedure

1. On the front side of a blank postcard, **draw** a scene of Earth. Use your scene to tell about Earth and about yourself. Be careful not to draw things that might confuse an alien being who is unfamiliar with Earth.

2. On the back side of the card, **draw** a diagram or map that might tell an alien being where your planet is located. Remember that residents of another planet may not be able to read English or any other Earth language. Use symbols that might mean something to an alien being.

Step 2

Analyze and Conclude

1. Exchange postcards with a classmate.

2. In your *Science Notebook*, make a list of all the things you are able to learn about Earth from your classmate's postcard. Look for as many things as possible.

3. Make a second list of all the things in the postcard that could be misinterpreted. Look at the card as if you were a being from another planet. You wouldn't even know when a picture was right side up!

4. **Share** your lists with your classmate. See if the two of you can think of ways to improve both postcards. Make a third postcard with ideas that you've thought up together.

5. **Infer** how easy or hard it might be for humans to communicate someday with beings from another planet. What might some of the problems be? What ways of communicating might work best? What things might alien beings and humans have in common that could help us understand one another?

▲ **How would you try to communicate with another species here on Earth?**

INVESTIGATE FURTHER!

EXPERIMENT

Plan an experiment that would test how humans communicate with another species, such as a chimpanzee or a dolphin. Begin by writing a hypothesis that you could test. Decide what steps you would take. Then list any special equipment you would need. How might your experiment be applied to communicating with beings from another planet?

Messages to the Stars

Reading Focus What are some ways scientists are trying to communicate with alien beings?

How would you talk to an extraterrestrial (eks trə tə-res'trē əl)? What would you say, and how would you say it? And just what *is* an extraterrestrial, anyway?

The word **extraterrestrial** can be used to describe anything that comes from beyond Earth. Meteorites, for example, are said to be of extraterrestrial origin. But when most people say *extraterrestrial*, they mean a living being from outer space.

Humans tend to think a lot about the possibility of life on other planets. Some people even believe that Earth has already been visited by aliens traveling in unidentified flying objects, or UFOs. But no proof exists that anything like this has ever happened.

Even though scientists are doubtful about the idea that aliens have visited Earth, many scientists do think it's possible for life to exist beyond our own planet. Some scientists have even gone so far as to try to send a message to any extraterrestrial civilization that might be out there, waiting.

One method of communicating with an alien civilization would be by using pictures, as is done in the activity on pages B86 and B87. That's what the

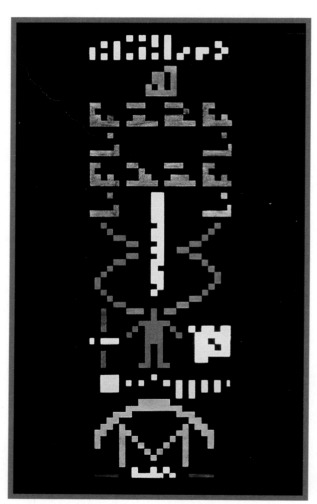

▲ **Frank Drake's radio message**

scientists did who launched the *Pioneer 10* and *11* space probes back in 1972.

Each Pioneer spacecraft was equipped with a gold plaque that was designed to tell any extraterrestrials it might encounter what the beings were like who made it and where it came from. On each plaque is a drawing of a man and a woman and a map of our solar system. A line shows the probe's course away from Earth.

Another way to communicate is to use radio or television signals. Without meaning to, humans have been broadcasting messages for decades! Ordinary radio and TV signals travel at the speed of light out into space. If there are any aliens out there, the first sign they get of intelligent life on Earth could be a broadcast of music!

Scientists have used a radio telescope to send messages out into space intended for any extraterrestrials they might reach. In 1974, astronomer Frank Drake sent out a pattern of on-and-off signals that could be decoded into pictures of a human, a DNA molecule, and our solar system.

The most elaborate message yet is one that relies heavily on sound. In 1977 this message was placed on board the *Voyager 1* and *2* probes which explored the outer solar system.

Each Voyager probe carries a disk made of gold-plated copper, designed to operate like an old-fashioned phonograph record. Called *The Sounds of Earth,* each 30-cm (12-in.) disk includes greetings spoken in 54 different Earth languages. There is also music that ranges from Beethoven to African and Mexican folk songs to jazz and rock. There are natural sounds such as a barking dog, the song of a whale, and the cry of a newborn baby.

Each Voyager record has instructions on how to play it. However, before the aliens can receive their message, they will have to figure out how to build their own record player! ■

▼ **The Voyager message disk**

▲ **A Voyager space probe receives its message disk.**

The Search for Intelligent Life

Reading Focus Do you think there is life on other planets?

Men and women from every era have spent time dreaming about the possibility of life existing on other planets. Despite possible evidence that tiny organisms may have once lived on Mars, scientists haven't found a single living cell from another planet. But every time we get a clearer peek into the universe, we come closer to answering questions about extraterrestrial life.

How We Search for Life

Radio telescopes are one of the major ways we get that clearer peek. A radio telescope is not a telescope in the visual sense at all. You can't look through one and see anything. Instead, a **radio telescope** is a gigantic antenna that receives radio signals.

The first radio telescope was built in 1931 as an aerial for studying static

Science in Literature

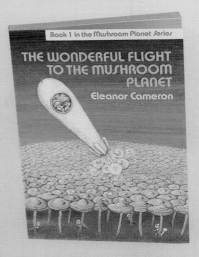

The Wonderful Flight to the Mushroom Planet
by Eleanor Cameron
Little, Brown and Company, 1954

SPACE SHIPS WANTED

"Wanted: A small space ship about eight feet long, built by a boy, or by two boys, between the ages of eight and eleven. . . . No adult should be consulted as to its plan or method of construction. An adventure and a chance to do a good deed await the boys who build the best space ship. Please bring your ship *as soon as possible* to Mr. Tyco M. Bass, 5 Thallo Street."

So begins the adventure of *The Wonderful Flight to the Mushroom Planet* by Eleanor Cameron. You can still enjoy this space adventure even though it was written a half century ago.

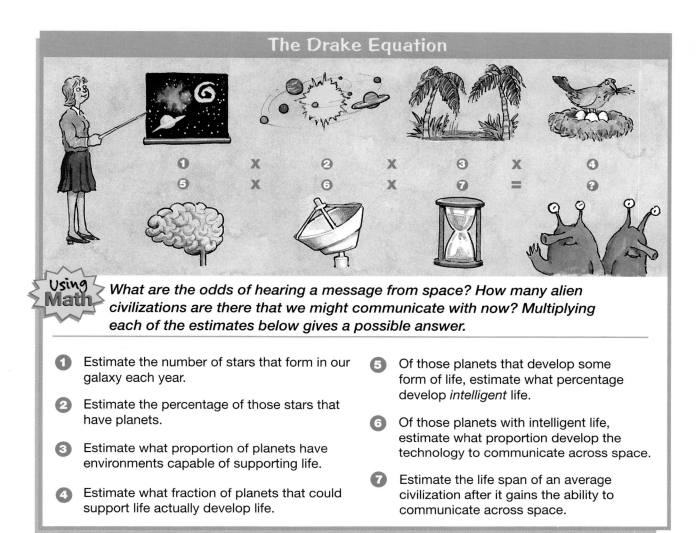

The Drake Equation

Using Math

What are the odds of hearing a message from space? How many alien civilizations are there that we might communicate with now? Multiplying each of the estimates below gives a possible answer.

1. Estimate the number of stars that form in our galaxy each year.

2. Estimate the percentage of those stars that have planets.

3. Estimate what proportion of planets have environments capable of supporting life.

4. Estimate what fraction of planets that could support life actually develop life.

5. Of those planets that develop some form of life, estimate what percentage develop *intelligent* life.

6. Of those planets with intelligent life, estimate what proportion develop the technology to communicate across space.

7. Estimate the life span of an average civilization after it gains the ability to communicate across space.

that was interfering with radio transmissions. Scientists found that this "static" was coming from the Milky Way. They soon discovered that radio waves are generated naturally by stars, planets, and other objects in space.

Astronomers interested in the possibility of extraterrestrial life realized that radio might be a good way to detect a distant civilization. If humans have been unintentionally sending radio signals out into space since the 1920s, perhaps alien beings have also been broadcasting news of their existence.

In the 1960s, astronomer Frank Drake began listening for radio signals from nearby stars that are like the Sun. This was the beginning of what we now call the search for extraterrestrial intelligence, or SETI. Today, SETI involves radio telescopes as large as 304 m (about 1,000 ft) in diameter that can pick up faint signals from as far away as 15,000 light-years.

Frank Drake has considered the odds that SETI might someday be successful. The equation he developed to estimate those odds is shown in the box above. Look especially at the last factor in the equation. Factor 7 may seem out of place with the rest, but it's one of the most important pieces of the puzzle.

10,000 years for message to reach Earth

10,000 years for Earth's reply to return

Another planet

Earth

Using Math

Think of Earth communicating with a planet 10,000 light-years away. Suppose a message from Earth was sent today and a return message was sent on the day it was received. In what year would it reach Earth?

Remember how large the distances between stars are? What if a civilization 10,000 light-years from Earth were to send a radio message in our direction? Traveling at the speed of light, that message would take 10,000 years to reach us. If aliens sent the message today, would humans still be here to receive it in 10,000 years? If they were, and if they immediately sent a reply, would the civilization that sent the first message still be around to receive the answer after another 10,000 years? That would be 20,000 years after they sent their first signal.

What if aliens had sent a message out 20,000 years ago? After a 10,000-year trip, the message would have reached Earth around 8000 B.C. Would anyone have had a radio back then to pick up the signal?

When you look at the Drake equation on the previous page, it should be clear to you that there are no firm numbers for any of its steps. Nobody knows how often planets develop or how often intelligent life evolves. Many scientists think it's probable that life exists elsewhere in the universe, but the chance that we'll have a two-way conversation with that life appears slim. If we keep on trying, however, someday we may just get lucky! ■

INVESTIGATION 3 WRAP-UP

THINK IT WRITE IT

REVIEW

1. What is a radio telescope, and what does it do?

2. What estimate does the Drake equation give?

CRITICAL THINKING

3. Describe ways in which humans have tried to send and receive messages from other worlds.

4. Suppose you're an astronomer who receives a signal from outer space. Would you respond? Give reasons for your answer.

REFLECT & EVALUATE

Word Power

Write the letter of the term that best completes each sentence. *Not all terms will be used.*

1. A huge antenna that receives radio signals is a/an ____.
2. The condition of very low gravity is ____.
3. The near-weightlessness that an astronaut experiences when in orbit is called ____.
4. A living being from outer space is known as a/an ____.

a. extraterrestrial
b. free fall
c. International Space Station
d. microgravity
e. refracting telescope
f. reflecting telescope
g. radio telescope

Check What You Know

Write the term in each pair that best completes each sentence.

1. An object in orbit stays in orbit because of (weightlessness, gravitational pull).
2. Astronauts in free fall become (shorter, taller).
3. The Drake equation estimates the odds of communicating with (beings from another planet, humans traveling to Mars).

Problem Solving

1. Suppose that scientists received a radio signal and determined that it came from alien beings on another planet. Do you think humans would be able to communicate with those who sent the signal? Why or why not?

2. What are some advantages and disadvantages of sending robots to do research in space?

Copy this drawing of the cannonballs and Earth. Explain why cannonball C orbits Earth but cannonballs A and B do not.

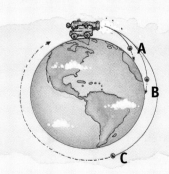

Drawing Conclusions

Writers often imply, or hint at, more information than they actually state. They give you clues and expect you to figure out the rest, using what you already know. Suppose an author writes "The car slid across the road, spun around, hit a fence, and came to rest in a snowbank." You can conclude that the road was slippery from snow or ice and that condition is what probably caused the accident.

> **Consider these questions as you draw conclusions.**
> • What did the author write?
> • What do I know?
> • What is my conclusion?

Read the paragraph. Then complete the exercises that follow.

Putting Telescopes in Space

Today there is a large telescope in orbit around Earth. The Hubble Space Telescope (HST) is positioned beyond our planet's atmosphere, so it avoids distortions caused by looking through the air. Even though the mirror in the HST is smaller than that of many telescopes on Earth, it can see more clearly and see objects that are fainter and farther away than telescopes on the ground can see. Space telescopes can even see wavelengths of light that aren't visible from Earth's surface.

1. **Which statement is a conclusion you can draw from the paragraph? Write the letter of that statement.**

   a. It was easy to place the HST in space.

   b. Earth's atmosphere limits what we can learn about space.

   c. The mirror in the HST is too small to see beyond Earth's atmosphere.

   d. The HST has changed our understanding of the Sun.

2. **What was the most important clue in helping you draw that conclusion?**

Using Math — Analyze Data

The table compares gravity on other planets to gravity on Earth.

Surface Gravity on the Planets								
Planet	Mercury	Venus	Earth	Mars	Jupiter	Saturn	Neptune	Uranus	Pluto
Gravity	0.38	0.90	1.00	0.38	2.64	1.14	0.91	1.20	0.04

 Notice that gravity on Earth is equal to 1.

Use the information in the table to complete the exercises that follow.

1. On which planet is gravity closest to Earth's gravity?

2. On which planet would an object weigh about the same as it would on Mars?

3. On which planets would your science textbook weigh less than it does on Earth? On which planets would it weigh more?

4. What is the difference in gravity between the planet with the greatest gravity and the planet with the least gravity?

5. Suppose a newly-discovered planet has gravity equal to three times that of Venus. In terms of its gravity, which of the known planets would the new planet be most like?

You may wish to use a calculator for Exercises 6 through 8.

6. Gravity on Saturn is about three times the gravity of which planets?

7. Gravity on Earth is about six times greater than gravity on the Moon. What decimal number might be used to represent the moon's gravity?

8. If a book weighed 1 pound on Pluto, how many pounds would it weigh on Earth?

WRAP-UP!

On your own, use scientific methods to investigate a question about the solar system.

THINK LIKE A SCIENTIST

Ask a Question

Pose a question about a planet, a star, or another object in the night sky that you would like to investigate. For example, ask, "If I am standing at the South Pole, can I see the star Polaris?"

Make a Hypothesis

Suggest a hypothesis that is a possible answer to the question. One hypothesis is that Polaris, also called the North Star, cannot be seen by someone standing at the South Pole.

Plan and Do a Test

Plan an experiment that uses models to determine whether Polaris can be seen from the South Pole. You could begin by using a globe of Earth and a paper circle to represent Polaris. Develop a procedure that uses these materials to test the hypothesis. With permission, carry out your experiment. Follow the safety guidelines on pages S14–S15.

Record and Analyze

Observe carefully and record your data accurately. Make repeated observations by moving the objects in your model.

Draw Conclusions

Look for evidence to support the hypothesis or to show that it is false. Draw conclusions about the hypothesis. Repeat the experiment to verify the results.

WRITING IN SCIENCE
Research Report

Research information about comets and what scientists hope to learn from them. Present your findings in a research report. Use these guidelines to prepare your report.

- Gather information from several sources.
- Organize the information in order of importance.
- Draw a conclusion from your research.

UNIT C

Matter and Energy

Theme: Models

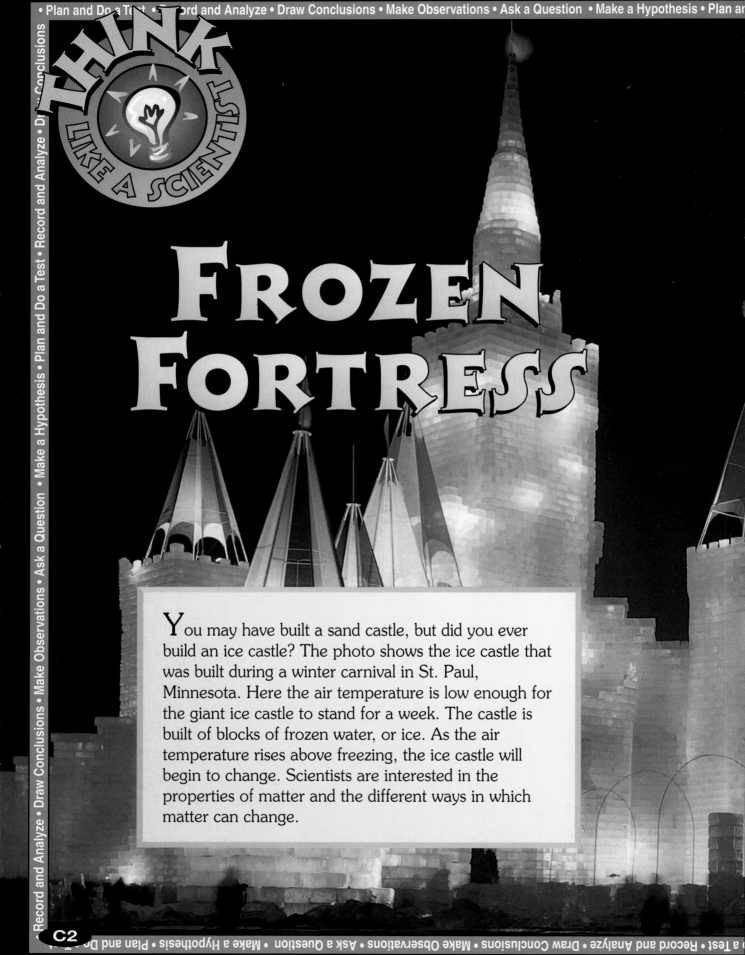

THINK LIKE A SCIENTIST

FROZEN FORTRESS

You may have built a sand castle, but did you ever build an ice castle? The photo shows the ice castle that was built during a winter carnival in St. Paul, Minnesota. Here the air temperature is low enough for the giant ice castle to stand for a week. The castle is built of blocks of frozen water, or ice. As the air temperature rises above freezing, the ice castle will begin to change. Scientists are interested in the properties of matter and the different ways in which matter can change.

THINK LIKE A SCIENTIST

Questioning In this unit you'll study what happens to water as it melts and freezes. You'll investigate questions such as these.

- What Are Some Different Forms of Energy?
- How Can Matter Change?

Observing, Testing, Hypothesizing In the Activity "Change This," you'll observe what happens to an ice cube and moist steel wool that are left overnight. You'll analyze what happened and also analyze other kinds of changes that occur in matter.

Researching In the Resource "The Same Stuff," you'll learn about the change of state that occurs in water as the temperature rises and falls. You'll also find out the meaning of a physical change.

Drawing Conclusions After you've completed your investigations, you'll draw conclusions about what you've learned— and get new ideas.

CHAPTER 1

DESCRIBING MATTER

What is matter? It's the stuff, or materials, that things are made of. That includes all of Earth and its living things. People use many different kinds of matter to make things, from highways and buildings to homes and works of art. In this chapter you'll explore the characteristics of matter.

Connecting to Science
CULTURE

The Anasazi The Anasazi (ä nə sä'zē) were Native Americans who lived thousands of years ago. In fact, the term *Anasazi* means "ancient ones." Remains of Anasazi dwellings can be seen at many sites in the southwestern United States. Today, the Pueblos of New Mexico are among the descendants of the Anasazi.

To build their homes, the Anasazi selected kinds of matter that had properties suited to construction. They used rocks held together with mud that later dried to make solid walls. They used clay, a kind of matter that can be shaped into different forms, to make pottery. Their pottery was both useful and beautiful. Today, Native American artists still make use of the properties of clay to make pottery in the tradition of the Anasazi.

Coming Up

◄ Pottery (*left*) made by Native Americans descended from the Anasazi and actual Anasazi dwellings (*above*)

How Can You Describe Matter?

Look around your classroom. List ten things you see that are made of matter. You probably named such things as pencils, desks, and people. Not everything around you, however, is matter. In this investigation you'll discover how to tell what is, and isn't, matter.

Activity

All Materials Matter

Have you ever made something from clay? What do you see that's made of wood or plastic foam? These materials are examples of matter. Find out what all kinds of matter have in common.

MATERIALS
- clay block
- plastic-foam block
- wood block
- balance and masses
- metric ruler
- *Science Notebook*

Procedure

1. **Observe** the color and texture of a clay block. Do the same for a plastic-foam block and a wood block. **Record** your observations in your *Science Notebook*.

2. Use a balance to **measure**, in grams, the mass of the clay block. Do the same for the wood block and then the plastic-foam block. **Record** the results.

See **Science** and **Math Toolbox** page H9 if you need to review **Using a Balance.**

Step 2

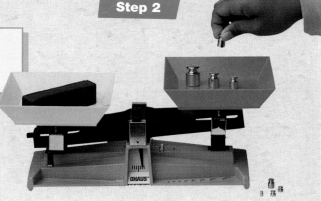

3. Make a **chart** like the one shown.

Material	Dimensions of Block		
	Length	Width	Height
clay			

Step 4

4. Use a metric ruler to **measure** the length, width, and height of each block. **Record** these measurements. Using your measurements, **calculate** the volume of each block. **Record** your results.

See **SCIENCE** *and* **MATH TOOLBOX** *page H10 if you need to review* **Using an Equation or Formula.**

Analyze and Conclude

1. Compare your observations of the blocks of the three materials. What characteristics, or properties, of matter do they all share?

2. In what ways are the blocks different?

3. Suppose you cut each block in half and then repeated the activity. **Infer** which observations would change. **Infer** which ones would not.

4. Infer whether the kind of matter in each block would change or remain the same if you cut each block in half.

INVESTIGATE FURTHER!

EXPERIMENT

What are some ways to classify matter by its properties? With your group, collect 20 or more samples of matter. Include a balloon full of air, a marble, a cup of juice, a rubber band, a plastic spoon, a bottle of vegetable oil, a piece of cloth, an index card, a screw, string, a piece of chalk, and other objects or materials. With your group, classify each sample according to its state: solid, liquid, or gas. Then brainstorm ways to classify the samples based on one or more other properties. Record your results in a chart.

Activity

Heat Conductors

Will a cup of hot soup still be warm after it stands awhile? It may depend on the kind of cup.

MATERIALS
- goggles
- plastic drinking glass
- metal can
- plastic-foam cup
- hot water
- 3 thermometers
- timer
- *Science Notebook*

- -

Procedure

1. Place a plastic drinking glass, a metal can, and a plastic-foam cup on your work surface. In your *Science Notebook*, **make a chart** like the one shown.

SAFETY //////
Wear goggles during this activity. Be careful not to touch the hot water.

Material of Container	Temperature		
	Empty	After filling with hot water	After standing five minutes

2. Your teacher will add hot water to the containers until each is three fourths full. Place a thermometer in each container. **Observe** and **record** the temperature of the water in each container.

See **SCIENCE** and **MATH TOOLBOX** *page H8 if you need to review* ***Using a Thermometer.***

3. Wait five minutes. Then **observe** the temperature in each container again. **Record** your observations.

Analyze and Conclude

1. **Compare** the temperatures of each container when first filled with hot water and after standing five minutes filled with hot water.

2. How well a material conducts heat is a property of that material. Based on this activity, what can you **infer** about how each of the materials tested conducts heat? Which material would make the best cup to keep soup warm?

Step 2

Activity

Electrical Conductors

A material that electricity can flow through is an electrical conductor. The wire of a lamp cord is a conductor, but its plastic covering is not. Test materials to find out if they are electrical conductors.

MATERIALS

- 3 insulated wires with stripped ends
- dry cell, size D, in holder
- light bulb in holder
- metal safety pin
- metal washer
- small plastic spoon
- rubber eraser
- wooden stirrer
- copper strip
- aluminum foil strip
- *Science Notebook*

Procedure

1. Use one wire to connect a dry-cell holder to a light-bulb holder. Attach a second wire to the light-bulb holder only, and a third wire to the dry-cell holder only, as shown.

2. Touch the free ends of the wires together. **Observe** what happens. In your *Science Notebook*, **record** your observations. **Infer** whether the wires in your system conduct electricity.

3. In your *Science Notebook*, **make a chart** like the one shown.

Object	Observation	Conductor	Nonconductor

4. Touch the free ends of both wires to a safety pin. **Observe** and **record** what happens. **Record** in your chart whether the safety pin is a conductor or nonconductor.

5. Repeat step 4 using a metal washer, a plastic spoon, a rubber eraser, a wooden stirrer, a copper strip, and an aluminum foil strip. **Record** your observations each time.

Analyze and Conclude

1. Which objects that you tested are conductors of electricity? Which are nonconductors?

2. Based on your results, what can you **infer** about the kinds of materials used to make electric wires?

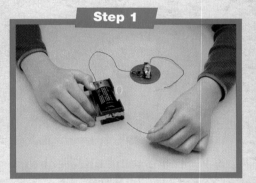

Step 1

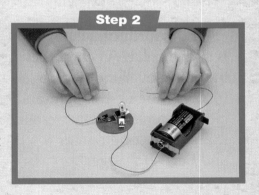

Step 2

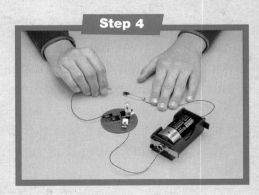

Step 4

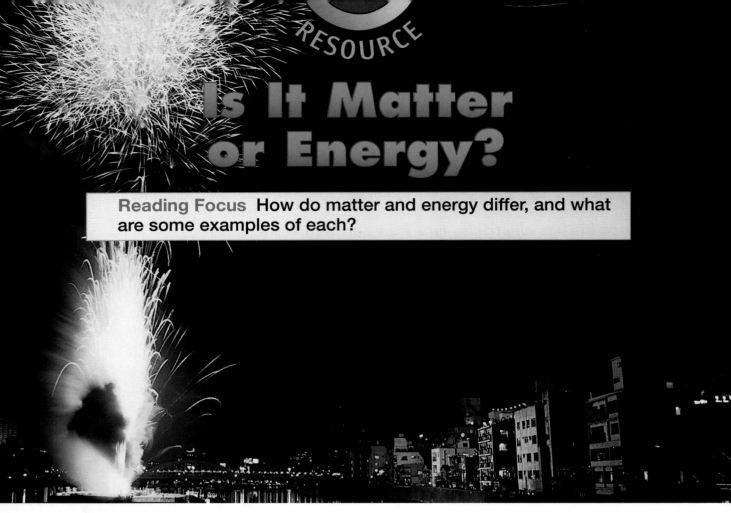

Is It Matter or Energy?

Reading Focus How do matter and energy differ, and what are some examples of each?

▲ **What are some different kinds of matter and energy involved in this display of fireworks launched from a river barge?**

The Fourth of July fireworks display is spectacular. As each rocket explodes in the air over the river, a loud boom follows the burst of light and color. The crowd watching from across the river roars! Everyone agrees it's the biggest and best show ever.

What's the Matter?

The chemicals in the rockets, the iron in the river barge from which the rockets are launched, and the oxygen in the air are all examples of matter. So are the water in the river and the people in the crowd watching the event. **Matter** is anything that has mass and takes up space.

Let's examine the two basic characteristics of all matter—mass and volume. **Mass** is a measure of how much matter there is in an object. The mass of a river barge, for example, is greater than that of a fireworks rocket. The amount of space an object takes up is its **volume**. Clearly, a river barge takes up more space than a fireworks rocket. So the volume of the barge is greater than that of the rocket.

Different kinds of matter have different characteristics, or properties. For example, being a good conductor of heat and electricity is a property of some of the materials used in the activities on pages C8 and C9.

Bits of Matter

Matter is made up of tiny particles called atoms, which are far too small to see, even with most microscopes. Scientists have discovered more than one hundred different kinds of atoms.

Each kind of atom is different from any other kind of atom. An atom of iron in a barge is different from an atom of oxygen in the air. An atom of copper in a penny is different from either iron or oxygen. You'll learn more about atoms later in this chapter.

Energy on the Move

Look again at the photograph of the scene on the Fourth of July. If you were watching this scene in a movie, what things would be moving? Things on the move, or in motion, have energy. **Energy** is the ability to cause change. Motion is a form of energy that would be evident in a movie. Light from the fireworks display is another form of energy.

Some other familiar forms of energy are sound and electricity. Energy can be "out of sight." For example, energy can be stored in chemicals. Look again at the photographs of the fireworks. Before the rockets are fired, the chemicals they contain have stored energy. During the display, light and sound are produced as the energy is released from chemicals.

Every day you see both matter and energy in different forms. Look at the photographs on this page. Name as many examples of matter as you can. Then name as many examples of energy as you can. Now look around you. What things that you see are matter? What things are energy? ■

▲ **Examples of matter and energy: blowing molten glass, lightning, pouring molten iron, sunset over water**

Properties of Matter

Reading Focus What are two sets of properties of matter and some examples of each?

▲ **Two hikers near a glacier on the side of a mountain**

Two hikers are making their way up a mountain. They have climbed nearly all day. Now they have pitched their tent in a beautiful spot near a glacier—a mass of ice that creeps across the land. These hikers are not just enjoying the scenery. They are also exploring the matter on the mountain—the rocks, the soil, the water, and even the air.

Matter on a Mountain

Imagine you are following these climbers. You watch and listen as they describe the matter around them. Their tools are their senses and some simple measuring devices. In the activity on pages C6 and C7, the same tools are used to observe some samples of matter. The climbers first examine the glacier. Their eyes tell them that the glacier's color is white. They can touch the glacier and observe that it's solid. But they also observe pools of liquid water where melting has occurred.

The climbers run their hands over the surface of the glacier. They observe that its texture, which is how it feels, is smooth and slippery.

C12

The air the climbers breathe is clear and invisible. They observe clouds which show that the air contains water vapor. This invisible gas can change to water droplets or ice crystals, forming clouds. The air also contains other invisible gases, such as oxygen and nitrogen.

Physical Properties

The climbers have described some of the physical properties of the matter on the mountain. A **physical property** is a characteristic of matter that can be detected or measured with the senses. You can observe a physical property of a material without changing the kind of matter that material is. Color, texture, and odor are physical properties.

One physical property of some materials, including all metals, is the ability to conduct heat and electricity. In the activities on pages C8 and C9, the metals are the conductors. Copper and aluminum are metals. Materials that are not metals, such as wood and plastic, are poor conductors.

Whether matter is solid, liquid, or gas—matter's physical state—is another physical property. The physical state of matter depends on the conditions, such as temperature, under which the kind of matter is observed.

The temperature at which a sample of matter changes state is also a physical property. Solid water, or ice, changes to liquid water at 0°C (32°F). This is the melting point of water. Liquid water that is being heated changes to water vapor at 100°C (212°F). This is the normal boiling point of water. You'll learn more about states of matter later in this unit.

Mass and Volume

One climber discovers a rectangular-shaped chunk of rock. The other hiker picks it up. The chunk of rock feels about as heavy as a hiking boot. The climber guesses that the rock might have a mass of 1,000 g (2.2 lb).

The climbers know that they could measure the dimensions of the rock. Then they would be able to calculate its volume, or the space it takes up. To find the volume of a regularly shaped object, you multiply its height by its width by its length.

 *Suppose one of the hikers found a rock that measured about 12 cm wide, 20 cm long and 10 cm high. What would be the approximate volume of the rock?*

Chemical Properties

All kinds of matter have a second set of properties, called chemical properties. A **chemical property** describes how a kind of matter can change into other kinds of matter. Are there any examples of such changes up here on the mountain? Outside the tent, the climbers light a kerosene lantern. The kerosene burns, but the glass and metal of the lantern do not. The kerosene is being used up. At the same time, soot and smoke rise out of the top of the lantern. The ability to burn is a chemical property of kerosene. The kerosene reacts with oxygen in the air and changes into other kinds of matter.

Most metals don't burn with flames and light. But metals sometimes do

▲ The ability of the kerosene in the lantern to burn is a chemical property of kerosene.

 # Science in Literature

AN ENDLESS VARIETY OF SNOWFLAKES

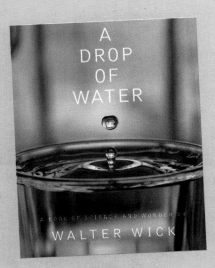

A Drop of Water:
A Book of Science and Wonder
by Walter Wick
Scholastic Press, 1997

"Many ice crystals grow into shapes that are just tiny slivers, rods, or clumps of ice. . . . But when weather conditions are just right, the crystals will grow into an astonishing variety of elaborate six-sided designs. . . . When a snow flake melts, its intricate design is lost forever in a drop of water. But a snowflake can vanish in another way. It can change directly from ice to vapor."

To learn more about water, read *A Drop of Water: A Book of Science and Wonder* by Walter Wick.

change into other kinds of matter. For example, the surface of an iron nail left outdoors will slowly change to rust. Iron and rust are two different kinds of matter. The surface of another metal, copper, tarnishes when exposed to the weather. A chemical property of both iron and copper is their ability to change to another kind of matter when exposed to air and moisture.

You're back home from your trip. Look around you. What are some properties of the matter you see? ■

▲ **How is the rusted iron nail different from the new iron frying pan?**

▲ **Before the copper coat of the Statue of Liberty tarnished, it was as shiny as a new penny.**

INVESTIGATION 1 WRAP-UP

REVIEW

1. How is *matter* defined? How is *energy* defined?

2. How is a chemical property different from a physical property?

CRITICAL THINKING

3. Write a story about an athletic event in which there is a great deal of action and excitement. Identify several examples of matter and energy that you might observe at the event.

4. Suppose you collected some rocks on your imaginary trip up the mountain. How might you use the properties of the rocks to tell one rock from another?

WHAT IS MATTER LIKE?

As you've read, there are more than one hundred kinds of atoms. But the number of different materials around you and everywhere else seems countless. The number is certainly far greater than one hundred! In this investigation you'll look at some of the forms in which matter can occur.

Activity

All Mixed Up

Can you separate the parts of a mixture made up of two black powders? Can you separate salt from a salt-water mixture that looks like plain water? Find out by doing this activity.

- - - - - - - - - - - - - - - - -

Procedure

1. In your *Science Notebook*, **make a chart** like the one shown.

Material	Observations
Charcoal	
Iron filings	
Charcoal-iron mixture	

2. **Observe** samples of charcoal and iron filings. **Record** your observations in your chart.

3. Use a stirrer to scrape some charcoal powder onto a paper plate. Add some iron filings to the charcoal. Use the stirrer to mix the powders together.

4. **Observe** the mixture on the paper plate. **Record** your observations in your chart.

5. **Talk with your group** and together **predict** whether you can separate the materials by using a stirrer, a magnet, or something else. **Record** your predictions and then **test** them. **Record** your results. Be sure to wash your hands after you handle the materials.

6. Add two spoonfuls of salt to a clear plastic cup of water. Use a clean stirrer to stir the mixture until the salt disappears or dissolves.

7. **Talk with your group** and together **predict** how you might use a clean plate to help separate the salt from the salt-water mixture. **Record** your prediction and then test it. **Record** your results in your *Science Notebook*.

Analyze and Conclude

1. **Draw a conclusion** about how mixing charcoal and iron filings affects the properties of these materials.

2. Were you able to separate the charcoal from the iron filings? What is your evidence?

3. **Draw a conclusion** about how mixing salt and water affects the properties of these materials.

4. Were you able to separate the salt from the water? What is your evidence?

UNIT PROJECT LINK

For this Unit Project you will work with classmates to collect, identify, and organize samples and pictures of matter in its various forms. The items in your collection should be suitable for display in the classroom. Begin now to look around your home and school for samples to start building your collection

Technology Link

For more help with your Unit Project, go to **www.eduplace.com**.

Activity

Small and Smaller

Centuries ago some Greeks suggested that all matter was made of tiny particles. The ancient Greeks lacked modern scientific methods and tools. Why would they make such a hypothesis about matter? Find some evidence they might have used.

MATERIALS
- goggles
- hand lens
- chalk
- 2 pieces of sandpaper
- 2 sheets of black construction paper
- piece of wood
- mystery liquid
- saucer
- *Science Notebook*

SAFETY //////
Wear goggles during this activity.

Procedure

1. Use a hand lens to **observe** chalk and a piece of sandpaper. In your *Science Notebook,* **record** the appearance of the chalk and the sandpaper.

2. Over a sheet of black construction paper, gently rub the chalk on the sandpaper several times. Use the hand lens to **observe** and **record** the appearance of the particles of chalk on the paper.

3. Use the hand lens to **observe** a piece of wood. **Record** the appearance of the wood.

Step 2

4. Over a clean sheet of black construction paper, gently rub a clean piece of sandpaper over the wood several times. **Observe** and **record** the appearance of the particles of wood on the paper.

5. Your teacher will pour a small amount of mystery liquid into a saucer. As soon as you are able to **observe** the liquid, **record** your observations.

Step 4

Analyze and Conclude

1. From your observations in steps 1 and 2, what can you **infer** about what makes up chalk?

2. From your observations in steps 3 and 4, what can you **infer** about what makes up wood?

3. In step 5, what property of the mystery liquid made it possible for you to detect it from a distance?

4. From your observations in this activity, what can you **hypothesize** about the structure of chalk dust and the structure of sawdust?

5. In step 5, suppose you could have seen what was happening in the air between you and the mystery liquid. **Make a drawing** to show what you **infer** was happening.

INVESTIGATE FURTHER!

RESEARCH

Democritus (di mäk′rə təs) was one of the ancient Greeks who hypothesized that matter was made of tiny indivisible particles. He called these particles atoms. In the library, find out where the word *atom* comes from. Through the centuries, scientists changed their ideas about what atoms are like. Find out about some of the different theories about atoms. Share what you find with the class.

States of Matter

Reading Focus What are the characteristics of the three states of matter?

▲ **In how many states of matter is the water in this scene?**

With a loud crack, a huge chunk of ice breaks off the Antarctic ice shelf and splashes into the sea. A group of penguins stand on the newly formed iceberg. One by one, they dive from the iceberg and swim to the shore. The iceberg begins to move slowly northward. Above, wispy clouds float in the crisp blue sky.

What State Is It?

The penguins are surrounded by water in its three states. The iceberg is water in the solid state. The sea around the iceberg is liquid water. Tiny drops of liquid water also make up the clouds above. The air contains water vapor, which is water in the gas state. Water is one of the few kinds of matter that is found in nature in all three states.

Changing State

Ice, liquid water, and water vapor can change from one to another. Think about some ways you can make such changes happen. Suppose you put liquid water in a freezer. The liquid will change to a solid, ice. If you leave ice at room temperature for a while, it will change to liquid water.

If you heat liquid water in a kettle until the water boils, some of the liquid changes into the invisible gas water vapor. Suppose, as the water boils, you hold a cold plate over the spout of the kettle. Almost at once any water vapor coming in contact with the plate would change to drops of liquid water.

Defining a State by Its Properties

The states of matter can be defined by their properties. Suppose you put an ice cube in a measuring cup. You'd notice that until it starts to melt, the ice cube keeps its shape. It was a cube when you took it from the freezer and it's still a cube. When you move the ice cube, its volume doesn't change either. These observations lead to a definition of a solid. A **solid** is matter that has a definite shape and a definite volume.

When the ice cube in the measuring cup melts into a liquid, the shape changes. The liquid water takes on the shape of the measuring cup. What happens if you pour the water from the cup into a graduated cylinder? The water still has the same volume, but it again changes shape. It takes the shape of the cylinder. A **liquid** is matter that has a definite volume but no definite shape. A liquid takes the shape of its container.

How can you describe the volume and shape of a gas? Suppose you pour the water from the melted ice cube into a kettle. You heat the water until it boils. The water vapor that forms spreads out through the whole room. A **gas** is matter that does not have a definite shape or volume. A gas always spreads out until it completely and evenly fills its container. ■

States of Matter

Solids A rock, a toothbrush, and a wooden statue are all matter in the solid state. Each has a definite volume and a definite shape.

Liquids Salad oil, cranberry juice, and milk are all matter in the liquid state. Each has a definite volume and takes the shape of its container.

Gases Neon in lights, air in a toy balloon, and helium in a blimp are all gases. Each takes the volume and shape of its container.

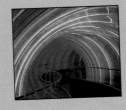

It's Elementary

Reading Focus What is an element, and how is each element different from every other element?

▲ **What element keeps this balloon afloat?**

The balloon in the picture is filled with a kind of matter called helium (hē′lē əm). What are some of the properties of helium that make it useful for inflating balloons? For one thing, helium is a gas. That's important. Because it's a gas, helium fills the entire balloon. Helium doesn't burn, so it's safe to use. Can you think of another property that makes helium perfect for use in balloons such as the one shown?

Helium is just one of 112 different basic kinds of matter. As you've read, matter is made up of tiny particles called atoms. An **element** is a basic kind of matter made up of just one kind of atom. So helium, which is made up of one kind of atom, is an element.

Parts of an Atom

An **atom** is the smallest particle of an element that has the properties of that element. Atoms are extremely tiny. They are so small that it would take millions of them to span the width of a hair on your head. Yet atoms are made up of even smaller parts. It is these smaller parts that make an atom of one element different from an atom of any other element. Using evidence that they collect from studying matter, scientists make models of atoms. The drawings show models of two kinds of atoms—carbon and helium.

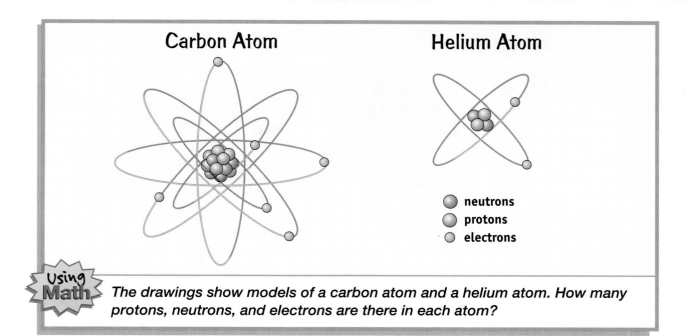

Carbon Atom

Helium Atom

- ○ neutrons
- ○ protons
- ○ electrons

Using Math The drawings show models of a carbon atom and a helium atom. How many protons, neutrons, and electrons are there in each atom?

Suppose you could shrink yourself so small that you could see an atom. Within the atom you would see the **nucleus** (n$\overline{oo}$′klē əs), which is the central part of an atom. Looking closer at the nucleus, you would find that the nucleus is made up of two kinds of particles—protons and neutrons. Protons have a positive electric charge. Neutrons have no electric charge.

If you could stand on the nucleus and look toward the outside of the atom, you'd see one or more electrons. Somewhat like planets speeding around the Sun, electrons move rapidly around the atom's nucleus. Electrons are much smaller than protons or neutrons and have a negative electric charge.

Atoms and Properties

The number of protons in an atom of an element determines the properties of that element. Look again at the models of the helium atom and carbon atom. You can see that a helium atom has two protons, and a carbon atom has six protons. The elements helium and carbon have very different

properties. Helium is a gas used in balloons like the one in the picture on page C22. Carbon is a solid. The powdered charcoal used in the activity on pages C16 and C17 is carbon.

Symbolic Meanings

Do you sometimes use just your initials when signing a note? Initials are a shorthand way of representing your name. A **chemical symbol** is a shorthand way to represent the name of an element.

Most chemical symbols come from the English names of elements. For example, the symbol C is the first letter of the word *carbon*. The symbol He consists of the first two letters of the word *helium*.

For some other elements, the symbol comes from the ancient language of Latin. For example, the symbol Fe comes from *ferrum*, which is the Latin word for iron. The chart on the next pages shows the names and symbols of several elements.

Internet Field Trip

Visit **www.eduplace.com** to find out more about many different elements.

Element and Symbol	Number of Protons	Some Properties	Examples of Use or Occurrence
Hydrogen H	1	colorless, odorless gas, burns easily, lighter than air	Hydrogen, which releases energy when burned, is used as rocket fuel.
Helium He	2	colorless, odorless gas, does not burn, lighter than air	Helium, which is lighter than air, and does not burn, is used to fill balloons and blimps.
Carbon C	6	black solid (charcoal, soot); gray greasy solid (graphite); clear crystal (diamond)	Charcoal briquettes, used as fuel, are a form of carbon.
Oxygen O	8	colorless, odorless gas, needed for breathing and burning	Hospitals use oxygen in tanks to help patients breathe.
Sodium Na	11	cream-colored, soft, solid metal	Sodium is present in table salt and baking soda.
Aluminum Al	13	shiny, hard silver-colored metal	Cookware and and foil are made of aluminum.
Silicon Si	14	brown powder or silver-colored metal	Some kinds of computer chips contain silicon.

Element and Symbol	Number of Protons	Some Properties	Examples of Use or Occurrence
Chlorine Cl	17	greenish-yellow gas	Chlorine can be added to water to kill germs.
Calcium Ca	20	gray, soft, solid metal	Calcium is present in seashells.
Iron Fe	26	gray hard metal	Steel girders, used in constructing buildings, are made of iron.
Copper Cu	29	orange-red, medium-hard metal	Copper is used in electric wires because it conducts electricity.
Silver Ag	47	silver-colored, solid metal	Its beautiful color is one reason that Native Americans use silver in making jewelry.
Gold Au	79	yellow medium-hard metal	Gold has been used since ancient times to make rings and other kinds of jewelry.
Mercury Hg	80	silver-colored liquid metal	This device uses the height of a column of mercury to measure blood pressure.

Compounds and Mixtures

Reading Focus How are a compound and a mixture alike, and how are they different?

Have you ever gone swimming in a lake or the ocean? Water covers about three fourths of Earth's surface. So water is a very plentiful kind of matter. Yet you won't find "water" on a list of elements. In fact, ocean water is a collection of matter that contains some elements and many other things.

Compounds

Scientists classify matter into three general kinds—elements, compounds, and mixtures. As you know, elements are the basic kinds of matter. But in most materials the elements are combined with other elements to form compounds. A **compound** is a substance made up of two or more elements that are chemically joined, or linked.

Scientists use the chemical symbols for elements as a shorthand way to represent compounds. A **chemical formula** is a group of symbols that shows the elements that make up a compound. Water is an example of a compound. The chemical formula for water

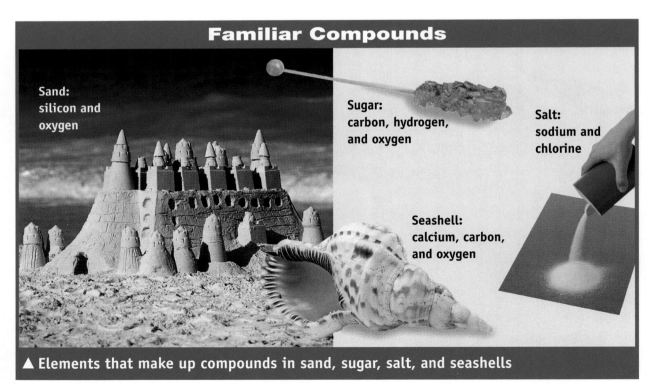

Familiar Compounds

Sand: silicon and oxygen

Sugar: carbon, hydrogen, and oxygen

Salt: sodium and chlorine

Seashell: calcium, carbon, and oxygen

▲ Elements that make up compounds in sand, sugar, salt, and seashells is H_2O. The formula tells you that a single particle of water is made up of two hydrogen atoms linked to an oxygen atom.

Scientists refer to both elements and compounds as *pure substances*. A substance is a type of matter that has a unique set of properties. For example, no other substance has exactly the same properties as water.

Look at the pictures on page C26. Each shows an example of a material that is entirely or mainly a compound. What elements are present in each compound shown?

Mixtures

As you've learned, air contains elements, such as nitrogen and oxygen. It also contains compounds, such as carbon dioxide and water vapor. Thus, the air you breathe is a mixture of elements and compounds. A **mixture** is matter made up of two or more substances. Most of the substances in the mixture we call air are gases. But mixtures can be made of any combination of gases, liquids, and solids.

When substances are combined in a mixture, each one keeps its own properties. The substances can be separated, using physical means.

Carbon and iron filings, for example, are two black powders. When mixed, as in the activity on pages C16 and C17, the two substances may look like one substance. But the iron is magnetic and the carbon in the mixture is not magnetic. So the two can be separated using a magnet. The ability to use physical means to separate these elements is evidence that the iron in the mixture is not joined chemically to the carbon. ■

Familiar Mixtures

birdseed

conglomerate rock

artist pallet

ice cream

salad

▲ In what way are mixtures, such as these, all alike?

Solutions

Reading Focus What is a solution, and what are its two main parts?

Have you ever made lemonade from "scratch"? Here's a good way to get the sugar to dissolve. Before you add lemon juice or ice, stir the sugar into warm water. When the sugar disappears completely, you've made a solution.

A Two-Part Solution

A **solution** is a mixture in which the different particles of matter are spread evenly. There are two parts in every solution. The substance that is present in the smaller amount is called the solute (säl′yo͞ot). In a solution of sugar in water, sugar is the solute. The substance that is present in the larger amount is called the solvent (säl′vənt). In a solution of sugar in water, water is the solvent.

Solutions may have properties that are different from those of the substances that make them up. For example, the freezing point of a solution of salt in water is lower than the freezing point of pure water. Thus, when salt is sprinkled on ice, it lowers the freezing point enough to melt the ice. If you live where streets get icy in winter, you may have seen people using salt in this way.

To make an orange-flavored drink, pour water into a glass (*left*), add orange-flavored sugar and stir the mixture (*center*). The drink that results (*right*) contains a solution in which sugar is the solute and water is the solvent. ▼

Types of Solutions

You're probably most familiar with such solutions as sugar dissolved in water. But not all solutions are made of a solid dissolved in a liquid. Each part of a solution may be a solid, a liquid, or a gas. For example, the solvent may be a liquid, such as water, and the solute may be a solid, such as salt. The table shows examples of some common solutions, the different solvents and solutes that make them up, and ways they are used.

Common Solutions

Solution	Solvent	Solute	Use
Saline solution	water (liquid)	salt (solid)	Saline, or salt, solution is used for cleaning contact lenses or for artificial tears.
Rubbing alcohol	isopropyl alcohol (liquid)	water (liquid)	A doctor rubs an area of skin with alcohol to clean it before giving an injection.
Carbonated water	water (liquid)	carbon dioxide (gas)	Soft drinks that contain carbon dioxide gas are called carbonated drinks.
Stainless steel	iron (solid)	carbon, chromium, and nickel (solid)	Stainless steel conducts heat evenly, making it a good choice for use in cookware.

Alloys

Look at the photograph of the bronze statue. Bronze is one of many metal mixtures known as alloys. An **alloy** is a solution of two or more metals with properties of its own. As you can see from the table, bronze contains both copper and tin. Bronze, which has the reddish color of copper, is both harder and more durable than either copper or tin.

All alloys are solid solutions. Like all solutions, alloys have properties that are different from those of the substances that make them up. ■

▲ **What metals make up bronze alloy in this statue?**

Common Alloys

Alloy	Metals It Contains	Some Uses
alnico	aluminum, nickel, cobalt	magnets
brass	copper, zinc	plumbing, hardware
bronze	copper, tin	jewelry, statues
chrome-vanadium steel	iron, chromium, and vanadium	auto parts
stainless steel	iron, chromium, nickel	knives, sinks
sterling silver	silver, copper	tableware, jewelry

INVESTIGATION 2 WRAP-UP

REVIEW

1. Distinguish among the three states of matter.

2. How are elements and compounds alike and different?

CRITICAL THINKING

3. A sample of powder is a mixture of two of these three substances—sugar, salt, and cornstarch. What tests would you do to help find out what the mixture contains?

4. "The smallest particle of a compound is not an atom." Do you agree or disagree with this statement? Explain your reasoning.

C30

Word Power

Write the letter of the term that best matches the definition. *Not all terms will be used*.

1. Central part of an atom
2. Anything that has mass and takes up space
3. Measure of how much matter there is in an object
4. Ability to cause change
5. Smallest particle of an element
6. Mixture in which the different particles are spread evenly
7. A shorthand way to represent the name of an element.

a. atom
b. compound
c. chemical symbol
d. energy
e. mass
f. matter
g. nucleus
h. solution
i. volume

Check What You Know

Write the term in each pair that best completes each sentence.

1. A state of matter that has a definite volume is a (solid, gas).
2. Matter made of just one kind of atom is (an element, a compound).
3. An example of a compound is (carbon, water).
4. Bronze and brass are examples of (alloys, compounds).

Problem Solving

1. Elements are the basic building blocks of matter. How is it possible that there are hundreds of thousands of different kinds of matter when there are only 112 known elements?

2. How is chopping ice into small pieces similar to melting ice? How are the two changes different?

BUILD YOUR PORTFOLIO

Study the drawing of an atomic model. Identify and describe the different parts of the atom. Then, in your own words, explain why this model is often called a *planetary* model of the atom.

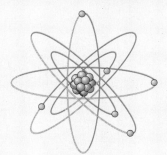

CHAPTER 2

ENERGY AND CHANGE

You're climbing ever so slowly upward. As you look skyward, your heart pounds, and you tightly clutch the safety bar over your lap. You finally reach the top, pause and then hurtle downward with terrifying speed! You're on a roller coaster, a ride that demonstrates how changes in energy can be put to use in a fun, exciting way.

PEOPLE USING SCIENCE

Mechanical Engineer

Ron Toomer is a mechanical engineer who designs roller coasters. He is president of Arrow Dynamics, Inc., of Clearfield, Utah. When Toomer designs a roller coaster, he first builds a model. Then, using a computer, he determines how to construct a safe, but exciting, roller coaster. What gives a roller coaster its energy? Find out through the investigations in this chapter.

Coming Up

◄ One of Ron Toomer's roller coasters

WHAT ARE SOME DIFFERENT FORMS OF ENERGY?

Make a list of all the examples of energy that are found in your classroom. In this investigation you'll explore these and other forms of energy and find out how energy travels.

Activity

It's a Stretch

Do you know how to store energy? In this activity you'll work with a balloon and a rubber band to explore how to store and release energy.

Procedure

1. Blow up a balloon and tie its neck so that no air escapes.

2. With the balloon resting on a flat surface, hold the balloon firmly out in front of you with your fingertips. At the same time, have your partner push the eraser end of a pencil into the balloon. Then you release the balloon. In your *Science Notebook*, **describe** what happens to the balloon.

MATERIALS
- goggles
- 2 small balloons
- pencil
- large rubber band
- *Science Notebook*

SAFETY

Wear goggles during this activity. When snapping rubber bands, be sure the bands are directed at the balloon only.

Step 2

3. Again place the balloon on a flat surface. Prepare to "snap" a rubber band at the balloon. Make a fist with your thumb pointed up and place a rubber band over the tip of your thumb. Stretch the rubber band back and aim it at the balloon, as shown.

Step 3

4. **Predict** what will happen if you release the rubber band. Release the rubber band and **observe** and **record** what happens.

5. Blow up a second balloon. Hold the neck tightly, but don't tie it off. **Predict** what will happen if you release the balloon. Release it and **observe** and **record** what happens.

Analyze and Conclude

1. Energy can be stored in matter by changing the matter in some way. How did you store energy in the balloon in step 2? in the rubber band in step 3?

2. Releasing stored energy often causes something to move. In this activity, **tell what evidence** you used to determine that stored energy was released.

3. Moving objects have energy. **Tell what evidence** you observed that indicated that stored energy can be changed to energy of motion.

INVESTIGATE FURTHER!

EXPERIMENT

Design your own experiment to investigate energy with a rubber band and a balloon. With your teacher's approval carry out your experiment. Be sure to wear your goggles. Describe the energy forms you observe.

Activity

Electricity to Go

A dry cell stores energy. In this activity, you can release some of the energy stored in a dry cell and get other forms of energy.

MATERIALS

- insulated wire with stripped ends
- magnetic compass
- tape
- dry cell, size D, in holder
- *Science Notebook*

SAFETY

Allow the wire to remain connected to the dry cell for only a short time.

Procedure

1. Wrap an insulated wire three times around a compass. Tape the wire in place.

2. Rotate, or turn, the compass until the needle is almost parallel to the wire, as shown.

 Math Hint *You will not need to rotate the compass more than 90°.*

3. Touch the bare ends of the wire to opposite ends of the dry cell. **Observe** what happens to the needle of the compass. **Record** your observations in your *Science Notebook*.

4. Reverse the positions of the ends of the wire. **Observe** what happens to the needle of the compass.

5. Remove one end of the wire from the dry cell. Then quickly touch this free end of the wire to the dry cell again. Do this quickly several times. **Record** your observations of the compass needle.

INVESTIGATE FURTHER!

EXPERIMENT

Plan an experiment to change electrical energy into light and heat. Use a dry cell, wires, and a light bulb in a holder. Get your teacher's approval and then try it!

Analyze and Conclude

1. Electric current produces magnetism. What evidence did you **observe** that electrical energy was present in the activity?

2. What kind of energy did you **observe** in the compass needle?

3. **List** all the forms of energy for which you observed evidence in this activity. Describe the evidence for each.

4. Based on this activity, what can you **infer** about the ability of energy to change form?

Step 2

C36

Forms of Energy

Reading Focus What are some forms of energy?

As thousands of people cheer, an athlete races down a narrow runway. At the end of the runway, she leaps upward and forward. A fraction of a second later, her heels dig into a sand-filled pit. The roar of the crowd becomes louder as fans realize that the athlete has broken a world record.

How did the athlete achieve her great feat? For one thing, she used energy to make things happen, or change. As a matter of fact, this is one way to describe energy. Recall from Chapter 1 that energy is the ability to cause change.

Changes Caused by Energy

If you were to watch a replay of the athlete's record-breaking leap, you might discover some of the changes caused by the energy she used. Look at the picture on this page. What changes do you see?

Energy can cause an object to change position. The athlete used energy in her muscles to move from the start of the runway to its end. That's a change of position.

Energy can make things change speed or direction. The athlete changed speed as she dashed down the runway.

What changes are caused by the athlete's energy? ▼

Sound energy can shatter glass (*left*) and damage eardrums (*right*).

She changed her direction when she jumped into the air.

Energy can also cause temperature to change. If you could have taken the temperature of the sand, you would have found that the temperature increased slightly when the athlete landed on it. Her energy of motion became heat energy.

Forms of Energy

There are many forms of energy, and each form can cause things to change. The athlete used mechanical energy to make things change. Mechanical energy includes everything that has to do with an object's motion.

If you watched the track event on television, you used electricity, another form of energy. In most power plants, coal or oil is burned to produce heat energy, which is used to make electricity. The burning of fuel releases energy stored in the chemicals of the fuel. This form of stored energy is called chemical energy. In the activity on page C36, the electricity in the wires comes from chemical energy that was stored in the dry cell.

The activity on pages C34 and C35 shows what happens when energy stored in a rubber band is released. You can store energy in this book just by lifting it up and holding it steady. When you let go of the book, it moves toward the floor. How did the book get energy to move? It got that energy when you picked it up. Was there more energy used to pick up the book than was released when the book fell? Actually, the energy of motion in the falling book is about equal to the energy used to lift it.

Think again about the track star. The energy she used in running and jumping came from chemical energy stored in food she had eaten earlier. Now it's time to "recharge her batteries." With rest and a balanced meal or two, she'll be ready to take another shot at the long-jump record. ■

Internet Field Trip
Visit **www.eduplace.com** to find out more about energy.

C38

Energy Transfer

Reading Focus In what three ways can energy be transferred?

A farmer shades his eyes from the blinding light of a summer day. Heated air rises from the fields around him. Sweat trickles down his tanned neck as he glances at a nearby thermometer. The thermometer reads a sizzling 35°C (95°F).

High in the sky over the farmer's head—150 million km (93 million mi) away—is the source of his discomfort. It's the Sun. Like most things that emit, or give off light, the Sun emits heat energy. Tremendous amounts of this light and heat energy travel outward from the Sun in the form of waves. Such energy is called electromagnetic (ē lek′trō mag net′ik) energy.

Energy Travels in Different Ways

Light is electromagnetic energy you can see. There are other kinds of electromagnetic energy you can't see, such as X-rays, ultraviolet radiation, and infrared radiation.

Electromagnetic energy can travel through empty space. You know this, because energy from the Sun reaches Earth. And there is little between Earth and the Sun except empty space. As stated earlier, electromagnetic energy travels as waves. The transfer of electromagnetic energy by waves is called **radiation** (rā dē ā′shən).

If you hold your hand near a hot object—a radiator, for example—you

Electromagnetic energy travels in waves from the Sun to Earth. ▼

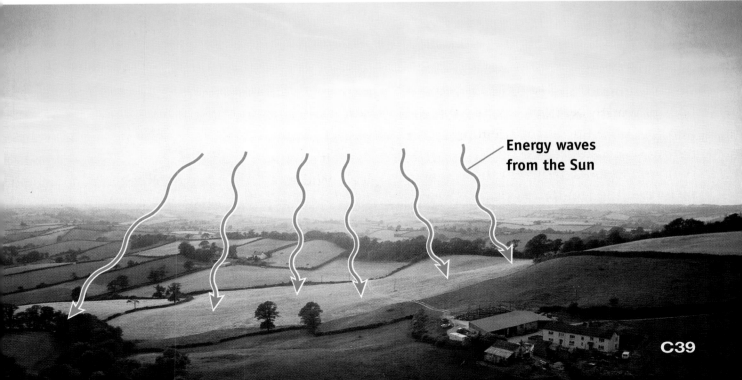

Energy waves from the Sun

▲ **Why does the last penny move from the row?**

can feel the heat without touching the object. Some energy leaves the radiator as infrared radiation. When this invisible form of electromagnetic energy reaches your hand, it is absorbed and changed to heat energy.

All forms of energy can travel from place to place. Electromagnetic energy can travel through empty space. Other forms of energy, such as heat energy or sound energy, can travel only by being carried along in some kind of material called a medium. Any solid, liquid, or gas can serve as a medium.

Moving Particles

Energy can travel through a solid, liquid, or gas by disturbing, or moving, the particles that make up the medium. In a solid, energy causes the particles merely to vibrate a bit and bump into nearby particles. The particles don't go anywhere. But the energy travels through the medium from particle to particle. In this way, energy moves through a solid.

To get an idea of how this transfer of energy works, lay down eight pennies in a row on a flat surface. Each penny should touch the next penny in line, as shown in the picture at the top of this page. Now take a ninth penny and snap it against a penny at one end of the row. What happens to the eight pennies?

When you struck the row of pennies, the last penny moved the most. The energy that you gave to the penny you hit is transferred through the row of pennies to the last penny. The other pennies served as the medium for the transfer of energy.

Heat and other forms of energy can be transferred through different mediums. Suppose you want to fry eggs in a pan with a metal handle. You place the pan on a hot stove burner. Soon the pan is hot. You drop in butter and eggs, and they begin to sizzle.

Suppose you continue to hold the handle of the pan. Soon something besides eggs begins to sizzle—your hand! This happens because heat is transferred through the metal pan to its handle.

Energy is transferred through solids such as the pan by conduction (kən-duk'shən). **Conduction** is the transfer of energy by direct contact between particles. The particles in a solid are packed close together. Energy is simply conducted, or passed along, from one particle to the next.

▲ **Heat travels through the metal of the pan from particle to particle.**

Warm air rises.

Air cools and sinks.

Air is heated.

Cool air pushes up warm air.

Cool air moves toward the stove.

Air in the room is heated by convection. Suppose you measured the air temperature in the center of this room both at the ceiling and at the floor. What might it measure at each place? Explain why.

Energy can also be transferred through fluids—liquids and gases—by the movement of particles from place to place. The transfer of heat energy through fluids by moving particles is called **convection** (kən vek′shən). The picture above shows how heat energy from a stove on one side of a room can warm the air on the other side.

Convection can occur in fluids because the particles in fluids can move about quite freely, carrying heat energy with them. Energy can't be transferred through solids by convection. That's because the particles in solids remain in fixed positions.

Energy can be transferred through solids, liquids, and gases in another way. Energy can travel through matter as waves. Think about the energy carried by ocean waves, for example. Sound energy travels through air as waves. Unlike electromagnetic waves, however, sound waves can't travel through empty space. Sound travels by "making waves" of air. ■

INVESTIGATION 1 WRAP-UP

REVIEW

1. Name three kinds of energy and give examples of how each kind can cause a change to occur.

2. Define and give examples of energy transfer by radiation, conduction, and convection.

CRITICAL THINKING

3. Explain how you could feel heat from a radiator by more than one method of transfer.

4. Explain why astronauts used radio waves (electromagnetic waves) rather than sound waves to communicate on the Moon.

INVESTIGATION 2

HOW CAN ENERGY CHANGE?

Think about a car being driven down a dark road. What forms of energy are being used? One form of energy, light, allows the driver to see the road ahead. The light is produced from another form of energy, electrical energy. Where does the electrical energy come from? In this investigation you'll explore examples of energy changing form.

Activity

To Bounce or Not to Bounce

A flashlight has energy stored in the chemicals of its batteries. An object on a high shelf also has stored energy. How can that energy change?

MATERIALS
- small rubber ball
- meterstick
- clay
- *Science Notebook*

SAFETY //////
Be careful not to lose your balance when standing on a chair.

Step 2

Procedure

1. Hold a rubber ball at a height of 1 m. Release the ball and have another student **measure** how high the ball bounces on the first bounce. **Record** the height of the bounce in your *Science Notebook*.

 *See* **SCIENCE** *and* **MATH TOOLBOX** page H6 if you need to review **Using a Tape Measure or Ruler.**

2. Stand on a chair and hold the ball at a height of 2 m. **Predict** how high the ball will bounce after it hits the floor. Release the ball and have a group member **measure** and **record** the height of its bounce.

3. Shape clay into a ball about the size of the rubber ball. Drop the clay ball from a height of 1 m. **Observe** and **record** how the clay looks after hitting the floor.

4. Reshape the clay into a ball and drop it from a height of 2 m. **Observe** and **record** how the clay looks after it hits the floor.

Steps 3 and 4

Analyze and Conclude

1. What evidence did you observe that the rubber ball and the clay ball had stored energy when held at a height of 1 m?

2. **Infer** what happened to the amount of energy stored in the balls as you raised them from a height of 1 m to a height of 2 m. Give reasons for your inference.

3. **Infer** what happened to the energy stored in the balls when you released them. Give reasons for your inference.

4. Some materials store energy when they change shape as they strike a surface. Then they release this energy. Which material, rubber or clay, stores energy this way? How do you know?

UNIT PROJECT LINK

Continue with your collection of samples of matter. Identify each item as an element, compound, or mixture. For each compound find out the names of some or all of the elements it contains. For each mixture find out the names of some or all of the substances it contains. Use this information to write labels for each sample. Organize the collection and display it under the heads "Elements," "Compounds," and "Mixtures."

TechnologyLink

For more help with your Unit Project, go to **www.eduplace.com**.

Activity

Roller Coaster Energy

A roller coaster car has stored energy when it is at the top of the first hill. How does the energy change as the car speeds down this hill and up the next?

MATERIALS

- BB or small marble
- aquarium tubing (about 3 m)
- masking tape
- *Science Notebook*

Procedure

1. Work with a partner. Place a BB inside a piece of aquarium tubing and seal the ends of the tubing with tape. You and your partner should each hold an end of the tubing.

2. Let the BB roll to one end of the tubing. Raise that end of the tubing to release the BB. **Observe** how its speed changes as it rolls down the tubing. **Record** your observations in your *Science Notebook*.

3. Remove the tape from one end of the tubing. Arrange the tubing in a series of hills (at least two) to model the form of a roller coaster track. The beginning of your model should represent the top of a hill. **Sketch your model** of a roller coaster.

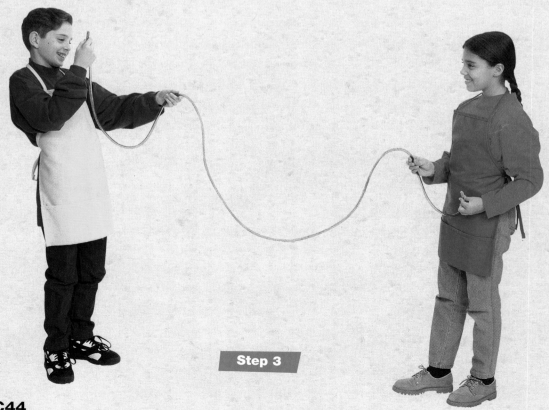

Step 3

4. Release the BB into the tubing. **Observe** and **record** how the speed of the BB changes as it moves.

Math Hint *To observe the changes in speed, note the speed of the BB near the top and near the bottom of the tubing.*

Analyze and Conclude

1. When does the BB speed up during its trip? When does it slow down?

2. When is the BB traveling the fastest in the tubing? When is it traveling the slowest?

3. At what point does the BB have the most energy of motion? When does it have the most stored energy? **Describe** the BB's trip along your model roller coaster in terms of the energy changes that take place.

INVESTIGATE FURTHER!

EXPERIMENT

Arrange aquarium tubing so that it has a loop in it. First draw the shape of the track. Then experiment with the track until the BB can make it through the entire loop. What factor seems to determine whether the BB moves all the way through?

Science in Literature

ENERGY TO DO WORK

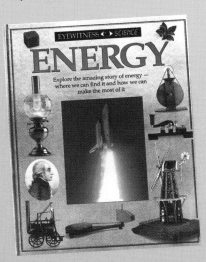

Energy
Jack Challoner
Dorling Kindersley, 1993

"Early civilizations used 'mechanical energy' to do work like lifting, grinding grain, building, and transporting people and goods. This mechanical energy could be obtained from wind or moving water. Wind and water flow are the most visible examples of natural energy on the Earth, but that energy originally comes from the Sun. The wind that turns the sails of a windmill and fills the sails of a sailing boat is caused by the Sun heating the Earth."

You will learn many interesting facts about energy when you read *Energy* by Jack Challoner.

Energy Changes

Reading Focus How can potential energy change to kinetic energy and back again?

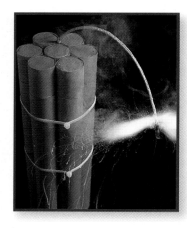

▲ **All of these objects contain stored energy.**

Look at the pictures on this page. What do the sugar, the dynamite, and the skier at the top of a steep hill have in common? They all have energy stored in them.

Sugar is a source of quick energy that can help you do a high-energy task, like run a race. Dynamite can blow rocks out of a moutainside. And when a skier on a hill moves to the top of the slope, he or she has enough energy to speed swiftly to the bottom of the hill.

So the sugar, the dynamite, and the skier on the hill contain enough energy to cause something to change position, or to move from one place to another. However, the energy in these things isn't being used. It's just waiting for something to set it loose. This energy-in-waiting is called potential energy. **Potential energy** is stored energy.

Chemical Storehouses

Energy is stored in different ways. Consider a packet of sugar and a stick of dynamite. One of these materials is sugar, a nutrient that can help living things grow. The other material, the explosive dynamite, can cause destruction. Both materials, however, store energy in the same way.

The energy in sugar and dynamite is stored in the chemical bonds that link their atoms. A bond can be compared to a spring in a pogo stick. Look at the pictures on page C47.

❶ The base of the pogo stick contains a spring. When the girl jumps onto the foot rests, energy is stored in the spring. As shown in the inset picture at the left, the spring becomes compressed.

❷ The spring pushes back, releasing the stored energy. As shown in the picture on the right, the girl bounces up.

1. The compressed spring of a pogo stick has stored energy.

2. When the spring pushes back, it releases its stored energy.

When you eat sugar, the chemical bonds that store energy in the sugar are broken down by chemicals in your body. This action releases energy that your body can use. In dynamite the bonds are broken down by a spark or a jolt of electricity. When these chemical bonds break, a great deal of energy is released very quickly. Because the energy in sugar and dynamite is stored in chemical bonds, it is called chemical potential energy.

How Much Energy?

How much energy is stored in that packet of sugar you read about earlier? If you read the label on a packet of sugar, you'll find that the sugar contains 16 Calories. But what does that tell you about the amount of stored energy in the packet of sugar?

A Calorie is a measure of energy. One Calorie is the amount of heat energy needed to raise the temperature of 1 kg of water 1°C. So if the stored energy in a packet of sugar were changed to heat energy, it could raise the temperature of 1 kg of water 16°C. The Calorie is a useful unit for finding the stored energy in different foods. But scientists deal with many different forms of energy, and they need a unit of measure that can be applied to all of them. The **joule** (jo͞ol) is the basic unit of energy used by scientists.

The joule is named after an English scientist who studied the relationship between heat energy and other forms of energy. One joule is the amount of energy that is needed to raise the temperature of 1 g of water 4.18°C.

Changing Energy

Look at the photo on page C48. A couple of seconds before the picture was taken, the two acrobats on the end of the seesaw were standing up on the platform to their right. The acrobat flying through the air was standing on the other end of the seesaw.

▲ **Where did the flying acrobat's energy come from?**

While standing on the platform, the two acrobats had potential energy because of their position above the ground. They stored that energy as they climbed up to the platform. Energy stored in an object because of its position above the ground is called gravitational potential energy. Such an object can be set in motion by the pull of Earth's gravity on the object.

As the two acrobats stepped off the platform, their potential energy was changed to kinetic (ki net'ik) energy. **Kinetic energy** is energy of motion. When the acrobats landed on the seesaw, their kinetic energy caused one end of the seesaw to move down. The other end was pushed up, launching the third acrobat into the air. The kinetic energy of the two acrobats had been transferred through the seesaw to the third acrobat.

Energy on a Roller Coaster

The thrills of a roller coaster ride depend on repeated changes in energy—from potential to kinetic and back again. These changes are similar to the changes that the BB in the activity on pages C44 and C45 goes through as it moves through the plastic tubing.

Energy changes in a roller coaster ride ▼

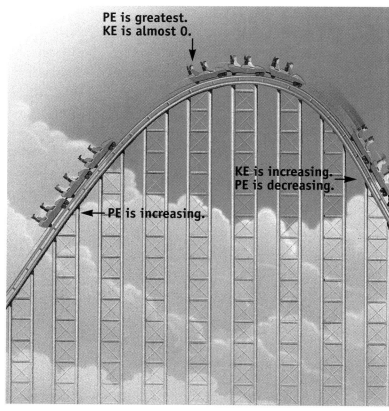

PE is greatest.
KE is almost 0.

KE is increasing.
PE is decreasing.

PE is increasing.

As a roller coaster ride begins, energy supplied by a motor pulls the roller coaster car up a track. As the car goes up, it gains potential energy. At the top of the hill, when its potential energy is greatest, the car is released.

What happens now? The car begins to roll down the hill. It gains kinetic energy. The potential energy the car had due to its position at the top of the hill is now changing back into energy of motion.

As the seconds flash by, more and more potential energy is changed into kinetic energy. How do you know this is happening? You know because the roller coaster car moves faster and faster down the track.

When the car reaches the bottom of the hill, all the potential energy it had at the top of the hill has been changed to kinetic energy. At this point the car is moving so fast it has enough kinetic energy to carry it all the way up to the top of the next hill.

But, as the car climbs that next hill, it slows down. Kinetic energy is being changed back to potential energy. When the car reaches the top of the hill, it begins a new plunge. Once again, potential energy changes into kinetic energy.

Engineers design roller coaster rides so that repeated changes, from potential to kinetic energy and back to potential energy, will keep all the cars in motion for the entire trip. And the changes, especially from potential to kinetic energy, will keep you screaming all the way. ■

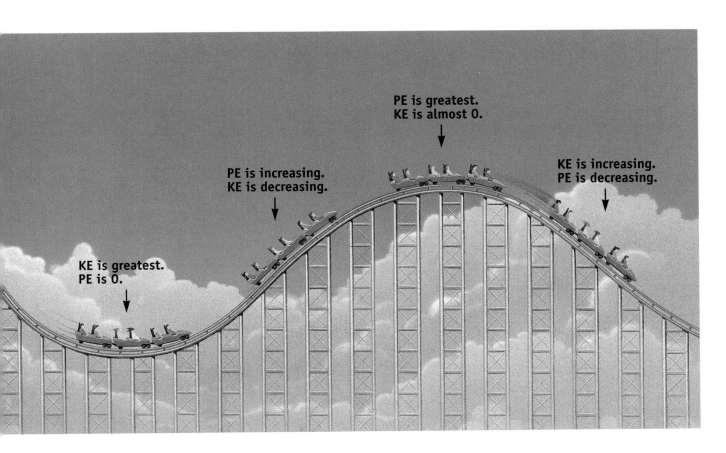

PE is greatest.
KE is almost 0.

PE is increasing.
KE is decreasing.

KE is increasing.
PE is decreasing.

KE is greatest.
PE is 0.

Green Plants: Energy Factories

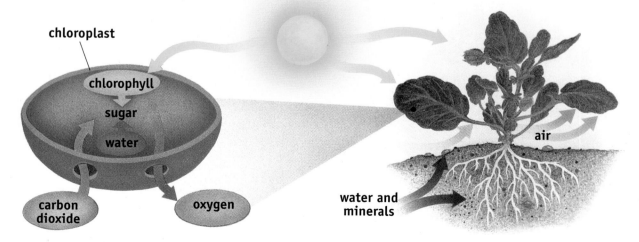

Reading Focus How do green plants change the Sun's energy into chemical energy stored in food?

Every country in the world is dotted with silent factories. In some places these factories cover the land as far as the eye can see. You may be thinking that these factories must be idle if they are silent, that no useful products are being made.

These factories, however, aren't idle. They make a product that the world's people could not live without. That product is food. Food contains the stored energy all living things need to carry out their life activities.

Unfortunately, in many countries of the world, there aren't enough of these energy factories to keep all the people healthy or even alive. What's more, many scientists fear that the situation

may get worse as the years pass. On the next page you'll find out why many scientists think this is true. But first take a brief tour of one of these energy factories to find out what it is and how it works.

The energy factories are green plants. Green plants make their own food. That food is also used by all living things that eat green plants. The plants are not actually single factories. Rather, each plant contains millions of tiny factories called chloroplasts (klôr'ə plasts).

Chloroplasts contain a chemical called chlorophyll. Chlorophyll captures, or absorbs, energy from the Sun. Using this energy, water from the soil and carbon dioxide from the air are combined to make a sugar called

The product made in this factory is sugar. ▼

chloroplast

chlorophyll

sugar

water

carbon dioxide

oxygen

air

water and minerals

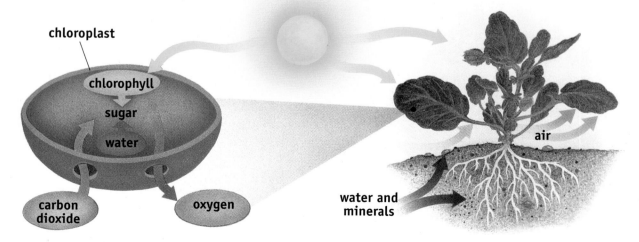

glucose (glōō'kōs). In this process, called photosynthesis (fōt ō sin'thə-sis), some of the Sun's energy gets stored in the glucose.

When you eat a leaf of spinach, a slice of whole-wheat bread, or any other plant product, you're taking in energy stored in glucose. Cells in your body are able to break down the glucose and release its stored energy. You're using some of that energy right now. You're using energy to move, to think, to breathe, and to do all the other things that keep you alive.

This thought brings us back to the problem that faces many people—hunger! Of the more than 6 billion people in the world, more than half a billion don't get enough food. Many people die each year from starvation.

In some places the human population is growing faster than farmers are able to grow the crops needed to feed the people. In a sense the energy factories aren't keeping up with the people

▲ **Bad weather can lead to crop failures.**

factories. Besides increasing populations, other factors that prevent farmers from growing enough crops include bad weather and poor soil.

Scientists and farmers all over the world are seeking solutions to the problem of hunger. New methods to increase crop production have been successful in some countries. But further efforts are needed to find ways to feed all the people in the world. ■

INVESTIGATION 2 WRAP-UP

REVIEW

1. Define and give two examples of potential energy.

2. Define and give two examples of kinetic energy.

CRITICAL THINKING

3. Trace the energy you get from eating an apple back to the Sun.

4. You give a friend on a playground swing one hard push. Describe the energy changes that the swing undergoes until it stops moving.

INVESTIGATION 3

HOW CAN MATTER CHANGE?

Matter changes in many ways that you can observe. Some of these changes are physical, and some are chemical. In this investigation you'll explore these kinds of changes.

Activity

Change This

If you crush a sugar cube, the kind of matter in the sugar doesn't change. But if you toast a marshmallow, which is mostly sugar, the kind of matter does change. The change to the sugar cube is physical. The change to the marshmallow is chemical. See if you can tell whether some other changes are physical or chemical.

MATERIALS
- goggles
- clay cube
- steel wool on plate
- ice cube on plate
- baking soda in cup
- new pencil
- wooden safety match on aluminum pan
- vinegar
- pencil sharpener
- *Science Notebook*

SAFETY //////
Wear safety goggles during this activity.

Procedure

1. In your *Science Notebook*, **make a chart** like the one shown on page C53.

See **SCIENCE** and **MATH TOOLBOX** page H11 if you need to review *Making a Chart to Organize Data.*

2. **Observe** the properties of each of these materials: a clay cube, steel wool, an ice cube, baking soda, a new pencil, a wooden match. **Record** your observations in your chart.

3. For each material, carry out the procedure described in the chart. **Observe** the results and **record** your observations.

Procedure	Observations		Analysis	Conclusion
	Properties before change	Properties after change	Change in kind of matter	Physical change or chemical change
Form a cube of clay into a sphere.				
Moisten steel wool and leave it overnight.				
Let an ice cube stand overnight.				
Pour vinegar on baking soda.				
Sharpen a pencil in a pencil sharpener.				
Your teacher will strike a match.				

Analyze and Conclude

1. Talk with your group about your observations. In each case, decide whether the kind of matter has changed. **Record** your decisions under *Analysis*.

2. Decide whether each change is physical or chemical. **Record** your decisions under *Conclusion*.

INVESTIGATE FURTHER!

EXPERIMENT

Plan an experiment to measure the melting and boiling points of water. Use ice cubes, a saucepan, a hot plate, and a thermometer. Have your teacher approve your plan, then try it!

The Story of Nuclear Energy

Reading Focus What are some important events in the history of the use of nuclear energy?

One day over a hundred years ago, a French scientist wrapped some photographic film in paper that blocked light. He then placed bits of rock on the paper. The bits of rock contained a compound of the element uranium (yōō rā′nē əm). Later the scientist developed the film. Images of the rocks appeared on the film. How could this happen? The scientist inferred that the uranium in the rocks gave off energy. He further inferred that the energy could go through the paper.

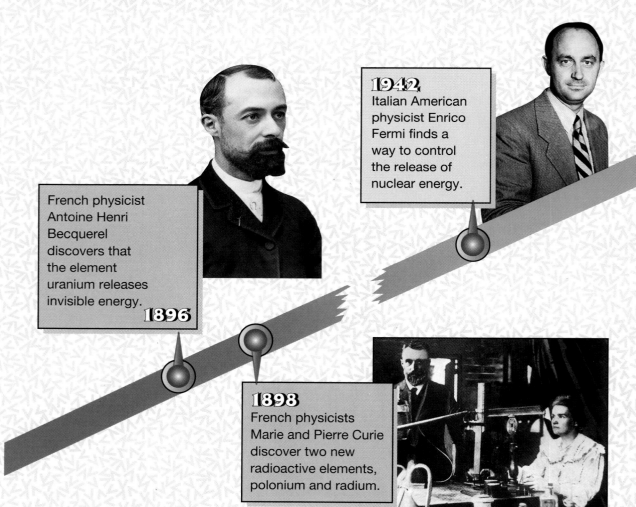

1942
Italian American physicist Enrico Fermi finds a way to control the release of nuclear energy.

French physicist Antoine Henri Becquerel discovers that the element uranium releases invisible energy.
1896

1898
French physicists Marie and Pierre Curie discover two new radioactive elements, polonium and radium.

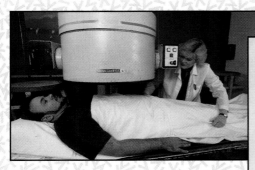

Nuclear energy is used in more and more tools for detecting and treating disease. Uses of radioactive elements also include killing bacteria in food, controlling insect pests, and making smoke detectors. **1990s**

BEYOND 2000

1954
The first ship powered by nuclear energy is launched. It is the U.S. Navy submarine *Nautilus*.

1970
A number of nations sign an agreement that forbids the giving or selling of nuclear weapons to countries that don't already have them. The agreement also forbids countries without such weapons to make them.

1956
The first nuclear power plant begins producing electricity at Calder Hall, England.

1945
The first nuclear bomb test takes place in the United States.

Uranium is now described as radioactive (rā dē ō ak′tiv). A **radioactive element** is one that releases energy and tiny particles from the nuclei of its atoms. The energy and particles can be powerful enough to pass through paper and other materials. Because the energy comes from the nuclei of atoms, it is called nuclear energy.

Since its discovery over 100 years ago, nuclear energy has been studied and used in a variety of ways. ■

The Same Stuff

Reading Focus What are three types of physical changes?

Nevado del Ruiz is a volcanic mountain in Colombia. One day in 1985 the volcano erupted. Smoke gushed out of its top. Rocks flew everywhere. Rivers of mud rushed down the mountainside. After the smoke cleared, most of the mountain's icecap and a huge chunk of the mountain itself were gone.

Case of the Missing Matter

Look at the photographs. Nevado del Ruiz is not as tall as it was before the eruption. And it has less ice on it than before. Where did the missing matter go? It seems to have vanished. Part of the rock that formed the top of the mountain became small bits and pieces of rock that were blown away. The kind of matter in the rocks did not change. What happened to the ice? The intense

heat energy coming from the volcano melted the ice. **Melting** is the change of state from a solid to a liquid. Some of the liquid water that formed mixed with soil to form mudflows.

Some of the liquid water evaporated, changing into water vapor in the air. **Evaporation** (ē vap ə rā′shən) is the change of state from a liquid to a gas. High above the mountain, the water vapor condensed into droplets of liquid water that formed clouds.

Condensation (kän dən sā′shən) is the change of state from a gas to a liquid. Changing the state of water does not change the kind of matter in water. Water vapor, liquid water, and ice are all the same kind of matter.

Think about the changes to the size and shape of the volcano's rocky struc-

Nevado del Ruiz *(left)* after its 1985 eruption and a mudflow *(right)* that formed from soil and melted ice during the eruption

ture. Then consider the changes in state that the water in the icecap underwent. The changes to both the rock and the ice were all physical changes. In a **physical change** the size, shape, or state of matter changes but no new substances are formed. In the activity on pages C52 and C53, the changes in the clay, the ice cube, and the pencil are all examples of physical changes.

Changes of State and Energy

Changes in the state of matter always involve heat energy. Heat energy from the volcano changed the solid icecap into a liquid and a gas. What's the connection between heat and these changes? Recall that matter is made of tiny particles. For water and most other compounds, these particles are called molecules (mäl′i kyo͞olz). A **molecule** is a particle made up of two or more atoms, which may be alike or different. Molecules are always moving. If the amount of energy in the molecules changes, their motion changes. And changes in particle motion may lead to changes in state.

Using Math *What is the difference in temperature between the freezing point and the boiling point of water?*

SOLID In a solid, molecules have only enough energy to vibrate. But they remain in fixed positions. Forces of attraction between the molecules hold them in place. When you raise the temperature of ice, the water molecules absorb heat energy. As a result, they start to vibrate faster.

LIQUID When enough heat is added to ice, the molecules move fast enough to flow over one another. The solid water changes to liquid water. The molecules are no longer in fixed positions. But the forces of attraction still hold the molecules together.

GAS If you keep raising the temperature of the water, its molecules gain more energy. As a result, they move faster and farther apart. Soon, the molecules are very far apart and are actually speeding through the air. The forces of attraction can no longer keep the molecules together. The water is now in the gas state.

Different Stuff

Reading Focus What is a chemical change?

"Ten, nine, eight . . ." a voice counts down. Clouds of white mist surround the rocket on its launching pad. "Four, three, two, one, ignition!" Flames burst from the bottom of the rocket. "Liftoff!" Imagine that you're watching explorers in a spacecraft blasting off to Mars. With the help of a chemical change, their adventure has begun.

A **chemical change** is a change in which one or more new substances form. In the change that sends the spacecraft aloft, hydrogen and oxygen combine. The new substance that forms is water. Just before liftoff, hydrogen gas and oxygen gas are mixed in a chamber. Then a spark ignites the mixture. The hydrogen burns rapidly in the oxygen. Hot water vapor rushes out of the bottom of the rocket.

What is the source of the energy released in this change? You've read that chemical bonds in sugar and dynamite contain chemical potential energy. So do the bonds in hydrogen and oxygen. When this mixture is ignited, the bonds break. The chemical energy of the bonds is changed to heat energy and then to kinetic energy as the rocket soars into space.

Using Math *In a water molecule, what is the ratio of hydrogen atoms to oxygen atoms? What is the ratio of oxygen atoms to hydrogen atoms?*

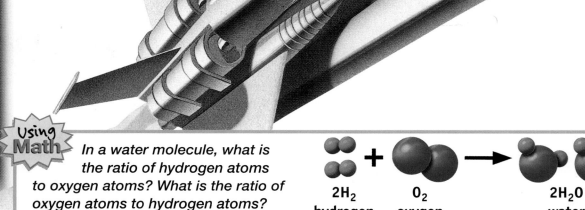

$2H_2$
hydrogen

O_2
oxygen

$2H_2O$
water

The Red Planet and Rust

Mars is often called the red planet. Long ago iron on the surface of Mars combined with oxygen to form the reddish compound iron oxide. This substance gives the planet its red color, as shown in the photograph. Iron oxide also forms as a result of chemical changes on Earth. In the activity on pages C52 and C53, the rusting of steel wool is a chemical change. Is energy released in this chemical change? Yes, but it happens slowly. It is usually too slow for you to be able to feel any heat energy coming from a rusting object.

How Things Burn

In the same activity a matchstick burns. You've probably watched wood logs burn. The burning of wood is a chemical change. Substances in the wood combine with oxygen in the air.

Energy is released in the form of heat and light. What was once wood and oxygen becomes gases, smoke, and ashes. These substances have different properties than wood. Unlike the slow chemical change that occurs when iron rusts, energy is released rapidly when wood burns.

The burning of any fuel is a chemical change. Natural gas, often used as a fuel in cooking, contains a compound called methane. Look at the drawing. It shows what happens when methane burns.

When methane burns, its molecules interact with oxygen molecules. Then molecules of water and carbon dioxide form. At the same time, energy that was stored in chemical bonds in the methane is released as heat and light. You might use the heat to cause chemical changes in pancake batter, or whatever else you may cook over that gas flame.

$$CH_4 + 2O_2 \longrightarrow CO_2 + 2H_2O$$

methane + oxygen ⟶ carbon dioxide + water

Chemical Changes in Living Things

Chemical changes occur in living things. In fact, to be alive means to be always changing chemically. For example, photosynthesis is a chemical change that occurs in green plants. In this process molecules of carbon dioxide and water combine to form molecules of glucose and oxygen. At the same time, energy from the Sun is stored in the bonds of glucose molecules.

In animals, the digestion of food involves many chemical changes. During digestion, complex molecules break down into glucose. The glucose is then used in cell respiration. In this process, molecules of oxygen and glucose change into molecules of carbon dioxide and water. At the same time, chemical energy that was stored in the glucose is released.

CO_2
carbon dioxide

O_2
oxygen

H_2O
water

$C_6H_{12}O_6$
glucose

▲ **The drawings show models of substances that take part in photosynthesis.**

Do leaves change color in the fall where you live? New substances form when a green leaf changes to red and then to brown. Look around you. What chemical changes can you observe? ■

INVESTIGATION 3 WRAP-UP

REVIEW

1. In a physical change, what changes and what doesn't change?

2. Give an example of a chemical change. Then explain what makes your example a chemical change.

CRITICAL THINKING

3. Apples picked too soon taste sour, but they may turn sweet if left to ripen on the tree. Is the change in an apple's taste physical or chemical? Explain.

4. Liquid water can change to water vapor. Hydrogen gas and oxygen gas can also change to water vapor. Which change is physical, and which is chemical? How is energy involved in each change?

REFLECT & EVALUATE

Word Power

Write the letter of the term that best completes each sentence. *Not all terms will be used*.

1. Nuclear energy can be obtained from a ——.

2. The change of state from a gas to a liquid is ——.

3. Energy of motion is ——.

4. The basic unit of energy is the ——.

5. The transfer of electromagnetic energy is ——.

6. Stored energy is ——.

a. condensation
b. radiation
c. evaporation
d. joule
e. kinetic energy
f. nuclear
g. potential energy
h. radioactive element

Check What You Know

Write the term in each pair that best completes each sentence.

1. Heat energy is transferred through fluids by (convection, radiation).

2. A change in size or shape of matter is a (chemical, physical) change.

3. Molecules in water vapor have (more, less) energy than molecules in liquid water.

4. An example of a chemical change is (evaporation, burning).

Problem Solving

1. A match is used to light the candles at a dinner party. Describe all the energy changes that were involved. What role did potential energy play in the lighting of the candles?

2. Suppose you put a pot of water on the stove to boil. Describe how heat is transferred from the stove burner to the water.

Copy the drawings of the models. Label each of your drawings with the name of the substance that the model represents. Then write a sentence that tells one way that substance is involved in a change in matter.

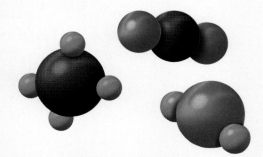

Using READING SKILLS

Cause and Effect

When you read, it is important to figure out what happens and why it happens. What happens is called the *effect*. Why things happen is called the *cause*.

Read the paragraphs below. Then complete the exercises that follow.

> **Use these hints to determine cause and effect.**
>
> • Look for signal words: *because, and so, as a result*
>
> • As you read, ask yourself why something is happening.

Changing State

Ice, liquid water, and water vapor can change from one to another. Think about some ways you can make such changes happen. Suppose you put liquid water in a freezer. The liquid will change into a solid, ice. If you leave ice at room temperature for a while, it will change to liquid water.

If you heat liquid water in a kettle until the water boils, some of the liquid changes into the invisible gas water vapor. Suppose, as the water boils, you hold a cold plate over the spout of the kettle. Almost at once any water vapor coming in contact with the plate would change to drops of liquid water.

Copy each statement. Write C in the blank after each cause. Write E in the blank after each effect.

1. Suppose you put liquid water in a freezer ___. The liquid will change into a solid, ice ___.

2. If you leave ice at room temperature for a while ___, it will change to liquid water ___.

3. If you heat liquid water in a kettle until the water boils ___, some of the liquid changes into the invisible gas water vapor ___.

Using MATH SKILLS

 Using Math **Equations and Formulas**

Density is the amount of matter in a given space. If you know the mass and the volume of an object or a substance, you can use the formula below to find the density of that object or substance.

density = mass ÷ volume

Suppose an object has a mass of 4 g and a volume of 16 cm³. Its density is 0.25 gram per cubic centimeter (0.25 g/cm³).

$$d = m \div v$$
$$d = 4 \text{ g} \div 16 \text{ cm}^3$$
$$d = \frac{4}{16} = \frac{1}{4} = 0.25 \text{ g/cm}^3$$

Use the density formula to complete the exercises that follow.

1. An object has a mass of 110 g and a volume of 20 cm³. What is the density of the object?

2. At a temperature of 4°C, the density of water is 1 g/cm³. If the density of an object is greater than that of water, the object sinks. If its density is less than that of water, the object floats. Suppose the temperature of water in a pail is 4°C. A block made of an unknown substance has a density of 0.78 g/cm³. Will the block sink or float? Explain.

3. Water at 20°C has a density of 0.998 g/cm³. A clear glass is filled with water at 20°C. A penny placed in the glass immediately falls to the bottom of the glass. What can you infer about the density of the penny?

You may wish to use a calculator for Exercise 4.

4. The density of gold is 19.3 g/cm³. The density of silver is 10.5 g/cm³. The density of nickel is 8.9 g/cm³. A block made of an unknown but pure substance has a mass of 634.125 g and a volume of 71.25 cm³. Is the material pure gold, silver, or nickel? Explain how you know.

WRAP-UP!

On your own, use scientific methods to investigate a question about matter and energy.

THINK LIKE A SCIENTIST

Ask a Question

Pose a question about matter and energy that you would like to investigate. For example, ask, "How does the temperature of water affect how much sugar can dissolve in it?"

Make a Hypothesis

Suggest a hypothesis that is a possible answer to the question. One hypothesis is that an increase in water temperature will increase the amount of sugar that can dissolve in that water.

Plan and Do a Test

Plan a controlled experiment to find out how much sugar can dissolve in water at room temperature and at 50°C (122°F). You could start with a thermometer, water, sugar, a measuring spoon, a graduated cylinder, a cup, and a stirrer. Develop a procedure that uses these materials to test the hypothesis. With permission, carry out your experiment. Follow the safety guidelines on pages S14–S15.

Record and Analyze

Observe carefully and record your data accurately. Make repeated observations.

Draw Conclusions

Look for evidence to support the hypothesis or to show that it is false. Draw conclusions about the hypothesis. Repeat the experiment to verify the results.

WRITING IN SCIENCE
Persuasive Essay

Write a persuasive essay that argues that plants, not fossil fuels, are the most important energy source on Earth. Use these guidelines to write your persuasive essay.

- Describe the importance of plants as an energy source.
- Compare ways that the two energy sources are used.
- Identify the many ways that plants are used as energy sources.

UNIT D

Populations and Ecosystems

Theme: Systems

THINK LIKE A SCIENTIST

THINK LIKE A SCIENTIST

BLOOMING DESERT

The Anza-Borrego Desert State Park, shown here, is a flowering desert stretching out below stark mountains in southern California. Scientists study things such as the temperature, the amount of rainfall, and the kind of soil that affect the organisms living in this desert. They also study how desert organisms behave and survive in an environment where temperatures can be high and water is scarce.

D2

a Test • Record and Analyze • Draw Conclusions • Make Observations • Ask a Question • Make a Hypothesis • Plan and Do a Test

THINK LIKE A SCIENTIST

Questioning In this unit you'll study how living and nonliving things in the environment interact. You'll find out how nonliving materials, such as water, carbon dioxide, and oxygen, cycle within the environment. You'll investigate questions such as these.

- How Do Earth's Major Ecosystems Differ?
- What Is Biodiversity, and How Is It Changing?

Observing, Testing, Hypothesizing In the Activity "Make a Mini-Biome!" you'll put together a biome of your choice. You'll observe how nonliving things affect the growth of living things in your biome.

Researching In the Resource "Earth's Biomes," you'll learn about diverse land environments and organisms that populate the land.

Drawing Conclusions After you've completed your investigations, you'll draw conclusions about what you've learned—and get new ideas.

CHAPTER 1

LIVING THINGS AND ENVIRONMENTS

Nature—it's amazing! Everything works together so smoothly. In every environment each plant and animal finds what it needs to survive. Together with other organisms in the environment, plants and animals form a busy, healthy community.

PEOPLE USING SCIENCE

Environmental Engineer Juho So (jōō hō tsä) works to clean up environmental pollution. For example, he has cleaned up water that was polluted by a company that made fertilizers. Since leaving his native Korea, Dr. So has monitored and corrected many kinds of water and soil pollution in the United States and England.

Dr. So first thought about cleaning up the environment when he was about ten years old. A pond where he played was filled with frogs and toads. One day he found the pond covered by a slick of oil from a nearby broken oil tank. A week later he was heartbroken to find that all the frogs and toads were gone. Today Dr. So cleans up environmental pollution after it happens. But he wants to prevent pollution from ever taking place.

Coming Up

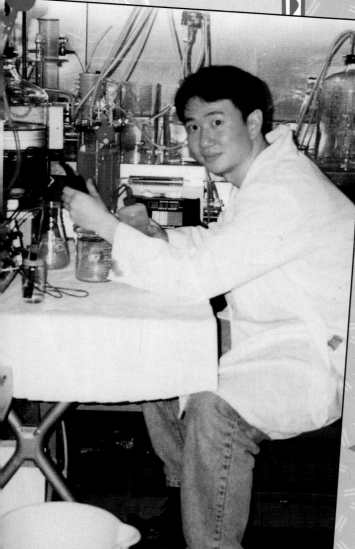

◀ Juho So at work in his laboratory

D5

WHAT IS AN ECOSYSTEM?

Do you need living things to survive? Do you need non-living things? If you answered "yes" to both questions, then you are part of an ecosystem. In this investigation you'll find out what an ecosystem is.

Activity

A Local Ecosystem

All ecosystems include living and nonliving things. How do these parts of an ecosystem affect each other, or interact? Study a plot of soil to find out.

Procedure

1. Use a meterstick to **measure** a plot of ground that is 1 m square. Push a wooden stake into the ground at each corner. Mark off the square by tying string around the four stakes.

 Math Hint *To make sure your plot of ground is reasonably square, measure the diagonals of the plot. The length of each diagonal should be about 1.4 m.*

2. **Predict** the kinds of living and nonliving things you'll find in your plot and how they'll interact. **Record** your predictions in your *Science Notebook*.

3. **Make a chart** like the one shown on page D7. Leave room to record your observations. **Describe** the location of your plot.

MATERIALS

- gloves
- meterstick
- 4 wooden stakes
- string (5 m long)
- garden trowel
- aluminum or plastic tray
- paper towel, moistened with water
- hand lens
- toothpick or probe
- *Science Notebook*

SAFETY

Wear gloves during this activity. Do not touch any plants until they have been identified as safe by your teacher. Some plants—poison ivy, for example—can cause skin rashes.

4. In your chart, **list** the number and kinds of living and nonliving things that you see in your plot.

	Living Things	Nonliving Things	Not Sure Whether Living or Nonliving	Interactions
Plot				
Soil Sample 1				
Soil Sample 2				

Step 7

5. **List** any interactions you see between living things and between living and nonliving things in your plot.

6. Place a moist paper towel in the bottom of a tray. Use a garden trowel to take a small sample of soil from the plot. Spread the soil on the towel.

7. With a hand lens and a toothpick or probe, gently probe the soil for living and nonliving things. Do not injure any living things you find. **List** living and nonliving things in your soil sample and **describe** any interactions between them that you see. **Record** your observations.

8. Empty the tray in the same spot from which you took the soil sample.

9. Take another sample of soil from a different part of your plot of ground and repeat steps 6 through 8. Be sure to **record** your observations in the chart.

Analyze and Conclude

1. **Write a paragraph** that describes which living and nonliving things make up the plot you observed and any interactions you noted.

2. How did your predictions about what you would find in your plot compare with your observations?

3. What do you think was the purpose of repeating part of the activity using a second sample of soil?

4. How do living things in the plot depend on and interact with nonliving things?

5. *Eco-* means environment. A *system* is made up of parts that interact. Was your plot an example of an ecosystem? **Provide evidence** to support your answer.

The Nature of an Ecosystem

Reading Focus In what ways are forest and water ecosystems alike and different?

Imagine that you have spent the night camping out in the woods. As the Sun rises, you are cozy in your sleeping bag. You hear insects drone and squirrels chatter. You look up and see broad green leaves overhead. What you hear and see is your environment.

All the living and nonliving things around an organism is its environment. The forest is the natural environment of organisms such as squirrels, birds, worms, insects, and many kinds of plants.

As seen in the activity on pages D6 and D7, organisms interact with their environment. In the forest, birds eat insects and worms, which feed on decomposing animals. Dead plants rot, adding nutrients (noo' trē ənts) to the soil. Nutrients are substances that living things need for growth. Skunks nest in hollow trees, and white-footed mice burrow underground. Organisms

interacting with one another and with their physical environment make up an **ecosystem** (ek'ō sis təm).

The living (and once-living) things in an ecosystem are called the biotic (bī ät'ik) factors. Biotic factors include trees, birds, insects, and all other organisms. The nonliving things in an ecosystem are called abiotic factors. Abiotic factors include soil, rocks, rain, snow, air and ground temperature, and sunlight.

Ecosystem Dwellers

Organisms that live together in an ecosystem make up a **community**. A community contains many different populations of organisms. Each **population** contains all the organisms of the same kind in a community. A forest may have populations of squirrels, maples, woodpeckers, blue jays, worms, and so on. Together with other populations, they form a community. All the members of a population are members of the same species (spē' shēz).

Organisms of the same species have the same general physical characteristics and other adaptations (ad' əp tā'shənz). An **adaptation** is a structure or behavior that enables a species to survive and reproduce in its environment.

The role that each species plays in a community is its **niche** (nich). Where an organism lives is part of its niche. Another part of its niche is how it obtains food. No two species in a community have exactly the same niche.

The niche of each species in an ecosystem is a result of its adaptations. For example, a redheaded woodpecker nests in a hollow tree. Its beak is an adaptation for digging insects out of dead wood. In the same community, a blue jay nests in living tree branches and is adapted to eat mainly flying insects. So each species of bird occupies a different niche.

Ecosystem Size

An ecosystem may be small, containing only a few interacting species. A puddle that forms on the sidewalk after a rain is a small ecosystem. It may contain four species of microbes. An ecosystem may be large, such as a rain forest, which stretches for thousands of kilometers. It may contain millions of different species, from monkeys to beetles, from moss plants to oak trees. Most ecosystems are made up of many smaller ecosystems.

A Watery Ecosystem

You climb out of your sleeping bag and explore your environment. You ramble through the forest and come upon a large pond. You hear the plop of jumping fish. Turtles sun themselves on a fallen log, and lily pads float on the water. In this ecosystem, plants and animals are living in and on water rather than land.

Changing Ecosystems

You continue to explore. You come to a place where the pond meets the cornfields of a farm. Human activity has changed this landscape—the cornfield was once part of the forest. The cornfield, like the forest, is an ecosystem.

Logging, farming, road construction, industries, and homes all change ecosystems. Marshes can be filled in, and houses, cars, and people can replace muskrats and mice. Forests can make way for factories. What did humans do to change the ecosystem shown below from a forest to a warehouse?

Humans aren't responsible for all changes to ecosystems. Ecosystems change naturally, too. Lightning strikes, starting a forest fire. An earthquake cracks open the ground. These natural events change physical environments and as a result change ecosystems. At first such events may appear to be disastrous. In fact, they are often called natural disasters. With time, however, the number of populations in these communities will increase again.

▲ The ecosystem of Mount St. Helens changed drastically—but naturally.

The Mount St. Helens volcanic eruption proved how suddenly an ecosystem can change without human interference. On May 18, 1980, the slopes of Mount St. Helens in Washington fell strangely still. The birds stopped singing. The squirrels ceased their chatter.

Suddenly the mountain burst apart. Hot rock, ash, and steam billowed into the air, then rained down on the forest.

Boiling mudflows surged down the mountain. Within minutes, trees were flattened and wildlife disappeared. From the air, the once-lush mountainside looked gray and lifeless.

▲ A forest ecosystem may be replaced.

▲ The new ecosystem may not support the earlier community.

▲ **What used to be living trees looked like giant toothpicks after the eruption.**

▲ **Regrowth soon began.**

Although the land looked dead, it was really just "napping." Before long, plants protected by a layer of unmelted snow began to grow. Shoots from underground roots poked through the ash. Frogs, salamanders, and crayfish, sheltered by a layer of ice, swam in mountain lakes. Ladybugs, springtails, and beetles, hidden safely inside rotting logs, returned to the soil and air. Bacteria thrived in pockets of water. Seeds and insects blew in. Large mammals wandered in, carrying hitchhiker seeds that sprouted. Small animals that were adapted to living underground survived and produced offspring. It's been more than 20 years since the eruption, and Mount St. Helens is again populated with a rich variety of species.

Ecosystems are constantly changing. Some changes might be hard to see. Other changes, whether caused by nature or by humans, are dramatic. ■

Internet Field Trip

Visit **www.eduplace.com** to see examples of animals in their niches.

INVESTIGATION 1 WRAP-UP

REVIEW

1. Define biotic and abiotic factors. Give an example of each kind of factor.

2. Distinguish between a community and a population.

CRITICAL THINKING

3. Analyze the adaptive characteristics of red-headed woodpeckers and blue jays. Describe how those characteristics result in each organism having a unique niche.

4. Predict some adaptations that enable an animal such as a bird to survive and reproduce in a desert ecosystem.

HOW ARE LIVING THINGS IN AN ECOSYSTEM RELATED?

How did you get energy this morning? Did you eat a bowl of cereal? Different kinds of organisms have different ways of getting energy. In this investigation you'll see how the members of an ecosystem are related by the ways they get energy.

Activity

A Meal Fit for an Owl

By examining the remains of an owl's meal, you can find out a lot about how owls are related to other organisms in their ecosystem.

MATERIALS
- goggles
- owl pellet
- paper towel
- hand lens
- tweezers
- toothpick
- *Science Notebook*

SAFETY
Wear goggles during this activity.

Procedure

Unwrap an owl pellet and place it on a paper towel. Observe the outside of the pellet with a hand lens. Predict what you will find inside the pellet. Record your predictions. Use your fingers, tweezers, and a toothpick to separate the pellet's contents. Examine the parts carefully with the hand lens. Record your observations.

Analyze and Conclude

1. How did your findings compare with your predictions?

2. Based on your observations, infer what an owl eats. In what kind of an ecosystem would this owl live?

Activity

Lunch Time!

If you don't eat lunch, you might not have enough energy to have fun after school. Find out how the members of an ecosystem get their energy.

MATERIALS

- marker
- paper
- collecting net
- hand lens
- *Science Notebook*

Procedure

1. With your group, go to the area that your teacher has selected. Look for every organism in the ecosystem. You may wish to use a collecting net to find insects.

2. Have one member of your group make a chart like the one below. Have that person **record** the data the group collects.

See **SCIENCE** and **MATH TOOLBOX** page H11 if you need to review **Making a Chart to Organize Data.**

Organism	How It Gets Energy

3. Have another member carry the hand lens and do "close-up" studies of the organisms you see. **Record** all observations.

4. Using what you have just learned about ecosystems, **discuss** with your group how each organism obtains energy.

5. Back in the classroom, copy your observations into your *Science Notebook*. Work with your group and other groups to **construct a map** of the area surveyed.

Step 3

Analyze and Conclude

1. **Infer** how most of the organisms studied got energy for life processes.

2. Name any organisms in the ecosystem that produced energy that was used by other organisms in the ecosystem.

The Sun: Life's Energy Supply

Reading Focus How is the Sun's energy used by living things on Earth?

▲ **The Sun provides energy for Earth's organisms.**

SCIENCE TECHNOLOGY & SOCIETY

You've probably heard people say, "It's so hot outside, you could fry an egg on the sidewalk!" Fry an egg? Don't you need a stove for that?

No, you don't need a stove. You just need plenty of heat energy. And sometimes, when it's sunny and extremely hot, it can feel as though there is enough heat energy from the Sun to fry an egg.

Energy from the Sun reaches Earth as light and other forms of wave energy, such as infrared rays. Much of this energy is changed to heat energy in Earth's air, land, and oceans. Day after day, year in, year out, the Sun lights and warms Earth. In fact, the Sun can be considered an inexhaustible energy resource for people and other living things.

Plants Convert the Sun's Energy

What do you think would happen to Earth's ecosystems if the Sun's energy were blocked? If you said that most life on Earth would soon disappear, you would be correct. Almost all life on Earth depends on the Sun for energy, either directly or indirectly. All plants depend directly on the energy of the Sun. Certain groups of plantlike organisms, many of which are microscopic, also depend on the Sun. Included in this group are organisms called algae (al'jē). Plants and plantlike organisms use light energy from the Sun to make food through a process called photosynthesis (fōt ō sin'thə sis). These living things take in water and carbon dioxide, a gas that is in the air and water, and change them to sugar and oxygen. The sugar is the plant's food and contains stored energy. So a plant actually "stores" the Sun's energy. When animals eat plants, they also use the solar energy stored in the sugar.

Organisms that carry out photosynthesis contain a chemical called chlorophyll (klôr′ə fil). Chlorophyll is the substance in plants that gives leaves and stems their green color. It also stores light energy from the Sun for use during photosynthesis. Organisms that do not contain chlorophyll can't store light energy and therefore can't produce food from carbon dioxide and water.

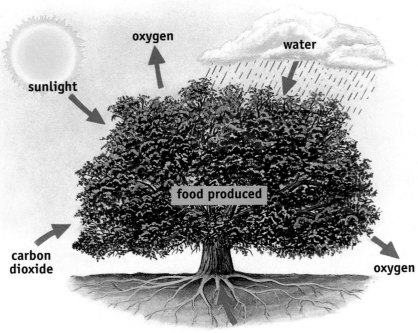

oxygen
water
sunlight
food produced
carbon dioxide
oxygen
water

▲ During photosynthesis, plants turn the energy in sunlight into food energy—the kind of energy that we need in order to live.

Nongreen Organisms Need the Sun

What would happen to nongreen organisms—such as you and your friends, a dog or a cat, or a mushroom—if the Sun's energy were blocked? You may think that you and these other organisms could get along just fine—after all, none of you contains chlorophyll or makes your own food. But think again!

Although animals and many other organisms can't use the Sun's energy directly, they still depend on the Sun. To obtain energy, animals must eat plants, or they must eat other animals that eat plants. Fungi (fun′jī), such as mushrooms, get energy by breaking

down the remains of dead animals and plants. You can see that nongreen organisms also depend on the Sun for energy. ■

INVESTIGATE FURTHER!

RESEARCH

The Sun is important to you in many ways. Find out whether solar power is used in your area. Hypothesize why it is a common or uncommon source of energy. In the library, research solar power. Decide whether a house in your area could be powered by solar energy alone.

What's to Eat?

Reading Focus In what ways do organisms in a forest obtain energy?

◀ **Great horned owls prey on small animals for food energy.**

It is mid-autumn, and the Sun is setting in the forest. A gray squirrel runs around the base of a maple tree, searching for food. Few acorns remain on the forest floor, so the squirrel ventures into a nearby clearing to nibble on fallen berries.

High above, a great horned owl perches on the branch of a red oak tree. The owl has begun its nightly search for prey. It hears the squirrel moving in the clearing. The owl focuses its eyes and prepares to attack.

The owl spreads its wings. In one swift silent swoop it seizes the squirrel in its talons.

Everyone Needs Food

Great horned owls thrive in forest ecosystems. There they find plenty of small mammals to feed on. In all ecosystems, each organism has its own way of getting food energy. Some organisms can use the Sun for food because they can carry on photosynthesis. These organisms are called **producers**. In forest ecosystems, producers include trees, vines, shrubs, ferns, and mosses.

Organisms that obtain energy by eating other organisms are called **consumers**. To get energy, consumers must eat producers or other consumers. Both owls and squirrels are consumers in a forest ecosystem. Squirrels eat acorns, berries, tree sap, and more than 100 kinds of plants. Owls eat squirrels, many other small mammals, and sometimes insects.

Another kind of consumer, called a **decomposer**, feeds on the wastes of living organisms and on dead, decaying plants and animals. Fungi, bacteria, and worms are forest decomposers. They release nutrients from animal waste and decaying matter and return those nutrients to the soil.

Three Kinds of Consumers

Consumers can be classified by the kinds of food they eat. Plant-eating consumers are called **herbivores** (hʉr′bə vôrz). Meat-eating consumers are called **carnivores** (kär′nə vôrz). Consumers that eat both plants and animals are known as **omnivores** (äm′ni vôrz).

Squirrels, deer, rabbits, mice, and most insects are examples of forest herbivores. Carnivores feed on herbivores and on other carnivores. The owl pellets in the activity on page D12 contain fur, bones, and other animal remains that owls cannot digest. You might be surprised to know that some owls can capture mammals as large as cats, rabbits, and skunks!

Omnivores eat both plants and animals. They often eat whatever is available. The forest-dwelling box turtle, for example, is an omnivore. It eats strawberries, blackberries, and mushrooms. It also eats insects and spiders.

Many forest birds are omnivores. For example, the wood thrush eats beetles, ants, and caterpillars as well as wild fruits and seeds. The Eastern bluebird feeds on grasshoppers and weevils. It also eats the fruits of holly, dogwood, and other plants.

Other ecosystems may contain organisms different from those of a forest. But all ecosystems contain producers, consumers, and decomposers. ■

UNIT PROJECT LINK

For this Unit Project you will make a science museum exhibit showing how ecosystems change over time. With other students brainstorm a list of living things you might find in your area. Devise a chart or make a map of the area. Then do a survey, marking the location of all the living things you find. You may use a camera to photograph some of these organisms in their environment. Compare your results with those of other students.

Technology Link

For more help with your Unit Project, go to **www.eduplace.com**.

▼ **Deer are herbivores.**

Wolves are meat eaters, or carnivores. ▶

Eat or Be Eaten

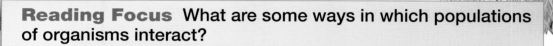

Reading Focus What are some ways in which populations of organisms interact?

The cycle of organisms eating and being eaten is a major part of life in an ecosystem. Every consumer has to eat in order to live. An organism that hunts and eats other organisms is called a predator (pred′ə tər). An organism that is hunted and eaten is called the prey.

The interaction between a predator and its prey is called a predator-prey relationship. Predator-prey relationships occur between populations of animals and other populations of animals.

The Size of a Population

As a predator population increases, it consumes more and more prey. Eventually, the prey become scarce. As a result the predators have trouble finding food. Then their population decreases. With fewer predators, the prey population increases again. In the evergreen forests of North America, the lynx and the hare have a predator-prey relationship. The lynx feeds on the hare. The lynx population increases

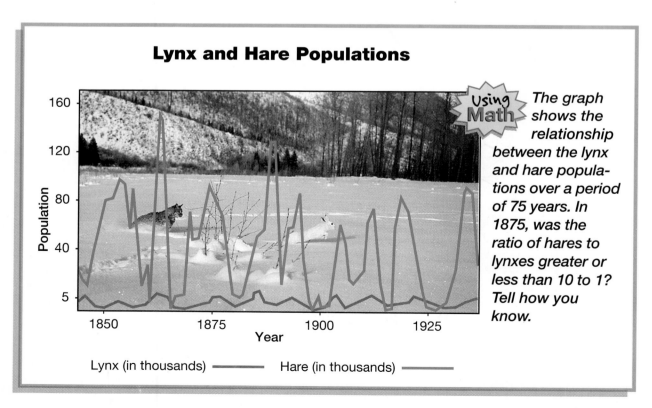

Lynx and Hare Populations

Using Math *The graph shows the relationship between the lynx and hare populations over a period of 75 years. In 1875, was the ratio of hares to lynxes greater or less than 10 to 1? Tell how you know.*

Population

Year

Lynx (in thousands) ——— Hare (in thousands) ———

when there are many hares. It decreases when hares are scarce.

Similar relationships take place between plants and animals. Elephants may eat so many plants in an area that the environment no longer contains enough food to keep animals alive. The elephants move on, allowing the plants in the environment to grow back.

It is not only predator-prey relationships that affect population size. Population size depends also on resources such as water and soil nutrients. For example, if a drought partly dries up a pond, the number of frogs in the pond will decrease. The size of a population of plants in a grassland depends on the supply of nutrients in the soil as well as the amount of rainfall.

For Better or for Worse

Some species form long-term close relationships with other species. This kind of relationship is called symbiosis (sim bī ō′sis). Symbiosis can occur between plants and microscopic organisms, animals and plants, and animals and other animals. The three kinds of symbiosis are explained below.

Ouch! That Hurts!

In **parasitism** (par′ə sīt iz əm), one organism lives in or on, feeds upon, and harms another organism. An organism that feeds on other organisms is called a parasite; the organisms that are fed upon are called hosts. A familiar example of parasitism is the relationship between a dog (host) and fleas and ticks

Science in Literature

The City Kid's Field Guide
by Ethan Herberman
Simon & Schuster, 1989

CITY BEES DRINK SODA

"It turns out that in addition to seeking out flowers, bees have made an important adaptation to city life by learning to drink soda and other sugary junk they find downtown and in city lots. The soda substitutes for nectar, of course; it allows the bees to make do with fewer flowers, although it's hard to imagine how the insects can stand it. Soda must taste awfully sour. Some nectar, after all, is at least four times as sweet."

This story about bees is from *The City Kid's Field Guide* by Ethan Herberman. The book tells you what goes on in vacant lots, parks, and garbage cans.

(parasites). Fleas and ticks live and feed upon dogs and other animals. The fleas and ticks benefit, and the dogs are harmed—and irritated!

No Harm Done

In **commensalism** (kə-men' səl iz əm), one species benefits, while the other species seems to be unaffected. Many kinds of animals have such relationships with plants. In some cases the animal resembles a certain part of a plant. When it is on that plant part, the animal cannot be seen by predators or prey. For example, a kind of crab spider resembles flower petals. The spider sits in a flower. When insects land on the flower, they are quickly eaten by the spider. While the spider profits, the flower is neither benefited nor harmed.

In **mutualism** (myoo'choo əl iz əm), all species that take part benefit from the relationship. For example, bees drink nectar from flowers. In the process they carry away pollen, which

▲ **A crab spider hiding in a flower (*left*) and lichens on a tree (*right*)**

pollinates other flowers. Both the bees and flowers benefit. Lichens are fungi and algae that live together. The algae produce sugars that the fungi use. The fungi supply the algae with water and nutrients.

Some microorganisms cause disease, but many are beneficial to humans. For example, large numbers of bacteria have mutualistic relationships with humans. In the human large intestine, bacteria live off parts of foods that humans can't use. These bacteria also make some nutrients that our bodies can use. ■

INVESTIGATION 2 WRAP-UP

REVIEW

1. By what basic process are the organisms in an ecosystem related?

2. Distinguish among herbivores, carnivores, and omnivores in an ecosystem.

CRITICAL THINKING

3. How might carnivores be affected by a decline in the number of producers in an ecosystem? Explain.

4. Classify an organism near your school or in a nearby park as a consumer, decomposer, or producer. Explain how the organism gets its energy. Describe its diet and the place where it lives.

REFLECT & EVALUATE

Word Power

Write the letter of the term that best matches the definition. *Not all terms will be used.*

1. Relationship that benefits one species and harms another
2. Organism that makes its own food
3. Animal that eats both plants and animals
4. Role of a species in a community
5. All the organisms living together in an ecosystem
6. Organism that eats only producers

a. community
b. herbivore
c. mutualism
d. niche
e. omnivore
f. parasitism
g. producer

Check What You Know

Write the term in each pair that best completes each sentence.

1. Soil and water in an ecosystem are (biotic, abiotic) factors.
2. Worms and bacteria in the soil are (producers, decomposers).
3. A meat-eating animal is a (carnivore, herbivore).
4. A community is made up of all the living things in a/an (niche, ecosystem).

Problem Solving

1. Like other organisms, you interact with your environment and are part of an ecosystem. Give three examples of ways that you interact with the living and nonliving parts of your environment.

2. Compare a fish and a turtle. What adaptations does each animal have to survive in a pond ecosystem?

BUILD YOUR PORTFOLIO

Study the photograph. Write the name of the type of relationship shown. Then write a paragraph explaining how the organisms benefit or are harmed by the relationship.

flea

cat's ear

2

ENERGY AND MATTER IN ECOSYSTEMS

An ecosystem is like a bustling city. Producers are busy storing energy. Consumers are always "shopping" for energy. And decomposers keep the city clean. The citizens of this "city" are plants, animals, and other living things.

PEOPLE USING SCIENCE

Ecologist Cynthia Wentworth is an ecologist, a scientist who studies how living things interact with each other and their environment. She works for the U.S. Forest Service.

Before becoming an ecologist, Wentworth spent 14 years as a medical technician. But her childhood love of the outdoors drew her away from the indoors and out into nature. Hoping to work at her first love, Wentworth returned to school to learn forestry. As an ecologist, Wentworth must be able to identify different species of plants and animals. Also, she must recognize animal habitats. Her work helps ensure that the environments she studies are preserved for their inhabitants.

Cynthia Wentworth studies living things, such as these mallard ducks, in their environment.

HOW DOES ENERGY FLOW IN AN ECOSYSTEM?

Energy moves through an ecosystem by being transferred from one organism to another. How does this happen? Find out in Investigation 1!

Activity

Energy in a Pond

A food chain shows the path that energy takes from the Sun through producers and consumers. You can trace some of the paths energy takes in a pond.

Procedure

1. The table lists pond organisms and their sources of food or energy. Use the information in the table to **identify** which organisms are producers and which are consumers. **Draw** a pond food chain. **Record** the data and the drawing in your *Science Notebook*.

2. You will work with three other students. Each person will choose one of the listed organisms and then play the role of that organism in the pond food chain. As you do this activity, remember that the organism whose role you play represents an entire population of that organism.

Organisms	Food or Energy Source
Pondweeds	sunlight
Algae	sunlight
Snails	pondweeds
Water fleas	algae
Minnows	snails, water fleas
Perches	minnows

3. A producer stores energy from the Sun in the food it makes. Use a 100-cm strip of paper to represent this stored energy. If you are the producer, measure and cut off 90 cm of the paper strip. This represents the amount of stored energy you use for growth and other activities.

Step 3

See **SCIENCE** and **MATH TOOLBOX** page H6 if you need to review **Using a Tape Measure or Ruler.**

4. If you are a consumer that eats the producer (a first-order consumer), take the 10 cm left from the 100-cm strip. This is the amount of stored energy available to you. Measure and cut 9 cm from the 10-cm strip. This represents the energy you use.

5. If you are a consumer that eats the first-order consumer (a second-order consumer), take the 1-cm strip from the first-order consumer. Measure and cut 9 mm from the 1-cm strip. This represents the energy you use. Pass the 1-mm strip on to a third-order consumer. This is the amount of stored energy left to pass on to that consumer.

Analyze and Conclude

1. Identify the producer and the consumers in your food chain.

2. About what percentage of the energy stored by producers is available to first-order consumers?

3. About what percentage of the energy obtained by first-order consumers is available to second-order consumers? About what percentage is available to third-order consumers?

4. Do you think this food chain could support a fourth-order consumer? Explain.

5. There are usually more producers than consumers in an ecosystem. Suggest a hypothesis to explain why this is so.

INVESTIGATE FURTHER!

Use the **Best of the Net— Science CD-ROM**, Life Sciences, *Nebraska Wildlife* site to learn the characteristics and habits of some of the animals that live in Nebraska. You'll also discover their habitat requirements and factors that can threaten their survival.

Activity

Weave a Food Web!

What happens when food chains overlap in an ecosystem? Do this activity and see for yourself!

MATERIALS

- goggles
- construction paper
- markers
- scissors
- bulletin board
- pushpins
- tape
- string
- *Science Notebook*

SAFETY

Wear goggles during this activity. Be careful when using pushpins.

Procedure

1. The table identifies feeding relationships in a grassland ecosystem. With your group, choose two food sources. **Predict** what would happen if they were removed from this ecosystem.

2. **Make a model** of a food web. **Draw** and **label** all the different grassland organisms and the Sun. Cut out the drawings and mount them on the bulletin board with pushpins. Leave space between the drawings.

3. Tape one end of a piece of string to any one of the drawings. Using the information in the table, connect the other end of the string to an organism that either eats it or is eaten by it.

4. **Draw** and cut out an arrow. Attach it to the string to indicate the flow of energy from one organism to another.

5. Use string to connect all the organisms according to their feeding relationships. Use arrows to show the direction of the energy flow. You have made a model of a food web.

Organisms	Food or Energy Source
Prairie dogs	roots of grasses grasshoppers
Snakes	mice, prairie dogs
Grasses	sunlight
Clover	sunlight
Hawks	snakes, mice, prairie dogs
Grasshoppers	grass, clover
Mice	grass seeds, shoots, grasshoppers
Fungi	dead plants
Bacteria	dead plants

Analyze and Conclude

1. Why is the term *food web* a good name for what you have just made?

2. Which organisms in your food web are the producers? Which are the consumers?

3. List three paths that the Sun's energy takes in this food web.

4. Suppose a disease killed all the grasshoppers. To show this, cut the strings that connect grasshoppers to all other consumers and producers. **Predict** how the death of the grasshoppers would affect other organisms in the ecosystem.

The Cycle of Food

Reading Focus What is the basic path that energy follows as it moves through an ecosystem?

Why do you eat lunch? If you didn't eat, you'd get very hungry, right? You'd probably also have trouble concentrating during the afternoon. You might even fall asleep in class!

All living things need energy to survive. This energy comes from food. The food you eat gives you the energy you need to move, breathe, and even think. But how does energy get into your food? The source of most life-giving energy is the Sun.

Capturing the Sun's Energy

Animals cannot use the Sun's energy to make food. But plants and other producers can do that job. Only producers can change energy from the Sun into food energy. Producers change the Sun's energy into food energy through a process called photosynthesis (fōt ō sin'thə sis). Much of this energy is used by the producer for growth and reproduction. Some of this energy is stored in the producer's cells for later use.

When a consumer eats a producer, some of this stored energy is passed on to the consumer. The consumer uses this energy to maintain its life. If this consumer is eaten by another consumer, energy stored in the first consumer's cells is passed on to the second consumer. This transfer of energy creates a food chain. A **food chain** is the path of energy transfer from one organism to another.

Using Math *People are consumers in food chains. Food energy is measured in units called Calories. One slice of bread contains about 75 Calories. Estimate the number of Calories you get from bread in one week.*

D27

Moving Up the Line

Plants are often the first link in a food chain. Because plants convert the Sun's energy into a usable form that can be passed on to other organisms, plants are called producers. Organisms that eat producers are called first-order consumers. Second-order consumers eat first-order consumers, and so on.

Trace the energy path in the ecosystem shown on page D29. When the crickets eat grass, they get only part of the energy that the grass received from the Sun. When the mice eat the crickets, the mice get only part of the energy that the crickets received from the grass. This pattern continues up to the hawks and the owls. Because less energy is available at each higher level in the food chain, there are fewer organisms at each higher level. So this ecosystem can support many more mice than owls or hawks.

Starting Over Again

All food chains include decomposers. Decomposers are organisms that get energy by breaking down dead plant and animal matter. Many decomposers, such

Fungi, such as mushrooms, are decomposers. ▼

as bacteria, fungi, and worms, can be found in soil. Where do you think decomposers are found in the salt marsh ecosystem?

Overlapping Food Chains

Most consumers and decomposers can get energy from more than one kind of food. An organism can be part of many food chains, causing food chains to overlap. In the activity on page D26, overlapping food chains form a **food web**. In a food web, an organism can be a first-order consumer in one food chain and a second- or third-order consumer in another food chain. What organisms in the salt marsh ecosystem are both second- and third-order consumers?

What About Us?

What is *your* place in food chains and food webs? Humans differ from many other consumers because of what they eat. Recall that herbivores eat only plants, and carnivores eat only animals. Humans, however, are omnivores. Omnivores eat both plants and animals.

As an omnivore, you can eat "high" or "low" on the food chain. If you eat animal foods, such as meat, eggs, and fish, you are eating high on the food chain. You are consuming other consumers. If you eat mostly plant foods, such as grains, fruits, and vegetables, you are eating low on the food chain. You are eating producers.

Internet Field Trip

Visit **www.eduplace.com** to find out more about organisms that are part of different food chains.

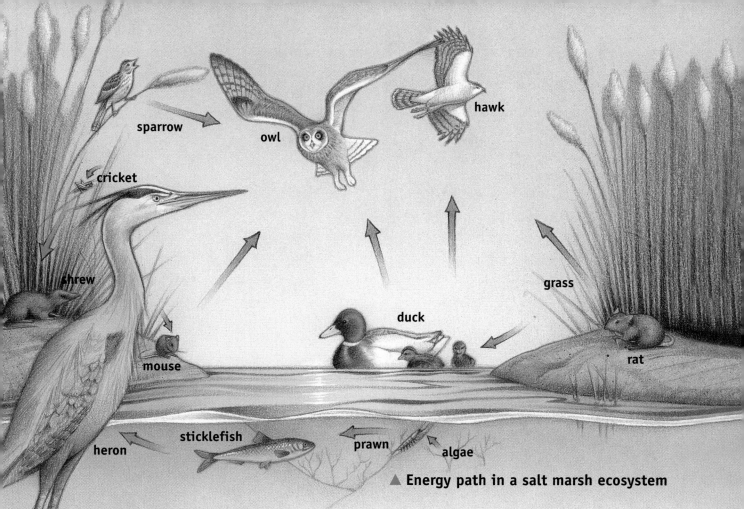

▲ **Energy path in a salt marsh ecosystem**

Many countries have abundant crops and the means to transport them. This enables people to eat fruits and vegetables, as well as meat, all year long. The climate of some regions, such as the Arctic, is harsh. Soil there does not support much plant growth. Because of the climate and the poor soil, these areas do not produce good crops. Unless fruits and vegetables are imported, people in these regions eat mostly fish and meat. In some places, then, there is a shortage of plant foods. So, energy is obtained high on the food chain. ■

INVESTIGATION 1 WRAP-UP

REVIEW

1. What is a food chain, and how is a food chain related to a food web?

2. Which type of organism, herbivore or carnivore, eats higher on the food chain?

CRITICAL THINKING

3. Describe a food web of which you are a part. What other organisms does your food web include?

4. Make a drawing that shows what happens to the amount of available energy in an ecosystem as the energy flows from producers through several levels of consumers.

Matter matters in ecosystems! Energy, although not used up, becomes unavailable as it moves through an ecosystem. Matter does *not* become unavailable. Instead, it cycles between living and nonliving portions of the ecosystem. How is this cycling done? Find out in Investigation 2.

Activity

Where's All the Water?

Water is matter. Plants help water cycle through an ecosystem. Find out how.

MATERIALS

- bean plant (in cup) with 4 or 5 leaves
- water
- small plastic bag
- rubber band
- *Science Notebook*

- -

Procedure

Your teacher will give you a bean plant in a cup. Add water to the plant so that the soil is moist. Loosely cover two or three of the leaves of the plant with a plastic bag. Place a rubber band around the bag and stem to hold the bag in place.

Leave the cup in a sunny spot for two days. Each day, **observe** the plant and **record** any changes in your *Science Notebook*. Note how the inside of the bag looks. **Observe** the leaves that aren't covered by the plastic bag.

Analyze and Conclude

1. What happened to the water in the soil over the two days?

2. Plants take in water and return some of it to the air through their leaves. What evidence do you have of this process?

Activity

Every Breath You Take

Your body uses the oxygen you inhale to release energy from the food you eat. You exhale one of the waste products, carbon dioxide. What happens to that carbon dioxide?

MATERIALS

- goggles
- beaker (250 mL)
- 2 wide-mouthed plastic cups
- water
- dropper
- bromothymol blue (BTB) solution
- plastic straw
- *Elodea* plant
- 2 test tubes
- timer
- *Science Notebook*

Procedure

1. Fill a beaker about two-thirds full with water. Use a dropper to add enough BTB solution to turn the water blue.

2. Using a plastic straw, blow into the BTB solution. **Record** in your *Science Notebook* what happens.

3. Put an *Elodea* plant in a test tube. Completely fill each of two test tubes with the BTB solution from the beaker.

4. Place your thumb over the mouth of the first test tube to seal it. Turn the test tube upside down and put it in a plastic cup, as shown. Do not let air get into the test tube. Do the same thing with the second test tube. Wash your hands.

5. Put the test tube setups in a sunny place for one hour. **Predict** what changes, if any, will take place. **Record** your predictions. After one hour, **observe** both test tubes and **record** your observations.

SAFETY

Wear goggles. Do not suck on the straw. If you accidentally do, do not swallow. Spit out the liquid. Rinse your mouth several times with tap water.

See **SCIENCE** *and* **MATH TOOLBOX** *page H14 if you need to review **Measuring Elapsed Time.***

Analyze and Conclude

1. In step 2, the carbon dioxide that you breathed out caused a change in the BTB. Describe that change.

2. In step 5, how did the BTB change after one hour? **Compare** it with the BTB in the other test tube. What can you **infer** about the carbon dioxide you breathed into the BTB?

3. In what way are you and plants cycling matter?

Step 4

The Carbon Dioxide–Oxygen Cycle

Reading Focus How do photosynthesis and cell respiration work together in the cycling of matter?

1 During cell respiration, living things use oxygen, given off by plants, to break down food and obtain energy. When organisms carry out this process, carbon dioxide is given off into the air and the water.

▲ **How carbon dioxide and oxygen are cycled in ecosystems**

Take a deep breath. As you inhale, you take in oxygen, as well as nitrogen, carbon dioxide, and water vapor in air. When you exhale, you breathe out less oxygen than you took in. You also breathe out more carbon dioxide than you took in. Each time you breathe, you take part in the worldwide **carbon dioxide–oxygen cycle**. Look at the drawing to follow the steps in the cycle.

Into the Soil

Did you know that soil is a major part of the carbon dioxide–oxygen cycle? Plant roots deep in the soil take in water. In the plant the water is combined with carbon dioxide to form sugar, a carbon compound rich in energy. Rotting plant and animal matter contain this carbon compound. Carbon is released as carbon dioxide when decomposers break down the plant and animal matter. The use of oxygen to break down carbon compounds and release energy is called **cell respiration** (res pə rā′shən). Carbon dioxide is a waste product of cell respiration. The activity on page D31 includes a test for carbon dioxide in exhaled breath. This is evidence of cell respiration.

2 During **photosynthesis**, plants use carbon dioxide, water, and energy from the Sun to make food in the form of sugar. They give off oxygen as a waste product.

4 As plants and animals decay, they add carbon compounds to the air and soil.

3 A plant breaks down some food for energy and stores the rest. This stored energy is passed from one organism to another in food chains.

Shells are storehouses of carbon and oxygen on the ocean bottom. ▶

Into the Ocean

Carbon dioxide and oxygen cycle through ocean ecosystems, too. For instance, in ocean food chains, algae are producers. Algae are plantlike organisms that carry out photosynthesis. The oxygen released during this process may be used by other sea creatures during cell respiration. Carbon dioxide is released into the water as a waste product.

The ocean acts as a storage site for carbon dioxide and oxygen. Some ocean organisms use carbon and oxygen, along with calcium, to make their shells. When these organisms die,

their shells settle on the ocean floor, trapping carbon.

The carbon dioxide–oxygen cycle is important to organisms in ecosystems on land as well as in water. Without the delicate balance of both carbon dioxide and oxygen, organisms could not survive. ■

The Water Cycle

Reading Focus What processes cycle water through the environment?

2 As water vapor rises, it cools and changes back into a liquid, forming clouds. Eventually the clouds release this water as precipitation.

1 An evaporating puddle is only a very small part of the world-wide cycling of water. The Sun's energy causes liquid water to evaporate from all over the Earth's surface.

▲ **How water is cycled in ecosystems**

Like carbon dioxide and oxygen, water moves in a continuous cycle through the land, oceans, air, and living things of Earth. This constant movement of water is called the **water cycle**. The Sun is the main engine that drives the water cycle.

Have you ever watched a puddle disappear after the Sun came out? Where does the water go? Some of it seeps into the ground. Much returns to the air as water vapor. The process by which liquid water changes to water vapor is **evaporation** (ē vap ə rā′shən).

Into and Out of the Air

Much of the water that evaporates from Earth's surface—about 84 percent—comes from the ocean. When water vapor reaches cool air above Earth, it changes to tiny droplets of liquid water that forms clouds. The process by which water vapor changes to liquid water is called **condensation** (kän dən sā′shən).

After water has condensed to form clouds, it can fall back to Earth in the form of precipitation (prē sip ə tā′shən) such as rain or snow.

3 Much precipitation falls into the ocean, lakes, and streams. Some water runs along the surface of the ground and ends up in bodies of water. Water also seeps into the ground.

4 Organisms take in water for their daily activities. Through transpiration, plants return some water back to the atmosphere. Both plants and animals also release water as a result of respiration.

The Role of Living Things

Living things are an important link in the water cycle. All living things need water to survive. Water carries nutrients, flushes away wastes, and is needed for life processes. Animals drink water or take in water in the food they eat. Some of this water is released back to the environment as waste products of digestion and cell respiration.

Plants also cycle water through ecosystems. Precipitation that seeps into soil may be taken in by plants through their roots. Recall that plants use some of this water, along with carbon dioxide

and sunlight, when they carry out photosynthesis and produce sugars. When the plants break down the sugars during cell respiration, water, along with carbon dioxide, is formed as a waste product. Water vapor is released through leaves in a process called transpiration (tran spə rā′shən). There is evidence of this process in the activity on page D30.

In places with a great many plants, such as tropical rain forests, as much as 90 percent of the rainfall is cycled back to the air by the plants. What happens to the water once it is again in the air? ■

RESOURCE

Recycling Waste Water

Reading Focus How do humans use water and care for water resources?

Water—we drink it, cook with it, bathe in it, and flush toilets with it. We swim in pools of it. We wash our clothes, dishes, and cars with it, and sprinkle our lawns with it. Farms and factories also use large quantities of water. An average of 2,000 L (500 gal) of water per person every day is used for all of these activities. How can people get along without water?

The answer is we can't. The human body is made up of about two-thirds water. In this way people are similar to most organisms. As the activity on page D30 shows, plants also need water. In fact, all living things contain water and need it to survive.

In addition to being vital to life, water is useful in many ways. And there's a lot of it around. In fact, about three fourths of Earth's surface is covered by water.

Some Uses of Water

Did You Know?

- Sugar cane plants need 681 L (180 gal) of water to produce 1 kg (2.2 lb) of sugar.

- It takes 1,242 L (328 gal) of water to produce .45 kg (1 lb) of rice.

- A hen must drink 769 mL (26 oz) of water to produce 1 egg.

- A cow must drink 3.78 L (1 gal) of water to produce 0.94 L (1 qt) of milk.

Using Math *How much water does a cow need to drink to provide a one-week supply of milk for you?*

D36

With all of the water on Earth, you might think that people never need to worry about having enough water. But this is not the case. Not all of Earth's water is usable. Much of it is salt water. Some water is frozen in polar icecaps or locked in soil. Also, when people use water, it can become dirty from soaps and detergents. When water combines with food wastes and human wastes, this used water becomes sewage.

When people dump sewage into rivers and lakes, these bodies of water get dirty. Soon there's less clean water for all organisms to use. That's why towns and cities build sewage treatment plants—places that clean up waste water.

Sewage treatment plants can't cure all sewage problems. For one thing, it may not be possible to remove all types of wastes that get added to water. Some disease-causing microscopic organisms that live in sewage may not be removed by the treatment process. Also, sewage treatment plants are costly to build and maintain. An accident can cause untreated sewage to be spilled back into Earth's waterways. And, in some places, towns are running out of money needed to treat their sewage.

Many people are trying to find new ways to solve the various sewage problems. They have found that natural processes of plants and of certain types of microscopic organisms, such as bacteria, can be used to help clean up sewage.

Science in Literature

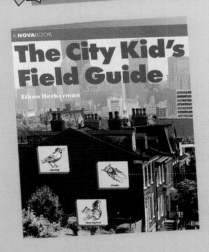

The City Kid's Field Guide
by Ethan Herberman
Simon & Schuster, 1989

THIRSTY ROACHES?

"Cockroaches will eat almost anything. . . . The roaches will live off the glue on postage stamps, the binding in books, the insulation in a TV. Or they will eat nothing. Assuming they get water, they will live two months on that. No water? One month."

Want to know more about cockroaches? Read *The City Kid's Field Guide* by Ethan Herberman. You'll also learn why a pill bug will die if a particular body part becomes too dry. And you'll find out more about what city living is like for plants and animals.

▲ Marshes are used in sewage treatment in Arcata, California.

One Town's Solution

The town of Arcata, California, has found a solution to its sewage treatment problems. Instead of using a huge sewage treatment plant, Arcata uses marshes that teem with wildlife to clean its water.

Arcata's sewage flows first into a holding tank. Next, it moves into a huge concrete tub, where solid materials settle to the bottom. The waste water is then drained from the tub into a large pond that has no plants. Here, bacteria begin to break down the harmful compounds in the water. When the water leaves the pond, it is treated with chlorine to kill the disease-causing organisms.

Next the water enters a series of marshes. These marshes are filled with many kinds of aquatic plants, including duckweed, cattails, and bulrushes. Bacteria and other small organisms cling to the underwater stems of these aquatic plants. These bacteria filter and clean the waste water. By the time the water flows into a nearby bay, it is cleaner than the bay water.

The people of Arcata have a sewage treatment facility that doesn't have a bad smell and doesn't break down. It's also not costly to maintain. It's a recreation area and wildlife preserve, attracting wildlife, joggers, and birdwatchers. Most importantly, the facility cleans waste water very well. ■

UNIT PROJECT LINK

Create a display of how the populations of living things in your neighborhood have changed. Find out how people lived there 200 years ago. Then find out how plant and animal populations have changed during the same time. Consider how human activities affected both living and nonliving things in your neighborhood. Also consider how the cycles of energy and matter may have changed over time.

Technology Link

For more help with your Unit Project, go to **www.eduplace.com**.

The Nitrogen Cycle

Reading Focus How is nitrogen cycled through the air and soil?

You know that living things need energy, oxygen, and water. Living things also need proteins. **Proteins** are compounds that act as the building blocks of living things. Some proteins control chemical processes that take place in the human body. Other proteins make up body parts including cells, hair, and nails.

Nitrogen is needed to make proteins. Earth's atmosphere is about 78 percent nitrogen gas. With all this nitrogen, you might think that your body could use the nitrogen that you inhale. But that isn't so. Nitrogen gas can't be used directly by most organisms. Before nitrogen can be used, it must be "fixed," or changed into nitrogen compounds.

The wastes that organisms produce, as well as the remains of dead organisms, are sources of nitrogen. Decomposers feed on waste products and dead organisms. The nitrogen they release is in the form of ammonia, which plants can use. Certain bacteria change ammonia into compounds that can also be used by plants. Unused compounds are broken down by bacteria that release nitrogen gas back to the air. Look at the diagram on the next page to see how nitrogen cycles through an ecosystem.

Look at the percentages of nitrogen in inhaled and exhaled air. Is nitrogen in air used directly to form protein? How do you know? ▼

nitrogen

78 percent

78 percent

21 percent

oxygen

17 percent

argon

0.03 percent

carbon dioxide

4 percent

other gases

Air breathed in

Air breathed out

1 In the **nitrogen cycle**, nitrogen gas is converted to a usable form and eventually returned to the atmosphere as nitrogen gas.

2 Lightning changes some nitrogen gas into nitrogen compounds. These compounds are washed to Earth in rain. Some of the nitrogen compounds enter the soil with rainwater.

5 Proteins in wastes and in the remains of dead organisms are broken down by decomposers to ammonia, nitrites, and nitrates. These compounds are used by plants or break down into nitrogen gas, which passes into the air.

3 Nitrogen is made usable by bacteria that grow on the roots of plants such as beans and peas. These bacteria turn nitrogen into ammonia. Other bacteria change ammonia into nitrates that can also be used by plants.

4 Plants use ammonia and nitrates to make proteins. Animals get nitrogen by eating plants or other animals.

▲ **How nitrogen is cycled in ecosystems**

INVESTIGATION 2 WRAP-UP

REVIEW

1. Sketch how water is recycled in ecosystems.

2. What are the roles of oxygen and carbon dioxide in cell respiration and photosynthesis?

CRITICAL THINKING

3. Modern farming practices speed up the decomposition of matter in soil. How might this affect the nitrogen cycle?

4. Compost, which is made from grass clippings, leaves, and food wastes that are broken down, can be used to enrich soil. What organisms must be part of a compost pile?

REFLECT & EVALUATE

Word Power

Write the letter of the term that best matches the definition. *Not all terms will be used.*

1. The use of oxygen to release energy from food
2. Overlapping food chains in an ecosystem
3. A group of compounds that are building blocks of living things
4. Consumer that eats only animals
5. Path of energy transfer from one organism to another
6. Process of changing water vapor to liquid water

a. carnivore
b. cell respiration
c. condensation
d. evaporation
e. food chain
f. food web
g. protein

Check What You Know

Write the term in each pair that best completes each sentence.

1. A carnivore's position on the food-chain is (high, low).
2. During cell respiration, oxygen is (used up, released).
3. Photosynthesis is an important process in the (carbon dioxide-oxygen, nitrogen) cycle.
4. Nitrogen is a substance found in (protein, sugar).

Problem Solving

1. Imagine that Earth stopped receiving light from the Sun. What effect would the lack of sunlight have on food chains and food webs? What effect would it have on the carbon dioxide–oxygen cycle? the water cycle? the nitrogen cycle?

2. Suppose you work on a farm. Identify three ways that you could improve the nitrogen content of the soil. What are the advantages and disadvantages of each of your proposed improvements?

Study the drawing. Then write a paragraph explaining each organism's role in food chains and food webs.

CHAPTER 3

DIFFERENT KINDS OF ECOSYSTEMS

Do you live in the American Southwest? If so, you may see cactuses outside your window. Perhaps you live somewhere else. You may see the Northeast's maple trees or the Southeast's palms. Wherever you live, you are part of a large ecosystem. If your ecosystem changes, your life and the life of every other organism will change, too.

PEOPLE USING SCIENCE

Biologist If you had visited Kenya in 1977, you would have seen a land stripped of trees. Ninety percent of Kenya's forests had been cut down. As the forests disappeared, so did Kenya's streams and wildlife. Wood for fuel had nearly vanished. Without fuel it was difficult to cook healthful foods. As a result, children were not eating well. The natural ecosystem was being destroyed. Every organism in the ecosystem suffered.

That same year a Kenyan biologist named Wangari Maathai began to save the ecosystem. She started a tree-planting project, called the Green Belt Movement, in which young trees are given to women farmers to plant. Maathai's idea has been a great success. In just the first ten years of the project, the Green Belt planted 5 million trees!

▲ Wangari Maathai's Green Belt Movement helped restore Kenya's ecosystem.

HOW DO EARTH'S MAJOR ECOSYSTEMS DIFFER?

Some ecosystems, like a backyard garden, are very small. Others, such as deserts or oceans, cover vast areas of Earth's surface. In this investigation you'll find out the characteristics that make each of Earth's major ecosystems unique.

Activity

Make a Mini-Biome!

Ecosystems that cover large areas of Earth's land surface are called biomes. In this activity you can make a model of the biome of your choice and see how abiotic factors affect it.

Procedure

1. From the table on the next page, choose the kind of plant you wish to grow. Your teacher will give you several specimens of that kind of plant.

2. Work on newspaper. Cover the bottom of a large jar with a layer of activated charcoal 0.5 cm thick. Use the table to find the kind of soil your plants need. Place a layer of this kind of soil, 3 cm deep, on top of the charcoal.

Math Hint

In step 2, remember that 0.5 cm equals $\frac{1}{2}$ cm.

MATERIALS

- goggles
- newspaper
- gardening gloves
- plants (several of the same kind)
- large plastic jar
- activated charcoal
- metric ruler
- potting soil
- sand
- grass seed
- water in a spray bottle
- *Science Notebook*

SAFETY

Use gardening gloves to handle plants that have needles or spines. Wear goggles when handling soil.

Kind of Plant	Soil Type	How Often to Water
Broad-leaved	potting	every 2–3 days
Cactus	sand	lightly, every 2 weeks
Grass	potting	every other day
Needle-leaved	potting-sand mixture	weekly

3. Carefully lift the plants out of their pots, making sure that most of the soil clings to the roots. Place the plant roots in the soil in the jar. Be sure the roots are completely covered so that the plant is well anchored. If you choose to grow grass, scatter the seeds on the soil and cover them with a thin layer of soil.

4. Place your mini-biome in a sunny spot. Use a spray bottle to moisten the soil. Use the table as a guide to watering the plants.

5. Observe your mini-biome daily. Record your observations in your *Science Notebook*.

6. Observe the mini-biomes of the other students. Compare the various biomes represented in your class.

Analyze and Conclude

1. The biomes varied as to the kind of plants, type of soil, and amount of watering. What abiotic factors were the same for all the biomes represented?

2. Which two biomes had the most similar growing conditions? Which two had the least similar conditions? Infer what would happen if you switched the plants growing under the least similar conditions.

3. What is the relationship between abiotic factors in a biome and the kind of plant life found there?

INVESTIGATE FURTHER!

EXPERIMENT

Plan your own experiment to find out how well the plants in your mini-biomes can live under different conditions (see Question 2 under Analyze and Conclude). Work with a partner to write a question you can test about what might happen to plants if you changed their conditions. Then write a procedure for your experiment that other students can follow.

Step 3

Earth's Biomes

Reading Focus What are some abiotic and biotic factors of each kind of biome?

The abiotic factors of an area include climate and soil type. Along with the biotic factors, such as plants and animals, abiotic factors determine an area's ecosystem. Ecosystems that cover large areas of land are called **biomes**.

The major biomes on Earth are the deciduous (dē sij' oo əs) forest, the desert, the grassland, the taiga (tī'gə), the tropical rain forest, and the tundra. This world map shows you where these biomes are found. Humans live in all biomes, but some biomes support human populations better than others do.

UNIT PROJECT LINK

Create a model of the biome where you live. Find out which biome you live in and how biomes can change over time. Work with others to create a model of your biome as it might have looked before any people inhabited it. Include any extinct plants and animals that once lived there.

Technology Link

For more help with your Unit Project, go to **www.eduplace.com**.

The largest number of people live in biomes that have abundant plant and animal resources. Many people also live in biomes with milder climates, such as temperate and tropical regions. Temperate and tropical regions are close to the equator. These biomes receive enough solar energy to support a great many living communities.

On the next two pages you'll find out about the abiotic and biotic factors of each biome. And you'll learn how these factors make each biome unique.

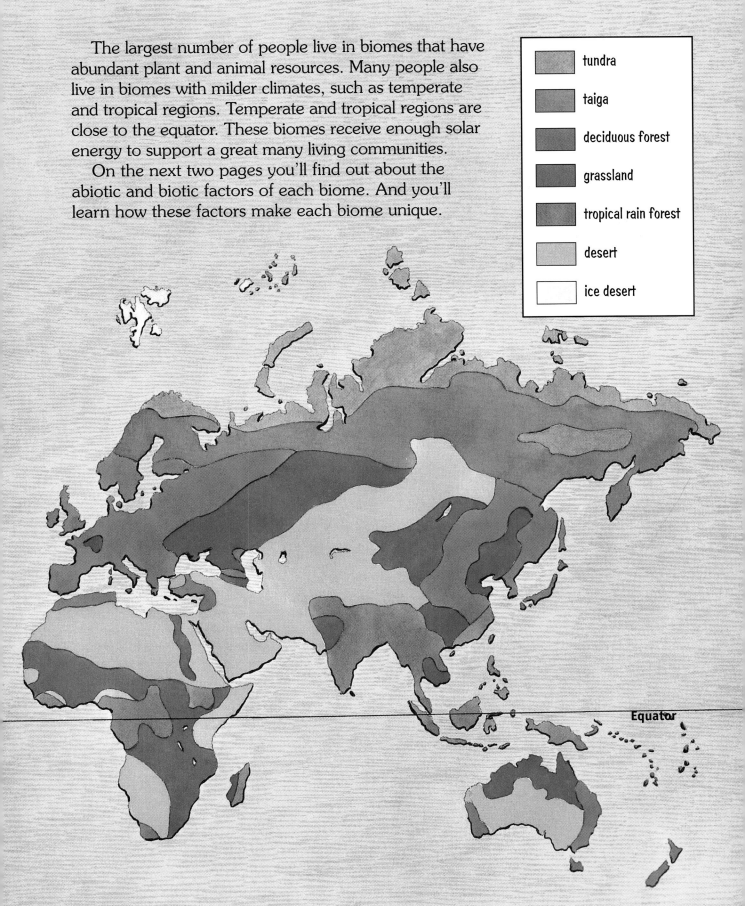

tundra

taiga

deciduous forest

grassland

tropical rain forest

desert

ice desert

Equator

toucan

◀ **TROPICAL RAIN FOREST Tropical rain forests** are lush and green year-round. Heavy rainfall and a warm climate create an environment in which an amazing variety of plants and animals thrive. These plants and animals live in "layers" of the forest, from the ground to the tops of trees. Tree branches form one layer known as the canopy.

GRASSLAND Grasslands are ▶ wide-open fields of grass that once covered vast areas of every continent except Antarctica. The kinds of grasses that grow in a grassland depend on the amount of rainfall in that particular grassland. Wetter areas have taller grasses; drier areas have shorter grasses. Grasslands attract grazing animals and rodents, as well as their predators.

field mouse

◀ **DESERT Deserts** can be either hot or cold, but they are always very dry. So desert plants and animals have to survive without much water. As a result, few types of plants grow in desert ecosystems. Animal populations also are not diverse.

horned lizard

D48

DECIDUOUS FOREST **Deciduous forests** grow where winters are cold and summers are warm and wet. The large leaves of deciduous trees—maple, oak, and birch, for example—carry out photosynthesis. Their leaves are lost in autumn. There is plenty of food for insects, birds, rodents, and other animals in these forests.

beetle

TAIGA The **taiga** contains ▶ coniferous forests where evergreens such as spruce, pine, and fir trees grow. In the taiga the winters are long and cold. On the forest floor are low-growing mosses and lichens. Many birds and mammals prey on needle-eating insects and seed-eating rodents.

lodgepole pine cone

◀ **TUNDRA** The **tundra** is the Arctic grassland north of the taiga where the subsoil is frozen year-round. The tundra has long, cold winters and cool summers. There is little precipitation. A thin layer of snow and ice covers the ground most of the year. The few plants and animals that live in the tundra survive a growing season that is only two to three months long.

saxifrage

Water Ecosystems

Reading Focus What are some abiotic and biotic factors of freshwater and saltwater ecosystems?

Look back at the map on pages D46 and D47. As you read earlier, about three fourths of Earth's surface is covered by water! There are two main kinds of water ecosystems: freshwater ecosystems and saltwater ecosystems. Each of these ecosystems includes a number of smaller ecosystems in which a great variety of organisms live.

Freshwater Ecosystems

Only 3 percent of the water on Earth is fresh. And over two thirds of that fresh water is locked in ice at the North Pole or the South Pole or at the tops of mountains. The remaining fresh water is in the ground or is surface water.

Fresh water fills all the lakes, ponds, rivers, streams, swamps, marshes, and bogs of the world. The variety of living things in a freshwater community depends on whether the water is still or flowing, slow-moving or fast-moving. It also depends on other abiotic factors, such as the water temperature, whether the water is clear or cloudy, and how much oxygen the water contains. All these factors are connected. Cold water, for example, holds more oxygen than warm water; fast-moving water holds more oxygen than slow-moving water. Look at the picture to get the idea about the variety of life forms some freshwater ecosystems support.

great blue heron

RIVER A river is running water that empties into a lake, an ocean, or another river. Some rivers are wide and slow-moving. Others are narrow and fast-moving. The underwater ecosystems of rivers vary a great deal. Rivers support freshwater fish, shrimp, plants, birds, and other life forms.

pickerelweed

Freshwater Ecosystems

deciduous trees

WETLAND A **wetland** is an area where land and water meet. The soil of a wetland is watery and the concentration of oxygen is less than in a river or lake. Many types of wetlands exist. A marsh has mostly grasses and cattails. A swamp is similar to a marsh but has mostly trees and shrubs. A bog consists primarily of mosses.

LAKE A **lake** is a large standing body of fresh water. Lakes range in size from huge expanses, such as Lake Superior, to small bodies of water. The place in which an organism lives is its habitat. A lake contains a variety of habitats, but each lake is different. Lake fish include perch and bass. Lakes also support frogs, insects, and other water life.

blue-winged teal

waterlily

cattail

leopard frog

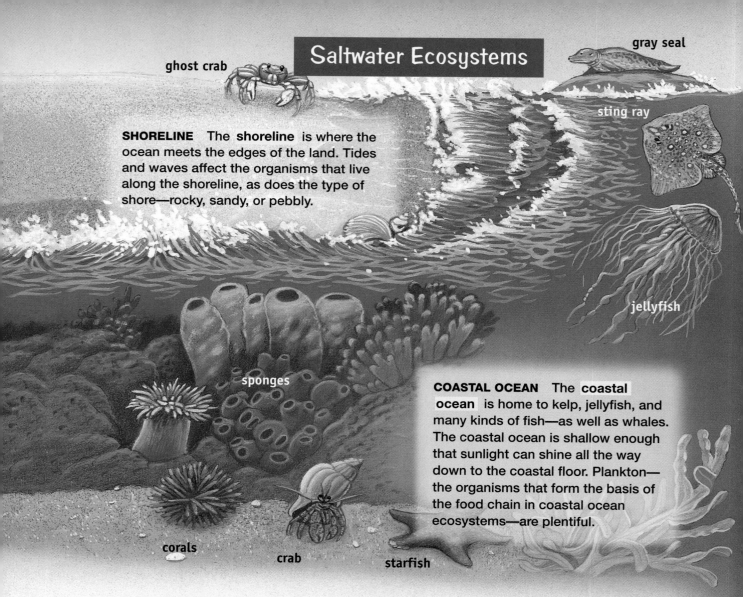

Saltwater Ecosystems

ghost crab

gray seal

sting ray

jellyfish

SHORELINE The **shoreline** is where the ocean meets the edges of the land. Tides and waves affect the organisms that live along the shoreline, as does the type of shore—rocky, sandy, or pebbly.

sponges

COASTAL OCEAN The **coastal ocean** is home to kelp, jellyfish, and many kinds of fish—as well as whales. The coastal ocean is shallow enough that sunlight can shine all the way down to the coastal floor. Plankton—the organisms that form the basis of the food chain in coastal ocean ecosystems—are plentiful.

corals

crab

starfish

Saltwater Ecosystems

Ninety-seven percent of Earth's water is salty ocean water. Actually, the oceans are one continuous body of water. The forms of life this ecosystem supports vary from tiny one-celled organisms to enormous mammals. In general, different organisms are found at different depths.

Ocean water generally contains about 3.5 percent salt, but this amount can vary. This variation is important. The amount of salt in water can either support organisms or kill them. Water pressure, temperature, and light also affect the types of organisms that live in salt water. So, there are really several different saltwater ecosystems.

The next time someone talks about the ocean as if it were one big ecosystem, you may want to set them straight. Explain that saltwater ecosystems are not as simple as they seem. To understand them, you must observe and study them. ■

Internet Field Trip

Visit **www.eduplace.com** to learn more about plants and animals in ocean ecosystems.

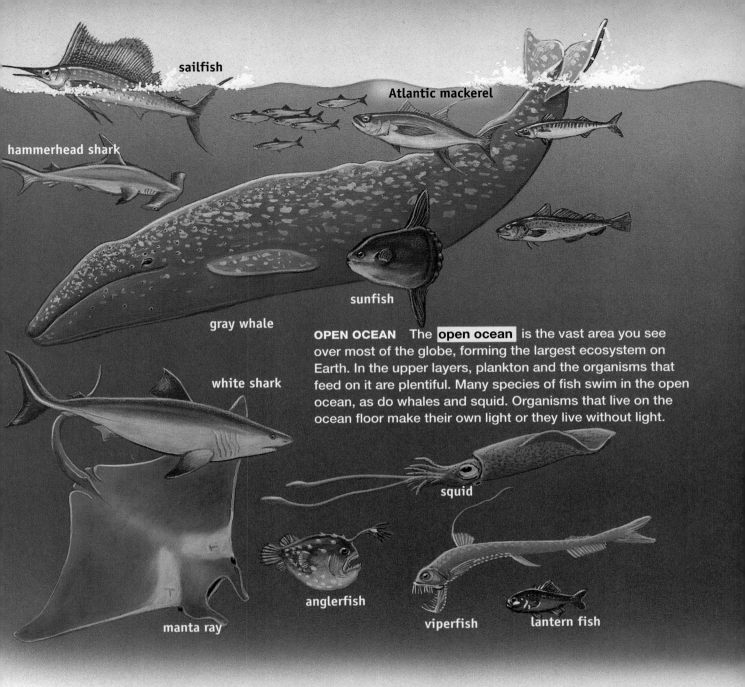

sailfish

Atlantic mackerel

hammerhead shark

sunfish

gray whale

white shark

OPEN OCEAN The open ocean is the vast area you see over most of the globe, forming the largest ecosystem on Earth. In the upper layers, plankton and the organisms that feed on it are plentiful. Many species of fish swim in the open ocean, as do whales and squid. Organisms that live on the ocean floor make their own light or they live without light.

squid

anglerfish

viperfish

lantern fish

manta ray

INVESTIGATION 1 WRAP-UP

REVIEW

1. Describe some abiotic and biotic factors that vary among different land biomes.

2. Give an example of each of the two main kinds of water ecosystems.

CRITICAL THINKING

3. Deciduous forests and grasslands have supported large human populations. Why do you think this is so?

4. Explain how desert plants and animals are adapted to live in their ecosystem.

INVESTIGATION 2

WHAT IS BIODIVERSITY, AND HOW IS IT CHANGING?

Earth's ecosystems are home to millions of species of living things. Each species in an ecosystem plays a role. In this investigation you'll find out about species diversity in ecosystems and how changes in this diversity affect an ecosystem.

Activity
Vanishing Species

When ecosystems change, some species may die out. Try to find one factor that has led to the decline of a rain forest in Ecuador.

Procedure

1. Look at the maps. They show how the area covered by tropical rain forests in Ecuador has changed since 1938. Forests are shown in green. In your *Science Notebook*, **describe** what has happened between 1938 and 1988.

2. Refer to the table on the next page. **Make a bar graph** that shows the change in Ecuador's forested area based on the data from 1961, 1971, 1991, and 1995.

See **SCIENCE** *and* **MATH TOOLBOX** *page H3 if you need to review **Making a Bar Graph.***

FORESTS OF ECUADOR 1938–1988

ECUADOR

SOUTH AMERICA

Equator

Forest Cover 1938
Quito
Guayaquil

Forest Cover 1958
Quito
Guayaquil

Forest Cover 1988
Quito
Guayaquil

N

Ecuador				
	1961	**1971**	**1991**	**1995**
Forest & Woodland	173,000 km²	153,000 km²	112,000 km²	110,920 km²
Human Population	5,162,000	7,035,000	10,782,000	11,920,000

3. Look again at the table. Notice how the human population in Ecuador had grown over the 34-year period. **Make a bar graph** that shows the change in Ecuador's human population based on the data from the table.

Analyze and Conclude

1. **Compare** the graphs you drew. What appears to be the relationship between the change in the human population and the change in the amount of forested land in Ecuador?

2. Based on your knowledge of food webs, **infer** what happens to a rain forest community when the trees are cut down.

Science in Literature

PROTECTING PANDAS

"Heavy mists and rains shroud bamboo and coniferous forests in the mountains of China's Sichuan province, home to giant panda bears. Of the estimated 750 pandas in the wild, more than half live in 12 reserves set aside for their protection. Farming, logging, and building have eliminated much of their habitat. . . . Since 1987, the death penalty awaits anyone convicted of killing giant pandas or smuggling their skins."

Bears
by Joni Phelps Hunt
Blake Books, 1993

This quote is from *Bears* by Joni Phelps Hunt. The book describes sloth bears, sun bears, spectacled bears, and other kinds of bears found in almost every part of the world. It shows some of the best bear photos ever taken!

Variety in Ecosystems

Reading Focus What is biodiversity?

Try to imagine 1,000 beetles, each a different species. Difficult, isn't it? But if you go to the forests of Central and South America, you can find more than 1,000 different beetles on a *single tree*. Now try to imagine *300,000* different species of beetles. Impossible! Yet there probably are at least that many. Scientists think they have, however, actually identified only a tiny fraction of all the species of beetles in the world.

Scientists believe our planet may be home to more than 100 million different species of organisms. So far only about 1.75 million species have been identified!

The great variety of different organisms that live on Earth is called **biodiversity** (bī ō də vur′sə tē). *Biodiversity* is a combination of the words *biological* and *diversity*. The term refers to the millions of species that can live in Earth's many ecosystems. Look at the circle graph on the next page. It shows known species of each major group of organisms. What fraction of the species is insects? Is it closer to one third or one fourth?

Biodiversity refers not only to the variety of species on Earth but also to diversity within a single species Think about how you are different from your mother, brother, neighbor, and classmates. Yet humans are members of the same species—*Homo sapiens.* Earthworms, regardless of differences in length or color, are all members of the same species—*Lumbricus terrestris.*

Diversity—A Lot or a Little?

The amount of biodiversity varies among ecosystems. One ecosystem may contain thousands of species; another, fewer than 50. What makes the difference? The biodiversity of an ecosystem depends on three major factors: its size, its land features, and its latitude, or distance from the equator.

Large ecosystems support more species than do smaller ecosystems. Over a larger area, abiotic factors tend to vary. For example, suppose that a small island covered by forests is home to 50 species of butterflies. Another island, which is much larger and also covered by forests, may contain 100 species of butterflies. Why? Perhaps a tall mountain rises on the larger island.

D56

Mountains can cause the amount of rainfall and the temperature to vary across the island. The result? The larger island has many more different ecosystems than does the smaller one. And different ecosystems have different populations of organisms. Thus, the larger island, with more varied abiotic factors and more ecosystems, also supports more species of butterflies.

Latitude also affects abiotic factors. As you move further away from the

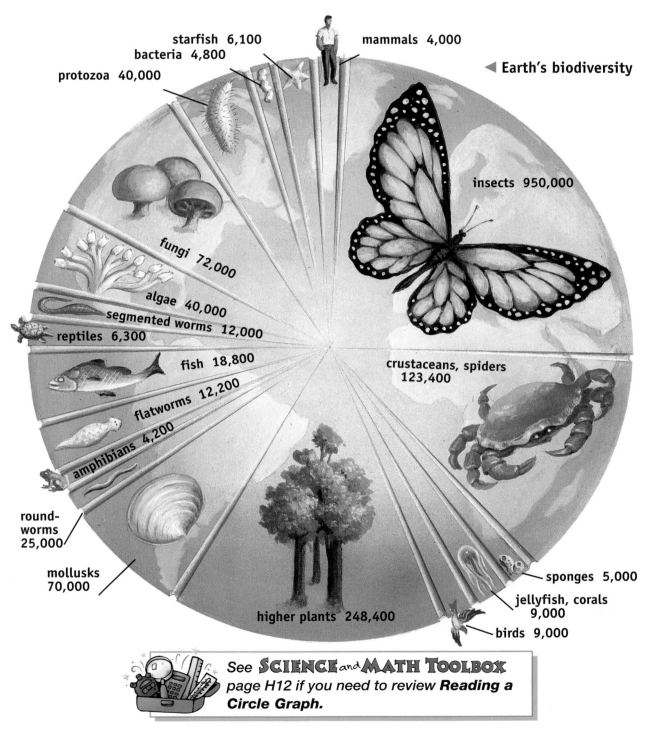

Earth's biodiversity

starfish 6,100
bacteria 4,800
protozoa 40,000
mammals 4,000
insects 950,000
fungi 72,000
algae 40,000
segmented worms 12,000
reptiles 6,300
fish 18,800
flatworms 12,200
amphibians 4,200
crustaceans, spiders 123,400
round-worms 25,000
mollusks 70,000
higher plants 248,400
sponges 5,000
jellyfish, corals 9,000
birds 9,000

See SCIENCE and MATH TOOLBOX page H12 if you need to review *Reading a Circle Graph.*

equator, temperatures are not consistently high. Sunlight is intense only part of the year, and precipitation is not as steady. These conditions become more extreme in ecosystems as the distance from the equator increases.

Close to the equator, temperatures are high, sunlight is intense, and rain is plentiful. Plants can grow all year. As a result, producers in tropical ecosystems are numerous and varied. They also can support more consumers, of a greater variety, than can the producers in colder or drier climates.

Most rain forests are in tropical locations. Thus, rain forests have the highest biodiversity of any ecosystem. Maps of the forests of Ecuador are shown in the activity on pages D54 and D55. In the forests of Ecuador, Colombia, and Peru—just 2 percent of the world's land surface—there are more than 40,000 species of plants!

The stable climate of the tropics has led to complex relationships among organisms, which also increases biodiversity. As you know, a single tree rooted in the ground is part of a forest. The tree also supports another whole

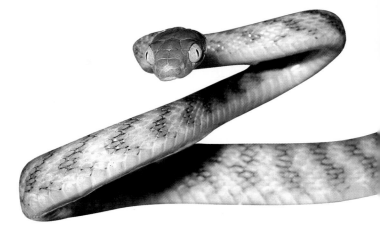

▲ **A brown tree snake**

ecosystem in its canopy layer. The canopy is laden with plant life—mosses ferns, orchids, and small trees. This miniature forest is home to a great many consumers, from one-celled organisms to snakes, frogs, mammals, and beetles.

Tinkering With Biodiversity

Do you think the dandelions in your schoolyard, the tumbleweed that rolls across the prairie, and the Norway maple in front of the library are "all-American"? If you said, "yes" you'd be wrong! Dandelions, tumbleweed, and Norway maples are three of the more than 3,000 species of plants that were brought, or introduced, to the United States by accident or on purpose.

Animal species have been introduced from other places, too. For example, the fierce brown tree snake was introduced to Hawaii from Guam in 1991. Scientists believe the snake survived a plane flight wrapped around the aircraft's wheels.

Native species can be driven out of their habitats by introduced species. Ecologists are trying to restore some ecosystems to their native biodiversity. ■

▼ **The rain forest canopy**

The Challenge of Biodiversity

Reading Focus Why should habitats of endangered or threatened species be preserved?

Have you ever seen a dinosaur? Did you ever hear of a dusky seaside sparrow? Have you ever heard anyone say "dead as a dodo"? The dodo was a bird that lived several hundred years ago. It was hunted until all members of its species were dead.

No one has ever seen a live dinosaur, and none of you ever will. Dinosaurs, dusky seaside sparrows, and dodos are all **extinct**. None remains alive. They are gone forever.

Some species, such as the giant panda, are not *yet* extinct. However, many species are **endangered** or threatened. Endangered species are

those in danger of becoming extinct. Threatened species are those that may soon become endangered. Eleven percent of the world's bird species are endangered.

The greatest threat to biodiversity is habitat destruction. For centuries, habitats have been destroyed in many ways, for many reasons. Many centuries ago, farmers cut down Europe's forests, destroying their native ecosystems. Settlers plowed under the prairies of the midwestern United States and planted crops. Today some developers fill in wetlands or cut down wooded areas to build housing developments.

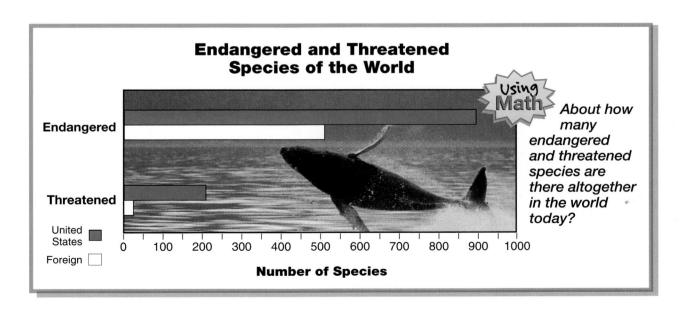

Endangered and Threatened Species of the World

Using Math *About how many endangered and threatened species are there altogether in the world today?*

Number of Species

United States | Foreign

Habitats can also be harmed without being destroyed. Pollution can poison a healthy habitat. The introduction of species can drive out native organisms.

But why should anyone care about biodiversity? Why should anyone care what happens to plants and animals, as long as people are all right? Why should anyone stop destroying habitats, as long as people's homes are safe?

Humans cannot live alone on Earth. Plants and animals provide people with food, raw materials for clothing, and building materials. More than 40 percent of all medicines come from living organisms. The complex web of plant life on Earth provides humans with oxygen for life processes. Decomposers keep the soil fertile for growing crops. Bacteria and other microscopic organisms break down wastes and purify water. These are just some reasons why people should care about biodiversity.

▲ Many species in the rain forests seem to be headed toward extinction, such as the red-leafed plant *Rafflesia arnoldii* shown.

Aside from these reasons, many people believe that human beings have a responsibility to preserve Earth. People have the power to destroy ecosystems and drive species to extinction. They also have the power—and the knowledge—to save ecosystems and encourage species' survival. You've learned about the consequences of doing both. What will you do? ■

INVESTIGATION 2 WRAP-UP

REVIEW

1. What does biodiversity mean on Earth and within a species?

2. What are the three major factors that affect biodiversity in an ecosystem?

CRITICAL THINKING

3. Why does biodiversity vary among ecosystems?

4. Identify a favorite species you have read about that you fear is in danger of becoming extinct. Why is it endangered? Can anything be done to save it?

REFLECT & EVALUATE

Word Power

Write the letter of the term that best completes each sentence. *Not all terms will be used.*

1. A species that is ___ has no living members.
2. In a ___ it may be hot or cold, but it is usually dry.
3. It is cold and there is low rainfall in a ___.
4. The great variety of life forms is called ___.
5. Rainfall is moderate and there are many conifers in a ___.
6. An area where land and water meet is a ___.

a. biodiversity
b. desert
c. endangered
d. extinct
e. grassland
f. taiga
g. tundra
h. wetland

Check What You Know

Write the term in each pair that best completes each sentence.

1. Most of Earth's water is (fresh, salty).
2. Whales live in the (coastal, deep) part of the ocean.
3. The number of species on Earth is closer to (2 million, 100 million).
4. The most species are supported by (rain forests, wetlands).

Problem Solving

1. Compare the variety of ecosystems in the ocean and on land. Suggest reasons why there is greater variety on land than in the ocean.

2. Explain how Earth's biodiversity has been affected by the development of civilization.

Draw or trace the animals shown. Cut out each drawing. Arrange the drawings on a sheet of paper. Identify each animal and the water ecosystem in which it lives. Then write a brief description of the main conditions of that ecosystem.

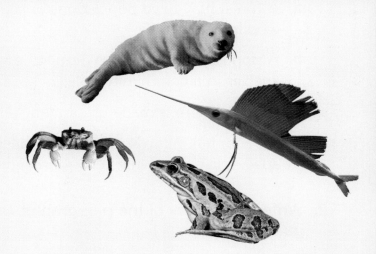

Summarizing

Summarizing helps you remember what you have read. A summary is a short paragraph that states the main points of a selection. Follow these guidelines to write a good summary.

Read the paragraphs. Then complete the exercises that follow.

Use these guidelines to write a summary.

- List topic sentences.
- Restate main ideas.
- Group similar ideas.
- Omit unimportant ideas.

Ecosystem Dwellers

Organisms that live together in an ecosystem make up a **community**. A community contains many different populations of organisms. Each **population** contains all the organisms of the same kind in a community. A forest may have populations of squirrels, maples, woodpeckers, blue jays, worms, and so on. Together with other populations they form a community. All the members of a population are members of the same species.

Organisms of the same species have the same general physical characteristics and other adaptations. An adaptation is a structure or behavior that enables a species to survive and reproduce in its environment.

1. Write the letters of two statements that you would put in your summary.

   a. A forest may have populations of squirrels, maples, and woodpeckers.

   b. A population is made up of members of the same species in a community.

   c. An ecosystem is made up of many different populations.

   d. An adaptation is a structure or behavior that enables a species to survive in its environment.

2. Write a summary of the paragraphs, using the guidelines.

Circle Graph

The circle graph compares the percentages of various plants and lichens found in Antarctica.

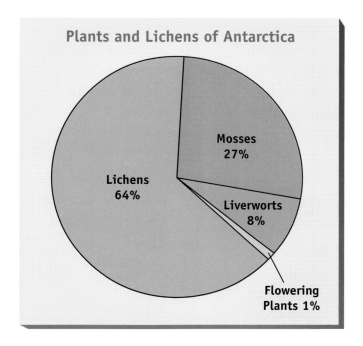

Plants and Lichens of Antarctica

Mosses 27%

Lichens 64%

Liverworts 8%

Flowering Plants 1%

Use the graph to complete the exercises that follow.

1. Which group of organisms is most common in Antarctica? Which is least common?

2. Do mosses, liverworts, and flowering plants make up more than one half or less than one half of all of the organisms shown? Tell how you know.

3. What percent of organisms shown in the circle graph are not flowering plants?

4. Represent each part of the circle graph as a decimal and as a fraction in simplest form.

5. Altogether, the circle graph above represents 312 species. About 200, or 64% of them, are lichens. About how many species of mosses do you think there are in Antarctica—15, 85, or 175 species? Explain.

UNIT D

WRAP-UP!

On your own, use scientific methods to investigate a question about a living thing in its environment.

THINK LIKE A SCIENTIST

Ask a Question

Pose a question about a living thing in its environment that you would like to investigate. For example, ask, "Could a land plant survive in the ocean?"

Make a Hypothesis

Suggest a hypothesis that is a possible answer to the question. One hypothesis is that a land plant would not survive if it was watered with only salt water (ocean water).

Plan and Do a Test

Plan a controlled experiment to find out the effect of ocean water (or water as salty as ocean water) on a land plant. You could start with 8–10 radish seedlings, fresh water, and ocean water. To simulate ocean water, dissolve 24 g of salt in 1 L of fresh water. Develop a procedure that uses these materials to test the hypothesis. With permission, carry out your experiment. Follow the safety guidelines on pages S14–S15.

Record and Analyze

Observe carefully and record your data accurately. Make repeated observations.

Draw Conclusions

Look for evidence to support the hypothesis or to show that it is false. Draw conclusions about the hypothesis. Repeat the experiment to verify the results.

WRITING IN SCIENCE
Note Taking

Prepare a list of different food chains that occur in a pond ecosystem. Use Internet searches and library resources to gather information. Follow these guidelines for taking notes.

• Write notes in your own words.

• Keep track of the name of each source and page references.

• Organize your notes into main topics.

• Draw conclusions based on the information you have reviewed.

The Solid Earth

Theme: Constancy and Change

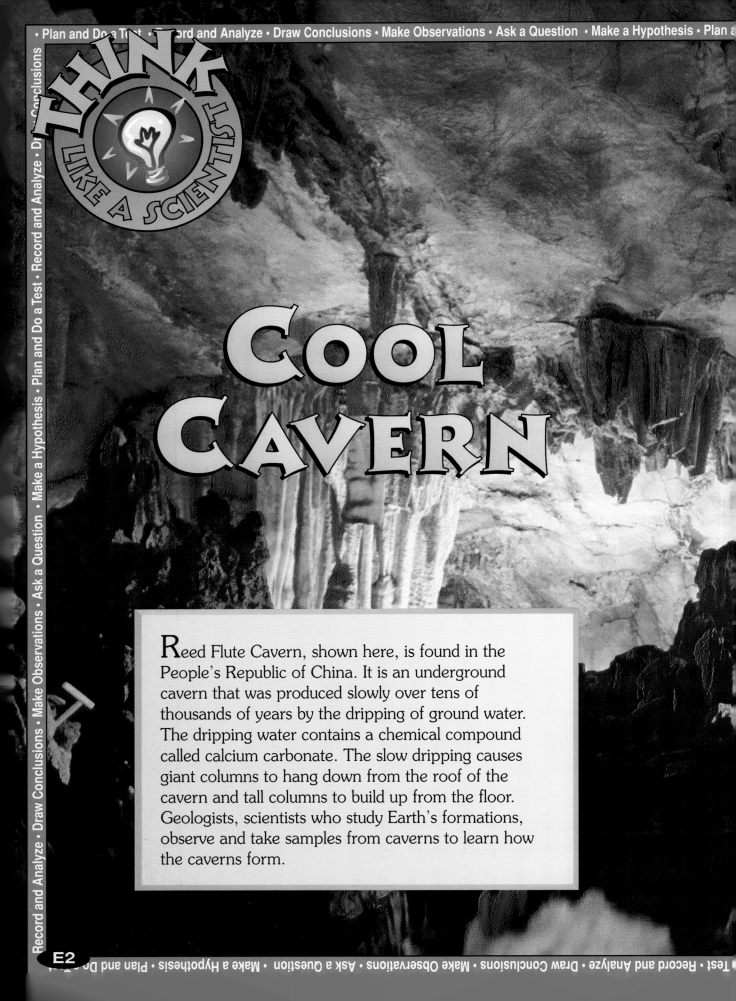

THINK LIKE A SCIENTIST

COOL CAVERN

Reed Flute Cavern, shown here, is found in the People's Republic of China. It is an underground cavern that was produced slowly over tens of thousands of years by the dripping of ground water. The dripping water contains a chemical compound called calcium carbonate. The slow dripping causes giant columns to hang down from the roof of the cavern and tall columns to build up from the floor. Geologists, scientists who study Earth's formations, observe and take samples from caverns to learn how the caverns form.

THINK LIKE A SCIENTIST

Questioning In this unit you'll study how rocks and minerals form, how they can be identified, how to tell how old rocks are, and even how mountains form. You'll investigate questions such as these.

- How Are Rocks Classified?
- How Do Rocks Change Over Time?

Observing, Testing, Hypothesizing In the Activity "Scratching Minerals," you'll test the hardness of minerals and find out how hardness can be used to classify minerals.

Researching In the Resource "Identifying Minerals," you'll learn to use a key to identify many minerals by their properties.

Drawing Conclusions
After you've completed your investigations, you'll draw conclusions about what you've learned—and get new ideas.

1

MINERALS

Have you ever visited a jewelry store or a museum and admired jewelry containing gemstones such as rubies or diamonds? Have you ever seen bracelets or necklaces made of shiny metals such as silver or gold? Both gemstones and metals have something in common. They are *minerals*.

Connecting to Science
ARTS

Wearable Art The beautiful jewelry pieces seen here are the work of Debbie Noiseux. She is a self-taught artist who has designed jewelry for many years. She uses colored gemstones, such as amethysts, opals, and garnets, in her work. Noiseux refers to her jewelry as wearable art.

The artist's fascination with colored gemstones shows in her designs. She carefully handpicks each gemstone according to its special properties. She gets ideas for how to use a particular stone from its color, texture, shape, and size. Her jewelry creatively displays the beauty of each stone.

In this chapter you'll study minerals such as those used in Debbie Noiseux's jewelry. You'll discover much about their physical and chemical properties.

Coming Up

◀ Gemstone jewelry designed by Debbie Noiseux

INVESTIGATION ①

HOW CAN YOU IDENTIFY MINERALS?

A mineral is a solid element or compound from Earth's crust that has a definite chemical composition and crystal structure. Now see if you can name this mineral. It is most often black or brown. It's used in tools for drilling. It's highly prized when it is colorless or blue-white. If you said "diamond," you are right!

Activity

The Way Minerals Look

Think about it—you identify most things just by looking at them. Minerals aren't any different. When you get to know them, you'll be able to look at them and name them. The key is getting to know them.

MATERIALS
- cardboard egg carton
- mineral set
- marker
- white unglazed ceramic tile
- *Science Notebook*

Procedure

1. Use an egg carton to store your mineral specimens. Open the carton and use a marker to number the pockets from 1 through 12.

2. **Observe** each mineral specimen. Does each look like it is made up of all the same kind of material? Is there any evidence of crystal structure in the minerals? **Record** your observations in your *Science Notebook.*

3. Make a chart like the one shown, with 8 columns and 12 rows. Any columns you don't fill in during this activity will be filled in during later activities.

MINERAL PROPERTIES							
Mineral Number	Luster	Color	Streak	Hardness	Cleavage	Special	Name

4. The way a mineral reflects light is called **luster** (lus'tər). Some minerals look like pieces of metal. They have a *metallic* luster. Others don't look like metal. They have a *nonmetallic* luster. Separate your minerals into two sets, one set with minerals that look like metal (such as brass, gold, or iron) and one with minerals that don't look like metal.

Step 5

5. Put each mineral in your egg carton. In your chart, **record** the number of the pocket you put each piece in. Then **record** *metallic* or *nonmetallic* under the column head *Luster*.

6. Inspect each mineral specimen and **record** its color in the next column of your chart. If needed, use more than one word, such as *yellow-brown* or *brass yellow*.

7. When a mineral is ground to a powder, its color is called its **streak**. **Predict** each mineral's streak. With each mineral, try to make a mark (like a pencil mark) on the tile. The color of the mark is the color of the streak. **Record** the color of each mineral's streak in your chart.

Analyze and Conclude

1. **Compare** the color and streak of each mineral in your collection. What conclusions can you draw about the color and streak of a mineral?

2. How are the properties of streak and luster useful in getting to know minerals?

INVESTIGATE FURTHER!

Use the **Science Processor CD-ROM**, *The Solid Earth* (Investigation 1, Who Am I?) to identify two unknown mineral samples.

Activity

Scratching Minerals

You may have noticed that some minerals are harder than others. Hardness is an important property in identifying minerals. Geologists test a mineral's hardness by seeing what objects will scratch or be scratched by the mineral. Try this scratch test yourself.

Procedure

1. Try scratching one mineral with another; make just a little scratch. Don't scrub the minerals together or you'll damage them. Can you find the hardest mineral in your set? How about the softest? **Record** your findings in your *Science Notebook*.

2. Geologists often use a set of tools to judge the hardness of a mineral. The tools include a piece of glass, a fingernail, a steel nail, and a piece of copper. **Predict** which of these items will be the hardest. Then scratch each tool with the others to rank the tools from softest to hardest.

3. Try to scratch each mineral with the edge of your fingernail. Always rub your finger over a mark to make certain it's a scratch and not a streak. A streak will rub off, but a scratch won't. If your fingernail scratches the mineral, **record** H < F for that mineral in your chart.

Math Hint *H < F means "the hardness is less than that of a fingernail."*

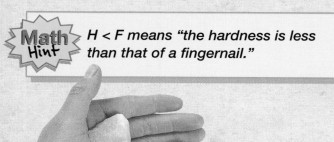

Step 3

Step 4

4. Find out if a copper wire will scratch the minerals that your fingernail did not scratch. For those that the copper scratches, **record** *F < H < C* (hardness is greater than that of a fingernail but less than that of copper) in your chart.

5. Now try a steel nail on those minerals that the copper didn't scratch. If the nail scratches the mineral, **record** this in the chart, using an *S* for "steel": *C < H < S.*

6. Finally, try scratching the glass plate with any mineral that was not scratched by the steel. **Record** those that scratch the glass as *H > G.*

 Math Hint *H > G means "the hardness is greater than that of glass."*

Analyze and Conclude

1. What was the order of hardness for your hardness tools?

2. Did your predictions match your results? Which mineral did you find to be the hardest? Which was the softest? **Compare** your results with those of your classmates. Did your classmates get the same results? If not, **hypothesize** why results varied. Then repeat the test and compare.

INVESTIGATE FURTHER!

RESEARCH

One important property of gemstones is that they are hard. After all, you wouldn't want to wear a gem if it scratched easily. Look up the hardness of diamonds, rubies, sapphires, emeralds, topazes, and garnets. How do they compare? What scale is used to compare hardness?

Activity

Minerals That Break Funny

If you have ever broken some glass, you were probably more concerned with cleaning it up than with how the glass broke. However, the way something breaks can tell us something important. Find out how minerals break.

Procedure

1. **Observe** some salt with a hand lens. Look for flat surfaces. They are called cleavage (klēv'- ij) planes. Like all minerals with cleavage planes, salt crystals always break along these planes. This property is called **cleavage**. Now pick out a large crystal and try to crush it with your pencil. **Observe** how the pieces are like the original crystal. **Record** your observations in your *Science Notebook*.

Step 1

2. **Observe** some large salt crystals with a hand lens. Look for cleavage planes inside the crystals. They often look like cracks. The cracks look as though the crystal might break along them. Sometimes you can see cleavage planes inside a crystal when you can't find them on the outside.

3. **Observe** your mineral samples. Look for flat surfaces where the mineral has broken. The surfaces are probably cleavage planes. Look for cleavage planes inside the mineral. If you find one or more cleavage planes on a mineral, **record** *yes* under *Cleavage* in your chart.

Analyze and Conclude

1. **List** the minerals that have cleavage planes.

2. **Compare** your mineral observations with those of your classmates. Do you agree on which minerals show cleavage? **Hypothesize** why you did or did not get the same results.

Activity

Name That Mineral

Now that you can recognize mineral properties, you can find out the name of each of the minerals in your mineral set.

• Mineral Properties chart

Procedure

1. Take mineral number 1 from its pocket in the egg carton. Use your chart to review the properties of the mineral.

2. Refer to the "Properties of Minerals" table on page E19. Look at the left column. Notice that the table is divided into two sections, minerals with metallic luster and minerals with non-metallic luster. Decide in which section of the table your mineral belongs. **Record** your observations in your *Science Notebook*.

3. Now move to the second column in the table. It is for hardness. Find the part of the column that describes the hardness of your mineral. Remember to stay in the section for the luster of your mineral when finding the hardness.

4. Move from left to right through the columns of the table. Information about streak and cleavage is sometimes in the column labeled *Special.* You should find the name of the mineral in the right-hand column. **Identify** the mineral. Then **record** its name in the last column of your chart.

5. Repeat steps 1–4 to **identify** all the other minerals in your set.

PROPERTIES OF MINERALS

Luster	Hardness	Color	Streak	Special	Name
Metallic	H > G	black	black	magnetic	MAGNETITE
Metallic	H > G	brassy yellow	black	fool's gold	PYRITE
Metallic	S < H < G	steel gray	red or reddish brown	may have reddish patches	HEMATITE
Metallic	C < H < S	brassy to gold yellow	black	often has blue, red, and purple tarnish	CHALCO-PYRITE
Metallic	F < H < C	silver gray	gray to black	heavy, shows cleavage (3)	GALENA

Luster	Hardness	age	Color	Special	Name
Non-metallic	H > G		white, pink, gray	hardness in very close	FELDSPAR
Non-metallic	H > G	yes			AMPHIBOLE
Non-metallic	H > G	yes (2)			PYROXENE
Non-metallic	H > G	no			QTZ
Non-metallic	C < H < S	yes (6)			
Non-metallic	C < H < S	yes (4)	purple, yellow	crystal are usually curved	
Non-metallic	C < H < S	yes (3)	white, pink	cleavage planes make parallelograms	CA
Non-metallic	F < H < C	yes (3)	colorless, white, yellow	tastes salty, breaks in cubes	HALITE
Non-metallic	H < F	yes (3)	colorless, white	sometimes transparent	GYPSUM
Non-metallic	H < F	yes (1)	colorless, white	peels in thin sheets, can be green	MICA
Non-metallic	H < F	yes (1)	colorless, silvery, black	usually flaky	TALC
Non-metallic	H < F	yes (1)	light green to white	looks like rust	LIMONITE
Non-metallic	H < F	no	yellow to brown	earthy	HEMATITE
Non-metallic	H < F	no	red		

Analyze and Conclude

1. Were you able to find the name of each of your minerals? **Hypothesize** why you were or were not able to find all of the minerals' names.

2. How are properties useful in identifying minerals?

E11

Mineral Properties

Reading Focus What are minerals, and what properties do they have?

Did you know that the "brain" of a computer, called a computer chip, is made from a mineral found in beach sand? A **mineral** is a solid element or compound from Earth's crust that has a definite chemical composition and crystal shape. Minerals can look very different from one another—colorless like quartz, silver or red like hematite, or shiny like gold and silver—but we find ways to use them all.

Look around and you'll see minerals being used. People may be wearing jewelry made of a gemstone such as a ruby, an emerald, or an opal. The walls in your home are probably made of wallboard, which is gypsum sandwiched between layers of paper. The windows in your classroom are made from quartz. The body powder you use may be made from the mineral talc. The point of your pencil is made of the mineral graphite. Your lunch may be wrapped in aluminum foil, made from the mineral bauxite. Perhaps you can think of other minerals you use every day. How many are there?

Why are minerals used in so many ways? They have different properties that make them right for many different uses. These same properties help scientists tell minerals apart. In the activities on pages E6 through E11, several properties of minerals are examined and tested.

▲ The mineral gypsum is used to make wallboard, or drywall.

▲ Talc is a mineral that you may sprinkle on your skin after a shower.

baby powder

USED IN HOSPITALS

WT 9 OZ (255g)

▲ A mineral's luster is a clue to its identity. Silver (*left*) has a metallic luster. Fluorite (*right*) has a nonmetallic luster.

Luster

Luster is one property that can be used to classify minerals. **Luster** refers to the way light reflects from the surface of a mineral. Look at the graphite in your pencil or at a piece of silver or gold jewelry. The shiny appearance of these minerals is called metallic luster. Any mineral that reflects light like metal has a metallic luster. All other minerals have nonmetallic luster. Minerals that have nonmetallic luster vary in the way they look. For example, the luster of a nonmetallic mineral may be dull like cinnabar, pearly like mica, or glassy and brilliant like diamond.

Hardness

A mineral's **hardness** is a measure of how easily it can be scratched. Talc is the softest mineral. It can be scratched by all other minerals. Diamond is the

Mohs' Scale of Mineral Hardness		
Mineral	**Hardness**	**Simple Test**
Talc	1	easily scratched by fingernail
Gypsum	2	scratched by fingernail
Calcite	3	barely scratched by copper
Fluorite	4	easily scratched by steel knife
Apatite	5	scratched by steel knife
Orthoclase feldspar	6	scratches glass with difficulty
Quartz	7	scratches glass and steel
Topaz	8	scratches quartz
Corundum	9	no simple test
Diamond	10	no simple test

Which mineral in the table has a hardness greater than that of quartz but less than that of corundum?

hardest mineral. It can scratch the surface of any other mineral, but no other mineral can scratch a diamond.

You can estimate a mineral's hardness by using Mohs' scale, shown in the table on page E13. This scale lists the hardness of ten common minerals. To test a mineral for hardness, find out which mineral on the scale is the hardest one that your mineral scratches. For example, a mineral that can scratch calcite but can't scratch fluorite has a hardness between 3 and 4.

In the activity on pages E8 and E9, you can test a mineral by using your fingernail, copper, steel, and glass. Using these materials and the scratch tests in Mohs' scale, you can estimate hardness. What would be the hardness of a mineral that can be scratched by copper but not a fingernail? Hardness is caused by the arrangement of matter in a mineral. For example, both diamond and graphite consist only of carbon. One arrangement produces the hardest natural mineral (diamond), and the other arrangement produces one of the softest minerals (graphite).

Color

Another mineral property is color. The elements making up a mineral determine its color. For example, chromium gives ruby its unusual red color. Although color is the easiest mineral property to observe, it's not the most reliable for identifying minerals. The variety of color of some minerals is due to the presence of tiny quantities of

Science in Literature

FASCINATING STONES

"The popularity of birthstones and the belief that they bring good luck reveal the fascination that rare and beautiful stones have exerted on people ever since the Stone Age. The most prized gemstones are diamonds (birthstones for April). They are formed at great depths and under tremendous pressure in a rock called kimberlite (blue ground)."

In *Rocks, Minerals and Fossils* by Keith Lye, you will find out just how fascinating minerals can be. Read this book if you are interested in starting a mineral collection or learning how beautiful gemstones form.

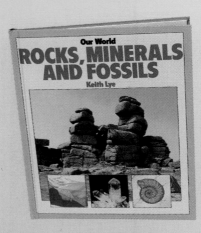

Rocks, Minerals and Fossils
by Keith Lye
Silver Burdett Press, 1991

other substances. Pure quartz is colorless, but traces of other substances within it can make it become white, pink, or purple.

Streak

Most minerals aren't as hard as a ceramic tile. When you scratch a mineral against a tile called a streak plate, some minerals crumble off as a powder. The color of this powder is the mineral property called **streak**.

The streak of most minerals is either colorless or the same color as the mineral. However, for a few minerals, the color of the mineral and the color of the streak aren't the same. For example, if you scratch silver-colored hematite on a streak plate, you'll find its streak is red! Apatite is a dark mineral with a white streak. Pyrite is brassy yellow and leaves a greenish-black streak.

Cleavage

Some materials split, or cleave, easily along flat surfaces, or planes. This property is called **cleavage**. The mineral

▲ **A mineral's streak may be different from its color.**

mica has cleavage planes that are all in the same direction. This allows mica to split easily into thin, flat sheets. Look at the photo of mica below. Can you see its cleavage planes?

Salt is a common name for the mineral halite. In the activity on page E10, halite is seen to have cleavage planes in three directions, producing cube-shaped pieces. Which mineral below resembles halite in its cleavage?

▲ **Calcite cleaves along three planes.**

▲ **Rubies, like many gemstones, have no cleavage.**

▲ **Mica cleaves along one plane, and peels in thin sections.**

You may think that all gemstones split naturally along several cleavage surfaces. But most gemstones do not. Gem cutters grind the gems to create the flat, shiny surfaces called facets. These facets give gemstones their different shapes and cause them to "sparkle" as they reflect light. The ruby shown on page E15 has been cut so that it sparkles.

Using Mineral Properties

How are mineral properties useful? If you were a gold miner, using the properties you just learned about might make you a fortune! You would need mineral properties to tell gold from other minerals you find.

Compare the samples of gold and pyrite shown. At first glance they may seem alike. Notice that they both have a brassy yellow color. They both also have a metallic luster, and neither mineral has cleavage.

Pyrite is known as fool's gold. Based on color, luster, and cleavage alone, you might easily mistake pyrite for gold. A smart gold miner would also compare the minerals' hardness and streak. Pyrite has a hardness of about 6, and gold has a hardness of about 3. Pyrite leaves a black streak; gold's streak is golden yellow. Gold has a greater value than pyrite, so it pays to be able to tell them apart. ■

▲ Pyrite, shown here, has some properties similar to those of gold.

▲ Gold, shown here, is softer than pyrite and has a different streak.

UNIT PROJECT LINK

For this Unit Project you will start a collection of minerals. There are many ways to get mineral samples. You could join a mineral club. There may be some collectors in your community who could help you. You could write to students in schools in other parts of the country and trade minerals through the mail. Or you could collect local mineral samples from road cuts and stream beds. To determine the name of any unknown minerals in your collection, see the activity on page E11.

Technology Link

For more help with your Unit Project, go to **www.eduplace.com**.

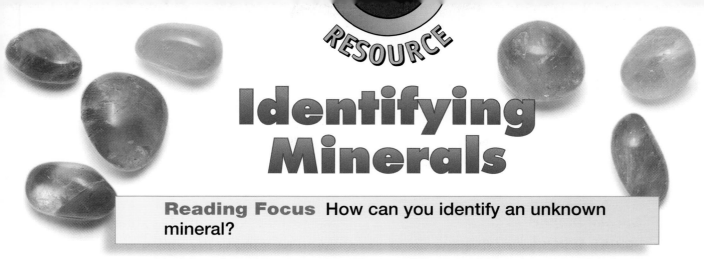

RESOURCE
Identifying Minerals

A key is an organizer designed to help you identify things. The table on page E19, "Properties of Minerals," is a key designed to help you identify minerals. To identify an unknown mineral, match the properties you observe in your sample with the properties listed in the table.

Try an example. Say you are given the unknown mineral shown below. What is it?

Using the Table: Nonmetallic Minerals

Step 1 Luster
How does it reflect light?

What kind of luster does your mineral have? It doesn't look like metal, so its luster is nonmetallic. Find in the table the column labeled *Luster* and locate all the nonmetallic minerals.

Step 2 Hardness
What scratches it?

You would use the tools listed in the activity on page E8 to test for hardness. Your mineral can be scratched with a fingernail. In the column labeled *Hardness,* only six minerals are both nonmetallic and softer than a fingernail. Your mineral must be one of those six.

Step 3 Cleavage
Does it split? In how many directions?

You can see that your sample has cleavage in one direction, or along one plane. You can rule out any of the minerals that don't cleave in one direction.

STEP 1	STEP 2	STEP 3
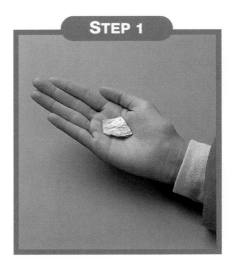	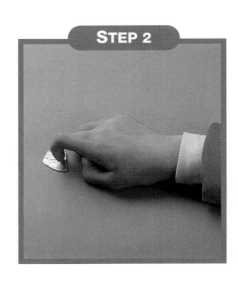	

Step 4 Color

What color is it?

Observe that your sample is colorless. Look under the column labeled *Color*. Two minerals fit that description: mica and gypsum. Which is it?

Step 5 Special Properties

Are there any special properties?

Find the column labeled *Special*. Since your sample peels easily in thin sheets, as is listed for mica, it must be mica. How might the procedure vary for a metallic mineral?

Using the Table: Metallic Minerals

Step 1 Luster

How does it reflect light?

Notice that the sample shines like metal. It has metallic luster. You can rule out all nonmetallic minerals, so cover that part of the table.

Step 2 Hardness

What scratches it?

If you could test it, you'd find that your sample can scratch glass. Look in the table to see which metallic minerals are harder than glass. Notice that there are only two minerals with this property: magnetite and pyrite.

Step 3 Color

What color is it?

Observe that your sample is black. Look under the column labeled *Color* and notice that pyrite is brassy yellow. Your mineral must be magnetite. But to make sure, check its other properties.

Step 4 Streak

What color is its streak?

If you could scratch your sample along a streak plate, you would see that its streak is black. This agrees with the data for magnetite under the column labeled *Streak* in the table.

Step 5 Special Properties

Are there any special properties?

If you had a magnet, you would see that your sample is attracted to it. You can use this property and others in the table to confirm that your unknown sample is indeed magnetite.

PROPERTIES OF MINERALS

Luster	Hardness	Color	Streak	Special	Name
Metallic	H > G	black	black	magnetic	MAGNETITE
Metallic	H > G	brassy yellow	black	fool's gold	PYRITE
Metallic	S < H < G	steel gray	red or reddish brown	may have reddish patches	HEMATITE
Metallic	C < H < S	brassy to gold yellow	black	often has blue, red, and purple tarnish	CHALCO-PYRITE
Metallic	F < H < C	silver gray	gray to black	heavy, shows cleavage (3)	GALENA

Luster	Hardness	Cleavage	Color	Special	Name
Non-metallic	H > G	yes (2)	white, pink, gray	hardness is very close to glass	FELDSPAR
Non-metallic	H > G	yes (2)	black, green, white	cleavage planes make a diamond shape	AMPHIBOLE
Non-metallic	H > G	yes (2)	black, green	cleavage planes make a square shape	PYROXENE
Non-metallic	H > G	no	colorless, white, pink, smoky, purple	looks glassy, chips or breaks like glass	QUARTZ
Non-metallic	C < H < S	yes (6)	yellow to brown or black	yellowish-white streak	SPHALERITE
Non-metallic	C < H < S	yes (4)	purple, green, yellow	crystals are cubes, transparent	FLUORITE
Non-metallic	C < H < S	yes (3)	white, pink	crystal faces are usually curved	DOLOMITE
Non-metallic	F < H < C	yes (3)	colorless, white, yellow	cleavage planes make parallelograms	CALCITE
Non-metallic	H < F	yes (3)	colorless, white	tastes salty, breaks in cubes	HALITE
Non-metallic	H < F	yes (1)	colorless, white	sometimes transparent	GYPSUM
Non-metallic	H < F	yes (1)	colorless, silvery, black	peels in thin sheets, can be green	MICA
Non-metallic	H < F	yes (1)	light green to white	usually flaky	TALC
Non-metallic	H < F	no	yellow to brown	looks like rust	LIMONITE
Non-metallic	H < F	no	red	earthy	HEMATITE

*Numbers in parentheses give number of cleavage planes.

Key: H—hardness; G—glass; S—steel; C—copper; F—fingernail; <—less than; >—greater than. **E19**

Diamonds

Reading Focus What are diamonds, and where are they found?

Have you ever passed a jewelry store window filled with sparkling diamond rings? Just what are diamonds and how are they mined? Diamond is the hardest mineral. It is made of pure carbon. It forms deep underground, where temperature and pressure are very great. Diamond forms in a rock called kimberlite (kim′bər līt). Most kimberlite forms long, tube-shaped rock bodies called pipes. Sometimes these pipes reach Earth's surface.

Mining Diamonds

Diamonds have been discovered in many parts of the world. The map shows areas that have provided the greatest number of diamonds. A limited number have been found in the United States, in northern California, southern Oregon, Arkansas, and the Appalachian Mountains.

Most diamonds are found in stream deposits called placers. A placer is a stream deposit that contains important mineral fragments. Diamond placers form when streams flow over kimberlite pipes and carry kimberlite particles downstream. Because diamonds are heavier than other rock particles, they drop to the bottom of streams and mix with sand and gravel on stream beds. Miners remove diamonds in the same way gold is panned.

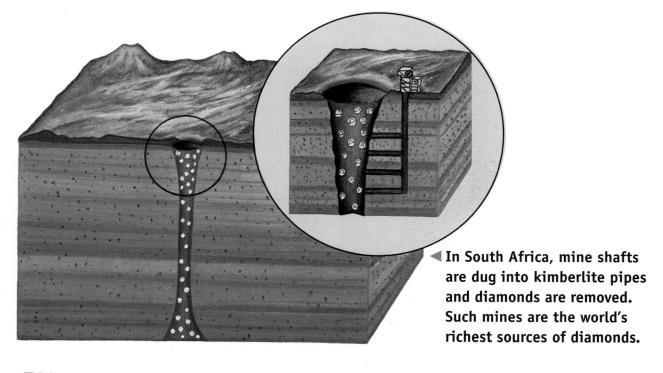

◄ In South Africa, mine shafts are dug into kimberlite pipes and diamonds are removed. Such mines are the world's richest sources of diamonds.

Diamonds are also mined directly from kimberlite. This is done by digging either surface pits or deep underground mine shafts. Once removed from the ground, the kimberlite is crushed and the rock is washed away, leaving behind only the harder diamonds. Any remaining traces of kimberlite are separated and removed by machines.

After mining, diamonds are sorted according to quality. Only two out of every ten diamonds are of good enough quality to be made into jewels. The rest are cut up for other uses, such as making abrasives, glass cutters, rock drill bits, and telecommunication products. The better-quality diamonds are then sorted, or graded, according to their color, size, and purity.

A Cut Above

After grading, diamonds are sent to a gem cutter. Gem-quality diamonds are cut because doing so shows off their brilliant nonmetallic luster. Next, the diamond is shaped. Finally, it is polished by holding it at an angle to a spinning disk coated with diamond dust. This step creates the sparkling facets highly prized in gemstones. ■

▲ Raw diamonds are often found in kimberlite.

▲ Gem cutters cut and polish selected diamonds.

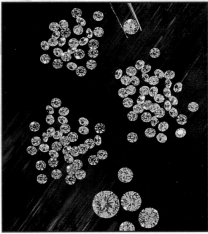

▲ Finished diamonds are sold around the world.

INVESTIGATION 1 WRAP-UP

REVIEW

1. What is a mineral?

2. Name five mineral properties.

CRITICAL THINKING

3. Describe how you would use mineral properties to distinguish quartz from calcite.

4. When trying to identify an unknown mineral, list all the questions you would need to answer about that mineral.

WHAT ARE MINERALS USED FOR?

Look around at your classmates. How many are wearing jewelry? You know that minerals are used to make much of that jewelry. Try to name as many minerals used in jewelry as you can. (Think in terms of gems and metals.) Can you think of other uses for minerals?

Activity

Growing Crystals

Mineral crystals are used in jewelry and in electronics. Some of these crystals are grown in laboratories. In this activity you can grow your own crystals!

- - - - - - - - - - - - - - - - - - - -

Procedure

1. Use a measuring cup to pour 500 mL of hot water into a large jar. Dissolve as much alum as possible in the water (about 100 g, or 3 to 4 oz). Put a lid on the jar and let it stand overnight.

See **SCIENCE** and **MATH TOOLBOX** page H7 if you need to review **Measuring Volume.**

2. The next day, pour a small amount of the solution from the jar into the bottom of a bowl and let it stand overnight. The next morning you should find some small crystals in the bowl. Use a spoon to remove one or two good crystals and pour the solution back into the jar.

MATERIALS

- goggles
- plastic gloves
- measuring cup
- large jar with lid
- hot tap water
- alum
- shallow bowl
- plastic spoon
- polyester thread
- large baby-food jar
- sheet of paper
- scissors
- metric ruler
- *Science Notebook*

SAFETY

Wear goggles and gloves at all times. Be sure to wash your hands after handling the alum.

3. Tie one of the crystals to the end of a piece of thread. Suspend the crystal in a baby-food jar.

Step 3

4. Nearly fill the baby-food jar with solution from the large jar. Be careful not to pour any crystals into the baby-food jar. Fold a square piece of paper to form a tent. Place it over the jar to keep the dust out. **Predict** how much the crystal will grow each day.

5. **Observe** your crystal growing. It may take a few days. Each day, **estimate** the size of the crystal. If the level of solution in the jar goes down, add more. When the crystal stops growing, remove it from the solution. **Make a drawing** of it in your *Science Notebook*.

Math Hint *Estimate the length and width of the crystal in millimeters or centimeters.*

Analyze and Conclude

1. About how large was the crystal when you started? How large was the crystal when you stopped growing it?

2. How many days did the crystal grow? Did your crystal grow by the same amount each day? **Describe** your evidence.

3. Think of ways people use crystals. **Infer** why scientists might want to grow crystals in a laboratory.

INVESTIGATE FURTHER!

EXPERIMENT

You can grow crystals from other substances. Instead of alum, try sugar, Epsom salts, or rock salt. Compare the shapes of the crystals and how easy or difficult they were to grow.

Quartz: A Versatile Mineral

Reading Focus What is quartz and how is it used?

If you've ever been to a beach or seen pictures of one, you know that beaches are made of sand. The words *sand* and *gravel* refer to the size of a grain of mineral or rock. Sand particles are smaller than gravel. Any rock or mineral can be broken into sand-sized or gravel-sized pieces.

The most common sand in the world is quartz sand. Quartz is also one of the most important minerals. It is made of only two elements, silicon and oxygen. The colors of common types of quartz include clear (rock crystal), pink (rose), white (milky), and gray (smoky). Some forms of quartz are semiprecious gemstones such as amethyst, agate, onyx, and opal. Native Americans used one form, flint, for tools such as arrowheads.

Building With Quartz

Quartz plays an important role in the building industry. Many building materials are made of rocks and minerals. **Concrete**, for example, is a rock material made of sand and gravel and a binder. The binder, called portland cement, is made by grinding limestone and shale, two kinds of rock, into a powder. This powder is baked at a high temperature until it forms balls called clinker. Cooled clinker is crushed to a powder and mixed with gypsum, another mineral. This mixture is then mixed with quartz-rich sand, gravel, and water and allowed to harden to form concrete. How have you seen concrete used in your neighborhood?

rose quartz ▶

clear quartz ▼

smoky quartz ▶

◀ milky quartz

▲ Concrete, a building material, is made with quartz and other minerals.

▲ Quartz is used to make glass.

Seeing With Quartz

Quartz is also used to make glass. In ancient times, people in the Middle East had a good understanding of quartz and its properties. Glassmaking probably began about 4,000 years ago in Egypt or Mesopotamia. Today the art of glassmaking is a worldwide industry.

Glass is easy to make if you have the proper tools. Powdered quartz is mixed with powdered limestone and soda (not the kind you drink, but a solid substance called sodium carbonate). This mixture is heated to about 1,600°C (2,912°F).

At this temperature the mixture melts. Then it is cooled quickly so that crystals cannot form. Crystals would make objects seen through the glass look wavy and distorted. Look around you. How many ways can you see glass being used?

The Computer Mineral

Quartz can be separated into its two parts, silicon and oxygen. From the silicon, crystals can be grown. Crystals are grown in the activity on pages E22 and E23. Silicon crystals can be cut into thin pieces. These pieces of pure silicon

◀ Quartz, a compound of silicon and oxygen, is one of the most abundant minerals in Earth's crust.

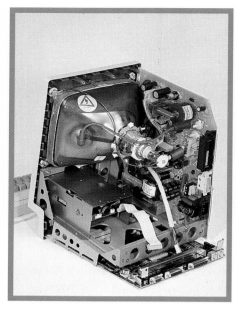

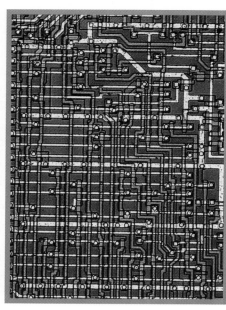

The brain of every desktop computer (*left*) is a silicon chip. Many chips, each the size of a fingernail, are obtained from silicon wafers (*center*). Each chip is etched with the electronic circuits (*right*) that carry out the calculations that make computers such timesavers.

are used in the electronics industry, which is a major part of the world's economy. Computer chips, which are the brains of computers, and solar cells, which power solar calculators, are made with silicon.

Perhaps the most amazing thing about quartz crystals is that they generate electricity. If the crystals are squeezed, they bend slightly and produce electricity. In addition, when a small electric current is put through a crystal, the crystal vibrates. The vibrations are very regular, making quartz

crystals ideal for keeping time. Many types of watches use quartz crystals.

Maybe you thought quartz was something you walked on as you viewed the ocean. But a world without window glass, portable electronic games, radios, CD players, computers, or concrete would be hard to imagine! ■

Internet Field Trip
Visit **www.eduplace.com** to find out more about quartz and other minerals.

◄ **You may be carrying a quartz crystal on your wrist. In a watch with a quartz crystal, the crystal's vibrations keep time more accurately than the spring that is used in other watches.**

How Iron Becomes Steel

Reading Focus Where does iron come from, and how is it made into steel?

In Arizona, there is a huge hole in the ground known as the Barringer Meteorite Crater. Scientists hypothesize that the crater formed about 25,000 years ago, when a chunk of iron from space, 18 m (59 ft) wide, collided with Earth. The chunk of iron from space shows that iron isn't found only on Earth. It's all over the universe! Maybe it should be called the universal metal!

Iron occurs in minerals. Magnetite and hematite are important iron-containing minerals. Minerals from which metals can be removed are called **ores**. An iron ore is made up of iron and other elements.

The most widespread source of iron is hematite, an ore made up of iron and oxygen. Over 2 billion years ago, hematite layers began to build up in the oceans. Over time the hematite was covered by layers of sediment. Later, parts of the ocean bottom were slowly lifted up to the surface. The iron deposits eventually became exposed. That was the easy part! For us, the hard part is getting the iron ores out of the ground and the iron out of the ores.

Iron ore is mined all over the planet. In the United States, most of the iron we use comes from hematite mined in Canada and South America. Magnetite

Iron is used to make many different products such as the blades of skates (*left*), the rails of roller coasters (*center*), and the hulls of ships (*right*).

is not as easy to find as hematite, but it's a purer source of iron. The world's largest magnetite mine is in Sweden. Others are located in Wyoming, New York, Utah, South Africa, Austria, Italy, and Russia.

The process of removing metal from ore is called **smelting**. The first smelting of metal may have occurred about 9,000 years ago. Around 3,500 years ago, iron smelting became widespread. Iron was often used in making cooking utensils and weapons. Because the intro-duction of iron affected cultures so greatly, that period of time was called the Iron Age. The diagram shows how a type of crude iron, called pig iron, is made.

Smelting Iron

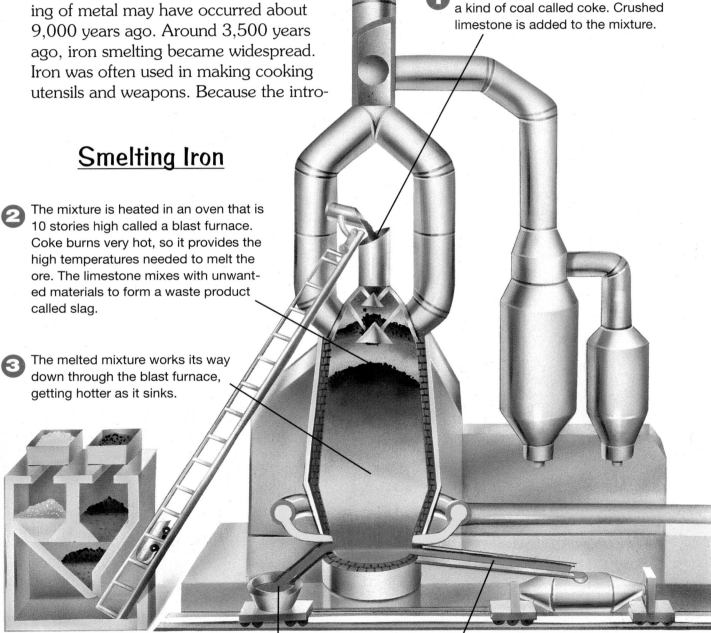

1 To smelt iron, iron ore is mixed with a kind of coal called coke. Crushed limestone is added to the mixture.

2 The mixture is heated in an oven that is 10 stories high called a blast furnace. Coke burns very hot, so it provides the high temperatures needed to melt the ore. The limestone mixes with unwanted materials to form a waste product called slag.

3 The melted mixture works its way down through the blast furnace, getting hotter as it sinks.

4 Wastes that are less dense separate and float on the molten metal. This slag is then drained off.

5 The remaining melted iron, called pig iron, is drained from the bottom of the blast furnace.

▲ Pig iron is remelted and mixed with a precise amount of carbon, making steel.

Impurities such as carbon are present in pig iron. These impurities make pig iron too brittle to be used for purposes requiring great strength. Instead it is remelted and poured into molds. Iron made in this way is called cast iron. Cast iron is used to make bells, wood stoves, bathtubs, railings, and other products.

Pig iron can also be remelted and converted into steel. In a furnace, melted pig iron is brought to a high temperature. Air

▲ The liquid steel is poured into molds and allowed to cool.

is blown over the iron to increase the heat and remove excess carbon. When the metal is free of carbon, a measured amount of carbon is mixed in. It may seem strange that carbon is removed only to be added again, but an exact amount of carbon is needed to make useful steel. Too much carbon makes the steel brittle, and too little makes it weak.

▲ Steel can be produced in a variety of forms, including rolled sheets.

Steel can be rolled into sheets or made into bars, blocks, and other shapes. It can be made as sharp as a razor or as blunt as a hammer. Other metals can be added to steel to make alloys, or mixtures of metals. For example, chromium is added to make steel rust resistant. Nickel is added to make steel stronger. Titanium makes steel more resistant to heat. Tungsten makes steel strong at high temperatures.

How did you get to school today? If you came by public transportation, car, or bike, steel helped you. What other uses for steel can you think of? ■

A World of Minerals

Reading Focus In what ways are Earth's mineral resources valuable?

Mineral resources are in the ground all over the world. But they are not evenly distributed. As the map shows, some countries have more mineral resources than others.

A country can mine its resources and use them to make products. That country can then sell some of its raw resources and products to other countries. The selling countries are called producers. Countries with few mineral resources must buy many resources or products. These buying countries are consumers. Consumers often buy raw resources to make products. If they sell these products to producers, the producers may actually be buying back their raw resources in a new form.

For example, raw iron ore may be shipped from the United States to Japan. A Japanese company turns the ore into iron, the iron into steel, and the steel into bike frames. Some frames are sold in Japan and some are sold in other parts of the world, including the United States.

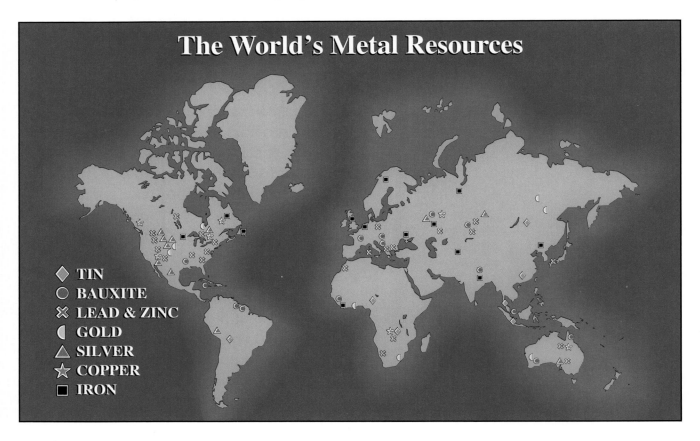

The World's Metal Resources

◇ TIN
◯ BAUXITE
✖ LEAD & ZINC
☾ GOLD
△ SILVER
☆ COPPER
■ IRON

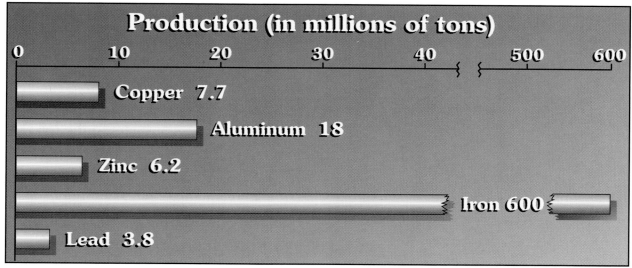

Production (in millions of tons)

0   10   20   30   40   500   600

Copper 7.7

Aluminum 18

Zinc 6.2

Iron 600

Lead 3.8

 Using Math *This graph shows the worldwide yearly production of selected metals. How does the amount of aluminum produced in one year compare to the total amount of copper, zinc, and lead produced in a year?*

Minerals and mineral products are an important part of the world trading market. There are few places on Earth where iron or steel isn't used in some way. Aluminum is important to the canning and cooking industries. Silver is valued for jewelry. What other ways are mineral resources used in the world?

A Limited Supply

A **natural resource** is any useful material or energy source found in nature. Some natural resources, such as sunlight and wind, are thought of as inexhaustible (in eg zôs'ta bəl). This means that they can never be used up.

Most natural resources are placed in one of two groups—renewable and nonrenewable. A **renewable resource** is one that can be replaced in a fairly short time. Trees are renewable resources. A **nonrenewable resource** is one that can't be replaced in nature. Once a nonrenewable resource is used up, it's gone forever.

Minerals are nonrenewable resources. Supplies of many minerals are limited and they are being used up fast. Items made from minerals are not really gone from our environment. The minerals are still here, ready to be recycled.

▲ Much of Earth's mineral wealth ends up in places like this.

Using Math *In the United States 1,500 aluminum cans are recycled every second. How could you estimate the number of aluminum cans that are recycled each year?*

World Issues

The way that mineral resources are handled in one country can affect many other countries. Look at the map on page E30 and the bar graph on page E31. Then discuss answers to the following questions with your classmates.

Which two metals are produced in the largest quantity? Do you think the United States has to import such resources? What happens when a nation doesn't have enough raw resources or money to trade evenly? What happens when countries are in competition for a product in limited supply? What happens when a country holds back on selling resources or products needed by other countries of the world? ■

Recycling Mineral Resources

Many communities in the United States have recycling laws. In addition to nonmineral products like paper and plastic, metals such as copper, steel, brass, and aluminum are recycled. Recycling doesn't solve the problem of using up a mineral resource, but it does extend our use of such resources.

INVESTIGATE FURTHER!

TAKE ACTION

Research and evaluate services for recycling minerals in your community. Then organize a recycling drive of those materials.

INVESTIGATION 2 WRAP-UP

THINK IT WRITE IT

REVIEW

1. Name six products made from minerals and at least one mineral used to make each product.

2. Where does iron come from, and how is it made into steel?

CRITICAL THINKING

3. List the materials made from minerals that you would use if you were building a house, and explain why you would use them.

4. Describe two ways you can help extend the use of a limited mineral resource.

REFLECT & EVALUATE

Word Power

Write the letter of the term that best completes each sentence. *Not all terms will be used.*

1. A building material made of sand, gravel, and a binder is ___.
2. The color of the powder left by a mineral on a ceramic tile is the mineral's ___.
3. The way a mineral reflects light is known as ___.
4. Metals can be removed from minerals called ___.
5. The way a mineral splits is a property called ___.
6. A measure of how easily a mineral can be scratched is its ___ .

a. cleavage
b. concrete
c. hardness
d. luster
e. mineral
f. ores
g. smelting
h. streak

Check What You Know

Write the term in each pair that best completes each sentence.

1. The hardest mineral is (diamond, talc).
2. Quartz is made up of silicon and (oxygen, carbon).
3. You can tell gold from pyrite by using the property of (streak, luster).
4. The end product of smelting is (concrete, pig iron).

Problem Solving

1. You are about to take a mineral-collecting field trip. You plan to identify all the minerals you collect. List the materials you will need to take and explain what property each will be used to identify.

2. What might happen if, from now on, all mineral resources found and used were recycled?

BUILD YOUR PORTFOLIO

Observe the properties of the mineral sample shown. This mineral's streak is gray to black. The mineral cannot be scratched by a fingernail but can be scratched by glass. Make a list of the mineral's properties. Then use the "Properties of Minerals" table on page E19 to identify this mineral.

CHAPTER 2

ROCKS

Rocks are made of minerals, and you find rocks of all kinds and sizes everywhere! They range from the sandstone pebbles in a city park to the gigantic granite face of a cliff. Most rocks appear sturdy and unchanging. Actually, however, natural processes are constantly changing rocks. People too can transform rocks.

PEOPLE USING SCIENCE

Stonecutter Edward Torres of Seaside Heights, New Jersey, is a stonecutter. He skillfully turns sheets of white, black, beige, red, or green marble into custom-made items. He crafts such things as fireplace mantels and counter tops.

A typical job for Torres begins when his material is delivered. A huge slab of marble is gently deposited onto his worktable by a forklift! Torres then uses a circular diamond-toothed saw to precisely cut the hard stone to the proper measurements. (Water cools the saw blade.) The fully processed piece, completed and polished, is a beautiful and useful item.

What natural processes change some materials into marble or into other kinds of rocks? What properties distinguish one kind of rock from another? In this chapter you'll explore these and other questions.

INVESTIGATION 1

HOW ARE ROCKS CLASSIFIED?

INVESTIGATION 2

HOW DO THE PROPERTIES OF ROCKS MAKE THEM USEFUL?

INVESTIGATION 3

HOW DO ROCKS CHANGE OVER TIME?

◄ Edward Torres, stonecutter

HOW ARE ROCKS CLASSIFIED?

Rocks are the "stuff" that makes up Earth. About 4 billion years ago, Earth was a molten ball of rock. Although some of Earth's rock is still molten, the rock in the outer layer is solid. You live on this rocky ball. In this investigation you'll find out how rocks are identified and classified.

Activity

Sort of Rocky

Rocks are made of minerals. Some rocks are made of only one mineral, but most rocks are made of more than one. In this activity you'll observe some properties of rocks and use those properties to classify the rocks.

MATERIALS

- paper punch-outs
- marker
- white glue
- set of rocks
- hand lens
- egg carton
- *Science Notebook*

Procedure

1. Number paper punch-outs from 1 to 12. With white glue, attach one punch-out to each rock specimen.

2. Put all the rocks together on your desktop. **Compare** the rocks to one another. **Classify** them by separating them into a dark-colored set and a light-colored set. In your *Science Notebook*, **record** the numbers for each set.

3. Mineral crystals in rocks are usually very small. They are shiny and have flat surfaces that look like tiny mirrors. Place all the rocks together and **observe** the rocks with a hand lens.

4. **Classify** the rocks into a set with crystals and a set without crystals. **Record** the numbers for each set.

5. Use the hand lens to study the rocks again. **Classify** the rocks into two new sets: one set in which the rocks appear to be made of more than one mineral and the other in which the rocks appear to contain only one mineral. **Record** the numbers for each set.

6. **Classify** the rocks with one mineral into two sets: rocks with crystals and rocks without crystals. Do the same for rocks with more than one mineral. **Record** your results.

7. Now **classify** each of the four sets from steps 4 and 5 into sets that contain dark-colored rocks and light-colored rocks. Then use an egg carton to store your rock specimens.

Analyze and Conclude

1. How many sets now contain only one rock?

2. List the properties that you used in this activity to classify rocks. **Infer** how these properties are used to classify rocks.

UNIT PROJECT LINK

Begin a rock collection. Rocks are easier to find than minerals. Get good clean rocks that are freshly broken so that you can see what the insides look like. Keep a numbered list of your rocks to tell where they came from. Try sorting them according to their properties.

Technology Link

For more help with your Unit Project, go to **www.eduplace.com**.

Activity
The Rock Key

A key is used in science to help identify something. The Rock Key will help you use the properties of rocks to find out their names.

Procedure

1. Choose a rock specimen. Look at the descriptions at the left side of the Rock Key. Find the description that matches your rock. Observe whether or not your rock has crystals. If it does, follow the line from "Rock has crystals" to the next level in the key. If it does not have crystals, follow the other line. Record all the properties of your rock in your *Science Notebook*.

2. At most levels in the key, two choices are given. Match a choice to your rock and follow the line to your next observation and choice. Eventually, you will arrive at the name of your rock on the right side of the key. Be sure to follow the lines in the key.

3. To test for hardness use glass, as you did with minerals. Hard rocks scratch glass; soft ones do not.

4. To find out if a rock with crystals is coarse-grained, medium-grained, or fine-grained, observe the size of the crystals. In a coarse-grained rock, most of the rock is made of crystals larger than a grain of rice. In a fine-grained rock, you need a hand lens to see crystals. In a medium-grained rock, you can see the crystals without a hand lens, but they are smaller than rice grains.

Math Hint *Compare the crystals to a typical grain of rice, which measures about 7 mm long and 2 mm wide.*

Step 4

5. Use the Rock Key to identify your rock. Record this information with your notes on the properties of the rock. Then repeat steps 1 through 5 for each rock in your set.

Analyze and Conclude

1. Which rocks did you find hard to identify?

2. Make an inference about what additional data would have helped you identify them.

THE ROCK KEY

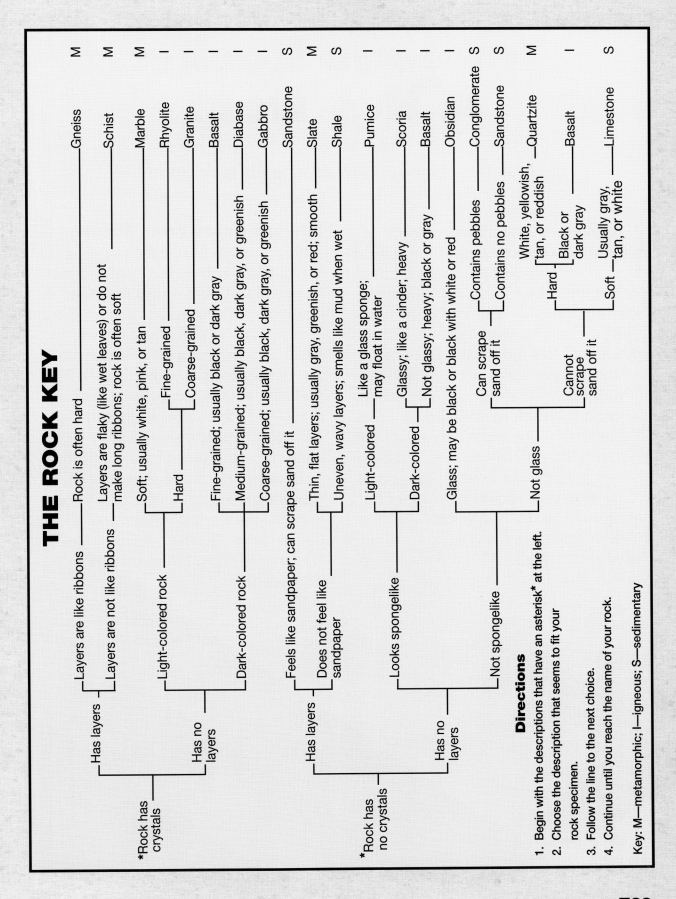

*Rock has crystals	Has layers	Layers are like ribbons	Rock is often hard	Gneiss	M
			Layers are flaky (like wet leaves) or do not make long ribbons; rock is often soft	Schist	M
		Layers are not like ribbons			
	Has no layers	Light-colored rock	Soft; usually white, pink, or tan	Marble	M
			Hard — Fine-grained	Rhyolite	I
			Hard — Coarse-grained	Granite	I
		Dark-colored rock	Fine-grained; usually black or dark gray	Basalt	I
			Medium-grained; usually black, dark gray, or greenish	Diabase	I
			Coarse-grained; usually black, dark gray, or greenish	Gabbro	I

*Rock has no crystals	Has layers	Feels like sandpaper; can scrape sand off it		Sandstone	S
		Does not feel like sandpaper	Thin, flat layers; usually gray, greenish, or red; smooth	Slate	M
			Uneven, wavy layers; smells like mud when wet	Shale	S
	Has no layers	Looks spongelike	Light-colored — Like a glass sponge; may float in water	Pumice	I
			Dark-colored — Glassy; like a cinder; heavy	Scoria	I
			Dark-colored — Not glassy; heavy; black or gray	Basalt	I
		Not spongelike	Glass; may be black or black with white or red	Obsidian	I
			Not glass — Can scrape sand off it — Contains pebbles	Conglomerate	S
			Not glass — Can scrape sand off it — Contains no pebbles	Sandstone	S
			Not glass — Cannot scrape sand off it — Hard — White, yellowish, tan, or reddish	Quartzite	M
			Not glass — Cannot scrape sand off it — Hard — Black or dark gray	Basalt	I
			Not glass — Cannot scrape sand off it — Soft — Usually gray, tan, or white	Limestone	S

Directions

1. Begin with the descriptions that have an asterisk* at the left.
2. Choose the description that seems to fit your rock specimen.
3. Follow the line to the next choice.
4. Continue until you reach the name of your rock.

Key: M—metamorphic; I—igneous; S—sedimentary

Igneous Rocks: A Hot Item

Reading Focus How do igneous rocks form?

Rocks are solid materials made of minerals. In the activities on pages E36 through E39, rocks are classified based on how they are similar and different. Scientists classify rocks into three types based on how they are formed. This system includes three types of rocks.

One of those types is called igneous (ig'nē əs) rock. These rocks are probably the most common rocks found on Earth. The word *igneous* comes from the Latin word for "fire." Knowing this, can you make a guess about how igneous rocks form? **Igneous rocks** form when hot, melted rock material cools and hardens. Rock that is melted to a liquid form is called molten rock. Where on Earth do you think molten rock is found?

Igneous Rocks From Magma

Deep within Earth, the temperature is much hotter than it is near the surface. It is so hot that rocks melt, or change from solid to liquid. This molten rock material that forms deep within Earth is called **magma**. Because it is less dense, or lighter, than the material around it, magma tends to slowly rise toward the surface of Earth. As magma rises, it sometimes cools and hardens before reaching the surface.

Because it is below the surface, magma cools very slowly. As it cools, mineral grains, or crystals, have a long time to form. So the mineral grains are large in rocks that are formed from magma.

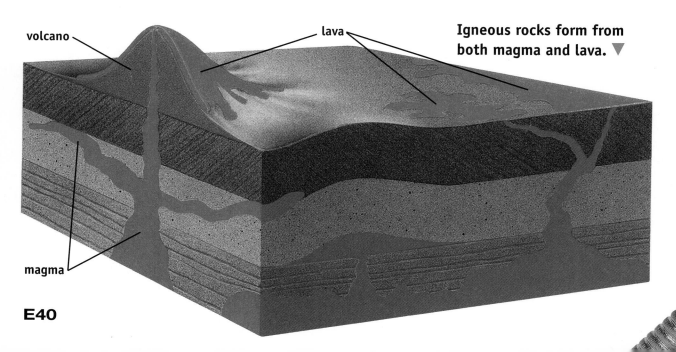

volcano

lava

magma

Igneous rocks form from both magma and lava. ▼

E40

One of the most common rocks formed from magma is granite, shown below. Notice that it consists of different minerals. The gray-colored mineral is feldspar, the white mineral is quartz, and the black mineral is mica. Notice the size of the mineral grains that make up granite. Have you seen granite used in your community? If so, how was this rock used?

Stone Mountain, which towers high above the surrounding land in the state of Georgia, is a mountain of granite. Where did this rock harden? How do you think this rock became exposed at Earth's surface?

Not all the igneous rocks that harden from magma are the same. They vary in the kinds of mineral grains that form. The kinds of minerals that form depend on what the magma is made up of.

Gabbro is another kind of igneous rock. Like all rocks that cool from magma, it has large mineral grains. But notice that gabbro is mostly made of dark-colored minerals, in this case pyroxene (pī räks'ēn) and olivine. It has few light-colored minerals, such as quartz.

▲ Stone Mountain, in Georgia

Igneous Rocks From Lava

You know that magma rises toward Earth's surface. What do you think might happen when it breaks through to the surface? Magma that reaches Earth's surface is called **lava**. Look back at the diagram showing lava and magma on page E40. An opening in Earth's surface through which lava flows is called a volcano. When lava cools and hardens at Earth's surface, it forms igneous rock.

Three kinds of rocks that formed from lava are shown on page E42. Compare them with the photograph of granite. How do the sizes of the mineral grains compare? Use what you have learned about igneous rocks to explain why the grains differ in size.

▼ Granite

Gabbro ▶

▲ Basalt

▲ Obsidian

Rhyolite ▶

Basalt is an igneous rock that forms when lava rich in dark-colored minerals cools and hardens. Find basalt on the chart below. Note that its composition, or makeup, is similar to that of gabbro.

Because it flows out onto Earth's surface, lava cools faster than magma. So rocks cooled from lava, such as basalt, have smaller grains than rocks cooled from magma, such as gabbro. Areas in the states of Washington and Oregon are covered by basalt, because of past volcanic activity.

Obsidian (əb sid'ē ən) is another igneous rock, often called natural glass. Lava that forms obsidian cools and hardens so quickly that mineral grains have very little time to grow. This rapid cooling gives the rock its glassy look. Native Americans once used obsidian to make cutting tools such as blades. That's because obsidian forms sharp edges when broken.

Look at the photograph of the igneous rock rhyolite (rī'ə līt). Find it on the chart. How do you think rhyolite forms? ■

COMPOSITION	Contains more light-colored minerals ◀	Contains more dark-colored minerals ▶
LARGE mineral grains: forms from MAGMA	**Granite**	**Gabbro**
SMALL mineral grains: forms from LAVA	**Rhyolite**	**Basalt**
NO mineral grains: forms from LAVA		**Obsidian**

INVESTIGATE FURTHER!

EXPERIMENT

Make a model of the slow flow of magma within the Earth. Mix equal amounts of water and white glue in a bowl. Slowly add powered borax to the mixture until it is no longer liquid. Handle the material and describe its properties. How does it resemble magma? How does it differ?

Sedimentary Rocks: Rocks From Pieces

Reading Focus How do sedimentary rocks form?

Sedimentary (sed ə men'tər ē) **rocks** are rocks that form at Earth's surface when sediments harden into rock. **Sediments** include bits of existing rocks, minerals, and organic materials. As you may know, things that are called organic were once living.

There are many different kinds of sedimentary rocks. In fact, you probably use one sedimentary rock every day in school. Can you guess which sedimentary rock is used by students and teachers in the classroom? You also may have used it to draw on the sidewalk. Chalk is a sedimentary rock.

Animal, Vegetable, or Mineral?

Just like igneous rocks, sedimentary rocks can be grouped according to how they form. There are three types of sedimentary rocks: clastic, chemical, and organic.

Clastic sedimentary rocks are those in which pieces of rocks, minerals, and organic materials are cemented together. The bits of sediment that make up clastic rocks can be as small as single grains of mud or as large as boulders! As you might expect, clastic sedimentary rocks are common on Earth's surface.

Clastic rocks are grouped according to the size of the sediments they contain. Conglomerate (kən gläm'ər it), shale, and sandstone are examples of clastic rocks. Study the photographs of these rocks. How do their sediment pieces compare?

Most clastic rocks form when wind, water, or ice carries and then drops

◄ **Conglomerate**

Sandstone ▶

▲ **Shale**

E43

sediments. Over time, these materials become compacted, or squeezed together. Minerals dissolved in water seep into spaces between the materials. As the water dries, the minerals are deposited. They bind, or hold together, the loose sediments into solid rock. This binding of sediments is called **cementation** (sē men tā'shən).

Sandstone, as you might have guessed, is made of small, sand-sized rock bits. Sandstone often feels gritty, like sandpaper. Where on Earth do you think sandstone might be forming? Can you think of any uses for sandstone?

Chemical sedimentary rocks form when water rich in dissolved minerals evaporates, leaving the minerals behind. These rocks also form when chemical changes form new minerals. Rock gypsum, rock salt, and some kinds of limestone are examples of chemical sedimentary rocks.

The type of limestone shown in the photograph below consists mostly of calcite, which formed when sea or lake waters evaporated. Limestone is ground

▲ **Rock gypsum**

and mixed with other materials to make certain kinds of cement.

Rock gypsum forms when water evaporates, leaving behind the mineral gypsum. Gypsum is used in plaster of Paris and plaster walls.

Rock salt, which is almost pure halite, is known to you as table salt. It does, however, have other uses, as you can see in the photograph below.

Limestone ▼

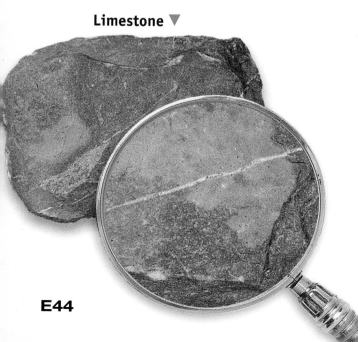

▲ **Rock salt is commonly used to melt ice and snow.**

The third type of sedimentary rock is called organic rock. Organic rocks form from the remains of plants and animals or from parts of organisms, such as shells. One type of coal is an organic sedimentary rock that forms when bits of dead plants are squeezed together over a long period of time. The squeezing removes all the water, leaving behind the carbon that forms coal. You'll find out more about coal later.

Limestones consist mostly of calcite. Some form when sea or lake waters evaporate. Others form when shells of sea animals become cemented together. Fine-grained limestones, like chalk, are the remains of tiny organisms that lived in the ocean.

Features of Sedimentary Rocks

Scientists, including budding scientists like you, can learn about how a sedimentary rock was formed by observing the features preserved in the rock. When sediments are dropped by water, wind, or ice, the sediments build up in layers. A layer can be as thin as a sheet of paper or as thick as a few meters! The layers harden over time. And as more sediments are dropped, more layers are formed. So most sedimentary rocks are layered. This layering is often called bedding.

Wind, water, ice and the shape of the land can affect the formation of beds of sedimentary rock. Use the chart on page E46 to compare how sediment beds form.

Science in Literature

CLUES TO EARTH'S PAST

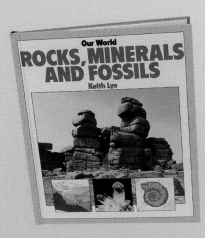

Rocks, Minerals and Fossils
by Keith Lye
Silver Burdett Press, 1991

"Sedimentary rocks and the fossils they contain provide much information about the climate when the rocks were formed. For example, limestones containing coral remains were formed in warm, shallow seas, while coal was formed in warm swamps. The fact that coal is found in Antarctica shows that the climate of that icy continent was once much warmer than it is today."

The sedimentary rocks of places like the Grand Canyon are more than amazing scenery. They are also a 3-D lesson on the history of Earth! Find out how to "read the rocks" in *Rocks, Minerals and Fossils* by Keith Lye.

Sediment Beds

◄ Notice that the surface of this sediment layer looks wavy. These wavy lines are called ripple marks. They are formed by moving water or wind. You may have seen ripple marks near a stream or on a beach. How might they become sedimentary rock?

◄ Most sediment beds, like these in shale, were deposited horizontally, resulting in the characteristic layering of sedimentary rock.

◄ The beds in this sandstone show cross-bedding. They formed when wind dropped sand on the curved slopes of sand dunes. Eventually, the sand beds hardened to form sandstone. What kinds of places can you think of that have sand dunes?

◄ Mud cracks are another feature sometimes preserved in sedimentary rocks. Mud cracks are evidence of wet periods followed by dry periods during the formation of a rock.

If you've ever gone rock collecting or to a natural history museum, you've probably seen fossils. A **fossil** is any remains or evidence of an organism from the past. Sedimentary rocks sometimes contain fossils. The photograph shows a fern fossil. Based on this fossil, what conclusions might you draw about how this rock formed?

The Rock Key on page E39 uses the letter S to show which rocks are sedimentary rocks. Try to classify the sedimentary rocks listed in the Rock Key as clastic, chemical, or organic, based on their properties. ■

Fern fossil ▶

Metamorphic Rocks: A Change of Identity

Reading Focus How do metamorphic rocks form?

The third major group of rocks is the metamorphic (met ə môr'fik) rocks. The word *metamorphic* is made of two word parts that together mean "to change form." In some ways metamorphic rocks are like sedimentary rocks because both kinds form from existing rocks. In other ways, metamorphic rocks are like igneous rocks because both kinds can form at high temperatures and pressures. So what qualities make metamorphic rocks different from both sedimentary and igneous rocks? Find out.

New Rocks

Metamorphic rocks are new rocks that form from existing rocks because of changes caused by heat, pressure, or chemicals. The existing rocks that are changed may be sedimentary, igneous, or other metamorphic rocks. The change from one rock type to another is called metamorphism.

Some changes that occur with metamorphism result in changes in texture. *Texture* refers to the size and shape of mineral grains and the way in which they are arranged in a rock. In other cases, changes in composition, or makeup, take place. The changes that occur during metamorphism can result from three different sets of conditions.

Contact metamorphism occurs when hot magma or lava comes in contact with rock. The rock gets "baked" by the molten

Metamorphic rocks form when existing rocks are changed by heat, pressure, and chemicals. ▼

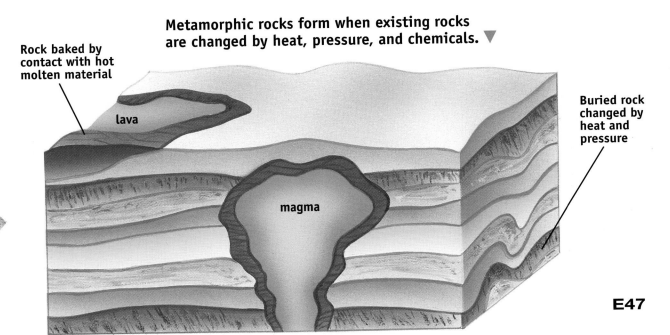

Rock baked by contact with hot molten material

lava

magma

Buried rock changed by heat and pressure

E47

material. So temperature alone, not pressure, causes the rock to change. Changes can occur in the kinds of minerals present and in the sizes of the grains. Liquids and gases escaping from the magma can also chemically change minerals in the surrounding rocks.

A second type of metamorphism is called regional metamorphism. It occurs in rocks that are buried deep below Earth's surface, where temperature and pressure are high. The texture of the rocks changes, particularly in the way the minerals are arranged. Mineral grains tend to become lined up in the same direction because of high pressures. Also, high temperatures cause changes in the original mineral makeup of the rocks.

Burial metamorphism causes the least amount of change in a rock. Burial metamorphism occurs when the weight of rocks and sediments burying a rock puts pressure on that rock. During burial metamorphism, the temperatures and pressures are not as high as they are with regional metamorphism. However temperatures and pressures are high enough to cause crystals to be altered and rock textures to change slightly. Such changes cause shale, a sedimentary rock, to be changed to slate, a metamorphic rock.

Banded Metamorphic Rocks

Metamorphic rocks are grouped according to their textures as banded or nonbanded. As you would expect, rocks with a banded texture look as if they contain bands, or thin layers. The bands may look wavy or straight. You are probably familiar with some banded metamorphic rocks. Gneiss (nīs) is a banded metamorphic rock that contains quartz, mica, and feldspar. Which igneous rock is made of these same three minerals? Look at the photograph of gneiss. Note the bands of mineral grains. In which direction do you think the pressure was applied during metamorphism?

Another banded metamorphic rock is slate. Recall that slate forms when shale, a sedimentary rock, is exposed to changes in temperature and pressure. Slate is used as a roofing material. Some chalkboards are made of slate. When exposed to more heat and pressure, slate can become another banded metamorphic rock, the kind called phyllite (fil′īt).

Gneiss ▼

Phyllite ▶

Slate ▶

▲ Marble

▲ Quartzite

Nonbanded Metamorphic Rocks

In nonbanded metamorphic rocks the mineral grains have not been lined up by pressure. The texture of these rocks is described as massive. Look at the photographs of the nonbanded rocks above. Contrast them with the photographs of banded rocks. Can you infer the meaning of the term *massive* as used to describe metamorphic rocks?

Marble is a nonbanded metamorphic rock. Marble forms when limestone is changed by metamorphism. Marble can be white, black, pink, gray, or green with streaks of other colors.

Another nonbanded metamorphic rock is quartzite (kwôrts'īt). Quartzite forms when sandstone that is rich in quartz is exposed to high pressures and temperatures. ■

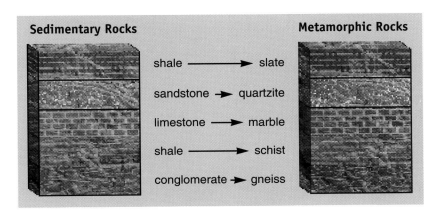

◀ The drawing shows some different parent rocks of metamorphic rocks.

INVESTIGATION 1 WRAP-UP

REVIEW

1. Name the three basic types of rocks and describe how each forms.

2. Name the three basic types of sedimentary rock and describe how each forms.

CRITICAL THINKING

3. How are rocks that form from magma and lava alike and different?

4. Fossils are found almost exclusively in sedimentary rocks. Suggest a hypothesis to explain this observation.

INVESTIGATION 2

HOW DO THE PROPERTIES OF ROCKS MAKE THEM USEFUL?

Make a rock! Punch small holes in the bottom of a paper cup. Pour a handful of sand into the cup. Dilute some white glue with a little water. Pour it into the sand. Let the water drain out. After the sand has dried, tear off the paper and behold your "rock." What are its properties? Find a use for it!

Activity

Comparing Properties of Rocks

Different kinds of rocks have different properties, which make the rocks useful in different ways.

MATERIALS
- rock set
- hand lens
- *Science Notebook*

- -

Procedure

1. Look at the Rock Key on page E39. In your *Science Notebook*, **make a chart** like the one shown. Include one row for each rock listed in the Rock Key.

Name of Rock	Group (I, S, or M)	Predictions	Observations

See **SCIENCE** *and* **MATH TOOLBOX** page H11 if you need to review **Making a Chart to Organize Data.**

2. **Classify** your rocks into three groups so that the first group has all the igneous rocks (I), the second group has all the sedimentary rocks (S), and the third group has all the metamorphic rocks (M). In the chart, **record** the names of all the rocks in each group.

3. **Predict** which groups will have layered rocks. Look for layered rocks and **record** your observations.

4. **Predict** which groups will have crystalline rocks (rocks with crystals). Look for crystalline rocks and **record** your observations.

5. **Predict** which rocks will be made of particles or fragments. Look for rocks that are made of particles or fragments. **Record** your observations.

6. **Compare and contrast** the rocks in your collection. **Record** as many properties as you can for each rock.

Step 2

Analyze and Conclude

1. In which group(s) of rocks do you find layers, and in which do you not find layers?

2. In which group(s) of rocks do you find crystals, and in which do you not find crystals?

3. In which group(s) do you find particles or fragments, and in which do you not find particles or fragments?

4. Consider the properties of the rocks in your collection. Then **make inferences** about some uses for the rocks.

INVESTIGATE FURTHER!

RESEARCH

How's your Unit Project rock collection coming? Do some research to find out how the types of rocks in your collection are used by people.

Rock Quarries

Reading Focus What are two kinds of rock removed from quarries and how are these rocks used?

Have you ever seen a fireplace built of rocks? How about a rock wall or a path lined with stones? Chances are, the rocks that make up these things came from a quarry (kwôr'ē). A rock **quarry** is an open pit at Earth's surface, from which certain rocks are removed. Billions of tons of granite, sandstone, limestone, slate, marble, and other types of rocks are removed each year from quarries all over the world.

Rock is removed from quarries in two forms. Dimension stones are slabs of rock that are removed from quarries in specific shapes and sizes. Most dimension stones are used to build things that will both last and look deco-rative, such as buildings. So the slabs must be solid and have an attractive texture, pattern, or color.

Most of the rock removed from quarries is in another form, called crushed stone. Crushed stone consists of bits and pieces of rocks. These rock pieces are primarily used in concrete, cements, and other construction materials.

You've probably tried to break or move a few big rocks at times. It isn't easy. So how do you suppose rocks are mined in quarries? How rocks are mined depends on how they'll be used. Most crushed stone gets blasted from solid rock with the use of explosives. First, holes are drilled into the rock. Then explosives are placed in the holes

Marble being cut at a quarry ▼　　**Marble slab being lifted by a crane** ▼　　**Transporting marble slabs** ▼

and set off, causing the rock to break up. Of course, this wouldn't be a great way to mine dimension stones, unless you are planning to cement the pieces back together!

In most quarries, dimension stones are cut from solid rock by using either a drill or a torch. Air moving through the drill makes the drill bit, or tip, spin rapidly. As it spins, the bit cuts away at the rock. A torch, on the other hand, cuts the rock by melting it. When cut with a torch, the edges of the slabs are smooth.

Once the dimension stones are cut, a huge crane is used to move them. The blocks of rock, which can weigh several tons each, are secured with hooks and chains. Then the crane is used to slowly lift and carry the stones.

From the quarry, loose slabs are taken to a processing mill. Many quarries that mine dimension stones have their own processing mills. At these mills the rock slabs are cut to size using steel wires and rock saws. The saw blades are often made with diamonds. As you learned in Chapter 1, diamond is the hardest known mineral. Diamonds can cut through even the hardest rocks.

Once the rocks are cut and sized, they may be polished. Polishing gradually smooths out any wire or saw marks left from the cutting stage. When the dimension stones are highly polished, they are ready to be shipped around the corner, around the country, or around the world.

The table shows some common dimension stones, where they come from, and what they are used for. Do any quarried rocks come from your state? What states might produce the marble for a counter top? Which stones might be used in monuments? ■

Dimension Stones

Rock	Where From	Uses
Granite	Vermont, Massachusetts, Maine, New Hampshire, Rhode Island, Minnesota, Wisconsin	monuments, buildings, grave markers
Sandstone	New York, Ohio, Pennsylvania, Kentucky, Connecticut	buildings, trim
Marble	Vermont, Georgia	monuments, buildings, flooring, counter tops, kitchen items
Limestone	Texas, Utah, Indiana, Missouri, Florida, Minnesota	decorative trims, buildings, monuments, park benches

A Ton of Bricks!

Reading Focus How are bricks made?

Although they are hard like most rocks and are made from minerals, bricks aren't actually rocks. Rocks are made of one or more minerals, and they form naturally. Since rocks are formed by nature, bricks cannot be rocks because bricks are made by people!

Brick Making Today

What, then, *are* bricks? Bricks are small, rectangular blocks made from a mixture of clays and other sediments. To make bricks, different kinds and amounts of clay are dug from river bottoms or other places on Earth's surface. These minerals are taken to a factory where they are crushed into a fine powder. Sometimes the powder is sifted to remove any large pieces. Water is added to the powder to make a thick, gooey paste. The paste is pressed into molds that are coated with sand or water. The coating helps to prevent the mixture from sticking to the molds, much as butter helps to keep cake batter from sticking to a pan.

Next, molds are placed in a kiln, or drying oven. When the clay mixture is completely dry, the molds are fired in another kiln. Firing chemically changes the clay blocks by heating them for up to 12 hours at temperatures above 800°C (1,500°F). Once fired, the bricks are cooled and taken to other parts of the factory to be packed and shipped.

Brick Making in the Past

People have used bricks for at least 60 centuries! The first bricks were probably simple mud blocks dried in the Sun. Adobe (ə dō′bē), or sun-dried brick, is thought to have first been made in dry areas of the world. Adobe bricks are made with a mixture of clay, sand, and sometimes, straw. The materials are mixed by hand, with bare feet, or with a simple tool. The mixture is then put into molds and allowed to dry for at least two weeks. When dry, the bricks are removed from the molds and used.

About 3,500 years ago, people began to fire bricks. They discovered that firing the clay blocks made them harder and longer-lasting.

▲ **This structure is made from adobe.**

Making Bricks

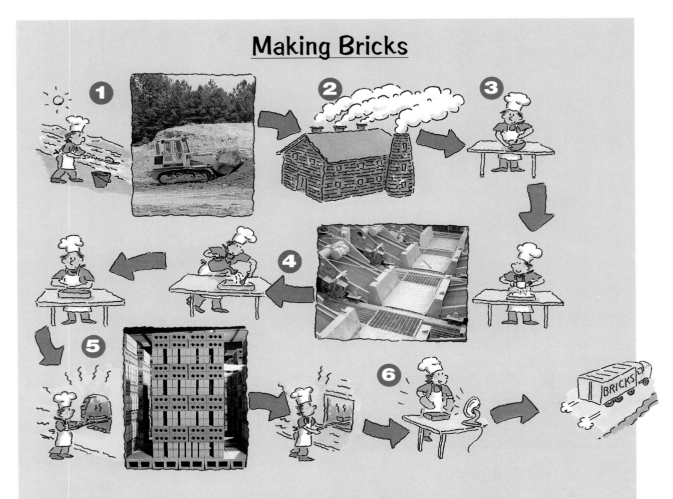

1. Clays and sediments are removed from Earth.

2. They are ground into powder in a factory.

3. The powder is mixed with water to form a paste.

4. The mixture is put into molds.

5. The molds are placed in ovens, called kilns, in which the mixture dries and changes.

6. The hardened brick is cooled.

INVESTIGATION 2 WRAP-UP

THINK IT WRITE IT

REVIEW

1. How are rocks mined in quarries?

2. What are four common types of dimension stones?

CRITICAL THINKING

3. Identify some ways in which rocks differ.

4. Suppose you were asked to recommend a type of rock that could be used to make a strong but attractive building. What rock would you choose? Use the Rock Key on page E39 for help. Give reasons to support your choice.

HOW DO ROCKS CHANGE OVER TIME?

It may seem that rocks last forever, but they don't. They change, just like everything else. Unwrap some broken crayons and set them on wax paper in the hot sunlight. What happens? What rock-forming change have you just modeled?

Activity

'Round and 'Round She Goes

It may take hundreds of thousands of years, even millions of years, but Earth materials go through changes called the rock cycle. In this activity you'll investigate this cycle.

MATERIALS

- Rock Cycle diagram
- rock set
- vial of sand
- vial of clay
- seashell
- *Science Notebook*

Procedure

1. Place the Rock Cycle diagram on your desk.

2. Granite, sandstone, sand, and quartzite form part of a loop in the rock cycle. Use those samples from your rock set to **make a model** of the rock cycle. Arrange the sand and rocks in their correct places on the Rock Cycle diagram. Then, in your *Science Notebook*, **draw** the part of the loop they make. **Label** your drawing to show the kinds of materials or rocks and the processes they undergo in changing from one to another.

3. Gneiss, sandstone, and sand make a complete loop in the rock cycle. Arrange those samples in order on the diagram. **Draw** and **label** this loop.

4. Basalt, slate, shale, and clay make another part of a loop. Arrange your samples in order on the diagram. **Draw** and **label** this loop.

5. Another part of a loop in the rock cycle is made by seashells, marble, and limestone. Get samples of these materials and arrange them on your rock cycle. **Draw** and **label** this loop.

Step 2

Analyze and Conclude

1. Explain why the loop in step 3 is a complete cycle that could happen over and over again.

2. In step 2, why don't the materials listed form a complete loop? What is needed to make this a complete loop in the rock cycle?

3. **Suggest a definition** of the rock cycle, based on how you think it works.

Technology
Link
CD-ROM

INVESTIGATE FURTHER!

Use the **Science Processor CD-ROM,** *The Solid Earth* (Investigation 2, Recycling Rocks) to explore the rock cycle.

Fossil Fuels

Reading Focus What are fossil fuels and how do they form?

How many ways did you use energy today? Most of the energy people use comes from fossil fuels. As you might suspect from its name, a fossil fuel is a material formed from plant or animal remains that can be burned for energy. Over millions of years, pressures and temperatures have squeezed and changed the remains. Left behind are substances rich in carbon and hydrogen that were once parts of organisms. When these substances are burned, energy is released.

Coal is one kind of fossil fuel. The drawings show the different stages in the formation of different types of coal. Peat and all types of coal are used as fuel. In the United States, coal provides about 20 percent of our energy needs.

Two other kinds of fossil fuel are oil and natural gas. Oil and natural gas

Millions of years ago

PEAT
60% Carbon
Coal begins to form when swamp plants die and are quickly buried beneath sediments and other plants. Tiny organisms called bacteria cause organic material to decay and change. Over time, a dark, watery organic material called peat forms.

peat layer

LIGNITE
70% Carbon
With time, the peat gets buried by more sediments. The weight of these sediments compacts the peat and squeezes water out. Eventually, the percent of carbon present increases and a sedimentary rock called lignite, a type of coal, forms.

lignite layer

form when ocean plants and animals die and their remains settle to the ocean floor. These remains become buried by sediments and, over time, the sediments become sedimentary rocks. Heat, pressure, and the action of bacteria change the organic remains into oil and natural gas. The oil and natural gas seep through cracks and spaces in the rocks. When they reach a rock layer that doesn't have cracks or spaces, the oil and gas become trapped. The oil collects in a layer of rock below the surface, and the gas collects in a pocket above the oil. ■

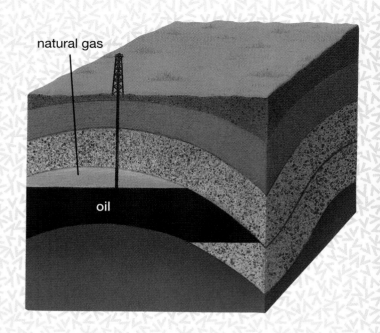

natural gas

oil

▲ **Oil and natural gas are often found trapped below the surface.**

Present Day

BITUMINOUS COAL
80% Carbon
As the rock becomes buried deeper, temperature and pressure increase. Nearly all of the water that was once in the plant parts gets forced out and bituminous (bi too′ mə nəs) coal forms. Bituminous coal, or soft coal, is a sedimentary rock that is mostly carbon.

ANTHRACITE
95% Carbon
With deep burying and great temperature and pressure, bituminous coal becomes metamorphosed to form anthracite (an′thrə sīt). Anthracite is a metamorphic rock. It has the highest percent of carbon of all the forms of coal.

bituminous layer

anthracite layer

E59

Rocks in Circles

Reading Focus How do rocks change over time?

 You learned that high temperatures and great pressures can change any rock into a metamorphic rock. But any kind of rock—igneous, sedimentary, or metamorphic—can be changed into another kind of rock, not just by metamorphism but also by other processes.

Heat and pressure are just two of Earth's agents of change. They act to change Earth's rock materials. The series of changes that rocks undergo is called the **rock cycle**.

Notice the ovals in the diagram of the rock cycle on the next page. They represent five kinds of rock materials: igneous rock, sedimentary rock, metamorphic rock, sediments, and molten rock (magma and lava). Between the ovals are factors that cause rocks to change. Among these factors are compacting, cementing, heat, pressure, melting, and cooling.

When you play most board games, you can move in only one direction around the board. But the rock cycle changes in many ways. Use the diagram to see how one type of rock changes into another. Start at any oval. Then move in the direction of any arrow coming out of the oval. Follow the arrows, and you can't go wrong.

Sedimentary to Metamorphic

As you can see from the diagram, there are many factors in the rock cycle that cause change. Find the words *Sedimentary Rock* on the diagram. What's one way in which sedimentary rock can change? You know that sedimentary rocks form at or near Earth's surface. What do you think happens when these rocks become buried? High temperatures and pressures deep below the surface change sedimentary rocks into metamorphic rocks. Follow this change on the diagram.

Metamorphic to Igneous

What do you suppose happens when the pressures and temperatures deep below the surface become very high? Melting, or the changing of a solid to a liquid, occurs. Melting changes metamorphic rock into molten rock. Find *Melting* on the diagram.

As magma or lava cools, minerals form. When different minerals, such as quartz and mica, form, they grow into different-sized crystals. So this step is sometimes called crystallizing.

Notice in the rock cycle diagram that magma and lava cool and crystallize to form igneous rock. On the diagram, follow the change from metamorphic rock to igneous rock.

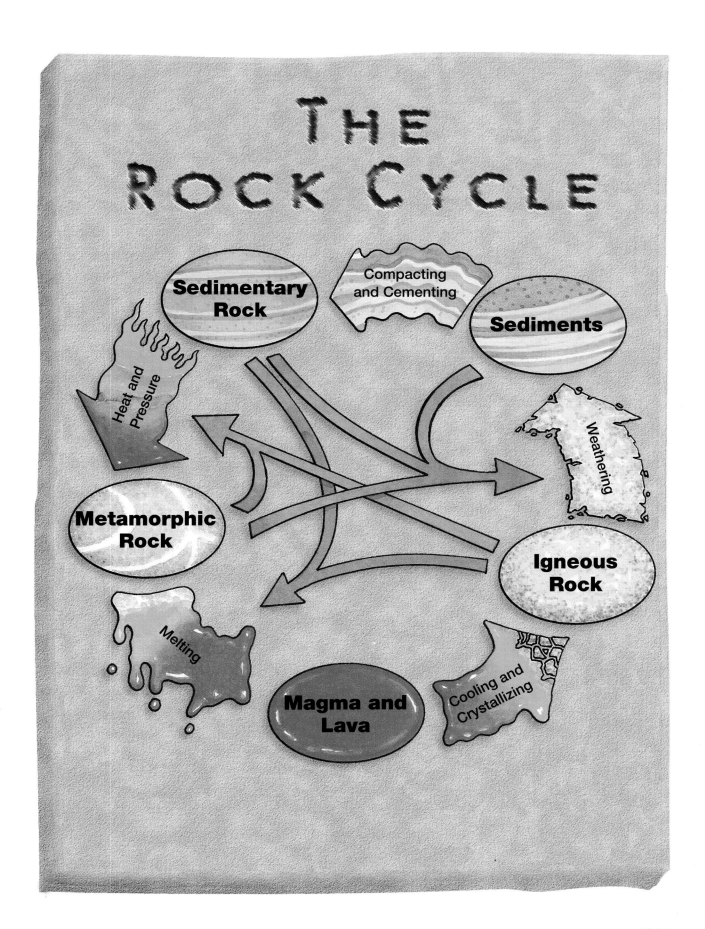

THE ROCK CYCLE

Sedimentary Rock

Compacting and Cementing

Sediments

Heat and Pressure

Weathering

Metamorphic Rock

Igneous Rock

Melting

Magma and Lava

Cooling and Crystallizing

Igneous to Sedimentary

What steps might igneous rock go through to become sedimentary rock? Any rock at Earth's surface is exposed to a number of conditions that cause the rock to break into small rock bits, or sediments.

Weathering is the breaking up of rocks into sediments. Through weathering, an igneous rock can eventually become sediment bits. Find the arrow labeled *Compacting and Cementing* in the diagram on page E61. Recall that when sediments are compacted, they are squeezed together. Cementing bonds sediments together. Compacting and cementing of sediments changes them into sedimentary rock. So, as you can see in the diagram, igneous rock must first weather to become sediment. Then the sediment is compacted and cemented and changed into sedimentary rock.

There are many other paths of change in the rock cycle. For example, how might sedimentary rock change into igneous rock? How might metamorphic rock become sediment?

▲ **When water mixes with hot lava that flows from a volcano, the lava cools, forming igneous rock, as the water becomes steam.**

By using the diagram on page E61, you can follow these changes. You can also use the diagram to find other ways rock materials change. What others can you find? ■

=== **INVESTIGATION 3 WRAP-UP** ===

REVIEW

1. What is the rock cycle?

2. Describe four ways rocks can change over time.

CRITICAL THINKING

3. Sand in a riverbed can become sandstone, and sandstone can become sand in a riverbed. Is this statement true or false? Explain your answer.

4. Describe how granite might become obsidian.

REFLECT & EVALUATE

Word Power

Write the letter of the term that best matches the definition. *Not all terms will be used.*

1. An open pit from which rocks are removed
2. Series of changes that rocks undergo
3. Rocks that form when sediments harden
4. Rocks that form from existing rocks
5. Bits of rocks, minerals, and organic materials
6. Rocks that form when melted rock material cools and hardens

a. fossil
b. igneous rocks
c. magma
d. metamorphic rocks
e. quarry
f. rock cycle
g. sedimentary rocks
h. sediments

Check What You Know

Write the term in each pair that best completes each sentence.

1. Granite forms when (lava, magma) cools.
2. Sandstone is an example of a (clastic, chemical) sedimentary rock.
3. Mineral grains of a rock tend to become lined up during (contact, regional) metamorphism.
4. Igneous rocks are changed into sediments through (weathering, compacting).

Problem Solving

1. You observe that a rock has large crystals and is unlayered. What type of rock would you infer it to be? Explain your inference.

2. Watch TV commercials or read advertisements of companies that provide coal, oil, or natural gas for heating homes. What can you infer about the safety of each product and the service offered by the companies?

Explain how the cycle shown could be never ending. Then describe an event that could break the cycle.

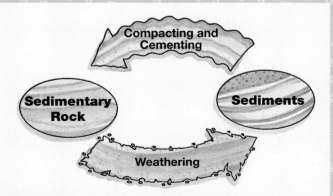

3

EARTH'S
STRUCTURES

Did you know that you can float with both feet on the ground? In fact, you're always floating—even when you think you're standing still. Here's why. The ground under your feet is drifting on a layer of hot, gooey rock. This rock is only one of the remarkable materials that make up Earth. Sometimes the drifting movement leads to earthquakes.

PEOPLE
USING SCIENCE

Geophysicist Scientists who study the physics of Earth are geophysicists (jē fiz' i sists). Some geophysicists, such as Dr. Rufus D. Catchings, study earthquakes and their effects on Earth. Dr. Catchings works for the United States Geological Survey. He is mapping the underground rock formations where earthquakes are likely to be felt.

Dr. Catchings is coordinating a project that "shoots" sound into the ground in order to find places where rock sections are likely to move. His team has mapped the area around the 1994 earthquake site in Northridge, California. On the opposite coast, his team is mapping an area in northern Delaware. In this chapter you'll learn more about where and why earthquakes occur.

Coming Up

◀ Dr. Catchings and a co-worker in earthquake territory.

E65

WHAT IS EARTH'S STRUCTURE?

How do rocks make up the sphere called Earth? What's at the center of that sphere? This investigation will help you answer such questions about Earth's structure by looking at what's inside as well as outside Earth.

Activity

A Model Earth

An apple makes a good model of Earth's structure. In science, a model is used to help understand something else. Sometimes a model helps scientists to ask better questions. In this activity you'll use an apple as a model of Earth.

MATERIALS
- wax paper
- apple
- plastic knife
- *Science Notebook*

Procedure

1. Place a piece of wax paper on your desktop. Put an apple on the wax paper.

2. Use the apple to **model** the interior of Earth. Cut the apple in half. Carefully **observe** the cut surface from the skin to the center of the apple. In your *Science Notebook*, **sketch** and **describe** what you see.

Step 2

3. Cut both halves in half again. The skin represents Earth's **crust,** or surface layer. The skin on three of the pieces is a model for the amount of Earth's crust that is covered by oceans.

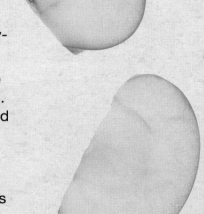

Step 3

 Recall that one half of one half is one fourth, so the apple is now divided into fourths.

4. Examine one of the pieces of apple carefully. Compare the thickness of the skin to the thickness of the rest of the piece.

Analyze and Conclude

1. Based on your model, how much of Earth's crust is covered by oceans? How much of the crust is land?

2. Earth has a layer below its crust called the **mantle.** The mantle covers a ball, called the **core**, in the middle of Earth. Infer which parts of the apple are models for the mantle and the core.

3. Compare the thicknesses of the crust, mantle, and core in your model. Based on your model, what can you hypothesize about the depths, or thicknesses, of the layers of Earth?

Technology Link
CD-ROM

INVESTIGATE FURTHER!

Use the **Science Processor CD-ROM**, *The Solid Earth* (Unit Opening Investigation, Down to Earth) to find out what it would be like to dig a hole through Earth's center.

The Sphere We Live On

Reading Focus What is the interior of Earth like?

When you hear the word *model*, what do you think of? You may picture a model airplane or a fashion model. In science, a **model** is something used to represent an object or an idea. In the activity on pages E66 and E67, an

> **Using Math**
>
> *Earth has four layers. The thickness of the layers add up to the radius of Earth. What is a reasonable estimate of Earth's radius in kilometers?*

apple is used as a model of Earth. What would happen if you took a huge knife and sliced right through Earth instead of through an apple? You'd see four layers instead of three—so the apple model is a bit too simple. Now take a look at another Earth model, shown below.

The Crust

Earth's outer layer is called the **crust**. It is the thinnest of all the layers, but it varies in thickness around Earth. It can be as thin as 10 km (6 mi) under the oceans and as thick as 65 km (40 mi) below the continents.

The crust is made up of solid rock. It is mostly granite, gabbro, and basalt, but it also includes all the igneous, sedimentary, and metamorphic rocks you have learned about. Much of the crust is covered by oceans, lakes, rivers, sediments, plants, and soil. The crust is broken into many large and small pieces called plates. These plates float like rafts on the layer below the crust. They can move very slowly

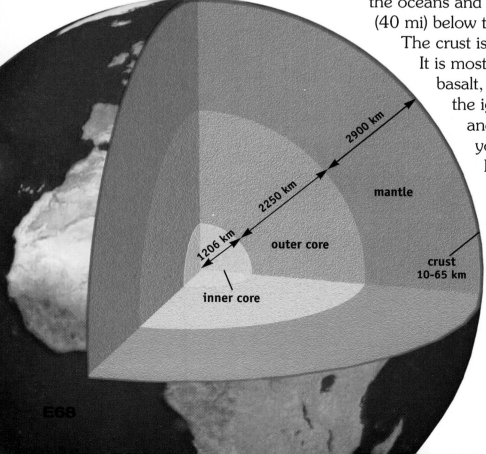

2900 km

2250 km

1206 km

mantle

outer core

crust
10-65 km

inner core

around Earth's surface, carrying the continents and oceans with them.

The Mantle

Below the crust is the **mantle**. The mantle is Earth's thickest layer.

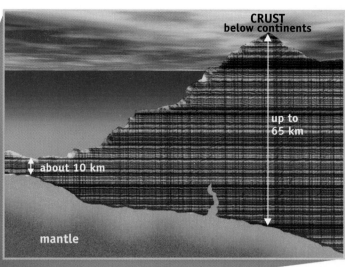

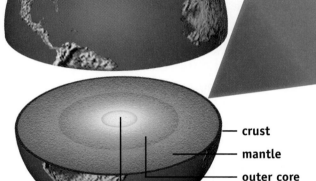

— crust
— mantle
— outer core
— inner core

▲ **Earth's crust is thicker beneath continents than beneath oceans.**

It takes up about 84 percent of Earth's volume. The part of this layer that is closest to the crust is made of solid rock. However, much of this solid rock has some properties of liquids. It can flow like syrup or be stretched out like putty.

Much of the mantle is composed of an igneous rock called peridotite (per ə dō′tīt). This rock is dark in color and rich in iron, magnesium, and silicon. When you studied about metamorphic rocks, you found out that temperature and pressure increase as you go deeper below Earth's surface. Temperature and pressure are much greater in the mantle than in the crust. As a result, some rock in the mantle melts. This molten rock sometimes makes its way to the surface as lava.

The Inner and Outer Core

Below the mantle is Earth's core. The **core** consists of heavy material that sank to Earth's center billions of years ago. The core is made up of a solid inner layer and a molten outer layer.

The outer core is made of molten iron, silicon, and carbon. Scientists think the boundary between the outer core and the mantle is wavy. They think the hills and valleys in this boundary are caused by the movement of molten rock between the outer core and the mantle. At Earth's center is the inner core, which is made of solid iron and nickel. Temperatures here may exceed 5,000°C (9,000°F)—almost as hot as the surface of the Sun! The extreme pressure here prevents the iron and nickel from melting.

Why Did Layers Form?

How do you think the different layers of Earth developed? One hypothesis is that billions of years ago, energy released by the breakdown of elements inside Earth caused the planet to grow hotter and hotter. Much of the iron and nickel found in Earth's rocks melted.

Because they are very heavy, the molten iron and nickel sank to the center of Earth. Extreme pressure turned these materials back to a solid. Lighter materials also melted, but they rose to the surface. As a result, a crust of light rock and a core of heavy metals formed, with the mantle layer in between.

Journeying to Earth's Center

Scientists know much about Earth's deep layers, even though they haven't been able to travel there! However, some rocks that have formed from magma make it possible for scientists to "see" the mantle. Rocks such as kimberlite, that were once magma in the mantle, give clues about the composition of the mantle.

How do scientists know where the layers begin and end? Think about trying to figure out what is inside a wrapped present. You can't see inside, but you could infer what is in the box. Scientists make inferences about Earth's layers by studying earthquake waves.

When you drop a stone in a pond, waves of energy move across the water's surface. In a similar way, when an earthquake occurs, waves of energy travel through Earth in all directions. Earthquake waves travel through some materials faster than others. Scientists measure the time it takes for the waves to arrive at different places around the world. Then they infer what kind of material the waves traveled through.

In 1909 a scientist named Andrija Mohorovičić (mō -hō rō'və chich) noticed that earthquake waves started to travel faster once they reached a certain depth below Earth's surface. He inferred that there must be a different kind of rock at this depth.

Two kinds of earthquake waves, called P waves and S waves, have also been used to make inferences about the properties of the core and its depth below the surface. Look at the drawing on the next page to find out what scientists have learned from the study of different kinds of earthquake waves.

INVESTIGATE FURTHER!

RESEARCH

As you have read, some forms of energy can be obtained from inexhaustible resources. One of these is called geothermal energy, which comes from hot water within the Earth's crust. Find out what heats up the water and how this energy resource is used.

How Earthquake Waves Travel

An earthquake occurs at this location.

S waves travel through the solid crust and through the mantle but not through the outer core. As a result, scientists concluded that the outer core is liquid.

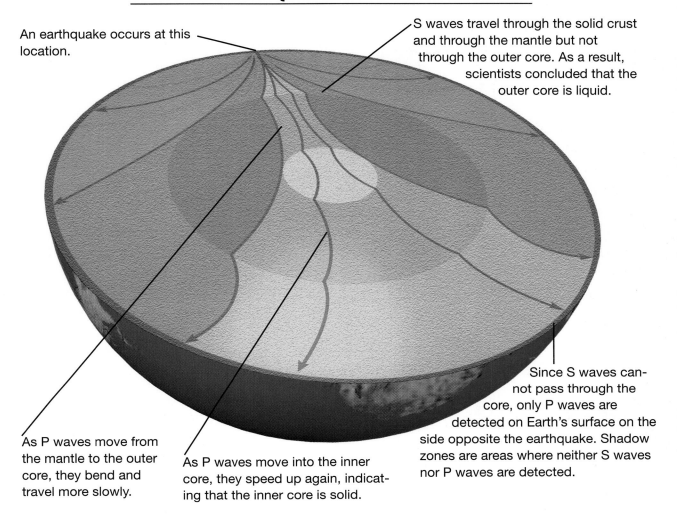

As P waves move from the mantle to the outer core, they bend and travel more slowly.

As P waves move into the inner core, they speed up again, indicating that the inner core is solid.

Since S waves cannot pass through the core, only P waves are detected on Earth's surface on the side opposite the earthquake. Shadow zones are areas where neither S waves nor P waves are detected.

Internet Field Trip
Visit **www.eduplace.com** to find out more about Earth's interior.

INVESTIGATION 1 WRAP-UP

REVIEW

1. Name and describe Earth's layers.

2. How do scientists find out about Earth's interior?

CRITICAL THINKING

3. Make a three-dimensional model showing Earth's layers. Identify the layers. Describe the materials you used for each layer.

4. Scientists know the mass and the volume of Earth. How could this information help them make inferences about the kind of matter that makes up Earth's interior?

HOW CAN FOSSILS HELP TELL US HOW OLD A ROCK IS?

Think of Earth as a book, with layers of rock stacked on top of one another like pages. How can you use the fossils in rocks to number the pages and read the book?

Activity
Layering Fossils

Scientists study rock layers and the fossils in them to learn about ancient forms of life. Find out what scientists can learn by doing this activity.

MATERIALS
- 3 different colors of modeling clay
- shell
- leaf
- twig
- *Science Notebook*

Procedure

1. Flatten three pieces of clay, each a different color.

2. **Make a model** of a fossil imprint by making an impression of a shell in one piece of clay. Make an impression of a leaf in a second piece of clay and a twig in a third piece of clay. Set aside the shell, leaf, and twig.

Step 2

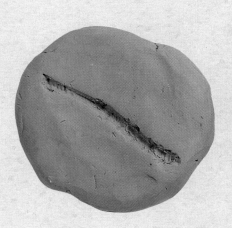

3. Each piece of clay represents a layer of sedimentary rock. Stack your rock layers one on top of the other. In your *Science Notebook*, **record** the order from top to bottom.

Analyze and Conclude

1. Based on what you have learned about how sedimentary rock forms, **infer** which of your "fossils" would be the oldest and which would be the youngest. Explain your reasoning.

2. Suppose that the twig is from a bush that lived after the shellfish died but before the tree from which the leaf was taken lived. Which fossil would be on the top of the stack? Which fossil would be on the bottom?

3. **Compare** your stack of fossils with the stacks made by other students. Are the fossils in the same order? If not, **infer** the relative ages of the fossils in each of the other stacks.

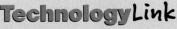

UNIT PROJECT LINK

Find out about fossils that have been collected in your community or that were discovered in your state. If possible, obtain examples of such fossils for your collection. Be sure to note the exact location where each fossil was found. If you can't get examples, make drawings of the fossils.

Technology Link

For more help with your Unit Project, go to **www.eduplace.com**.

Sorting Through Time

Reading Focus What did William Smith use to identify rock layers of the same age?

People have been digging up fossils for centuries. But not until the 1700s did the idea that fossils were the remains of creatures from the past begin to be accepted. You can bet that William Smith, an English geologist, didn't at first realize that his hobby of fossil collecting would show a way of matching rock layers by age!

While surveying land in England, Smith observed many rock layers and collected fossils. He noticed that rock layers lie stacked in a set order. Next, he saw that each layer of sedimentary rock contained different types of fossils. He soon realized that fossils could be used to recognize rock layers of the same age in different places. Scientists today use fossils to do just that!

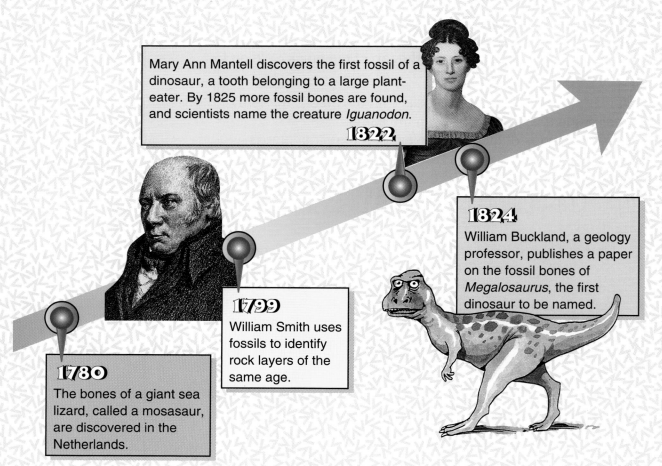

Mary Ann Mantell discovers the first fossil of a dinosaur, a tooth belonging to a large plant-eater. By 1825 more fossil bones are found, and scientists name the creature *Iguanodon*.
1822

1824
William Buckland, a geology professor, publishes a paper on the fossil bones of *Megalosaurus*, the first dinosaur to be named.

1799
William Smith uses fossils to identify rock layers of the same age.

1780
The bones of a giant sea lizard, called a mosasaur, are discovered in the Netherlands.

Fossils Tell Tales!

Reading Focus What clues do fossils provide about Earth's history?

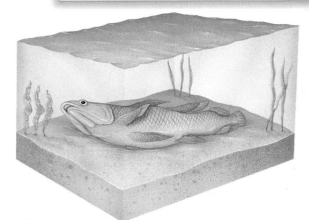

1 An organism dies.

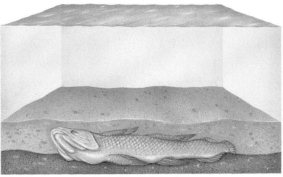

2 The remains get buried quickly by sediment. The soft parts decay.

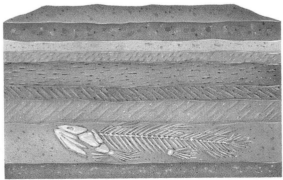

3 Over time, the hard parts get replaced with minerals. The sediment layer gets buried deeper and is compacted and cemented to form sedimentary rock.

There aren't many things more exciting than coming face to face with a dinosaur—a dinosaur skeleton, that is. Our knowledge of dinosaurs has come from studying fossils. Recall from Chapter 2 that fossils are remains or traces of living things from the past. What clues do you think a fossil might provide about Earth's past? A fossil can give clues about the environment where an organism once lived, how it may have moved, what it ate, what it looked like, and the age of the rock it was found in.

You Old Fossil!

How does a fossil form? Many fossils form when plants and animals die and are quickly buried by clay, sand, and other sediments. Look at the drawings to see how a fossil might form.

In some cases, bone and other hard materials are replaced by minerals. Other

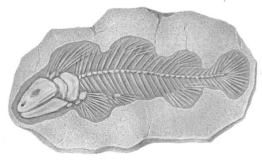

4 A fossil is later exposed due to the carrying away of weathered rock.

A cast ▶

A mold ▼

fossils form when plants and animals leave imprints in soft sediment. Over time, the organic material dissolves and the imprint gets filled with minerals or sediments. The imprint, or hollow part of the fossil, is called a mold. The material that fills in the imprint is called a cast. In the activity on pages E72 and E73, the imprints left in modeling clay by a shell, a leaf, and a twig are all examples of molds.

Relative Age

Scientists began studying fossils partly in the hope that fossils would help them estimate the age of Earth's rocks. There are many clues, including fossils, that you can use to learn about the ages of the rocks you see.

One clue to look for is the position of the rock layers. Recall that most sedimentary rocks begin as horizontal sediment layers. Think about books you might stack before putting them away. The first book you put down is on the bottom of the stack. It's the same with rock layers. The oldest rock layer was laid down first and is on the bottom. The youngest rock layer was laid down last and is on the top.

When you can say that one rock is older than another, you have found its relative age. A rock's **relative age** is how old it is compared to other rocks.

In addition to a rock's position, scientists also use certain kinds of fossils, called **index fossils**, to help them tell the relative ages of rock. Plant and animal species that lived for only a short time (perhaps only a few million years) but that could be found in large numbers over much of Earth make very helpful index fossils.

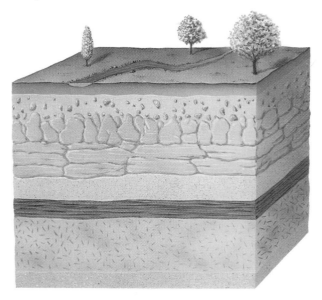

▲ The sequence of rock layers can be used to determine the relative ages of rocks.

The fossil shown below is a trilobite (tri′lō bīt). Many kinds of trilobites lived in oceans all over the world. Since certain kinds lived only at certain times in the past, they make good index fossils. When scientists find two rocks in two different places that both contain the same kind of trilobite fossils, they know that both rocks are about the same age.

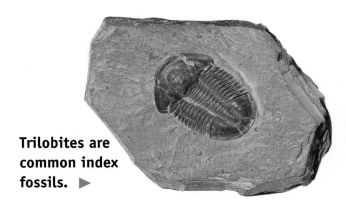

Trilobites are common index fossils. ▶

Absolute Age

When someone asks how old you are, you probably say, "I'm 11 years old," rather than "I'm older than my sister." At times, scientists need to know more than a rock's relative age. They need to know its **absolute age**, or how old the rock really is.

Some elements found on Earth are not stable. These elements decay, or break down, into other elements at a known rate. Scientists measure how much of a decaying element is present in a rock layer. They also measure how much of the new element, into which it decays, is present. The amount of time required for this level of decay provides the rock's absolute age.

Potassium is an element found in rocks. Some of the potassium found in igneous and metamorphic rocks breaks down to form the element argon. Scientists have used the amount of potassium and argon in rocks to find the absolute age of those rocks. Some are as old as a few billion years! ■

Technology Link
CD-ROM

INVESTIGATE FURTHER!

Use the **Science Processor CD-ROM**, *The Solid Earth* (Investigation 3, Can You Dig It?) to dig for and identify fossils.

INVESTIGATION 2 WRAP-UP

THINK IT

WRITE IT

REVIEW

1. How do fossils form?

2. How are index fossils used to date rocks?

CRITICAL THINKING

3. Suppose you found fossils in different layers of sedimentary rock. What can you conclude about which fossil formed first? How do you know?

4. A layer of shale is 3 million years old, and a layer of sandstone below it is 4 million years old. What can you conclude about the relative and absolute ages of each layer?

How Do Rocks Bend?

Tonight, before you get into bed, place your hands flat on top of your covers. Then push the covers 20 cm (8 in.) across the bed. Make them push up into folds. How are these folds, or bends, like mountains?

Activity

Big Wrinkles

The Appalachian Mountains in the eastern United States are folded mountains that are worn down. Geologists read them like a book. Here's how.

Procedure

1. Flatten three pieces of clay, each a different color, into slabs about 2 cm thick. Each slab represents a layer of rock. Stack the layers. In your *Science Notebook*, make a sketch to show the order of the colors from top to bottom.

 *See **SCIENCE** and **MATH** **TOOLBOX** page H6 if you need to review **Using a Tape Measure or Ruler.***

2. Gently press the ends of the stack together, folding the layers upward into a mountain. Continue pressing until the sides come together.

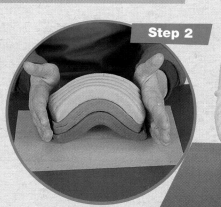
Step 2

3. In step 4 you will cut off the top of your mountain. **Predict** what the cut surface will look like. **Make a sketch** of your prediction.

4. In the process of **erosion**, weathered rock materials are carried away. **Model** erosion by cutting the top off your mountain. Use a plastic knife and cut so that you can see all three layers in the cut surface. **Observe** the cut surface and **compare** it with your prediction. **Draw** the eroded top. **Label** the layers by color and title your drawing "Upward Fold."

5. Separate the three colors of clay. Flatten each lump again and make another stack. Keep the order of the colors the same as in step 1.

6. Fold the left and right ends of the stack upward until they meet, forming a mountain.

7. **Model** erosion by cutting the top off your mountain. **Draw** the eroded top. **Label** the layers and title your drawing "Downward Fold."

Analyze and Conclude

1. Where was the oldest layer of rock in the stack in step 1? in the upward fold (step 4)? in the downward fold (step 7)?

2. Suppose you know the relative ages of rock layers on an eroded surface. Explain how you can tell if an upward folding of rocks or a downward folding of rocks has occurred.

UNIT PROJECT LINK

Walk around your community to observe natural landforms. A landform is a feature of Earth's surface, such as a hill, a valley, or a plain. Make a list of the landforms you observe. Try to identify the types of rocks that make up the different landforms. Can you tell which rock layers are oldest?

Technology Link

For more help with your Unit Project, go to **www.eduplace.com**.

Activity
Dome Questions

Some rocks get pushed up to form a geologic structure called a dome. Investigate how bending rocks can form this structure.

MATERIALS
- 3 different colors of modeling clay
- small ball (table tennis or golf ball)
- plastic knife
- *Science Notebook*

Procedure

1. Flatten and stack three layers of clay, each a different color. Then press the stack down over a small ball to make a dome.

Step 1

2. **Predict** what the pattern of layers will be when you cut the top off the dome. In your *Science Notebook*, **make a sketch** of your prediction.

3. **Model** erosion by cutting the top off the dome, but do not cut so deep that you can see the ball. **Observe** the pattern of layers and **compare** it to your prediction. **Make a sketch** of the actual pattern and title it "Dome." Be sure to **label** the order of the layers.

Analyze and Conclude

1. What does the pattern of layers in a dome look like?

2. **Infer** what forces could cause a dome to form. Explain your inference.

INVESTIGATE FURTHER!

RESEARCH

With a model dome made of clay, it takes only a short time to model erosion. But in nature, erosion can take a very long time. Research how long it took for the Appalachian Mountains to weather and erode from jagged peaks to smooth-topped mountains.

All Bent Out of Shape

Reading Focus What processes caused the Appalachian Mountains to form?

No matter how hard you try, you will probably never be able to bend a rock. But mountains all over the eastern United States formed because rocks can and do bend. Explore how this comes about.

Forces Bend Rocks

Every time you push open a door or pull a window shut, you apply a force. A force is a push or a pull. In the activity on pages E78 and E79, forces are applied to layers of clay, pushing the clay layers in different directions.

Sometimes forces in nature push on rocks in the same way. If the forces are strong enough and are applied long enough, they can cause rock layers to bend. A bend in a rock layer is called a **fold**.

Most forces that bend rock layers are caused by Earth's moving plates. Recall that Earth's crust consists of huge plates that move slowly around the surface. When two plates come together, their edges may become folded. Over millions of years the folds become higher and the folded rock forms mountains.

Folded mountains form as rock layers bend and are pushed upward. ▼

The Appalachian Mountains

The Appalachian Mountains in the eastern part of North America formed from folded rock. This mountain range stretches from Newfoundland in Canada to Alabama in the United States. The Appalachians formed as the plate carrying Africa collided with the plate carrying North America about 250 million years ago. With time, the folded rock formed high hills and deep valleys.

When rock layers bend, some layers fold up and some layers fold down. An **anticline** is an upward fold of rock layers. A **syncline** is a downward fold of rock layers. An anticline and a syncline are modeled in the activity on pages E78 and E79.

The process of weathering wears all rocks at Earth's surface into sediments. The carrying away of these weathered rock materials is called **erosion**. Wind, moving water, ice, and gravity all erode rocks. Since the time that folded rocks formed the Appalachians, it has taken many millions of years for them to weather and erode to their present height and shape.

Notice in the diagram on page E83 that the oldest rock layers of an anticline are found near the center of the fold. The layers get younger and younger as you move away from the center of the anticline. Now compare this to an eroded syncline. When a syncline is eroded, where is the youngest rock located?

Science in Literature

A Mountain Adventure

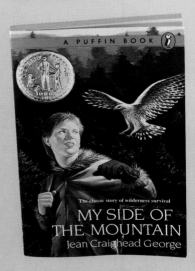

My Side of the Mountain
by Jean Craighead George
Puffin Books, 1991

"I landed with an explosion on my seat. The jolt splintered the ice and sent glass-covered limbs clattering to earth like a shopful of shattering crystal. As I sat there, and I didn't dare to move because I might get hurt, I heard an enormous explosion. It was followed by splintering and clattering and smashing. A maple at the edge of the meadow had literally blown up."

In *My Side of the Mountain* by Jean Craighead George, Sam Gribley escapes his city home to find a new life on a mountain. This exciting tale tells how Sam survives the dangers he faces.

The Appalachian Mountains are made up of many anticlines and synclines. All areas do not weather and erode at the same rate. Some rocks don't wear away easily. Rocks such as sandstone and conglomerate resist weathering. Where they are exposed at the surface, these rocks form ridges. Rocks such as limestone and shale wear away easily. These rocks form valleys. The combination of folding, weathering, and erosion has made the Appalachian Mountains a varied and beautiful landscape. ■

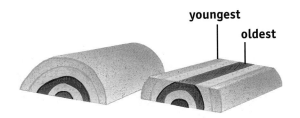

▲ **The oldest rock layers of a weathered and eroded anticline are near the center.**

The oldest rock layers of a weathered and eroded syncline are farthest from the center. ▶

▲ **The Appalachian Mountains have a varied landscape because of folding, weathering, and erosion.**

The Black Hills

Reading Focus How do dome mountains form?

Forces pressing on rock from opposite sides can cause rock layers to fold. Over time, the folds may form mountains such as the Appalachians. A mountain called a dome mountain can also form from folded rock layers. The Black Hills of western South Dakota and eastern Wyoming are an example of dome mountains.

A dome mountain forms when forces deep within Earth push rock layers upward. Recall that magma can flow into existing rock. Sometimes the magma pushes the rock layers above it upward, creating a dome.

The wearing down of the top of a dome exposes other rock layers. More weathering and erosion may expose igneous rock formed from magma.

In the Black Hills, the magma that created the domes is now granite and is exposed at the surface. The center of the dome is granite surrounded by schist. How do you think the schist formed? Around the center are rings of sedimentary rock, including limestone and sandstone. The sandstone is very hard and resists weathering, forming steep ridges sometimes called hogbacks. People have also shaped the Black Hills—by carving the faces of four presidents into Mount Rushmore!

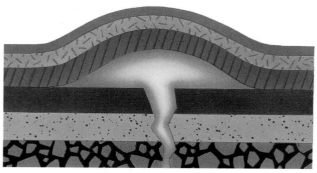

1 A dome forms when a vertical force, such as rising magma, pushes up.

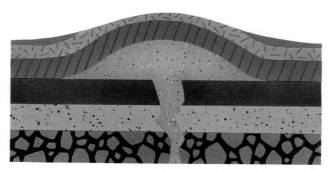

2 In a dome, the youngest rock is the igneous rock formed from the magma.

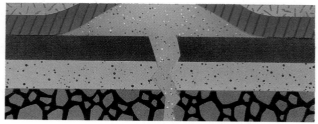

3 Weathering and erosion of a dome may expose the igneous rock formed from the magma.

Mr. President...

How many of the likenesses of former presidents carved into this mountain's granite wall can you identify? The national memorial on Mount Rushmore's northeastern side is just over 1800m high. Each head is about 30m tall.

A Real Jewel...

Jewel Cave National Monument is a 100-km long maze of underground rooms and passageways. Its caves formed long ago when water seeped underground and eroded the limestone rock layers.

INVESTIGATION 3 WRAP-UP

REVIEW

1. How did the Appalachian Mountains form?

2. How do dome mountains form?

CRITICAL THINKING

3. How are folded mountains different from dome mountains? How are they alike?

4. Suppose you see some folded rock layers that were exposed by weathering and erosion. How would knowing the ages of the layers help you tell if the folding was an anticline or a syncline?

INVESTIGATION 4

WHAT IS A FAULT, AND HOW CAN IT MAKE MOUNTAINS?

Mountains are big blocks of rock. You already know that rock can be bent to make mountains. In this investigation you'll find out about another way that mountains are made.

Activity

It's Your Fault

Cracks and breaks in sidewalks are common. Sometimes a section of sidewalk is actually thrust up above nearby sections. Sections of rock are also thrust up to make mountains at times!

Procedure

1. A place where rock has moved on one or both sides of a crack is called a **fault**. To **model** how a fault starts to form, have a partner hold one end of a meterstick down on a table, with most of the stick extending off the table.

 Math Hint *Hold the meterstick so that about 70 cm of it extends off the table.*

Step 2

2. Apply a gentle downward force to the free end of the meterstick. In your *Science Notebook*, **describe** what you **observe**. **Predict** what would happen if you used more force.

E86

3. Make two identical stacks of books, each consisting of two books of different sizes. The book stacks are models of rock layers.

4. Hold one stack on your right hand and the other stack on your left hand. Hold the books so that the top surfaces are level. The open sides of the books should face each other.

5. Move the books so that the edges of the covers in your left hand are just under the edges of the covers in your right hand.

6. The separation between the two stacks of books represents a fault. To model the motion along a fault, slowly raise your left hand a distance equal to the thickness of one book. Observe what happens, especially to the covers. Record your observations.

Analyze and Conclude

1. The meterstick in step 2 represents rock in Earth's crust. What happens to rock if a force strong enough to bend it is applied?

2. After you raised the books in step 6, which books were beside each other on opposite sides of the fault? Infer what happens as layers of rock move vertically along a fault.

3. In step 6, did the covers of the books catch on each other? How might this be like the rocks along a fault?

INVESTIGATE FURTHER!

RESEARCH

The mountain ranges in the Great Basin of the western United States were created by faults in blocks of rock. In which states are these mountains located? What mountain ranges are part of the Great Basin?

It's So Grand

Reading Focus What forces created the Grand Canyon?

Name the natural wonder that is 446 km (268 mi) long, up to 29 km (17 mi) wide, and more than 1.6 km (1 mi) deep. If you guessed the Grand Canyon, you're right! The Grand Canyon is cut into thousands of meters of rock! What kinds of forces could have created this amazing place? Read on to find out.

If you could peer over the edge of the canyon rim, you would see layer upon layer of rock. Long before the canyon existed, all these rock layers were formed. Recall that when rock layers are stacked one on top of the other, the oldest layer is on the bottom. The oldest rocks exposed at the very bottom of the Grand Canyon are metamorphic and igneous rocks that were formed as many as 1.5 billion years ago. The youngest rocks at the top of the rim are limestone that formed on an ocean floor 225 million years ago.

The Grand Canyon ▼

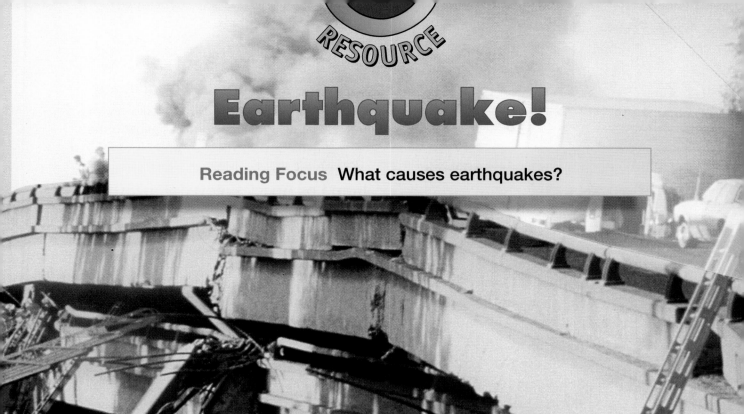

RESOURCE

Earthquake!

Reading Focus What causes earthquakes?

▲ **Bridge damaged by the 1994 Los Angeles earthquake**

Can you imagine how scary it must be to wake up with the room shaking around you? That's what happened to millions of people around Los Angeles in 1994. The ground was shaking because an earthquake had begun along a fault in California.

Why did this happen? As you have learned, forces within Earth can cause rock to break and move. When this occurs, energy is released. As a result, the ground shakes. This shaking of the ground is called an earthquake. Movement along a fault is not the only thing that causes an earthquake, although it is the most common cause.

The place where movement first occurs along a fault is below Earth's surface and is called the focus. The place on Earth's surface above the focus is called the epicenter. Find the fault, the focus, and the epicenter in the drawing.

Have you ever struck a bell to make it ring? If so, you know it starts to vibrate. In the same way, waves of energy move out from the focus of an earthquake and start the ground shaking. These waves damage land and buildings. In general, as the depth of the focus increases, so does the size of the area that will be damaged by the earthquake waves.

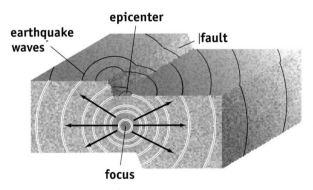

▲ **Earthquakes occur when there is movement along a fault.**

▲ **Signs of movement along the San Andreas Fault**

Why do you think earthquakes don't occur all the time along the system of faults under California? Faults are jagged and rough. So as plates move, sections of rock on either side of the fault catch on each other and lock together. Eventually enough force builds up so that the rocks unlock and slip past each other. This sudden movement causes an earthquake.

Most earthquakes occur at shallow depths, above 650 km (390 mi). Below this depth, temperature and pressure are so high that all rock bends and flows rather than breaks. Along the famous San Andreas Fault, most earthquakes occur at depths that are less than 30 km (18 mi).

There have been major earthquakes along the San Andreas Fault. In 1857 a section of the fault 120 km (72 mi) from Los Angeles moved 9 m (30 ft). In 1906 the fault shifted 6 m (20 ft), and the earthquake that resulted destroyed San Francisco. Over the past 20 million years, there have surely been many major earthquakes along the same fault.

Slow movement occurs along the San Andreas Fault all the time. Each year, crust along the fault moves several centimeters. Scientists believe that in about 10 million years, Los Angeles will have moved so far north that it will sit just across the fault from San Francisco! In about 60 million years, Los Angeles will be completely separated from the rest of California. As long as the crust along the San Andreas Fault continues to move, earthquakes will happen. And the residents of California must keep expecting them. ■

Internet Field Trip

Visit **www.eduplace.com** to explore earthquakes.

_____ **INVESTIGATION 4 WRAP-UP** _____

REVIEW

1. What are the three types of faults?

2. How do faults result in the formation of mountains?

CRITICAL THINKING

3. Along what type of fault is a mountain not likely to occur? Explain your answer.

4. You find a 6-million-year-old conglomerate above a 4-million-year-old shale. Explain this arrangement of rock layers.

REFLECT & EVALUATE

Word Power

Write the letter of the term that best matches the definition. *Not all terms will be used.*

1. A bend in a rock
2. Earth's thickest layer
3. A break in rock along which movement has occurred
4. A downward fold of rock layers
5. Actual age of an object
6. Earth's outer layer

a. absolute age
b. anticline
c. core
d. crust
e. fault
f. fold
g. mantle
h. syncline

Check What You Know

Write the term in each pair that best completes each sentence.

1. Extreme pressure keeps the inner core (molten, solid).
2. An imprint of a trilobite is called a fossil (mold, cast).
3. In a weathered and eroded anticline, the center contains the (oldest, youngest) rock layers.
4. When forces on rock pull in opposite directions, a break known as a (reverse, normal) fault can form.

Problem Solving

1. Compare and contrast folding and faulting.
2. Make a sketch of a syncline and an anticline. Then make a sketch showing the weathered and eroded top of each formation. Label the rock layers from oldest to youngest in each sketch.
3. How would folding make it hard to find the relative ages of rock layers?

BUILD YOUR PORTFOLIO

The drawing shows a model of Earth. Copy the drawing. Then label the layers of Earth on your drawing. For each layer, write a short paragraph that describes its thickness, the kind of material it contains, and any other information about that layer that interests you.

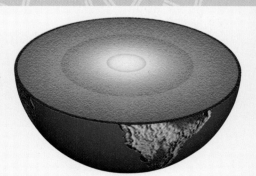

Using READING SKILLS

Detecting the Sequence

Sequence is the order in which things happen. To keep track of the sequence, look for signal words such as *first*, *then*, *next*, and *later*. When a passage doesn't contain signal words, look for other clues, such as numbers in the text or numbered steps in a diagram.

Look for these clues to detect the sequence.

- Signal words: *first, then, next, later*
- Numbers in the text
- Numbered steps in a drawing

Read the following paragraph. Then complete the exercises that follow.

A Cut Above

After grading, diamonds are sent to a gem cutter. Gem-quality diamonds are cut because doing so shows off their brilliant nonmetallic luster. Next, the diamond is shaped. Finally, it is polished by holding it at an angle to a spinning disk coated with diamond dust. This step creates the sparkling facets highly prized in gemstones.

1. **Which statement tells what happens to a diamond just before it is finally polished? Write the letter of that statement.**

    a. It is sent to a gem cutter.

    b. It is cut to show off its brilliant nonmetallic luster.

    c. It is shaped.

    d. It is polished by holding it at an angle to a spinning disk coated with diamond dust.

2. **List each clue that helped you keep track of the sequence.**

MATH SKILLS
Using

Using Math — Bar Graph

The heights of selected mountains in Colorado and Alaska are shown in the graph below.

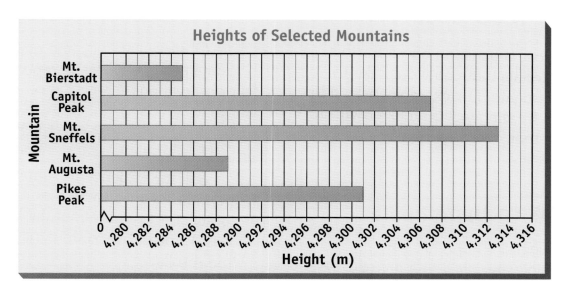

Heights of Selected Mountains

Use the graph to complete the exercises that follow.

1. Write the names of the mountains from lowest to highest. How much taller is the highest mountain than the lowest?

2. Which mountain is nearest in height to Pikes Peak?

3. Which is greater—the average height of the mountains or the median height of the mountains? Tell why.

4. Estimate the total number of meters you would climb if you climbed to the summits, or tops, of all of the mountains shown in the graph. Explain your answer.

5. Mount McKinley at 6,194 m (20,320 ft) in Alaska is the highest mountain in the United States. Estimate the height of this mountain in miles. Remember, 1 mi = 5,280 ft.

6. Make a bar graph that shows the following heights of mountains: Ellingwood Point, 4,280 m; Mt. Langley, 4,275 m; Snowmass Mountain, 4,295 m; Split Mountain, 4,285 m; Sunlight Peak, 4,285 m.

WRAP-UP!

On your own, use scientific methods to investigate a question about Earth's materials, structure, or changes.

THINK LIKE A SCIENTIST

Ask a Question

Pose a question about Earth's materials that you would like to investigate. For example, ask, "How can freezing water break down, or weather, rocks?"

Make a Hypothesis

Suggest a hypothesis that is a possible answer to the question. One hypothesis is that freezing water can crack rocks, weathering them.

Plan and Do a Test

Plan a controlled experiment to find out if freezing water can weather, or break down, rocks. You could start with four pieces of limestone or four other rocks that have cracks, four sealable plastic bags, water, and a freezer. Develop a procedure that uses these materials to test the hypothesis. With permission, carry out your experiment. Follow the safety guidelines on pages S14–S15.

Record and Analyze

Observe carefully and record your data accurately. Make repeated observations.

Draw Conclusions

Look for evidence to support the hypothesis or to show that it is false. Draw conclusions about the hypothesis. Repeat the experiment to verify the results.

WRITING IN SCIENCE
Interview

To learn about valuable gems, interview an expert such as a gemologist or a jeweler. Write up your interview as an article for a class newsletter. Follow these guidelines.

- Prepare questions before the interview.
- Take notes and, with permission, record the interview.
- Use a question-and-answer format in writing up the main points of the interview.

UNIT F

Light and Sound

Theme: Models

THINK LIKE A SCIENTIST

BRILLIANT SOUND

What kind of show uses both light and sound energy? A laser light show at a concert, of course! The photo shows laser lights displayed during a performance of the Sacramento Symphony Orchestra. With the help of computers, the sequence of laser-light images are timed to go with the music. The laser images are produced by sending a laser beam through a series of lenses and mirrors. The laser beams produce a brilliant kaleidoscope effect.

THINK LIKE A SCIENTIST

Questioning In this unit you'll find out about the nature and properties of waves of light and waves of sound energy. You'll investigate questions such as these.

- How Does Light Travel?
- How Does Matter Affect How Sound Travels?

Observing, Testing, Hypothesizing In the Activity "How Mirrors Affect Light," you'll find out how mirrors change the direction of light. You'll hypothesize how the various shapes of mirrors affect how light travels.

Researching In the Resource "Bouncing Light," you'll find out why light changes direction when it bounces off concave and convex mirrors.

Drawing Conclusions After you've completed your investigations, you'll draw conclusions about what you've learned—and get new ideas.

PROPERTIES OF LIGHT

Black lamps don't seem to give off much light. But shine them on surfaces covered with a certain kind of paint and see what happens! What is light, anyway? How can light be black?

PEOPLE USING SCIENCE

Lighting Designer Richard Green is founder of Wildfire Incorporated, a company in Los Angeles that creates lighting effects for music videos, television commercials, theme parks, and movies. Green, a lighting specialist, designs and produces lighting for shows and other events.

One popular lighting technique involves making objects fluoresce, or glow. Green covers objects with fluorescent paint and then shines a black light on them. The objects seem to glow! He says that people experience fluorescent objects in different ways. For some it is like stepping into an animated cartoon world of bright, crazy colors. For others the color and light seem to appear from nowhere.

Coming Up

◀ These people seem to glow because of fluorescent paint and black lights.

WHAT IS LIGHT, AND WHERE DOES IT COME FROM?

Have you ever been home when the electric power went off? A power failure can make you stop and think about something you take for granted—light! In this investigation you'll find out about light you can see and its relatives you can't see.

Activity

MATERIALS

• *Science Notebook*

Seeing the Light

There are lights all around you. Try a "scavenger hunt" to find some of them.

Procedure

Work with a group of other students to investigate light sources in various places. Look for all possible light sources. **List** the locations and the light sources in your *Science Notebook*. **Record** the kind of energy you think is being used to produce the light.

Rank the light sources from brightest to dimmest, using 1 for the brightest. Note whether any heat was given off from each light source.

Analyze and Conclude

1. What were the light sources your group found?

2. For each source, what kind of energy change produces the light? What can you **infer** about the connection between light and heat?

Activity

All Aglow

A simple electric circuit contains one dry cell, a light bulb, and a couple of connecting wires. What changes can you see in the light as you experiment with the different parts of the circuit?

MATERIALS
- light bulb *A*
- 3 dry cells (size D) in holders
- 4 insulated wires (ends stripped)
- light-bulb holder
- light bulb *B*
- *Science Notebook*

Procedure

1. Insert light bulb *A* into a light bulb holder. Connect one dry cell to light bulb *A*, using copper wire.

2. **Observe** what happens when you complete the electric circuit. Carefully note if the bulb is warm. **Record** your observations in your *Science Notebook*.

3. **Predict** what will happen if you add a second dry cell to the circuit. **Record** your prediction. Then add the second dry cell, connecting the cells positive to negative. **Record** your results.

4. Add a third dry cell to the circuit and again **record** your observations.

5. Replace light bulb *A* with light bulb *B*. Repeat steps 1–4. **Record** the results.

Step 1

Analyze and Conclude

1. In step 3, how did your prediction match what happened?

2. What happened when you added more dry cells to the circuit? **Suggest a hypothesis** to explain what you observed.

3. What change occurred when you replaced bulb *A* with bulb *B*? Why did this change occur?

4. What do you think is flowing from the dry cells to the bulb through the copper wire?

5. What causes the bulbs to glow? Were the bulbs warm?

6. What evidence do you have that light is energy?

Lighting the Way

Reading Focus What are some natural ways and artificial ways light energy is produced?

Imagine that it is summertime and you are lying on a sandy beach. Through your sunglasses you cán see the light of the Sun. You can feel the heat of the Sun on your bare skin. The Sun's rays provide Earth with light and heat, which are both forms of energy. You may recall that **energy** is the ability to do work or cause a change in matter.

The Sun, a star, supplies nearly all of Earth's natural light energy. From Earth you can see other stars during the night, but the amount of light from those stars is very small compared to the amount received from the Sun. Moonlight, the light Earth receives from the Moon, is really sunlight that has bounced off the Moon's surface.

Energy From the Sun

The Sun gives off huge amounts of energy that travel to Earth through the vacuum of space. The energy given off by the Sun is called **electromagnetic radiation** (ē lek′trō mag net′ik rā′dē-ā′shən). There are many kinds of electromagnetic (E-M) radiation; some kinds you can see, and others you can't see. **Visible light** is the type of E-M radiation that you can see.

Most types of E-M radiation are invisible. For example, infrared radiation and ultraviolet radiation are two types of invisible E-M radiation. Infrared radiation from the Sun causes you to feel warm when you stand in sunlight. Infrared lamps produce heat for personal and industrial uses.

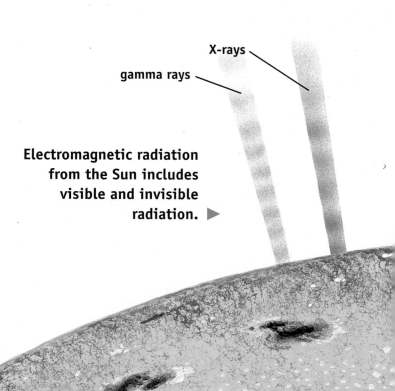

X-rays

gamma rays

Electromagnetic radiation from the Sun includes visible and invisible radiation. ▶

Ultraviolet (UV) radiation is sometimes called black light because an ultraviolet lamp looks dark to us when it is on. But when UV light shines on some materials, they glow, or give off visible light. That painful sunburn you get from lying in the Sun too long is caused by ultraviolet radiation.

Electromagnetic radiation can cause changes in matter. For example, sunlight heats water in the oceans. Light can also be used to heat water in solar collectors. Have you ever seen a solar calculator? When light shines on the calculator's solar cells, electricity to run the calculator is produced. In both the solar collector and calculator, light is changed to other forms of energy.

Light starts many chemical reactions. One of the most important reactions

▲ Certain minerals glow under ultraviolet (UV) radiation (*left*). The same minerals are shown under normal light (*right*).

started by light is photosynthesis, the food-making process of plants. During photosynthesis, plant cells convert carbon dioxide and water to oxygen and sugar. In this reaction, light energy is stored as chemical energy in sugar.

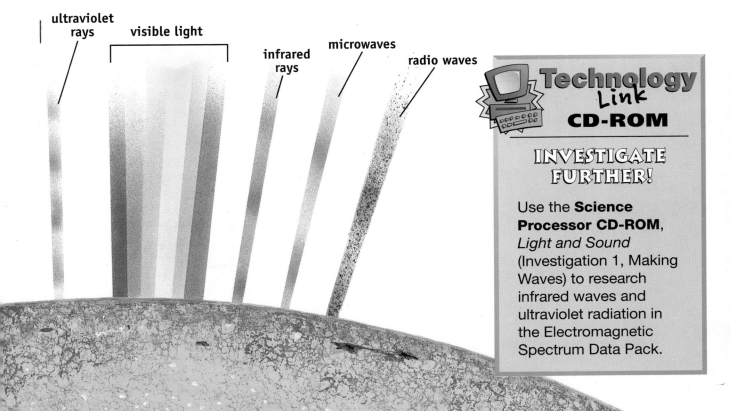

ultraviolet rays

visible light

infrared rays

microwaves

radio waves

Technology Link CD-ROM

INVESTIGATE FURTHER!

Use the **Science Processor CD-ROM**, *Light and Sound* (Investigation 1, Making Waves) to research infrared waves and ultraviolet radiation in the Electromagnetic Spectrum Data Pack.

Making Light

How many light sources can you think of other than the Sun? Light bulbs are the most common sources of artificial light. But fire was the first source of light that humans were able to control.

Fire is a rapid chemical reaction that gives off light. When a substance burns, some of the energy stored in it is given off as heat and light. The matter being burned is not destroyed—it is changed to other substances.

▲ A campfire is a chemical reaction in which light and heat are given off.

Most of the chemical reactions that give off light also produce heat. With a campfire, you may be more interested in the heat than in the light. With a lamp, however, you're interested in the light given off. In the activity on page F7, chemical energy in a dry cell is changed to electrical energy. A light bulb changes some electrical energy to light. But more of this energy is changed to heat, which is wasted.

Have you ever carried a "light stick"? People often take these plastic tubes along on camping trips for emergency lights. The plastic tubes contain two sets of chemicals. When you bend the light stick, you break a small tube inside it. When the inner tube breaks, chemicals mix. A reaction occurs that gives off light. This reaction does not make much heat, so the tube does not get hot.

The kind of light bulb commonly used in homes is an incandescent light bulb. In this type of light bulb, there is a very thin wire, called a filament, that

A light stick before its chemical reaction (*left*); breaking the tube releases chemicals that mix, causing a chemical reaction (*center*); the glowing light stick (*right*).

Sources of light: fluorescent light bulbs (*left*); lightning bolt (*center*); sparks given off during welding (*right*)

carries electricity. The wire gets very hot when the electricity goes through it. This makes the wire glow. But only about 2 percent of the electrical energy is changed into light.

Your classroom probably is lighted by fluorescent (floo ə res′ənt) lamps. These electric lights don't contain a filament. Instead, they contain a gas that gives off ultraviolet radiation when electricity flows through it. Remember that you can't see ultraviolet radiation. To make visible light, the fluorescent tube is lined with chemicals that glow when ultraviolet radiation strikes them.

Fluorescent lights do a much better job of changing electrical energy into light energy than do incandescent lights. About 30 percent of the electrical energy is changed into light. This means that less energy is changed to heat. So, fluorescent bulbs don't get as hot as incandescent bulbs do.

One familiar source of light doesn't last very long, but it can be very bright. What is it? Lightning! Lightning is a very bright electrical spark that has enough energy to run a 100-watt light bulb for three months. Perhaps you've seen a lightning flash light up the night sky so that it's as bright as day. ■

INVESTIGATE FURTHER!

RESEARCH

Examine the packaging of long-lasting energy-efficient light bulbs and regular incandescent light bulbs. Compare the prices, light output, energy used and average life span. Decide which light would be the best buy. Present your findings to your class.

Light Through the Ages

Reading Focus How has artificial lighting changed through the ages?

For thousands of years the only sources of light humans had were the Sun and fire. Progress in producing artificial light occurred very slowly over long periods of time. Finally, in the mid-1700s, real strides were made. In recent years the advances in light technology have been fantastic!

Follow the time line to see the changes that have occurred in artificial light through the ages.

Kerosene replaces whale oil in house lamps.

1850

Whale blubber oil is used in oil lamps.

1800-1900

Sumerians use oil-burning lamps. Candles and oil lamps are used to light homes for many centuries.

3000-2500 B.C.

EARLY 1800s

Gaslights are used in cities. The gas is carried to buildings by a series of pipes. As cities grow, gas lighting becomes common in homes and apartments. At twilight, lamplighters go around the city, lighting gas-fueled street lamps.

18,000 B.C.

People learn to make torches out of pieces of wood tipped with flammable tree resin.

A.D. 1786

First attempts are made to provide inside gas lighting in Germany and England.

BEYOND 2000

Lewis Howard Latimer, an African American inventor, invented an improved, long burning carbon filament. 1881

Fluorescent light bulbs are invented. 1927

1980
The halogen light, an incandescent lamp that burns more brightly than standard lamps, is invented.

1911
Tungsten filament is invented.

1879
Thomas Edison (American) and Joseph Swan (British) invent an improved light bulb. Both Edison and Swan experiment with light bulbs. On October 21, 1879, Edison demonstrates a light bulb that uses a carbon filament made from a burned cotton thread. Unlike earlier light bulbs, this one lasts for many hours before the filament burns out.

Building a Better Light Bulb

Since 1980, scientists have invented different kinds of lighting that are brighter or use less energy. One of these energy-efficient light sources is the compact fluorescent bulb. It uses 75 percent less energy than an incandescent light bulb and can last for about 10,000 hours! ■

INVESTIGATION 1 WRAP-UP

THINK IT WRITE IT

REVIEW

1. Describe two different ways that you can produce light.

2. Explain why fluorescent bulbs don't get as hot as incandescent bulbs do.

CRITICAL THINKING

3. Discuss how advances in lighting technology have affected how people spend their time.

4. Imagine that you are an engineer who is designing an improved light bulb. Describe the characteristics of your improved light bulb.

HOW DOES LIGHT TRAVEL?

Have you ever been in a sports stadium when one section starts a "wave"? Think about how the motion travels from one part of the stadium to another. The way light travels is a little like the way the human wave travels around a stadium.

Activity

Light Waves

Light is a form of energy that travels in waves. Can you imagine what a light wave looks like? This activity will show you a model of the way a light wave travels.

Step 1

MATERIALS

- goggles
- large plastic coil spring
- tape measure
- *Science Notebook*

SAFETY

Wear goggles during this activity.

Procedure

1. Work with a partner. Stretch a plastic coil spring between yourself and your partner. Be careful that you don't overstretch and damage the coils. Have a classmate measure the distance between you and your partner.

 See **SCIENCE** *and* **MATH TOOLBOX** page H6 if you need to review *Using a Tape Measure or Ruler.*

2. While your partner holds one end of the coil spring still, make one quick motion to the side and back to the center position. **Observe** the wave that you have created. **Record** your observations in your *Science Notebook*.

3. Repeat step 2 several times and **record** your observations.

4. Predict what will happen if you move the coil spring up and down. **Record** your prediction. Then try moving the coil spring up and down. **Record** how the wave moves this time. **Make a sketch** of the wave.

Analyze and Conclude

1. Write a statement describing two ways the coil spring moves.

2. What evidence is there that the wave carries energy as it travels along the coil?

3. How far did the wave travel? Did any single coil travel that distance? How do you know?

Step 4

UNIT PROJECT LINK

For this Unit Project you will use your investigations of light and sound to help you plan and produce a puppet show. Start by making a catalog of the different shadows you can create with common objects. Choose objects with interesting shapes. Look around your classroom or your home for the objects.

Darken the room. Shine a flashlight at the objects from different angles to produce different shapes. Try moving the flashlight far away from the objects and then near them to see what happens. Choose one object. On a sheet of white paper, trace the different shadows you can make from that object. Remove all the objects. Then see if anyone can guess the object that made the shadows.

Technology Link

For more help with your Unit Project, go to **www.eduplace.com**.

Lasers

Reading Focus How does laser light differ from ordinary light?

What do supermarket checkouts, CD players, and rock concerts have in common? Lasers! Laser beams are used in the scanners that make barcode readers and CD players work. Laser beams are also used in concert light displays. How does a laser work? What makes laser light different from ordinary light?

All light beams tend to travel in a straight line, but ordinary light beams spread out as they travel. And ordinary light beams aren't as bright after they spread out. Laser beams, however, spread out very little, allowing them to travel a long distance without getting dim.

Laser lights at rock concert

One use for lasers is in communications. Lasers are used to send signals along telephone and television cables. The cables are made of optical fibers, which are long, thin strands of glass. Even if the fibers are bent, the light bounces off the sides of the fiber wall and follows the bending pathway.

Today, laser beams and optical fibers are used in medicine. For example, laser light can help repair a detached retina in the eye. It can cut and seal blood vessels or destroy skin cancers. Optical fibers and lasers make microsurgery possible. Doctors can use optical fibers to operate through a small cut in the body. ■

PARTS OF A LASER This laser contains a ruby crystal surrounded by a coiled tube from which light flashes. As the light flashes, energy builds up in the crystal. When enough energy has built up, an intense beam of laser light is released.

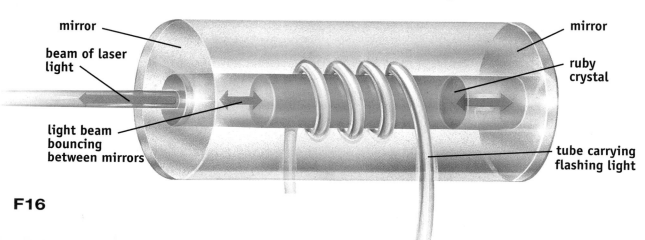

mirror

beam of laser light

light beam bouncing between mirrors

mirror

ruby crystal

tube carrying flashing light

Light as a Wave

Reading Focus How are light waves similar to other kinds of waves?

A **wave** is a disturbance that moves away from its starting point. As a wave moves, it transfers energy. Think about what happens if you drop a stone into a pond. As the stone hits the water, it creates waves that travel out across the pond from that spot. The waves carry energy, but the water itself does not move across the pond.

Light also travels as a wave. Light waves are different from water waves in an important way. Without water, there would be no water waves. But light waves don't need water or air or any kind of matter to carry them. Light waves can travel through a vacuum. A **vacuum** is a region that is empty of any matter.

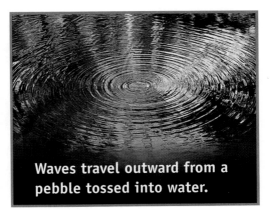

Waves travel outward from a pebble tossed into water.

Light waves from the Sun travel through space without being carried by matter.

Parts of a Wave

You can see light, but you can't see light waves. Still, scientists know that light waves do many of the same things that other kinds of waves do. In the activity on pages F14 and F15, a plastic coil spring is used to model light wave behavior. To use and understand the wave model of light, you need to know the parts of a wave. Refer to the drawing below.

Measuring Light Waves

The lengths of light waves can be measured. **Wavelength** is the distance

Parts of a wave ▼

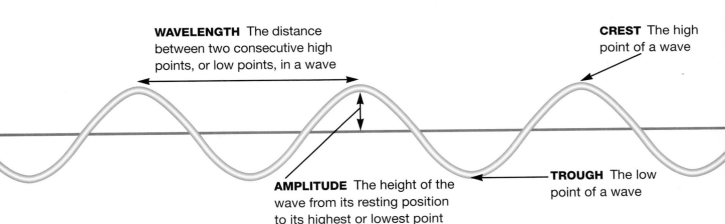

WAVELENGTH The distance between two consecutive high points, or low points, in a wave

CREST The high point of a wave

AMPLITUDE The height of the wave from its resting position to its highest or lowest point

TROUGH The low point of a wave

from one crest of the wave to the next crest. Of course, you can't place a ruler next to a light wave because you can't see the waves. But the wavelength of light has been measured in the laboratory. Scientists have found that each color of light has a different range of wavelengths. The wavelengths of visible light are shown in the table. Because light wavelengths are so short, they are measured in a tiny unit called a nanometer (nm). One nanometer equals one billionth of a meter.

Wave Frequency

The number of waves produced each second is the **frequency** of a wave. Wave frequency is measured in a unit called the **hertz** (Hz). If ten waves are produced each second, the frequency of the wave is 10 per second, or 10 Hz. The frequency of light waves is measured in a unit called a megahertz (MHz). One megahertz is equal to 1 million hertz.

Speed of Light

Although each color of light has a different range of wavelengths and frequencies, all light waves travel at exactly the same speed. The speed of light is 300,000 km/s (186,000 mi/s).

Wavelengths of Light

Color of Light	Wavelength (nm)
Violet	350–400
Indigo	400–450
Blue	450–500
Green	500–550
Yellow	550–600
Orange	600–650
Red	650–700

Using Math *If a wavelength of light is 575 nm long, what color is the light?*

Imagine light traveling through an optical fiber wrapped around Earth's equator. Light travels so quickly that it could travel around the world 7.5 times in just one second! Light traveling from the Sun, which is 150 million km (about 93 million mi) away, takes 500 seconds, or 8.3 minutes, to reach Earth.

The electromagnetic spectrum ▼

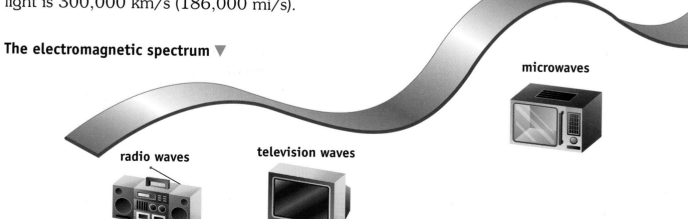

radio waves television waves microwaves

The speed of light depends on the material through which it moves. The rate 300,000 km/s is the speed of light traveling in a vacuum.

The Electromagnetic Spectrum

As you know, light is only one kind of electromagnetic radiation. E-M radiation also includes gamma rays, microwaves, infrared waves, X-rays, radio waves, and other kinds of waves.

From the drawing below, you can see that radio waves have the longest wavelengths and gamma rays have the shortest wavelengths. How do the wavelengths of visible light compare to those of radio waves? of microwaves?

The energy of electromagnetic radiation is related to its wavelength—the shorter the wavelength, the more energy carried by the wave. How does UV light compare with visible light in terms of energy?

Although the wavelengths, frequencies, and energy levels of electromagnetic waves vary, E-M waves have two things in common. (1) When traveling through space, all E-M waves travel at the same speed. (2) All E-M waves can travel through a vacuum. ■

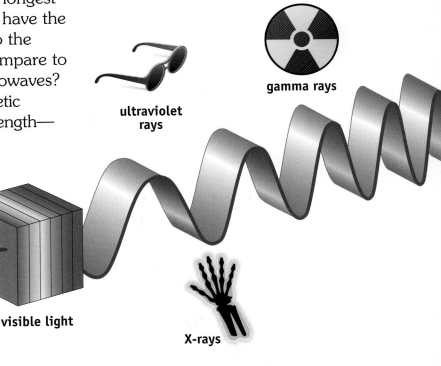

gamma rays

ultraviolet rays

infrared waves

visible light

X-rays

INVESTIGATION 2 WRAP-UP

REVIEW

1. Describe visible light in terms of (a) its speed in a vacuum, and (b) how the colors of light differ.

2. Draw a light wave and label its wavelength, crest, and trough.

CRITICAL THINKING

3. How do the wavelength and frequency of ultraviolet light compare to those of visible light?

4. How do the wavelengths and frequencies of radio waves and visible light compare?

HOW DOES LIGHT BEHAVE?

Have you ever used mirrors to look around a corner or over a wall? If so, you know that some kinds of matter can change the direction in which light travels. In this investigation you'll find out under what conditions light bounces and bends.

Activity

How Mirrors Affect Light

In this activity you'll see how three different kinds of mirrors change the direction that light travels.

MATERIALS

- flashlight
- plane mirror (flat)
- large piece of cardboard
- concave mirror (curves inward)
- convex mirror (curves outward)
- *Science Notebook*

Procedure

Darken the room. Turn a flashlight on and point it at an angle toward a plane mirror. Hold a large piece of cardboard at the edge of the mirror, as shown. **Record** your observations in your *Science Notebook*.

Repeat the above procedure, but this time use a concave mirror. **Observe** and **record** your results. **Predict** what will happen with a convex mirror. Try it. **Observe** what happens and **record** your results.

Analyze and Conclude

Describe the effect of each mirror on the light beam. What uses can you think of for each mirror?

Activity

The Bending Pencil

Sometimes things aren't quite what they appear to be. That's the idea behind many of the tricks that magicians perform. With some water and oil, you can "break" a pencil in two. To do the trick, you have to learn how to bend light.

MATERIALS
- pencil
- tall narrow jar
- water
- paper towel
- vegetable oil
- *Science Notebook*

Step 2

Procedure

1. Place a pencil in a jar. Observe the jar and pencil from the side. In your *Science Notebook*, draw the jar and pencil. Label the drawing *Step 1*.

2. Keep the pencil in the jar. Then fill the jar almost to the top with water. Observe the jar and pencil from the side and from above. In your *Science Notebook,* draw pictures of what you observe from the side and from above. Use a dotted line to show where you think the pencil in the water *actually* is. Label the drawings *Step 2*.

3. Remove the pencil from the jar. Pour out the water. Use a paper towel to dry the inside of the jar. Now, fill the jar almost to the top with vegetable oil. Predict how the pencil will look from the side and from the top. Record your prediction. Then place the pencil back in the jar. Observe and draw as you did in step 2. Label the drawings *Step 3*.

Analyze and Conclude

1. What is the difference between the way the pencil looked in step 1 and in step 2? What evidence is there that light changes direction as it leaves the water?

2. Describe the difference between the appearance of the pencil in water and its appearance in vegetable oil. Give a reason for any difference.

INVESTIGATE FURTHER!

EXPERIMENT

Predict what would happen if you used other liquids in this activity. Try several liquids and compare the results.

Bouncing Light

Reading Focus What happens to light when it strikes a surface?

▲ **Image in a fun-house mirror**

You see objects because light coming from them enters your eyes. The Sun, lamps, and burning candles produce light, but most objects don't. You can see such objects because of reflected light.

Reflection (ri flek'shən) is the bouncing back of light from a surface. Think of light from a lamp hitting a chair. The chair absorbs some of the light. But the chair also reflects some of the light that strikes it. It is this reflected light reaching your eyes that allows you to see the chair.

Any smooth surface that reflects most or all of the light that strikes it can act as a mirror. The activity on page F20 shows how the shape of a mirror can affect the way the mirror reflects light.

Plane Mirrors

The type of mirror you are most familiar with is called a plane mirror. A **plane mirror** is a mirror with a flat surface.

Light reflects from a plane mirror in the same pattern and at the same angle

Reflection in a plane mirror ▼   **Image in a plane mirror** ▼

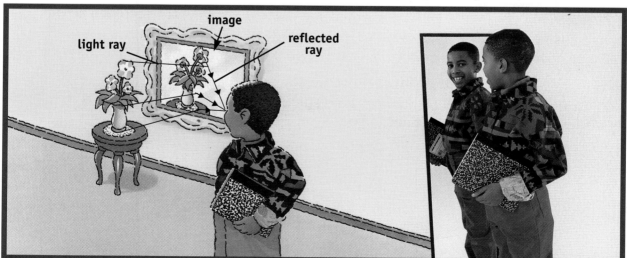

at which it strikes the mirror's surface. However, the light changes direction as it is reflected. If you stand in front of a mirror, light bouncing off your body strikes the mirror's surface and is reflected back to your eyes. Because light reflects from the mirror in the same pattern as the light that struck the mirror, you see an image.

The image you see in a plane mirror is right side up and the same size as the object being reflected. The image is not distorted, or out of shape. But it is reversed from left to right, so you don't see yourself exactly as others do.

Use the drawing on page F22 to follow the path that light takes to form an image in a plane mirror. Some light rays from the object travel toward the mirror. As these light rays strike the mirror, they are reflected. These rays enter your eye and form an image. Your brain forms a mental picture of where the light seems to come from. Because your brain "assumes" the light has traveled in a single straight line, the image seems to be behind the mirror.

Concave Mirrors

The images you see in curved mirrors often are distorted and are usually not the same size as the object. There are two kinds of curved mirrors—concave and convex. A **concave mirror** curves inward at the middle. When an object is close to a concave mirror, the image formed in the mirror is larger than the object. That's why shaving and makeup mirrors are often concave. Concave mirrors are also used as reflectors to concentrate light. The reflected light rays come together and are focused at one point. In a solar oven a concave mirror is used to focus rays of sunlight to cook food.

Convex Mirrors

A **convex mirror** curves outward at the middle. A convex mirror produces an image that is smaller than the object. It also allows you to see much more of an area than other kinds of mirrors do. Because convex mirrors reflect light from such a wide area, they are useful as side-view mirrors on cars and trucks. ■

▼ **Concave mirror and the image it produces**

▼ **Convex mirror and the image it produces**

Bending Light

Reading Focus What happens to light as it passes from one material to another?

A Change in Direction

In the activity on page F21, light passing through different materials is seen to produce a strange image—like a broken pencil. The illusion occurs because light rays bend, or change direction, as they travel from one material into another. This bending of light as it passes from one material into another is called **refraction** (ri frak'shən). In the activity, light is refracted as it passes from water into air.

The speed of light changes as it passes from one material into another. For example, light travels at close to 300,000 km/s (186,000 mi/s) in air and at 225,000 km/s (140,000 mi/s) in water.

A Change in Speed

When light waves pass from air into water, they slow down. This change in speed of the light waves is what causes the light to refract, or change direction. In the drawing on page F25 you can see how light waves change direction as their speed increases when they pass from water into air.

In the photograph below you can see how a glass prism affects a beam of white light passing through it. The light slows down as it enters the left side of the prism, causing the beam of light to refract. But the different colors of light are bent at different angles. So a rainbow, or spectrum, is produced as the light leaves the right side of the prism.

▲ **A beam of white light is refracted as it passes from air through a glass prism.**

Tricks With Refracted Light

Have you ever used a net to catch a fish in a fish tank? If you looked at the fish from above at an angle to the water's surface, you probably had trouble. The fish looks closer to the surface than it is. Look at the drawing of the fish tank. Light reflecting from the fish is refracted as it leaves the water. The light enters your eye, and your brain "assumes" that the light has traveled in a straight line. So your brain forms an image of where the fish seems to be. But that isn't where the fish really is! The refraction of light fools you.

When someone in a pet store tries to net a fish, it's likely that person will look at the fish through the side of the tank.

▲ **Refraction of light in water can fool you. Where is the fish?**

By looking straight into the water, that person has a better chance of catching the fish. When light rays move from one material to another along a line that is perpendicular to the surface, there is no refraction. Since the light rays don't bend, you don't get fooled.

Science in Literature

CRACKLE, CRACKLE, POP, POP

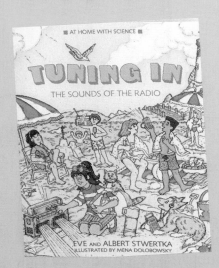

**Tuning In:
The Sounds of the Radio**
by Eve and Albert Stwertka
Illustrated by Mena Dolobowsky
Julian Messner, 1993

"Lightning creates radio waves. The next time there is an electrical storm, turn on your radio. Listen for the crackling sound you hear whenever there is a bolt of lightning. The radio waves produced by the lightning interfere with the waves produced by the normal broadcast."

Radio waves are a form of electromagnetic radiation that can not only travel at the speed of light but can also be bounced and bent like light. Find out how radio waves behave and how they are put to use by reading *Tuning In: The Sounds of the Radio* by Eve and Albert Stwertka.

Air Bends Light

Have you ever ridden in a car on a hot, dry day and thought you saw a pool of water in the road? Was your mind playing tricks on you? Actually, the mirage you see is a result of light traveling at different speeds through cool air and warm air. Light from the Sun was refracted toward your eyes by the heated air near the road's surface.

The pool you saw was really refracted sunlight. In effect, you were seeing an image of the sky on the road surface ahead of you. Your brain interprets the light as coming to you in a straight line from the road. ■

Internet Field Trip

Visit **www.eduplace.com** to learn more about optical illusions.

Seeing a Mirage

We often notice mirages during summer months, when air near the ground is much warmer than air higher in the atmosphere.

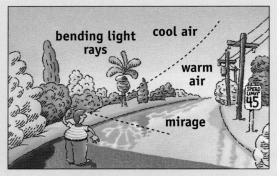

bending light rays

cool air

warm air

mirage

As light waves from above pass into the layer of warm air near the surface, the light bends, or refracts. If these light waves enter your eyes, you see an image of the sky, but you see it on the road surface.

INVESTIGATION 3 WRAP-UP

REVIEW

1. What are three things that may happen to light that strikes an object?

2. Explain what happens when light strikes a prism like the one on page F24.

CRITICAL THINKING

3. You are in water up to your knees in a local swimming pool. You see a coin through the water, at the bottom of the pool. You reach down to pick it up, but it's not there. What happened?

4. Compare and contrast the reflection of light with the refraction of light.

REFLECT & EVALUATE

Word Power

Write the letter of the term that best matches the definition. *Not all terms will be used.*

1. A unit used to measure wave frequency
2. Wave energy produced by the Sun and some other objects
3. A mirror that curves inward at the middle
4. A disturbance that carries energy and moves away from its starting point
5. The bending of light as it passes from one material to another

a. concave mirror
b. convex mirror
c. electromagnetic radiation
d. frequency
e. hertz
f. reflection
g. refraction
h. wave

Check What You Know

Write the term in each pair that best completes each sentence.

1. The distance between one crest of a wave and the next crest is (frequency, wavelength).
2. An image in a (convex, concave) mirror can look larger than the object being reflected.
3. Most types of electromagnetic radiation are (visible, invisible).

Problem Solving

1. Sketch the energy path that leads to light in a flashlight. Write a description of your sketch.
2. Make a sketch that shows a wave of red light and a wave of violet light. Label the sketch and explain how the waves differ.
3. Use a diagram to show that light travels in straight lines, even when it refracts, or reflects off a surface.

BUILD YOUR PORTFOLIO

Suppose you were the person on the pier in the drawing. Draw a picture to show where the snorkeler would appear to be. Write an explanation of why the snorkeler would not be where he appeared to be.

CHAPTER 2

LIGHT, LENSES, AND COLOR

Corrective lenses change the direction of light that passes through them. Through the use of such lenses, over 100 million people in the United States are able to see more clearly. Scientists use lenses in many other tools to control light. Devices such as telescopes and microscopes improve how we see ourselves, our planet, our solar system, and even the universe.

PEOPLE USING SCIENCE

Optometrist As a child Dr. Tanya Carter visited the office of an optometrist, or eye doctor, where she was impressed by the warm and open relationship the doctor had with his patients. She learned that optometrists test vision, color perception, and how well their patients focus and coordinate their eyes. Using the results of these tests they prescribe eyeglasses and contact lenses, and carry out treatment for eye disorders. Dr. Carter decided to pursue a career in health sciences and studied to be a doctor of optometry.

Being an optometrist has been rewarding for Dr. Carter. She enjoys seeing a child's face light up after receiving eyeglasses, or having students thank her for helping them to see the chalkboard more clearly. She has been impressed with how improving someone's vision can change that person's whole outlook on life.

Coming Up

◄ The instrument behind Dr. Tanya Carter is called a refractor. It is used to prescribe eyeglasses.

HOW DO LENSES HELP CONTROL LIGHT?

Do you know someone who wears contact lenses? A contact lens changes the direction of light passing through it. This investigation should help you understand how lenses help a person see more clearly.

Activity

Becoming Focused

You've seen that as light passes from one material to another it can change direction. When a material such as glass is shaped into a lens, it directs—or redirects—the path of light. Explore how lens shape affects the way light passes into and out of the lens.

Procedure

1. In your *Science Notebook,* make a chart with two wide columns. Title the chart "Comparing Convex and Concave Lenses." Record all observations during this activity in the chart.

 See **SCIENCE** *and* **MATH TOOLBOX** *page H11 if you need to review Making a Chart to Organize Data.*

2. Use a piece of tissue to feel the shape of the convex lens. Make a sketch of the lens.

3. Darken the room. Using a manila folder as a screen, place a flashlight about 30 cm from the screen. Point the flashlight toward the screen.

4. Place the convex lens between the flashlight and the screen so that the light passes through the lens and shines onto the screen.

5. **Observe** what happens on the screen as you move the lens back and forth between the light and the screen. **Infer** how the lens is affecting the light. **Record** your inference.

Step 4

6. Stand with your back toward a window. Hold the lens in one hand and extend your arm so that direct sunlight from the window passes through the lens.

7. Have a classmate hold the screen so that the light passing through the lens shines on the screen. Move the screen and lens as needed until a clear image appears on the screen. **Observe** the image carefully and **record** your observations.

Step 7

8. Place the convex lens on a sheet of newspaper over printed words. Raise the lens slowly and **observe** the print. **Record** your observations.

9. Repeat steps 2–8, using a concave lens. In the chart, **record** your observations about the concave lens.

Analyze and Conclude

1. In step 5, how did the appearance of the beam of light on the screen change for each lens?

2. **Describe** the image you saw on the screen as you moved each lens back and forth in step 7. What was unusual about the image?

3. How does a convex lens affect light when it focuses light to a point? How do convex and concave lenses differ in the way they affect light?

UNIT PROJECT LINK

With your group, put on a puppet show using different-colored lights to produce special visual effects. Cover a flashlight with cellophane of different colors. Experiment with blue, red, and green, in turn. Create situations to act out, using your puppets. Decide which colors of light to use to create the right emotion for each situation. Then give your show.

TechnologyLink

For more help with your Unit Project, go to **www.eduplace.com**.

Light and Lenses

Reading Focus How is light affected by concave and convex lenses?

How Lenses Bend Light

You've probably had fun playing with a hand lens. Held close to an object, a hand lens lets you see details you didn't know were there. Held at arm's length, it shows a world turned upside down! What "magic" is at work here?

Actually, you already know something about this "magic." When light passes from one transparent, or clear, material into another, the light bends, or changes direction. A **lens** is a transparent object with at least one curved surface. Lenses come in a variety of shapes, but all types refract light that passes through them.

Lens Shape

A lens that is thicker in the center than it is at the edges is called a **convex lens**. Such a lens brings parallel light rays together at a point known as the **focal point**. The more a lens curves, the more it bends light. So the more a lens curves, the closer the focal point is to the lens. In the activity on lenses on pages F30 and F31, the image of a near object viewed through a convex lens appears right side up and larger than the object. This is how hand lenses work. It's refraction that produces a larger image. If a convex lens isn't very close to an object, the image that forms is small; it's also upside down!

A lens that is thicker at the edges than at its middle is called a **concave lens**. A concave lens causes parallel light rays to spread apart. The image of an object viewed through a concave lens is smaller than the object, but the image formed is always right side up.

The Eye and a Camera

Both the human eye and a camera contain convex lenses. An important difference between your eyes and a camera is that a camera takes only one picture at a time. But your eyes are constantly "taking pictures."

A convex lens brings light rays together at a focal point (*left*); a concave lens causes light rays to spread apart (*right*).

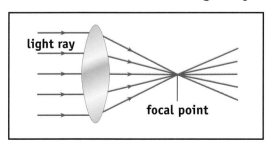

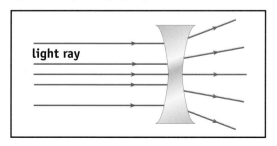

COMPARING THE HUMAN EYE TO A CAMERA

How a Camera Works

A camera contains one or more lenses. Here's what happens when you take a picture.

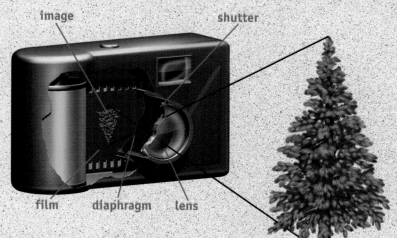

image   shutter

film   diaphragm   lens

1. Point the lens toward an object. Press a button on the camera, and the shutter behind the lens opens.

2. Light from the object passes through the lens.

3. The diaphragm controls the amount of light entering the camera.

4. The lens bends the light so that it comes together or focuses, on the film.

5. The light causes chemical changes in the film. These changes form an image on the film.

How the Human Eye Works

The human eye is like a camera. The eye has a convex lens. Here's how you see.

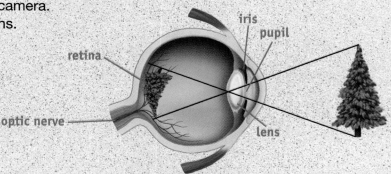

retina   iris   pupil

optic nerve   lens

1. Look at an object. Light from the object passes through a hole in the eye called the pupil.

2. The pupil is surrounded by the iris, which acts like the camera's diaphragm. Tiny muscles in the iris make the pupil smaller or larger. This controls the amount of light entering the eye.

3. The light passes through the lens. The lens bends the light so that it comes together, or focuses, on the retina, forming an image.

4. The light causes nerve impulses to travel down the optic nerve to the brain. The image is interpreted, or "seen," in the brain.

When you look at an object the lens of your eye focuses an image on the retina (ret´´n ə). The **retina** is the light-sensitive layer at the back of the eye. It sends nerve impulses to the brain along the optic nerve. The brain then interprets the pictures and figures out what you're seeing.

Another difference between your eyes and a camera is in how the eyes focus. You can focus on objects that are close to you and on objects that are far away, but the eye's lens can't move in and out the way a camera lens does. Instead, the lens of the eye changes shape. When you look at something nearby, muscles in the eye pull on the edges of the lens and make it less curved. When you look at something far away, the muscles relax, and the lens gets more curved again.

Correcting Vision

Many people wear eyeglasses. Nearsighted people can see nearby things clearly, but cannot see distant objects clearly. As the drawings below show, the eyes of a nearsighted person focus images in front of the retina. Eyeglasses with concave lenses correct such a condition by spreading out the light rays before they enter the eye. The eye's lens then focuses the light rays on the retina.

People who are farsighted see faraway objects clearly, but they have trouble seeing nearby things. This condition is corrected with convex lenses, which bring the light rays closer together before they enter the eye. The lens of the eye then properly focuses the light rays on the retina.

NEARSIGHTED

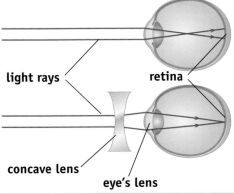

light rays   retina

concave lens

eye's lens

▲ Correcting nearsightedness

FARSIGHTED

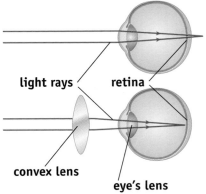

light rays   retina

convex lens

eye's lens

▲ Correcting farsightedness

Contact Lenses

Many people wear contact lenses instead of *eyeglasses*. **Contact lenses** are clear, thin lenses that are placed on the eye in front of the cornea. Contact lenses float on a thin layer of tears that covers the cornea.

Like eyeglasses, contact lenses change the path of light. But with contact lenses, concave lenses are used for both near-sighted and farsighted people. Because contact lenses are so close to the *eye*, they don't need to be thick to bend the light enough to correct a person's vision.

The earliest contact lenses were made of rigid plastic and were often uncomfortable. In 1965 soft contact lenses were invented. These lenses are flexible and more comfortable than the older lenses. Most soft contact lenses must be removed and cleaned each day. The removal also allows oxygen to reach the living tissue of the cornea. Some soft contact lenses let oxygen pass through, so they can be worn for many days at a time. When they are taken out, they also must be carefully cleaned. ■

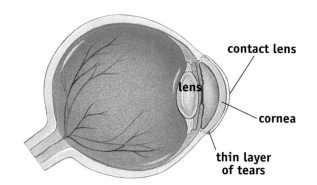

▲ **A contact lens floating on a layer of tears**

INVESTIGATE FURTHER!

EXPERIMENT

To see how the iris responds to the brightness of light, work with a partner. Take turns observing each other's eyes in dim light. Then turn on bright lights or move toward a sunny window. Observe the pupils of your partner's eyes. How did the pupils look in dim light? How did they change in bright light?

INVESTIGATION 1 WRAP-UP

REVIEW

1. Sketch how a lens can correct the vision of a farsighted person.

2. Describe how a camera records the image of an object on film.

CRITICAL THINKING

3. Compare and contrast the way light is changed as it moves through convex and concave lenses.

4. A convex lens projects an image that is upside down. If the image on your retina is upside down, why doesn't the world look upside down to you?

HOW ARE LENSES USED IN TELESCOPES AND MICROSCOPES?

Lenses can be used to see things too small or too far away to be seen with our unaided eyes. Much of what we know about life on Earth and objects in space is a result of combining lenses and mirrors.

Activity

Telescopic View

In the 1600s, lens makers in Europe placed two lenses of different sizes in a tube, forming a telescope. You can build a telescope very much like the ones they built.

Procedure

1. Use scissors to cut a cardboard tube into two sections. Make one section 12 cm long and the other section 15 cm long. In the shorter tube, make a lengthwise cut as shown.

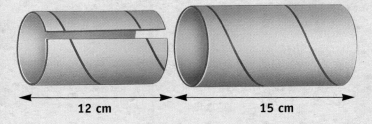

Step 1

12 cm   15 cm

See **SCIENCE** and **MATH TOOLBOX** *page H6 if you need to review Using a Tape Measure or Ruler.*

MATERIALS

- scissors
- cardboard tube
- metric ruler
- tape
- convex lens *A*, 15 cm focal length
- convex lens *B*, 5 cm focal length
- modeling clay
- *Science Notebook*

SAFETY /////

NEVER LOOK DIRECTLY AT THE SUN! Be careful when handling glass lenses.

2. Overlap the cut edges of the shorter tube, making it slightly narrower. Tape the cut edges as shown in the drawing in step 3.

3. Use modeling clay and tape to attach lens *A* to one end of the longer tube. Use more clay to attach lens *B* to one end of the shorter tube. Place the open end of the shorter tube into the open end of the longer tube. You have just made a simple telescope!

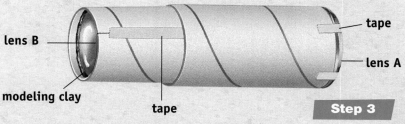

lens B

modeling clay

tape

tape

lens A

Step 3

4. Hold the telescope up to your eye and look through the lens that is in the shorter tube.

5. Use the telescope to **observe** various objects outdoors. Move the shorter tube back and forth inside the longer tube until the image of the object you are observing is clear.

Analyze and Conclude

1. **Describe** in your *Science Notebook* how the objects you observed looked when viewed through your telescope.

2. **Make sketches** of how several objects look when viewed directly and when viewed through a telescope.

INVESTIGATE FURTHER!

EXPERIMENT

Look in your daily newspaper to find out which planets are visible at this time. Then use your telescope to observe the Moon and these planets.

The Telescope— From Galileo to Hubble

Reading Focus What is the difference between a refracting telescope and a reflecting telescope?

No one knows for certain who made the first telescope. Evidence suggests that it was probably constructed in Holland in the early 1600s.

Galileo (gal ə lē′ō) Galilei was the first person to use a telescope to study the sky. An Italian scientist who lived from 1564 to 1642, Galileo built his first telescope in 1609. He had been studying the stars and planets for many years and was eager to get a better look. Galileo's telescope magnified by 32

times what he saw. With the telescope he was able to see mountains and craters on the Moon. When he studied the planet Jupiter through his telescope, he discovered four of its moons.

Galileo's telescope was a **refracting telescope**. As the name suggests, this telescope used lenses that refracted light to make an image. The drawing on the next page shows a refracting telescope that uses two lenses. Light from a faraway object first passes through the objective lens, or lens closer to the object, forming a very

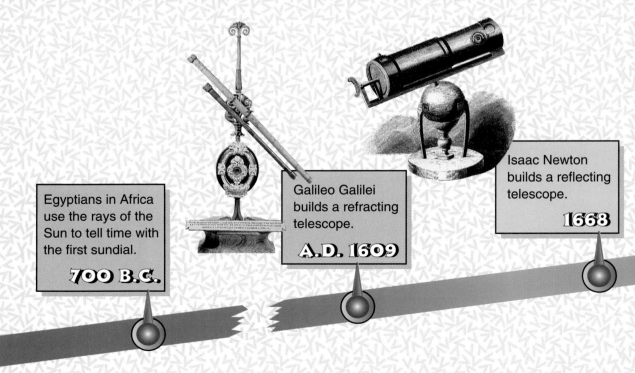

Egyptians in Africa use the rays of the Sun to tell time with the first sundial.

700 B.C.

Galileo Galilei builds a refracting telescope.

A.D. 1609

Isaac Newton builds a reflecting telescope.

1668

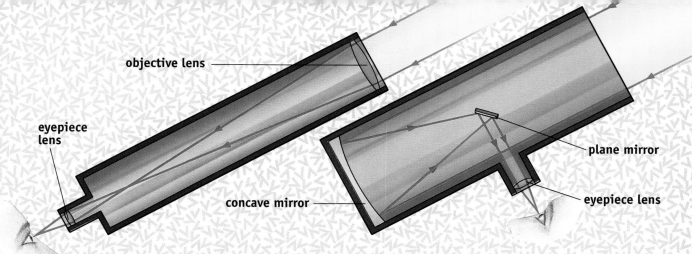

objective lens

eyepiece
lens

plane mirror

concave mirror

eyepiece lens

▲ **A simple refracting telescope**

▲ **A simple reflecting telescope**

small image. Then the eyepiece lens, or lens nearest the eye, magnifies the first image.

In 1668, Isaac Newton made a reflecting telescope, using a concave mirror. In a **reflecting telescope**, light strikes a mirror and is reflected to a focal point, where an image forms. A small flat mirror is used to reflect this image to a lens that magnifies the image.

The mirror in Newton's telescope had a diameter of only about 3 cm (1.2 in.). A larger mirror can focus on

smaller or more distant objects. The reflecting telescopes used by modern astronomers are much larger than Newton's.

The Hubble Space Telescope, also a reflecting telescope, is in orbit above Earth's atmosphere. The advantage of having a telescope in orbit is that the light from distant objects doesn't have to pass through air, which changes the light. The Hubble Space Telescope was named in honor of United States astronomer Edwin P. Hubble. ■

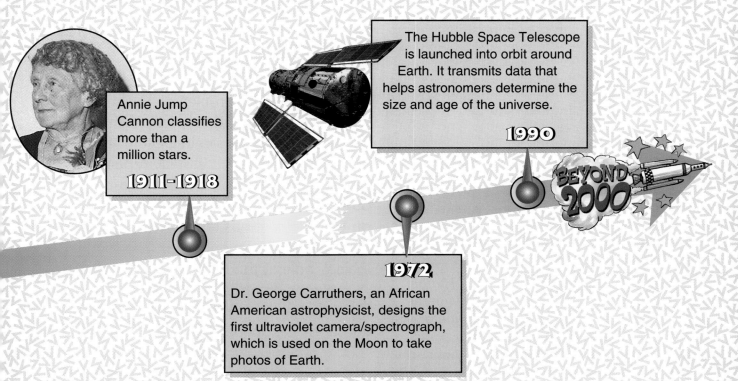

Annie Jump Cannon classifies more than a million stars.

1911–1918

The Hubble Space Telescope is launched into orbit around Earth. It transmits data that helps astronomers determine the size and age of the universe.

1990

BEYOND 2000

1972

Dr. George Carruthers, an African American astrophysicist, designs the first ultraviolet camera/spectrograph, which is used on the Moon to take photos of Earth.

Lyman Spitzer and His Magnificent Dream

Reading Focus Why can the Hubble Space Telescope observe greater detail than other reflecting telescopes?

STS
SCIENCE TECHNOLOGY & SOCIETY

In 1946, Lyman Spitzer wrote that a telescope in space could avoid the blurring effects of the Earth's atmosphere. It could provide the information needed to answer some very difficult questions: How big is the universe? What is the structure of galaxies? What is the nature of the planets?

In 1957 the Soviet Union launched the *Sputnik* satellite. The following year the United States space agency, the National Aeronautics and Space Administration (NASA), was started. In the 1960s and 1970s, two observatories carrying telescopes were placed in orbit by NASA. The success of these telescopes in space showed that Spitzer's idea for a large space telescope could work.

In 1990 the telescope known to the world as the Hubble Space Telescope was finally placed in orbit. While it did give scientists some good information, the telescope had problems. The mirror had not been shaped correctly. During a space shuttle mission in December 1993, astronauts successfully repaired the telescope. It is now able to observe objects 50 times fainter than telescopes on Earth can. It has taken photographs of Pluto and its moon. It has also found a black hole at the core of a galaxy.

Spitzer's dream has become a reality. The information needed to answer his questions is now being gathered. ■

Using Math *The primary mirror of the Hubble Space Telescope has a diameter of 240 cm (96 in.). What is the diameter of the mirror in meters?*

The Microscope

Reading Focus How do a simple microscope, compound microscope, and electron microscope differ?

During the 1600s, making lenses was a popular hobby. Anton van Leeuwenhoek (lā′vən hōōk) was a Dutch cloth merchant and lens grinder. From one of the many lenses he ground, he made a **simple microscope**. The photo at right shows a girl holding a model of this microscope. Leeuwenhoek's microscope had only one lens that was held between two metal plates. The object to be examined was stuck on the end of a pin placed beside the lens. A person using the microscope had to bring it up close to the eye. The lens could magnify objects more than 200 times their normal size.

With his microscope, Leeuwenhoek looked at insect parts, hair, ivory, and droplets of pond water. In the water, he found tiny organisms that could not be seen with only the human eye. He called these organisms *tierken*, which is Dutch for "little animals."

After Leeuwenhoek reported that he had found parasites on fleas, the English writer Jonathan Swift wrote:

So naturalists observe, a flea
Has smaller fleas that on him prey;
And these have smaller still to bite' em;
And so proceed *ad infinitum*.

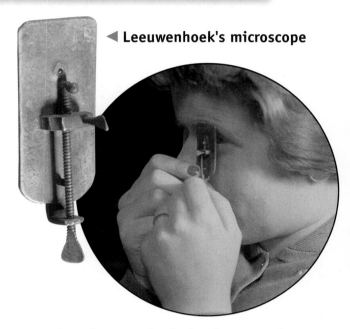
◄ **Leeuwenhoek's microscope**

What do you think Swift meant by these four lines of poetry?

A few years prior to Leeuwenhoek, Zacharias Janssen had invented a compound microscope. The **compound microscope** uses two convex lenses. A mirror reflects light toward an object that is on a clear glass slide. Light transmitted through the object enters the microscope tube containing the lenses. Light passing through the objective lens forms the first image. Light rays from this image pass through the eyepiece lens, which enlarges the image.

Robert Hooke, an English scientist, studied many objects through a compound microscope that he built. In

F41

1665, Hooke published the book *Micrographia* which contained his drawings of the things he had seen. One of the objects he had looked at was cork. Hooke noticed that the cork was made of tiny boxes. He called the boxes *cells*. The cells Hooke saw weren't living. What he saw were the outer parts of the cells that had once been alive.

The compound microscope made it possible for people to see, for the first time, the structures of living things— tiny living things that they never even knew existed. Scientists today use microscopes to study organisms that cause diseases. In fact, microscopes have had a far greater impact on human life than most people realize.

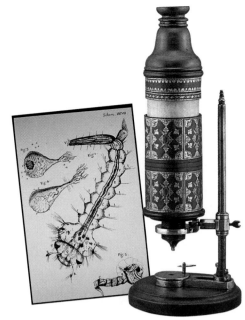

Hooke's compound microscope ▲

Modern compound light microscopes can magnify as much as 2,000 times. The **electron microscope** uses a

![Science in Literature]

Science in Literature

YOU ARE NOT ALONE!

"Do you remember the last time you felt lonely? The next time you think you're all alone, think again. Even if your room looks empty, you've got company. Millions of living critters are hidden in places you never thought to look: inside your intestines and your vacuum cleaner. . . . Just because you can't see them doesn't mean they're not there."

Extremely Weird Micro Monsters
by Sarah Lovett
John Muir Publications, 1993

You can look at 22 of these colorful creatures too small to see without the aid of a microscope in *Extremely Weird Micro Monsters* by Sarah Lovett. Do you get the feeling that microscopes make the world seem much more crowded?

Flu virus seen with this microscope ▼

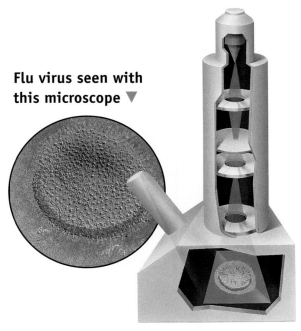

Transmission electron microscope ▲

Insect seen with this microscope ▼

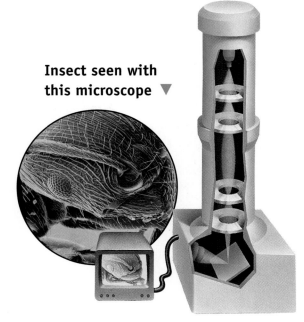

Scanning electron microscope ▲

beam of electrons instead of a beam of light. An electron microscope can make things appear hundreds of thousands of times bigger than they actually are. Scientists have used electron microscopes to see objects as small as bacteria, viruses, and even atoms.

There are two kinds of electron microscopes. A transmission electron microscope passes electrons from an electron gun through the object and onto a fluorescent screen. The microscope often displays the object in white

against a black background. The flu virus shown here had color added to it.

A scanning electron microscope moves electrons across the object being viewed. Then the electrons enter a collector and produce an enlarged image on what looks like a television screen. This kind of microscope is excellent for showing objects in three dimensions. ■

Internet Field Trip

Visit **www.eduplace.com** to learn more about microscopes.

━━━ INVESTIGATION 2 WRAP-UP ━━━

REVIEW

1. Explain how refracting and reflecting telescopes are different. How are they similar?

2. Compare a simple microscope, a compound microscope, and an electron microscope.

CRITICAL THINKING

3. One way to study a leaf is to look at very thin slices of the leaf under a compound microscope. Why is it useful to view a thin slice and not the whole leaf?

4. How are microscopes and refracting telescopes similar? How are they different?

HOW ARE LIGHT AND COLOR RELATED?

Have you ever been at a school show where red or blue lights were shone on the stage? A stage crew probably used filters of different colors. Did the performers and scenery change color, too? How do you think filters cause color changes?

Activity

Circles of Light

You have probably mixed paints of different colors together. Think back to what happened. Do you think the same colors will result when you mix different colors of light? Try this activity and find out.

MATERIALS

- 3 flashlights
- 3 rubber bands
- red, blue, and green acetate sheets
- *Science Notebook*

Procedure

1. Cover the lens of a flashlight with a red acetate sheet. Fasten the sheet tightly over the lens with a rubber band.

2. Repeat step 1 with two other flashlights. Cover one flashlight with a blue acetate sheet and cover the other flashlight with a green acetate sheet.

Step 2

3. Darken the room. Direct the light from the flashlight covered with the red acetate sheet onto a white wall or screen. Repeat with each of the other two flashlights.

4. **Observe** the wall and **record** your findings in your *Science Notebook*.

5. **Predict** what will happen when you direct red and green light from the flashlights onto the wall or screen so that the circles of light overlap. Try it. **Record** your observations.

Step 6

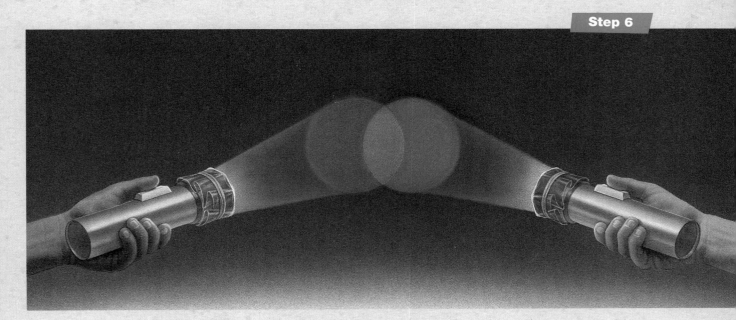

6. Repeat step 5, using all the possible combinations of two colors of light. **Record** your results.

7. **Predict** what will happen if you make all three circles of color overlap. Then overlap the circles of color. **Observe** what happens and **record** your results.

Analyze and Conclude

1. Did your predictions of what would happen match what actually happened? If they did not, explain why.

2. What color light results from mixing red and blue light? red and green light? blue and green?

3. What color light results from mixing all three colors of lights?

4. What conclusion can you draw about white light?

Technology Link CD-ROM

INVESTIGATE FURTHER!

Use the **Science Processor CD-ROM**, *Light and Sound* (Investigation 2, Mixing Colors) to find out what new colors are produced by different combinations of primary-colored lights.

Seeing Color

Reading Focus What determines the colors you see when you look at an object?

"Look, it's a rainbow!" That brilliant, multicolored band arching across the sky usually causes people to stop and stare. You probably know that a rainbow comes from white light. White light is made up of all the colors of the visible spectrum.

Making Rainbows

What causes a rainbow? Sunlight passing through water droplets in the air is refracted by these "natural" prisms, or lenses. The different colors are refracted in different amounts, so the colors spread out and are then reflected off of the inside of the droplets to your eyes— treating you to a rainbow.

You can make a rainbow by shining light through a prism. When you do, you separate white light into red, orange, yellow, green, blue, indigo, and violet.

As you saw earlier, the color of visible light is related to its wavelength. Violet light has the shortest wavelength. Red light has the longest wavelength. So your eyes and your brain are really responding to differences in wavelengths of light and interpreting these differences as colors.

A prism separates white light into many colors. ▶

white light

prism

The Colors of Objects

When you look at a red apple, what color of light is reaching your eye? You may need to think about this question for a moment. The answer involves knowing what happens to the light that strikes an object.

Most objects are **opaque** (ō pāk′), which means that they do not let light pass through them. Wood, books, and apples are opaque. When light strikes an opaque object, some of the light is absorbed, or taken in, by the object. This light changes to heat in the object, warming it. Some of the light is reflected. If the object is a red apple, red light is reflected and the other colors are absorbed.

Some objects, including lenses, are **transparent**. Light passes through them. Transparent matter is said to transmit light. Clear glass and shallow water are transparent. They absorb very little light. They do reflect some light, but most light passes through. In the photos of shirts, which screen lets the most light pass through?

Colored glass is partially transparent. It allows only certain colors of light to pass through. Red glass absorbs all colors of light except red. Some red light is reflected, but most passes through the glass. Remember, an object's color is the color that reflects off or passes through the object. It's the color that reaches your eye.

Translucent objects, such as frosted glass and wax paper, let light pass through them. However, the light does not follow one straight-line path through the material. It is scattered in many directions. This scattering makes it impossible for you to see clearly through translucent materials. But the colors of objects behind the translucent material can be seen.

Making Colors by Adding Light

During a live stage show, colored lights are often used to create special effects. Stage lights have a colored transparent material in front of the bulb. These colored materials, or **filters**, absorb some colors of light and let others pass through. Each kind of filter transmits a different color. The most common filters used are red, blue, and green. By shining several of these different-colored lights on the same

▲ **An opaque screen**

▲ **A transparent glass**

▲ **A translucent screen**

spot, the stage crew can make other colors, or even white light.

Look at the photograph of overlapping circles of colored light on page F48. Mixing red light and green light produces yellow light. Combining red

▲ **Examples of color addition, the mixing of light**

light and blue light makes magenta light. Combining blue light and green light makes a blue-green color called cyan (sī′an). Mixing colored light in this way is called color addition because colored lights are combined, or added together. The activity on page F44 includes experiments on color addition.

As the photograph at the right shows, shining red, green, and blue light onto the same area of a screen produces white light. These three colors are called primary colors because you can mix them to make other colors.

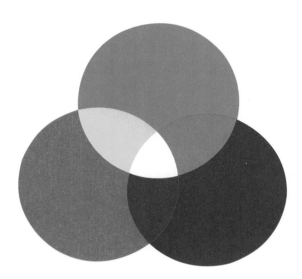

▲ **The effect of overlapping primary colors of light**

INVESTIGATION 3 WRAP-UP

REVIEW

1. Explain the difference between transparent and translucent objects.

2. What filters should a stage crew use to produce a white light?

CRITICAL THINKING

3. For each different area of the U. S. flag, tell what colors of light are reflected and absorbed.

4. Why does a blue flame look blue? Why does white light passing through a blue filter look blue?

REFLECT & EVALUATE

Word Power

Write the letter of the term that best matches the defintion. *Not all terms will be used.*

1. A material that lets light through but scatters it
2. The point at which light rays passing through a lens come together
3. A viewing instrument that uses two convex lenses to magnify tiny objects many times
4. A transparent object with at least one curved surface that bends light as it passes through it
5. The light-sensitive layer at the back of the *eye*
6. A material that does not let light pass through

a. compound microscope
b. focal point
c. lens
d. opaque
e. refracting telescope
f. retina
g. simple microscope
h. translucent

Check What You Know

Write the term in each pair that best completes each sentence.

1. A (convex, concave) lens is thicker in the middle than at the *edges* and brings light rays together.
2. Frosted glass is (translucent, transparent) because light does not follow straight-line paths through it.
3. A microscope that can magnify objects as much as 2,000 times is a/an (simple, compound) microscope.

Problem Solving

1. Make sketches showing the lens shape when the eye is focused on a nearby object and when it is focused on a distant object.
2. Microscopes have become more and more powerful. How do you think this has affected the kinds of things scientists study with microscopes?

Study the drawing. Then write a description of how light is absorbed, reflected, or transmitted by the objects. Tell if each object is transparent, translucent, or opaque.

CHAPTER 3

PROPERTIES OF SOUND

The community where you live has landmarks that make it special and give it character. Your community also has soundmarks. A soundmark is a unique sound that people recognize and remember. It might be a sound made by a clock, bell, whistle, or horn. What are some soundmarks in your community?

Connecting to Science

ARTS

Sound Designs Have you ever seen a sound sculpture? If so, it might have been the work of sonic architects Bill and Mary Buchen. They design and build interactive sound sculptures, games, and playgrounds. One of their playgrounds is at Candlestick Point Recreation Area in San Francisco, California.

At each of their playgrounds children can explore a variety of instruments. The wind gamelan is an instrument played by the wind. The sound observatory is a series of stainless steel drums played with the feet. Big Eyes/Big Ears is an echo chamber that amplifies and transmits captured sounds and allows children to explore the sounds of their neighborhoods. If the chamber were in your neighborhood, what captured sounds would you hear?

Coming Up

◀ A student explores the sounds that can be made on steel drums.

WHAT IS SOUND?

Have you ever sat perfectly still and listened to the sounds around you? Try it sometime and you may be amazed at what you hear. In this investigation you'll see how sound is produced and how it travels. In the process, you may hear some sweet—and sour—sounds!

Activity

Rubber-Band Banjo

How are sounds produced? Construct a simple banjo and use it to find out.

MATERIALS
- goggles
- rubber band
- ruler
- 2 pencils
- *Science Notebook*

SAFETY
Wear goggles during this activity.

Procedure

Stretch a rubber band lengthwise over a ruler. Then insert a pencil under the rubber band at each end of the ruler so that the rubber band is lifted away from the surface of the ruler. Pluck the rubber band at any point between the two pencils. **Observe** what happens. **Record** what you see and hear in your *Science Notebook*. Press your finger at different points along the rubber band, plucking it each time. **Describe** the sounds produced.

Analyze and Conclude

1. Hypothesize how the rubber band produces sound.

2. How did the sound change when you pressed the rubber band at different points on the ruler?

Activity

Waves and Sound

Sound is a form of energy that travels through different objects and materials. In this activity you'll build a model of the way a sound wave moves.

Procedure

1. Use a piece of string to tie one end of a coil spring to a table leg. Stretch the coil spring and use another piece of string to tie the other end to another table leg. Make sure that the spring is stretched tightly enough so that it doesn't touch the floor.

2. Fold 10 pieces of colored yarn in half. Starting at one end of the spring, hang a piece of yarn on every tenth coil.

3. Predict what will happen to the yarn if you pinch the five coils at the end together and then release them. Discuss your prediction with your group. Record your prediction in your *Science Notebook*.

4. Pinch together five coils at one end of the spring and quickly release them. Record your observations of the coil spring and the hanging pieces of yarn.

5. Repeat step 4 several times. Record your observations each time.

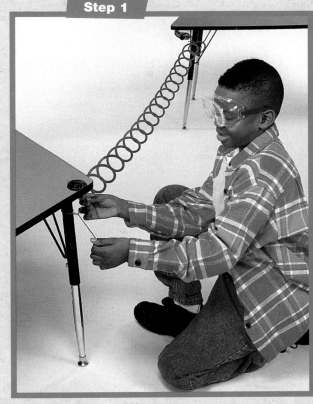

Step 1

Analyze and Conclude

1. Write a general statement about the way the coil spring behaved when you pinched and then released the five end coils.

2. What evidence did you observe that energy was transferred along the spring coil?

The Nature of Sound

Reading Focus How can you describe sound waves?

The melody of a popular song, the roar of the crowd at a basketball game, and the clatter of a jackhammer cutting a hole in a sidewalk all have something in common. They all are produced by vibrations. **Vibrations** (vī brā'shənz) are back-and-forth movements of matter.

If you pluck a stretched rubber band, as suggested in the activity on page F52, or if you pluck a guitar string, you can see the rubber band or string vibrate as you hear the sound that the vibrations cause. Air carries the vibrations to your eardrums and causes them to vibrate. The vibrations in your ears produce nerve impulses that are carried to your brain. There the impulses are interpreted as sounds.

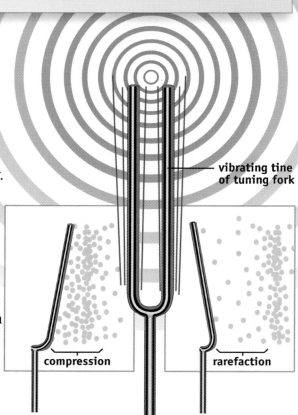

vibrating tine of tuning fork

compression

rarefaction

Sound Waves

Sound is a form of energy that you can hear and that travels through matter as waves. Anything that is in motion has energy, and sound is certainly in motion. If you tap a tuning fork with a rubber hammer, you transfer energy from the moving hammer to the tines of the tuning fork.

Parts of a sound wave ▼

crest

amplitude

rarefaction

wavelength

compression

wavelength

amplitude

trough

F54

The back-and-forth motion of the tines pushing against air particles around them creates sound waves. These sound waves travel outward in all directions from the tuning fork. The region where the particles have been pushed closer together is called a **compression** (kəm presh′ən). Air pressure is greater than usual in this region. The region where there are fewer particles than normal is called a **rarefaction** (rer ə fak′shən). Air pressure is lower than usual in this region. A sound wave is a series of compressions and rarefactions moving outward from the source of a vibration.

A sound wave can be represented as a more familiar up-and-down wave, as shown at the bottom of page F54. In the drawing, the **crests** represent the compressions of a sound wave, or regions of greater air pressure. The **troughs** represent the rarefactions, or regions of lower air pressure.

When a sound wave travels from its source to your ear, the particles that carry the wave do not travel along with the wave. Like the coils of the spring in the activity on page F53, the particles in air move back and forth. But after the wave passes, the particles are still in the same general location, much as the coils remained where they were.

Measuring Sound Waves

The distance from one compression to the next is the **wavelength** of a sound wave. Wavelength depends on the frequency of vibration of the source of the sound. **Frequency** is the number of complete waves produced in a unit of time, such as a second. A high sound is one that has a high frequency. In a high sound a great many waves are produced each second. A low sound has a low frequency. In a low sound fewer waves are produced each second. The **amplitude** (am′plə tōōd) of a wave is the distance from rest to a crest or from rest to a trough. It is a measure of the amount of energy in a sound

Sound wave of a loud sound, such as the whistle of a freight train ▼

Sound wave of a soft sound, such as a whisper ▼

wave. A loud sound is represented by a sound wave with a large amplitude. A soft sound is represented by a sound wave with a small amplitude.

Quality of Sound—Timbre

The drawing on page F54 shows a simple sound wave. It represents a pure sound made by a tuning fork. A tuning fork produces a tone, or sound, with a single frequency and a simple wave pattern. But most of the sounds you hear, such as music on the radio and TV, are very complex. They are made up of several waves that combine to form complex sounds.

Whether produced by a vibrating string or a vibrating air column, musical instruments have complex sounds. The sound of a musical instrument is made up of a basic tone (simple wave pattern) and overtones (other wave patterns). **Overtones** are softer, higher tones that are mixed with the basic tone. The blending of basic tones and overtones is what makes the sounds of different instruments unique. This blending also makes the voices of different people unique.

When two instruments produce the same note, or tone, you can tell that one sound comes from a flute, for example, and one comes from a trumpet. The special sound produced by a musical instrument is its **timbre** (tam′bər). Musicians often use words such as *mellow*, *bright*, or *tinny* to describe differences in timbre.

Science in Literature

BALLOON ROCKS AND ROLLS

"Try this. . . . Blow up a balloon and tie the opening. Tune a radio to your favorite station and turn up the volume loud. Hold the balloon gently between your finger tips near the speaker of the radio. Feel the sound waves making the balloon vibrate."

You can find this and other interesting experiments with sound when you read *Tuning In: The Sounds of the Radio* by Eve and Albert Stwertka. You might want to write about your experiments and share them with your class.

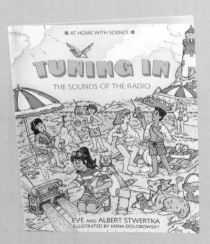

**Tuning In:
The Sounds of the Radio**
by Eve and Albert Stwertka
Illustrated by Mena Dolobowsky
Julian Messner, 1993

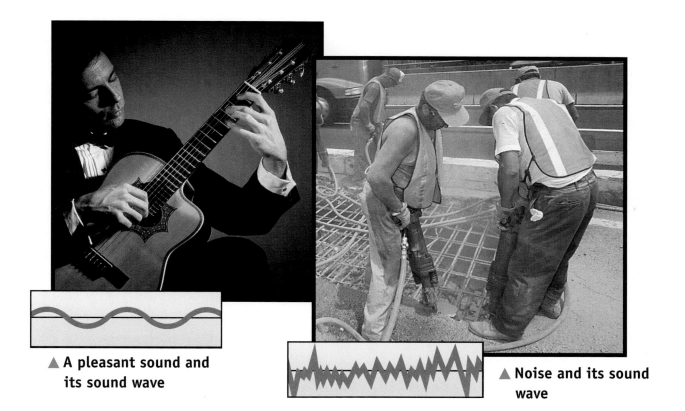

▲ A pleasant sound and its sound wave

▲ Noise and its sound wave

Noise

You may disagree with your family and friends about what is "good" music. But you'll probably agree that the tones and overtones of most music combine in very pleasant ways. On the other hand, many sources of sound produce combinations of waves that are unpleasant. You would probably agree that the sounds of jackhammers, squealing brakes, or a tray of dishes being dropped are unpleasant. Unpleasant sounds, or noises, have irregular sound waves. Look at the drawings below the photographs. You can see that the wave pattern of music can be smooth and form a repeating pattern. The wave pattern of noise can be irregular. ■

Internet Field Trip

Visit **www.eduplace.com** to learn more about sound.

INVESTIGATION 1 WRAP-UP

REVIEW

1. Describe three main characteristics of a sound wave.

2. Why is sound called a form of energy?

CRITICAL THINKING

3. Make sketches of sound waves to represent (a) a shout and a whisper; (b) a bird's chirp and a lion's roar; and (c) music and noise.

4. How might a hearing-impaired person keep perfect time to music from a piano he or she cannot hear?

INVESTIGATION 2

HOW DOES MATTER AFFECT HOW SOUND TRAVELS?

Have you ever gone swimming and noticed that sounds are different under water? As you experiment with sound, you'll find out how the material through which sound passes affects the properties of sound.

Activity

Ear to the Wall

Press your ear to a wall. What can you hear? Does sound travel better through some materials than through others?

Procedure

Tap your fingernails on your desk. Then place your ear on your desktop. Again, tap your fingernails. Compare the two tapping sounds. Record your observations in your *Science Notebook*. Next, place an empty plastic cup upside down on the desk. Press your ear against the bottom of the cup. Tap lightly on the desk. Repeat, using an empty aluminum can. Discuss your observations with your group. Record your findings.

Analyze and Conclude

1. What can you infer about how well sound travels through wood, plastic, and metal?

2. Why can you often hear a conversation in another room when you press your ear to the wall?

Activity

A String Phone

You might have made string telephones when you were younger. In this activity you'll figure out how they work.

MATERIALS
- 2 paper cups
- sharpened pencil
- 6 m of strong string
- 2 paper clips
- *Science Notebook*

- -

Procedure

1. Use a pencil to punch a hole in the center of the bottom of two paper cups.

2. Put one end of a piece of string through the hole in one cup and tie the string around a paper clip on the inside of the cup.

3. Repeat step 2 with the other end of the string and the other cup.

4. Stand far apart from your partner and have your partner say something quietly. **Observe** how well you can hear what your partner says. **Record** your observations in your *Science Notebook.*

5. Now hold the cup up to your ear. Have your partner quietly say something into the other cup. **Record** your observations.

Step 3

6. Reverse roles with your partner and repeat steps 4 and 5.

7. There are at least two variables that must be controlled for you to hear clearly with a string telephone. Try to discover what they are.

Analyze and Conclude

1. **Compare** how well you could hear your partner with and without the string phone.

2. Through what did the sound travel to reach your ear each time?

3. What variables did you need to control to make the string phone work?

4. **Hypothesize** how you could improve this telephone. **Test** your hypothesis.

INVESTIGATE FURTHER!

EXPERIMENT

Plan an experiment to show that an electrical circuit can produce a sound. Use dry cells, a buzzer, and a setup similar to the one on page F7. Have your teacher approve your plan, then try it!

When Sound Travels and When It Doesn't

Reading Focus What determines the speed of sound through matter?

The pitcher winds up and then releases the ball. The batter swings, and the bat connects with the ball right over home plate. But you don't hear the bat hit the ball until about a second later. Why does this happen?

At the Speed of Sound

Sound waves travel much more slowly than light waves do. The speed of sound waves in air is about 346 m/s (1,142 ft/s). The speed of light is about 300 million m/s (990 million ft/s)—almost 900,000 times greater than the

Why don't you *hear* the bat hit the ball at the same time that you *see* it? ▼

F60

speed of sound! The speed of sound varies with the material through which it moves. The table on page F61 compares the speed of sound in several different materials. In the activity on page F58, the sound of fingers tapping on a desk is much louder when you place your ear directly on the desktop. Less sound energy changes to other forms of energy in wood than in air. So the sound of fingers tapping is louder with your ear on the wood desktop. Sound travels faster through wood than it does through air. The closely packed particles in wood are springy and transmit sound more quickly than do the particles in air.

The speed of sound also varies with the temperature of the material through which the sound moves. From the table, compare the speed of sound in air at 0°C and at 25°C. Particles of matter move faster at higher temperatures than at lower temperatures. Why does this difference affect the rate at which sound travels? As the temperature rises, particles take less time to collide with one another. As a result, they pass along the wave energy more quickly.

Matter Is a Must

Unlike light waves, sound waves can travel only when there is matter to carry

The Speed of Sound in Different Materials	
Material	**Speed (m/s)**
Air (at 0°C)	331
Air (at 25°C)	346
Pure Water (at 25°C)	1,498
Sea water (at 25°C)	1,531
Wood (oak)	3,850
Copper	3,100
Brick	3,650
Glass	4,540
Steel	5,200

About how much faster is the speed of sound through air at 25°C than at 0°C?

▲ **Sound waves travel through air.**

▲ **Sound cannot travel through a vacuum.**

them. You can see the light from the Sun because it travels through the vacuum of space. But you don't hear the roaring nuclear explosions that are the source of the Sun's energy. You can't hear them because sound waves require matter in order to travel.

Sound waves cannot travel through a vacuum. If you put a ringing alarm clock inside a jar filled with air, you'll hear the alarm going off as the boy in the drawing does. Then if you slowly pump air from the jar, you'll find that the sound gets fainter and fainter until you can no longer hear it. So the girl in the drawing does not hear the ringing clock. ■

INVESTIGATION 2 WRAP-UP

REVIEW

1. In which material—wood, glass, or steel—does sound travel the fastest? the slowest?

2. Why can't you hear the sound of explosions on the Sun?

CRITICAL THINKING

3. Explain how the matter through which sound travels affects the sound. Give an example to support your explanation.

4. After lunch you put your head down on your desk to rest. You hear very loud footsteps that you hadn't noticed before. Why are the footsteps so loud now?

HOW DO HIGH SOUNDS DIFFER FROM LOW SOUNDS?

When your best friend calls you on the telephone, you know his or her voice right away. You can also tell the difference between a guitar and a trumpet. What makes sounds different? How can you tell one sound from another?

Activity

Highs and Lows

The pitch of a sound is its highness or lowness. What are some ways you can vary pitch?

MATERIALS

- 3 identical small-necked plastic bottles
- water
- *Science Notebook*

SAFETY

Clean up spills immediately.

Procedure

Put water into two identical bottles. Fill one bottle. Half fill the second bottle. Leave a third bottle empty. **Predict** what will happen if you blow across the top of each bottle. **Discuss** your prediction with your group. Then blow across the top of each bottle until you hear a clear tone from it. **Infer** why there were differences between the tones. **Record** your observations in your *Science Notebook*.

Analyze and Conclude

1. How did the sounds in the three bottles compare? How did the quantity of water affect the pitch?

2. Infer what was vibrating—the water, the air, or the bottle. Explain your inference.

3. Hypothesize about what causes the pitch of a sound to vary.

Activity

Changing Pitch

In this activity you'll explore ways to change the pitch of a vibrating rubber band. What do you think some of the ways might be?

- -

Procedure

1. Stretch three rubber bands lengthwise over a box as shown in the picture.

2. **Predict** how the pitch of each of the three rubber bands, when plucked, will differ. **Discuss** your predictions with your group.

3. Pluck each rubber band and listen to the pitch. **Record** your observations in your *Science Notebook*.

4. Select one of the rubber bands and slide a pencil under it near one end of the box. Turn the pencil to twist and tighten the rubber band.

5. Pluck the rubber band and **record** your observations.

6. Repeat step 5 three times, each time turning the pencil a little bit more. **Record** your observations.

7. Repeat steps 4, 5, and 6 with each of the other rubber bands. **Record** your observations.

Step 1

Analyze and Conclude

1. How is the thickness of a rubber band related to the pitch of the sound it produces when plucked?

2. **Compare** the sounds produced by the rubber bands in steps 3, 5, and 6. What can you conclude about any differences?

3. What did you do to the rubber band when you twisted the pencil? How did this affect the pitch of the sound produced when it was plucked?

4. Imagine that the rubber bands are strings on a guitar. What general statements can you make about the pitches of sounds produced by guitar strings?

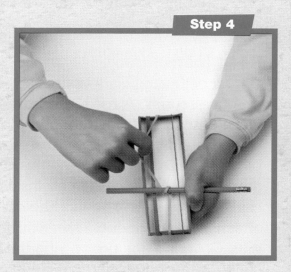

Step 4

Wind Instruments

Reading Focus How do wind instruments produce sound?

In Japan, it's called a *fuye* (f$\overline{oo}$'yä); in South Africa it's known as the *naka ya lethlake* (nä'kä yä le-lä'kä); in China, the *ti-tzu* (di dz$\overline{oo}$). What is it? All of these words describe the same thing—the musical instrument you know as the flute. Wind instruments in different parts of the world vary in shape and sound. But they are all alike in one way—they depend on a vibrating column of air to produce sound.

Recall that pitch is the highness or lowness of a sound. The pitch made by the vibrating air depends on the length of the air column, as demonstrated in the activity on page F62. A shorter column produces a sound with a higher pitch; a longer column produces a lower pitch.

Reed Instruments

The orchestral clarinet uses a reed to produce sounds. A reed is a short, thin piece of wood attached to the mouthpiece. When you blow into the mouthpiece, the reed vibrates, and this vibration causes the column of air inside the clarinet to vibrate. The mouthpiece is attached to a cylindrical tube with holes in it. Covering and uncovering the holes changes the length of the column of air, thereby changing the note that is played. The sound comes out the bell at the base of the tube.

Compare the orchestral clarinet with the *zummara* (z$\overline{oo}$ mä'rə), shown below. The zummara, a reed instrument made of cane, has two joined pipes with six holes in each pipe. It is played in Tunisia, a country in northern Africa.

Brass Instruments

You have seen that a wind instrument such as the clarinet uses a reed to make the air vibrate. Brass instruments such as the trumpet and the trombone have no reeds. The player's lips vibrate against the mouthpiece, causing the air in the instrument to vibrate.

Orchestral clarinet ▶

▲ **Zummara, a double-pipe reed instrument from Tunisia**

The orchestral trumpet uses valves to control the length of the air column and to control the pitch of the sound. The trombone has a slide that changes the length of the air column. In some parts of the world, musicians play trumpets that do not use valves. Instead, the trumpeters use only the vibration of their lips to change the pitch. Such an instrument is the *neku*, shown below.

Kinds of Flutes

Flutes also lack reeds. A narrow opening cut in the tube produces sound when air passes over the opening or through it. In an orchestral flute, this opening is on the side of a long, thin tube. The multiple flute has more than one pipe. This *dvojnice* (dvoi'nē tsə) has a twin wood pipe, a mouthpiece, and finger holes. However, it does not have keys, and the air is blown in from the top rather than from the side.

Wind instruments from around the world look and sound different. But people from any country can enjoy the music from these instruments. ■

UNIT PROJECT LINK

Instruments and other devices are used to create music and sound effects in shows. Work with your team to plan a show based on a folk tale, using puppets. After you decide which folk tale you'll use, try telling the tale from a different point of view.

Plan the sound effects that you will need. You may even want to build your own instruments and sound-effects devices. Add lighting, using acetate-covered flashlights.

Technology Link
For more help with your Unit Project, go to **www.eduplace.com**.

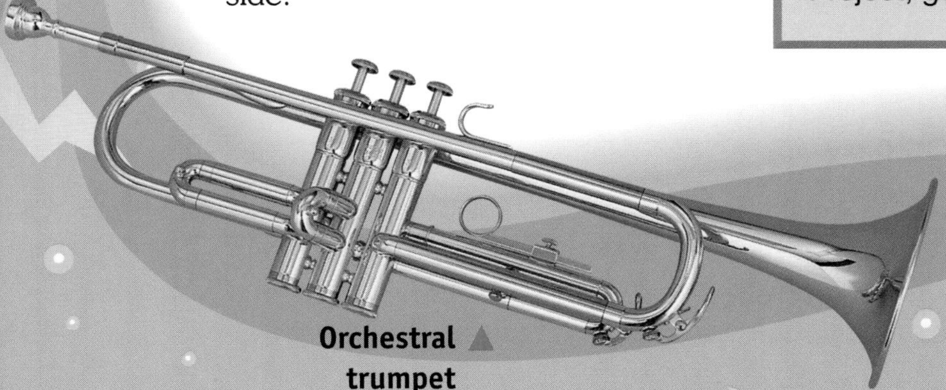

Orchestral flute ▶

Orchestral trumpet ▲

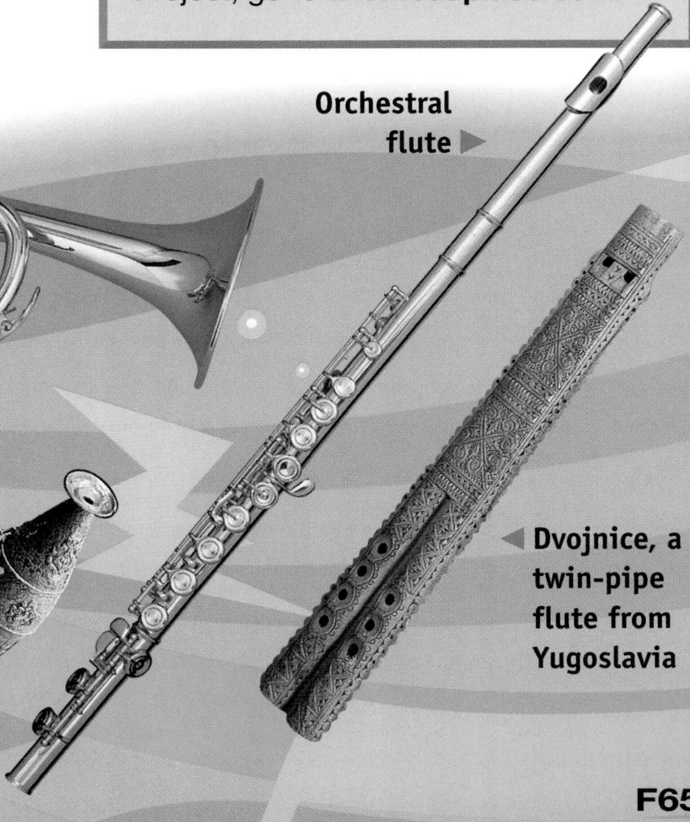

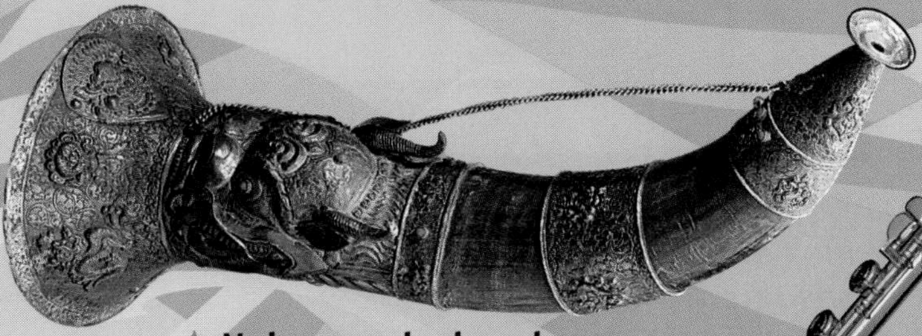

▲ **Neku, a valveless brass instrument from Nepal**

◀ **Dvojnice, a twin-pipe flute from Yugoslavia**

F65

Pitch

Reading Focus How is the length of your vocal cords related to the pitch of your voice?

Singing the American national anthem is not easy for many people, especially when it comes to hitting the high notes. But a good singer can sing the notes having the highest and lowest pitches. **Pitch** is the highness or lowness of sound. It is related to the frequency of the sound waves produced. The frequency of a sound wave is the number of waves passing a location, such as your eardrum, each second. High-pitched sounds produce many sound waves per second and so have a high frequency. Low-pitched sounds produce fewer sound waves per second and so have a lower frequency.

The frequency of a sound wave is measured in a unit called the **hertz** (Hz), or cycles per second. Some animals, including humans, have a certain range of frequencies that they can hear and a range that they can produce. Look at the graph below. People can hear sounds as low as 20 Hz and as high as 20,000 Hz. How does this compare with what bats can hear?

Pitch and Music

Do you play the piano, organ, or electric keyboard? If you do, you know that the keyboard is divided into octaves. Each series of eight notes makes up an

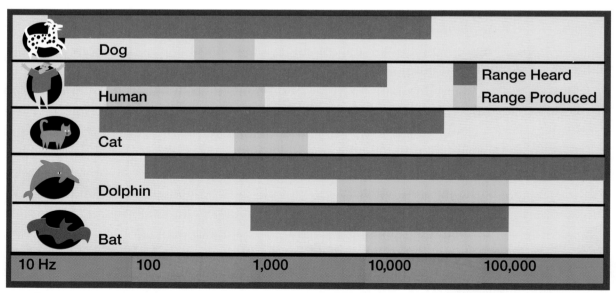

This bar graph shows the ranges of frequencies heard and produced by certain animals and humans. Which animal can hear the highest frequency? the lowest? What are those frequencies?

F66

99 Hz	110 Hz	124 Hz	132 Hz	148 Hz	165 Hz	176 Hz	198 Hz	220 Hz	248 Hz	264 Hz	297 Hz	330 Hz	352 Hz	396 Hz	440 Hz	495 Hz	528 Hz	594 Hz	660 Hz	704 Hz	792 Hz
G_2	A_2	B_2	C_3	D_3	E_3	F_3	G_3	A_3	B_3	C_4	D_4	E_4	F_4	G_4	A_4	B_4	C_5	D_5	E_5	F_5	G_5

Middle C

▲ **The frequency of notes on a piano keyboard. Middle C, which has a frequency of 264 Hz, is in the center of the keyboard.**

octave (äk'tiv). The keyboard above shows the frequencies of notes of several octaves. Notice that middle C, which has a frequency of 264 Hz, is written as C_4. The note that is one octave below middle C is another C, written C_3. The C note that is one octave above middle C is written C_5. A similar method is used to show octaves for other notes.

Look at the frequencies of C_3, C_4, and C_5. Note how the frequencies are related. Each time you go up an octave, the frequency of the note doubles. How might this explain why we hear all these notes as C? Is this pattern also true of other notes that are one or two octaves apart, such as E_3 and E_4 or G_3 and G_4? Check the frequencies of the notes on the keyboard to find out.

The graph below shows the frequency range for a number of musical instruments and for human voices. In general, men have longer, thicker vocal cords than women do. As a result, men find it easier to sing notes with lower pitches.

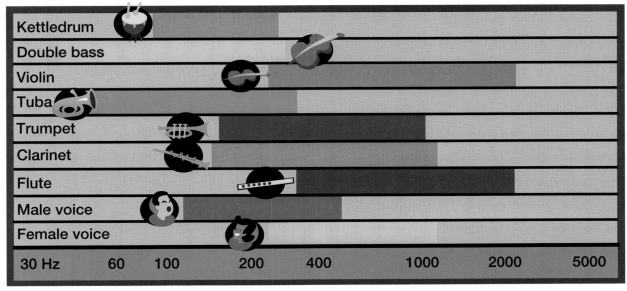

Kettledrum								
Double bass								
Violin								
Tuba								
Trumpet								
Clarinet								
Flute								
Male voice								
Female voice								
30 Hz	60	100	200	400	1000	2000	5000	

Using Math

This bar graph shows the range of frequencies produced by various instruments and the human voice. Which instrument produces the smallest frequency range? the largest?

▲ When the guitarist strums the full length of a string, she produces a low note.

▲ When she presses her finger on a string, she shortens it, and produces a higher note.

Women can more easily sing notes of higher pitches. Because the vocal cords of children are shorter than those of adults, children tend to speak and sing at higher pitches than adults do.

Musical Highs and Lows

If you've ever played a guitar, you know that the thicker strings produce the lower notes, and the thinner strings produce the higher notes. The guitar player changes the length of a string by holding the string down against the frets, the bars on the guitar neck. When a string is held against a fret, the part of the string that vibrates is shorter, so the pitch is higher.

At the top of the guitar are the pegs that change the tension on the strings. If a string is tightened, the pitch gets higher. If the string is loosened, the pitch gets lower. This change in pitch was shown by tightening rubber bands in the activity on page F63.

The pitch of the sounds produced by wind instruments depends on the length of the vibrating column of air. The shorter the column of air, the greater the frequency of vibration and the higher the pitch. As the graph on page F67 shows, the frequency ranges of instruments differ.

Controlling Loudness

The amplitude of the sound waves produced by musical instruments is heard as loudness. For stringed instruments the loudness depends on how a string is plucked or bowed. The harder you pluck or bow the string, the louder the sound. For wind instruments the harder the musician blows, the louder the sound. For percussion instruments, such as drums and cymbals, the loudness depends on how forcefully the instruments are struck. ■

Technology Link
CD-ROM

INVESTIGATE FURTHER!

Use the **Science Processor CD-ROM**, *Light and Sound* (Investigation 3, Sound of Music) to learn more about sound frequencies. You will be able to "pluck" a guitar string to learn how changes in the length of the string relate to the sound it plays.

Synthesizing Sound

Reading Focus What are some ways that sound synthesizers can be used?

A **sound synthesizer** is an electronic device that can produce a wide variety of sounds. The first electronic sound synthesizer was developed by Harry Olson and Herbert Belar at Radio Corporation of America (RCA) in 1955. Olson and Belar built the synthesizer to carry out research on the properties of sound. But a number of composers saw the great potential for sound synthesizers to produce music.

Music Synthesizers

Today synthesized music is produced using a keyboard or a sound bank that creates specific groups of sound waves. Synthesizers can create sounds that are like many instruments, such as pianos and flutes. They can also combine tones to form new sounds. Some synthesizers can produce special effects, including echoes.

A synthesizer can produce the sounds of all musical instruments fairly well. So it can sometimes be used to replace a band or an orchestra. Many musical compositions are written especially for the music sythesizer. It has become a popular means of providing music for radio, television, movies, and live concert performances.

Speech Synthesizers

Did you ever call directory assistance for a telephone number and hear a robot-like voice? That was synthesized speech! Synthesized speech has many uses. It can provide instructions to children on how to use a computer. It can alert pilots, astronauts, and drivers about conditions that may need their attention. A speech synthesizer can be used by people with various kinds of disabilities.

How does a speech synthesizer work? It stores sounds that are later combined to produce words and sentences that sound like those spoken by a human voice. Most speech synthesizers use the basic sounds of a language

Music synthesizer ▼

F69

such as English. Each of the sounds, when spoken into a microphone, produces a distinct electrical pattern. The electrical pattern can be stored in a computer as part of a magnetic pattern. A computer can then select and combine the stored patterns, as needed, to reproduce different sounds such as syllables, words, and sentences. The speech synthesizer can then produce the sounds of a human voice.

When you hear the voice of a speech synthesizer, you can usually tell that it is not a real person speaking. But the computer programs of synthesizers are improving, and the voices produced by these new programs are becoming more humanlike in quality.

Recognizing Voices

The sound waves that form when people speak can be changed to electrical pulses by a microphone. Some computers have been successfully programmed to respond to the electrical signals produced by voice com-

mands. Instead of typing commands, a person can talk to the computer and get it to to bring up a certain file. For example, with some telephone systems, you just say someone's name into the phone and the system finds that person's number in your directory. You don't even have to dial! ■

The boy is learning to use a speech synthesizer. ▼

_____ **INVESTIGATION 3 WRAP-UP** _____

REVIEW

1. How is pitch related to frequency?

2. How does a speech synthesizer work?

CRITICAL THINKING

3. Imagine that you are looking inside a grand piano. Compare the appearance of the strings that produce low notes with that of the strings that produce high notes.

4. A piccolo is an instrument that looks like a short flute. Would you expect a piccolo to produce higher or lower sounds than a flute? Explain your answer.

REFLECT & EVALUATE

Word Power

Write the letter of the term that best completes the sentence. *Not all terms will be used.*

a. crest
b. compression
c. overtone
d. pitch
e. sound
f. timbre
g. trough
h. wavelength

1. The region in a sound wave where particles have been pushed closer together is the ___.
2. The highest point of a wave is its ___.
3. A form of energy that you can hear that travels through matter as waves is ___.
4. The highness or lowness of a sound is its ___.
5. The distance from one compression to the next is the ___.

Check What You Know

Write the term in each pair that best completes each sentence.

1. A high sound is one that has a high (frequency, amplitude).
2. A loud sound is represented by a sound wave with a large (frequency, amplitude).
3. All sound is produced by (rarefactions, vibrations).
4. You can identify the sound of a flute by its (octave, timbre).
5. Sound waves cannot travel through (a vacuum, water).

Problem Solving

1. Why would a motorboat sound closer when you're underwater than it actually is when you come to the surface?
2. In many science-fiction movies, a *whooshing* sound is heard as a spacecraft moves by. Imagine you are in a real spacecraft in space and another flies by. Explain whether you would—or would not—hear a sound.

BUILD YOUR PORTFOLIO

Study the photograph of the recorder, a simple wind instrument. Then use the photograph to explain how the recorder produces the highest pitch and the lowest pitch.

CHAPTER 4

HEARING AND RECORDING SOUND

Some of the things that people enjoy most in life are sounds. We hear a special person's voice, the laughter of a child, our favorite music. All these are possible because of the existence of sound.

PEOPLE USING SCIENCE

Electrical Engineer There are about 28 million Americans who have some type of hearing impairment that could be helped by the use of a hearing aid. But only one in four of these people actually gets one. Many people simply don't like the appearance of the traditional hearing aid that rests in the cup of the outer ear. Now scientists, led by electrical engineer Henri Garcia, have developed the first "invisible" hearing aid. It consists of a tiny cylinder about .64 cm (.25 in.) wide and 1.3 cm (.5 in.) long.

This hearing aid is so small that it can be planted inside the ear canal, almost touching the eardrum, where it's hard to see. A hearing aid makes sound louder. In what other ways can sound be changed or controlled?

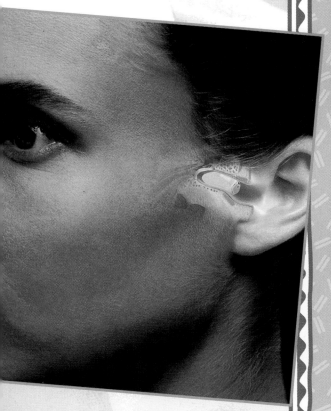

◄ Henri Garcia holds the technology award he received for inventing the "invisible" hearing aid. The tiny device, made of spongy material, fits into the ear canal, as shown.

INVESTIGATION 1

How Can You Control Sound?

Have you ever been to a rock concert? If you have, you know how loud sounds can be made. People often control sound—making it louder, softer, higher, or lower. In this investigation you will explore some of the ways sound can be controlled.

Activity

Directing Sound

Outdoors, bands sometimes play in front of a curved band shell. How does a band shell control sound?

MATERIALS
- meterstick
- large sheet of construction paper
- *Science Notebook*

Procedure

With your class, go to an open area outdoors. Have one student stand about 50 m away, face the class, and make an announcement. In your *Science Notebook*, **record** how well you heard him or her. Next, have the student cup both hands around his or her mouth and repeat the announcement at the same volume. **Record** how well you heard him or her.

Finally, have the student make a megaphone by rolling a sheet of construction paper into a cone shape. Have the student make the announcement through the megaphone. **Compare** this sound to the sounds made the other two times he or she spoke.

Analyze and Conclude

1. When could you best hear the student speak? Why?

2. Where are megaphones used? What is their purpose?

3. **Infer** how a megaphone and a band shell are alike.

Activity

Muffling Sound

Have you ever been kept awake by a ticking clock? Maybe you muffled the sound with a pillow. Which materials work best to muffle, or absorb, sound?

MATERIALS
- small empty cardboard box with top removed
- wind-up alarm clock with loud ticking sound
- meterstick
- sound-absorbing materials (cloth, cotton, bubble packing, shredded newspaper, plastic-foam peanuts)
- *Science Notebook*

Procedure

1. Place a small cardboard box on its side with the opening toward you. Place a ticking clock inside the box.

2. Walk away from the box in a straight line until you can no longer hear the clock ticking. **Measure** this distance with a meterstick. **Record** the distance in your *Science Notebook*.

 See **SCIENCE** and **MATH TOOLBOX** page H6 if you need to review **Using a Tape Measure or a Ruler.**

3. With the alarm clock in place, fill the box with one of the sound-absorbing materials. **Predict** how far you will be from the box when you will no longer be able to hear the clock ticking. **Record** your prediction. Repeat step 2.

4. Repeat step 3, using a different material. Continue until all the materials are used.

5. Rate the materials, from best to worst. (*Best* means "best at muffling sound.") **Compare** your results with those of other groups in your class.

Step 3

Analyze and Conclude

1. Do some materials muffle sound better than others? **Give evidence** to support your answer.

2. **Classify** which of the materials best muffled the sound. Which materials best conducted the sound?

3. **Hypothesize** what effect adding more material would have on the sound. Then plan and carry out an experiement to **test** your hypothesis.

Turn Up the Sound

TURN DOWN THAT RADIO!

Reading Focus How can you reduce unwanted or harmful sounds?

"Turn down that radio!" "Could you please turn up the TV a little?" What are you changing when you turn the radio "down" or the TV "up"? You are changing the volume, or loudness of the sound. **Volume** describes how loud—or soft— a sound is. It is related to the **intensity** of the sound, which is a measure of the amount of energy of a sound wave. Recall from Chapter 3 that if you make a drawing of a sound wave, a loud sound will have a wave with a large amplitude. A soft sound will have a wave with a small amplitude.

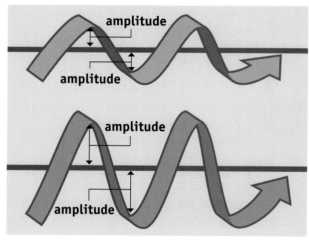

▲ Sound wave of a soft sound (*top*); sound wave of a loud sound (*bottom*)

Using Math *Sounds vary in intensity, or volume. The intensity of sound is expressed in decibels (dB). Calculate the difference in the decibel level between the intensity of sound inside a home and a jet taking off at 30 m.*

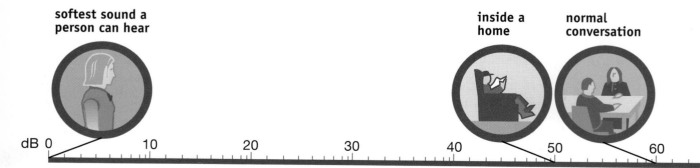

softest sound a person can hear

inside a home

normal conversation

dB 0   10   20   30   40   50   60

F76

Measuring Sound Volume

The **decibel** (des'ə bəl) is the special unit used to measure sound intensity, or volume. A sound that most people can just barely hear has an intensity of 0 decibels, or 0 dB.

The table on this page lists various common sounds and their intensity, or volume, in decibels. The sound of normal breathing or rustling leaves, at 10 dB, is 10 times louder than a sound that a person can just barely hear at 0 dB. A 20-dB sound is 10 times as loud as a 10-dB sound and 100 times as loud as a 0-dB sound. Every increase of 10 decibels means the intensity of the sound has increased by a factor of 10.

Of course, whether a sound is loud enough to disturb you depends on other factors. The sound of a rustling newspaper is 10 times as loud as the sound of a whisper, but a whisper may disturb you if you're trying to study. The sound of street traffic is 10,000 times as loud as the sound of a rustling newspaper, but you may ignore it if you're playing ball on the playground. And devices such as megaphones, which direct sound toward you, can make sounds seem louder than they actually are.

Source Sounds	Intensity (dB)
Barely audible	0
Breathing	10
Whispers	20
Rustling newspaper	30
Quiet conversation	40
Inside quiet car	50
Normal conversation	60
Street traffic	70
Vacuum cleaner	80
Rush-hour traffic	90
Subway (near)	100
Thunder (near)	110
Loud rock music	120
Jet airplane (near)	140
Rocket engine (near)	180

A sound of 120 dB is loud enough to cause pain in the ears. Such sound is 1 billion times as loud as the 30-dB sound of a rustling newspaper. Where might you hear a sound this loud?

Noise Pollution

The growth of cities and technology has led to sounds and sound volumes that were unheard of until recent centuries. Studies have shown that

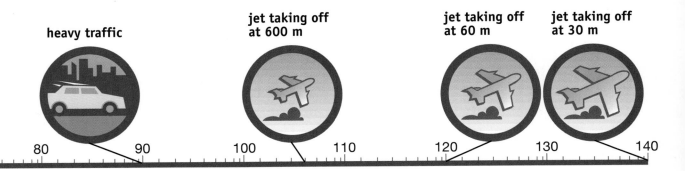

heavy traffic   jet taking off at 600 m   jet taking off at 60 m   jet taking off at 30 m

80   90   100   110   120   130   140

exposure to loud noise or loud music can become physically painful and damage a person's hearing. Besides causing damage to the ear itself, noise can cause stress-related disorders such as hives, ulcers, or high blood pressure. The occurrence of loud or unpleasant sound in the environment even has a name— **noise pollution**.

An understanding of the properties of sound can help you reduce noise pollution. Like light, sound is absorbed by some materials and reflected by others. Materials that are hard, such as concrete or brick, reflect most of the sound that reaches them. Highway engineers take advantage of this property by building wooden or concrete barriers

▲ In a recording studio a complex control panel allows the sound engineers to control sounds produced by the recording artists.

Science in Literature

"QUIET ON THE SET!"

"With the camera and tape recorder rolling, the actors begin to play the scene. Technicians check the sound recording levels and make adjustments as the scene progresses. When the shot is complete, the director yells, 'Cut!'"

**That's a Wrap:
How Movies Are Made**
by Ned Dowd
Simon & Schuster
Books for Young Readers, 1991

Find out more about how a movie is made by reading *That's a Wrap: How Movies Are Made* by Ned Dowd. You'll learn how the stunts and special effects are recorded. From a whispered secret to an explosion, sounds make movies thrilling.

between highways and surrounding homes. These barriers help reduce noise by reflecting it. Plants growing on or near these barriers can also help reduce noise by absorbing it.

In the activity on page F75, different materials are used to muffle the sound of a ticking clock. Materials that are soft, such as cloth, plastic foam, and acoustical plaster, absorb much of the sound that reaches them. In many buildings, ceilings and walls are built of such sound-absorbing materials. The hanging banners in school gymnasiums help absorb sound so that you can hear the gym teacher speaking. ■

A restaurant is often a quiet place because its chairs, floors, and walls have sound-absorbing materials (*left*). A large cafeteria can be a very noisy place if it has no materials to absorb sound (*right*).

INVESTIGATION 1 WRAP-UP

REVIEW

1. Describe at least two specific ways that people can control sound.

2. How would the volume of a sound change as the intensity of the sound changed?

CRITICAL THINKING

3. An office manager wants to reduce noise pollution in an office. What kinds of floor and window coverings would be best to use? Explain your answer.

4. Draw and explain a scale that shows sounds around you expressed in decibels.

INVESTIGATION 2

HOW DO PEOPLE HEAR?

Every day you are bombarded by sound. You may wake up to the jarring noise of an alarm clock. On the street, recyclers may be collecting your used glass. How can you tell one sound from another? This investigation explores hearing—and not hearing.

Activity

Identifying Sounds

How distinctive are sounds? Are there any two voices—or sounds—that are exactly alike? In this activity you'll test how well you can tell one sound from another.

MATERIALS

- blindfold
- assorted sound makers (bells, whistles, rattles)
- *Science Notebook*

Procedure

1. Blindfold one member of your group. Then have each student in your group, one by one, say a word or phrase. Have the blindfolded student identify each person who speaks. **Record** in your *Science Notebook* whether the blindfolded student could identify each person.

2. Repeat step 1. This time, have each student whisper the same word or phrase. **Record** whether each person was identified. **Discuss** your findings with your group.

3. Blindfold a different group member. Have each student, one by one, make a sound with a different sound maker.

4. **Record** whether the blindfolded student identified each sound maker. **Discuss** your findings as a group.

Step 3

Analyze and Conclude

1. In step 1, could the student correctly identify each person who spoke? What do you think allowed the blindfolded student to identify the speakers? If the student couldn't identify each person, give a reason why not.

2. In step 2, could the blindfolded student identify each student who spoke? Why might it have been difficult to identify the speakers?

3. Could the blindfolded student identify each sound maker? Which ones couldn't be easily identified?

4. In general, what properties of a sound can be used to identify it?

UNIT PROJECT LINK

Plan a soundtrack for the folk tale you have begun rehearsing. Include the instruments and other devices needed for the sound effects. Choose a narrator to tell the story. Decide how long the show will last. Then make an audiotape of the soundtrack, including the narration. Make sure the puppets' movements go along with the soundtrack.

Technology Link
For more help with your Unit Project, go to **www.eduplace.com**.

American Sign Language

Reading Focus What makes American Sign Language a unique way of communicating?

"I even got to ride on an elephant!" Sara was excited as she told her parents about the trip to the zoo that day. She described the antics of the monkeys and the sheep, but she didn't say a word. How did Sara tell her story? She used American Sign Language—a method of communication that uses the hands, face, and body to express ideas.

People who can hear acquire language by listening to people around them and imitating what they hear. Deaf people need another way to learn language. They often use one of the many sign languages from around the world.

One form of sign language, American Manual Sign Language, uses hand gestures to spell out the letters of words. When using this sign language, a person must "sign" each letter of the word he or she wishes to express. The letters are put together to form words.

By contrast, American Sign Language, or ASL, uses signs to express single words or groups of words that are often used together. But ASL is not just a direct translation of English into signs. It is a language all its own, with unique expressions and ideas. Many of these expressions cannot be directly translated into the spoken word.

Many members of the deaf community prefer ASL over American Manual Sign Language because it offers more freedom of expression. ■

A girl signing "I sign in American Sign Language." ▼

| I | sign | in | American Sign Language |

How the Ear Works

> **Reading Focus** How are sound vibrations transmitted to the brain?

The Structure of the Ear

How do you hear sound? Sound waves are collected by the parts of the outer ear. Then the sound waves move to the middle ear, where they cause the eardrum to vibrate. The eardrum is connected to three tiny bones that transmit the force of sound vibrations from the eardrum. The last of the three bones pushes against a membrane that separates the middle ear from the inner ear.

In the inner ear, vibrations are transmitted to the cochlea. The cochlea (käk′lē ə) contains fluid, which also vibrates. A membrane that runs along the entire length of the cochlea has about 30,000 tiny hair cells (not the same as the hairs on your head). When the fluid in the cochlea vibrates, some of these hairs move. Their movement causes nerve impulses to travel along the **auditory nerve**, which connects the ear to the brain. The brain interprets the nerve impulses as sounds.

A Tunnel and Balance

The **eustachian tube** (yo͞o stā′kē-ən to͞ob) is a tunnel-like structure that

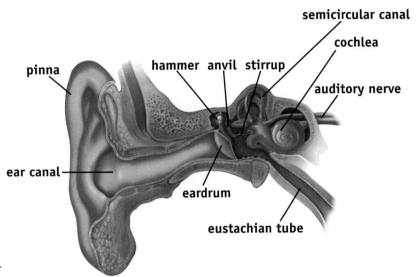

pinna — hammer anvil stirrup — semicircular canal — cochlea — auditory nerve — ear canal — eardrum — eustachian tube

▲ **The outer, middle, and inner ear**

connects the middle ear to the throat. It allows air to pass between the middle ear and the throat, which helps keep air pressure within the ear the same as the outside air pressure. Have your ears ever hurt while you were flying in an airplane? The pain is caused when the air pressure inside your ear is different from the air pressure around you.

Your inner ear, especially the **semicircular canals**, help you keep your balance. These canals are filled with fluid and contain hair cells that respond to movement. Nerve impulses from these cells give the brain the information needed to keep the body balanced. ■

F83

Help for Hearing Loss

Reading Focus What role does electricity play in aiding people with hearing loss?

About 10 percent of the population has some form of hearing loss, or deafness. There are several kinds of loss. Some people can't hear certain frequencies of sound; others hear all sounds but hear them more faintly than they are heard by people with normal hearing.

Hearing loss has many causes. A damaged eardrum can cause hearing loss, as can injury to the auditory nerve—the nerve leading from the ear to the brain. Damage to the auditory nerve cannot be corrected. But most deafness, including that due to nerve damage, can be helped through hearing aids and sometimes with surgery.

If your great-grandparents had hearing problems, they may have used an ear trumpet. This device, similar to a reverse megaphone, was used to funnel sound into the ear.

Today, most hearing loss can be at least partially helped with a battery-powered hearing aid. A hearing aid is a small device that increases the volume of a sound. The hearing aid receives sound waves and converts them into electrical impulses. The electrical signals are amplified, or made stronger. Next they are converted back to sound waves. The sound waves are channeled to the eardrum through a plastic piece molded to fit inside the outer ear. The hearing aids are so tiny that it's difficult to tell if someone is wearing one.

Before hearing aids were invented, ear trumpets were used to funnel sound to the ear. ▶

Two kinds of electronic hearing aids are shown on this page. Both are comfortable and help with certain kinds of hearing loss. As you read on page F72, a new, tiny hearing aid is now available. This hearing aid is implanted deep in the ear canal. Because the device is placed very close to the eardrum, it prevents many of the problems of standard hearing aids. People who use this device find that they can understand normal conversation much more easily. The aid allows people to hear high-frequency sounds that are often distorted by other hearing aids.

Not all people with hearing loss can use this hearing aid. For example, some may have ear canals that are not the right shape to hold the hearing aid. Fortunately, engineers are always working on new ways to help hearing-impaired people. ■

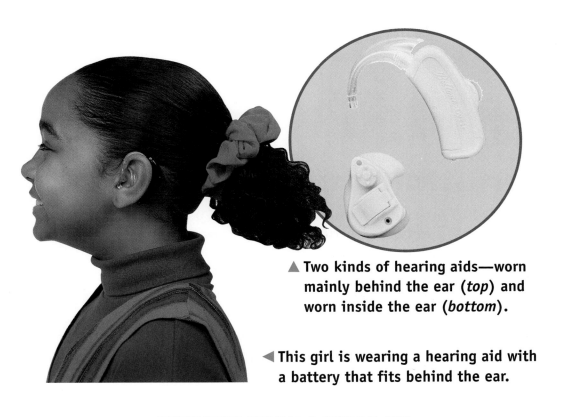

▲ Two kinds of hearing aids—worn mainly behind the ear (*top*) and worn inside the ear (*bottom*).

◄ This girl is wearing a hearing aid with a battery that fits behind the ear.

INVESTIGATION 2 WRAP-UP

REVIEW

1. How does a hearing aid work?

2. How do your ears help you keep your balance?

CRITICAL THINKING

3. Imagine that you are a sound wave traveling through a human ear. Describe your trip.

4. How is a hearing aid somewhat like a compact microphone and stereo set?

HOW IS SOUND TRANSMITTED AND RECORDED?

Inventors achieved a longtime goal when they were able to record the performances of great artists so they could be heard by future generations. This investigation explores how sound is transmitted and recorded today. It also explores some ideas for the future.

Activity

Magnetic Sounds

MATERIALS
- blank audiocassette
- bar magnet
- *Science Notebook*

You've probably purchased audiocassettes of your favorite recording artists. Perhaps you've taped your own voice. Do you have any idea how sounds are recorded? This activity will give you a hint about how it happens.

Procedure

Carefully **examine** the tape inside a blank audiocassette. In your *Science Notebook*, **record** your ideas about how sound is recorded on the tape. **Discuss** these ideas with your group. Then place a bar magnet close to the exposed part of the tape. **Observe** what happens and **record** your observations.

Analyze and Conclude

1. What happened when you brought the bar magnet close to the tape?

2. Based on your observations, what can you **infer** about the nature of the tape?

Activity

Tape Recording

In general, audiocassettes should be kept away from magnets. But in this activity you will deliberately place a bar magnet near an audiocassette that contains a recording. What do you think will happen?

MATERIALS
- blank audiocassette
- tape recorder
- bar magnet
- pencil
- *Science Notebook*

Step 1

Procedure

1. Tape-record the voices of the members of your group. Have each student say at least one sentence.

2. Rewind the tape and then play back the taped sentences.

3. In your *Science Notebook*, record how each student sounds. For example, record whether the taped students' voices sound the same as in normal conversation.

4. Remove the audiocassette from the tape recorder. While holding a bar magnet near the surface of the exposed tape, use a pencil to rewind the tape completely. Predict what will happen. Discuss your predictions with other members of your group.

5. Now play the tape. In your *Science Notebook*, record what you hear on the tape. Note whether there are any changes in the students' voices.

Analyze and Conclude

1. Compare how the students' voices sounded in step 2 and step 5. Account for any differences you heard.

2. If you heard any differences in the voices, make a hypothesis to explain what happened.

3. Write a statement about the effect of a bar magnet on tape-recorded sound. Why should you keep magnets away from audiocassette tapes?

RESOURCE

Recorded Sound

Early Recordings

Thomas A. Edison had a knack for inventing devices that fascinated the public. In 1877 he invented the **phonograph** (fō'nə graf), a device that recorded and reproduced sound. To record sound, he used a thin metal disc that vibrated when sound waves struck it. A metal penlike device, called a stylus, was attached to the disc. The tip of the stylus touched a sheet of metal foil that was wrapped around a rotating cylinder.

When sounds made the disc vibrate, those vibrations were transferred to the stylus. As the stylus vibrated, the sound was recorded as a pattern of tiny hills and

cylinder

▲ **An early phonograph**

valleys in a spiral track on the cylinder. By reversing the recording process, it was possible to hear the sounds on the cylinder. As the cylinder was turned, by hand, a stylus rose and fell over the hills and valleys in the recorded soundtrack. The

Thomas A. Edison and the phonograph he invented ▼

vibrations produced sounds that traveled out through a megaphone attached to the stylus.

Edison's phonograph was a wonderful invention, but it did have some problems. The sound reproduction was poor, and the cylinders wore out after being played only a few times. Only one cylinder could be recorded at a time. A singer had to sing each time a recording was made on a cylinder.

Invention of the Record

In 1888, Emile Berliner dramatically improved sound recording by inventing the disc record. Berliner produced a "master" copper plate that contained all of the patterns of the recording.

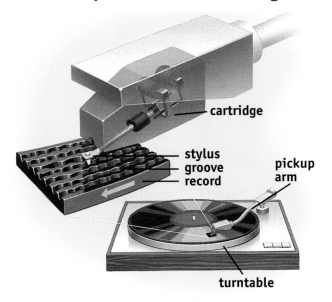

▲ A long-playing record (LP) on a turntable

This copper plate could then be used to stamp out large numbers of copies on shellac resin discs. From then on, a singer had to sing a song only once—for the master disc. After that, many more copies of the recording could be made. The great opera singer Enrico

Caruso made a recording that sold more than a million copies by 1900!

Inventions Improve Recordings

When plastics were developed, they were used to replace the shellac resin records. Plastic records were lighter and were less likely to break. But the greatest advantage of plastic records was that they could be made with narrower and more closely packed soundtracks. Only one song could fit on the old shellac resin records, but several songs could be recorded on one plastic record. Plastics led the way to long-playing records (LPs), which first appeared in 1948.

Sound in Stereo

Ten years later, stereophonic (stereo) records were introduced. Two separate microphones were used during the recording, and two separate soundtracks were cut in the recording disc. When a stereo record was played, each soundtrack was connected to a separate loudspeaker. The two speakers produced sound that was like a live performance. People quickly replaced their old one-speaker record players with new "stereos."

Sound on Tape

But then a new method for recording sound was developed—coating plastic tapes with a magnetic material such as iron oxide. Today, many people use audiocassettes, miniature versions of the older reel-to-reel tapes for entertainment. An **audiocassette** is a small container that holds magnetic tape used for playing or recording sound.

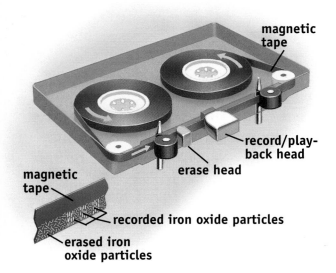

magnetic tape

record/play-back head

erase head

magnetic tape

recorded iron oxide particles

erased iron oxide particles

▲ **An audiocassette, showing the magnetic tape on small reels**

When you record sound on tape, as in the activity on page F87, electric currents are produced by sound waves entering a microphone. The current is sent through the coil of an electromagnet (the recording head). The changing electric current in the coil causes changes in the magnetic field of the recording head. As the tape moves through the changing magnetic field of the head, a magnetic pattern is formed. This magnetic pattern is formed in the tiny crystals of iron oxide on the surface of the tape.

How do you hear the sounds recorded on the tape? The tape is passed through another head, called the playback head. Weak electrical signals are produced that are made stronger, or amplified. When these amplified electrical signals are fed to a loudspeaker, they reproduce the sounds that first entered the microphone.

By the mid-1980s, audiocassettes were outselling records. This was due mainly to

Internet Field Trip

Visit **www.eduplace.com** to learn more about how sound is recorded.

their convenience. Tapes could be played anywhere—even in a moving car.

Compact Discs (CDs)

Tapes store a magnetic "image" of sounds. Today, digital signals can also be used to store sound. In a digital recording, the electrical signal from the microphone is changed to a series of on-or-off electrical pulses. These pulses are recorded as strong or weak magnetic fields.

A **compact disc**, or CD, is a small disc on which sounds are digitally recorded and played back by a laser beam. Along the very thin recording track of the disc, the "offs" are recorded as pits. The "ons" are recorded as the flat surface of the disc. As the disc spins on a CD player, the codes of offs and ons along the track are scanned by a laser beam and changed to electrical signals. These signals are then sent to the speakers. Today, CDs have replaced audiocassette tapes in popularity. What do you think might replace CDs? ■

A compact disc (CD), showing an enlargement of "pits" (holes) and "flats" (flat surfaces) ▼

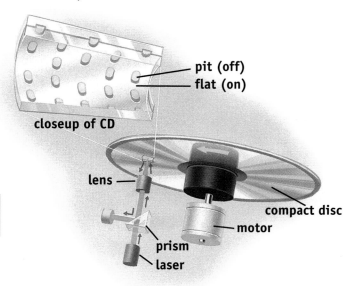

pit (off)
flat (on)

closeup of CD

lens

compact disc

motor

prism

laser

F90

Delivering Information

Reading Focus What are some uses of the Internet?

STS
SCIENCE
TECHNOLOGY
& SOCIETY

Television provides the world with an amazing variety of entertainment. You can enjoy comedy, drama, music, and sports all on the same day in the comfort of your home. Satellites in orbit above Earth make it possible for people in nearly all parts of the world to view an Olympic event as it happens.

Through TV, you can see world leaders in action and observe the effects of wars and natural disasters. You can also see that even though people have different backgrounds and cultures, people all over the world have many of the same needs and interests.

The television is just part of our ever-growing communication system that includes the telephone, computer, fax machine, and wireless hand-held devices. This system links people together in a way that was never before possible. Imagine being part of a worldwide network providing communication, entertainment, and information.

The Internet

Small but powerful computers linked by telephone lines and television cable systems allow users to access information from all around the world. The Internet is a communications system that connects a global network of government, education, business, and home computers. The Internet links over 50 million users in the United States alone.

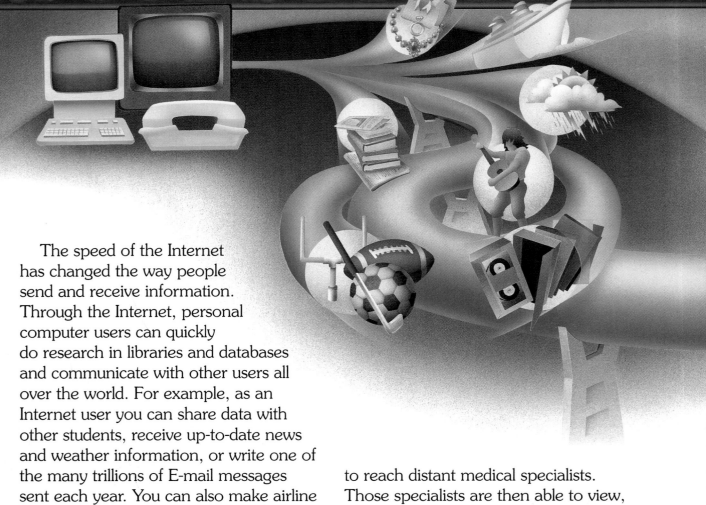

The speed of the Internet has changed the way people send and receive information. Through the Internet, personal computer users can quickly do research in libraries and databases and communicate with other users all over the world. For example, as an Internet user you can share data with other students, receive up-to-date news and weather information, or write one of the many trillions of E-mail messages sent each year. You can also make airline and hotel reservations as well as shop for your favorite CD—all while never having to leave your home.

Doctors can provide their patients with better care by using the Internet to reach distant medical specialists. Those specialists are then able to view, examine, and talk with the doctors and their patients.

What lies beyond the current uses of the Internet? In another two or three decades, you'll know! ■

INVESTIGATION 3 WRAP-UP

REVIEW

1. Choose a sound-recording system, either old or new, and describe how sound is recorded on this device.

2. What was the advantage of plastic long-playing records over shellac resin records?

CRITICAL THINKING

3. How are the hills and valleys on Edison's cylinders similar to the pits and flats on a CD?

4. Describe how you think your life is affected by your home or school being linked to the Internet.

REFLECT & EVALUATE

Word Power

Write the letter of the term that best matches the definition. *Not all terms will be used.*

1. A measure of the amount of energy of a sound wave
2. The loudness or softness of a sound
3. A small device that increases the volume of a sound
4. A small disc on which sounds are digitally recorded and played back when read by a laser beam
5. The occurrence of loud or unpleasant sound in the environment
6. A device that records and reproduces sound

a. audiocassette
b. auditory nerve
c. compact disc
d. hearing aid
e. intensity
f. noise pollution
g. phonograph
h. volume

Check What You Know

Write the term in each pair that best completes each sentence.

1. A unit used to measure sound intensity is the (hertz, decibel).
2. The (semicircular canal, eustachian tube) in your inner ear helps you keep your balance.
3. American Sign Language uses signs to express single (letters, words).
4. A small container holding magnetic tape that is used for playing or recording sound is (an audiocassette, a compact disc).

Problem Solving

1. One thing that actors must learn is to speak loudly enough to be heard by the audience. This skill is called "projecting the voice." Why do actors have to project more when an audience is present than at rehearsals?

2. Devices such as LPs, cassette tapes, and CDs do not actually "store" sound itself. Explain what is meant by this statement.

Make a copy of the graph. Suggest a sound that could be placed at 20 dB and another at 30 dB.

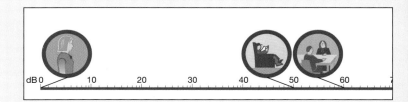

dB 0   10   20   30   40   50   60   7

Compare and Contrast

Making comparisons when you read is a good way to understand new ideas. As you read, compare each new idea to an old, familiar idea.

Read the passage and complete the exercise that follows.

Look for these signal words to help you compare and contrast.

- To show similar things: *like, the same as*

- To show different things: *different from, instead*

The Eye and a Camera

Both the human eye and a camera contain convex lenses. An important difference between your eyes and a camera is that a camera takes only one picture at a time. But your eyes are constantly "taking pictures." When you look at an object, the lens of your eye focuses an image on the retina. The **retina** is the light-sensitive layer on the back of the eye. It sends nerve impulses to the brain along the optic nerve. The brain then interprets the pictures and figures out what you're seeing.

Another difference between your eyes and a camera is in how the eyes focus. You can focus on objects that are close to you and on objects that are far away, but the eye's lens can't move in and out the way a camera lens does. Instead, the lens of the eye changes shape. When you look at something nearby, muscles in the eye pull on the edges of the lens and make it less curved. When you look at something far away the muscles relax, and the lens gets more curved again.

Write the letter of each statement that is true of both the eye and a camera.

    a. Both have convex lenses.

    b. In both the lens moves in and out to focus.

    c. Both have a sensitive area where the light is focused.

    d. Both take only one picture at a time.

Using Math Analyze Data

The number of seconds that elapse between a flash of lightning and the sound of thunder can be used to estimate your distance from a thunderstorm. The table below provides data that can help you make such an estimate.

Computing Distance From a Thunderstorm						
Elapsed Time Between Lightning and Thunder (s)	0	1	2	3	4	5
Distance (m)	0	346	692	1,038	?	1,730

Use the table to complete the exercises that follow.

1. How far from a thunderstorm are you if 3 seconds elapse between the time you see a flash of lightning and the time you hear the sound of thunder?

2. If exactly 4 seconds elapse between the time you see a flash of lightning and the time you hear the sound of thunder, how far are you from a thunderstorm?

3. Estimate the speed at which sound travels through air. Use a pattern from the table to explain your answer. Based on your estimate of the speed of sound, how many meters would sound travel in 6 seconds?

4. Explain how you could estimate if it would take 2, 3, or 4 seconds for the sound of thunder to travel 1 km.

You may wish to use a calculator for Exercise 5.

5. Suppose you are 3,500 m from a thunderstorm. How many seconds will elapse between a flash of lightning from that thunderstorm and the sound of thunder? Round your answer to the nearest second.

WRAP-UP!

On your own, use scientific methods to investigate a question about light or sound.

THINK LIKE A SCIENTIST

Ask a Question

Pose a question about light or sound that you would like to investigate. For example, ask, "How is the sound produced by a plucked string affected by the material the string is made of?"

Make a Hypothesis

Suggest a hypothesis that is a possible answer to the question. One hypothesis is that the material the plucked string is made of affects the pitch of the sound produced.

Plan and Do a Test

Plan a controlled experiment to find how the materials two different strings are made of affect the sound produced by each string. You could begin by using a metal string and a plastic string of the same length and thickness. Develop a procedure that uses these materials to test the hypothesis. With permission, carry out your experiment. Follow the safety guidelines on pages S14–S15.

Record and Analyze

Observe carefully and record your data accurately. Make repeated observations.

Draw Conclusions

Look for evidence to support the hypothesis or to show that it is false. Draw conclusions about the hypothesis. Repeat the experiment to verify the results.

WRITING IN SCIENCE
Summary

Write a summary of "Recorded Sound," pages F88-F90. Use these guidelines in writing your summary.

- State the main ideas.
- Include only the important details for each main idea.
- Sum up the content in a brief statement.

Share your summary with a partner.

SCIENCE and MATH TOOLBOX

Using a Microscope

A microscope makes it possible to see very small things by magnifying them. Some microscopes have a set of lenses that magnify objects by different amounts.

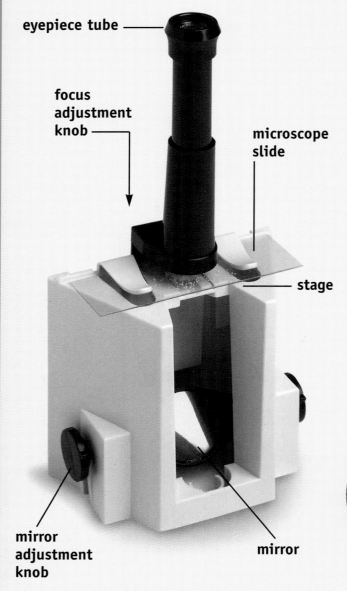

eyepiece tube

focus adjustment knob

microscope slide

stage

mirror adjustment knob

mirror

Examine Some Salt Grains

Handle a microscope carefully; it can break easily. Carry it firmly with both hands and avoid touching the lenses.

1. Turn the mirror toward a source of light. **NEVER** use the Sun as a light source.

2. Place a few grains of salt on the slide. Put the slide on the stage of the microscope.

3. Bring the salt grains into focus. Turn the adjustment knob on the back of the microscope as you look through the eyepiece.

4. Raise the eyepiece tube to increase the magnification; lower it to decrease magnification.

Salt grains magnified one hundred times (100X)

Making a Bar Graph

A bar graph helps you organize and compare data. For example, you might want to make a bar graph to compare weather data for different places.

Make a Bar Graph of Annual Snowfall

For more than 20 years, the cities listed in the table have been recording their yearly snowfall. The table shows the average number of centimeters of snow that the cities receive each year. Use the data in the table to make a bar graph showing the cities' average annual snowfall.

Snowfall	
City	Snowfall (cm)
Atlanta, GA	5
Charleston, SC	1.5
Houston, TX	1
Jackson, MS	3
New Orleans, LA	0.5
Tucson, AZ	3

1. Title your graph. The title should help a reader understand what your graph describes.

2. Choose a scale and mark equal intervals. The vertical scale should include the least value and the greatest value in the set of data.

3. Label the vertical axis *Snowfall (cm)* and the horizontal axis *City*. Space the city names equally.

4. Carefully graph the data. Depending on the interval you choose, some amounts may be between two numbers.

5. Check each step of your work.

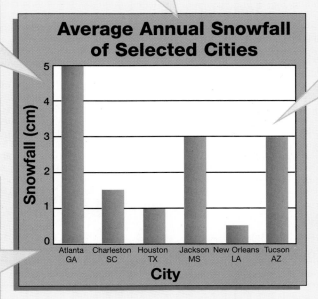

Using a Calculator

After you've made measurements, a calculator can help you analyze your data. Some calculators have a memory key that allows you to save the result of one calculation while you do another.

Add and Divide to Find Percent

The table shows the amount of rain that was collected using a rain gauge in each month of one year. You can use a calculator to help you find the total yearly rainfall. Then you can find the percent of rain that fell during January.

1. Add the numbers. When you add a series of numbers, you need not press the equal sign until the last number is entered. Just press the plus sign after you enter each number (except the last).

2. If you make a mistake while you are entering numbers, press the clear entry (CE/C) key to erase your mistake. Then you can continue entering the rest of the numbers you are adding. If you can't fix your mistake, you can press the (CE/C) key once or twice until the screen shows 0. Then start over.

3. Your total should be 1,131. Now clear the calculator until the screen shows 0. Then divide the rainfall amount for January by the total yearly rainfall (1,131). Press the percent (%) key. Then press the equal sign key.

Rainfall	
Month	**Rain (mm)**
Jan.	214
Feb.	138
Mar.	98
Apr.	157
May	84
June	41
July	5
Aug.	23
Sept.	48
Oct.	75
Nov.	140
Dec.	108

214 ÷ 1131 % =

The percent of yearly rainfall that fell in January is 18.921309, which rounds to 19%.

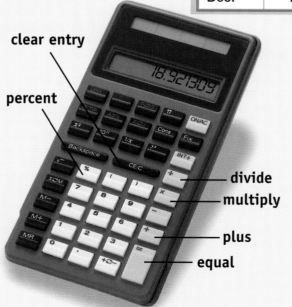

clear entry

percent

divide

multiply

plus

equal

Finding an Average

An average is a way to describe a set of data using one number. For example, you could compare the surface temperature of several stars that are of the same type. You could find the average surface temperature of these stars.

Add and Divide to Find the Average

Suppose scientists found the surface temperature of eight blue-white stars to be those shown in the table. What is the average surface temperature of the stars listed?

Surface Temperature of Selected Blue-white Stars	
Blue-white Star	**Surface Temperature (°F)**
1	7,200
2	6,100
3	6,000
4	6,550
5	7,350
6	6,800
7	7,500
8	6,300

1. First find the sum of the data. Add the numbers in the list.

$$
\begin{array}{r}
7,200 \\
6,100 \\
6,000 \\
6,550 \\
7,350 \\
6,800 \\
7,500 \\
+\,6,300 \\
\hline
53,800
\end{array}
$$

2. Then divide the sum (53,800) by the number of addends (8).

$$
\begin{array}{r}
6,725 \\
8\,\overline{)\,53,800} \\
-48 \\
\hline
58 \\
-56 \\
\hline
20 \\
-16 \\
\hline
40 \\
-40 \\
\hline
0
\end{array}
$$

3. $53,800 \div 8 = 6,725$
The average surface temperature of these eight blue-white stars is 6,725°F.

Using a
Tape Measure or Ruler

Tape measures, metersticks, and rulers are tools for measuring length. Scientists use units such as kilometers, meters, centimeters, and millimeters when making length measurements.

Use a Meterstick

1. Work with a partner to find the height of your reach. Stand facing a chalkboard. Reach up as high as you can with one hand.

2. Have your partner use chalk to mark the chalkboard at the highest point of your reach.

3. Use a meterstick to measure your reach to the nearest centimeter. Measure from the floor to the chalk mark. Record the height of your reach.

Use a Tape Measure

1. Use a tape measure to find the circumference of, or distance around, your partner's head. Wrap the tape around your partner's head.

2. Find the line where the tape begins to wrap over itself.

3. Record the distance around your partner's head to the nearest millimeter.

Measuring
Volume

A graduated cylinder, a measuring cup, and a beaker are used to measure volume. Volume is the amount of space something takes up. Most of the containers that scientists use to measure volume have a scale marked in milliliters (mL).

Measure the Volume of a Liquid

1. Measure the volume of some juice. Pour the juice into a measuring container.

2. Move your head so that your eyes are level with the top of the juice. Read the scale line that is closest to the surface of the juice. If the surface of the juice is curved up on the sides, look at the lowest point of the curve.

3. Read the measurement on the scale. You can estimate the value between two lines on the scale to obtain a more accurate measurement.

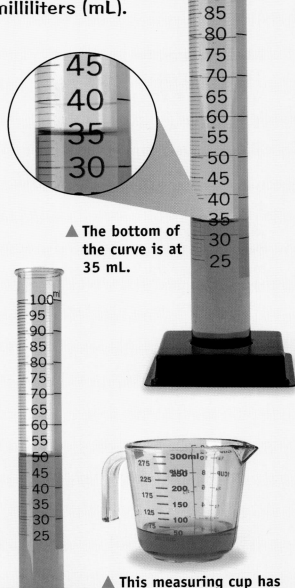

▲ The bottom of the curve is at 35 mL.

This beaker has marks for each 25 mL. ▶

This graduated cylinder has marks for every 1 mL. ▶

▲ This measuring cup has marks for each 25 mL.

Using a
Thermometer

A thermometer is used to measure temperature. When the liquid in the tube of a thermometer gets warmer, it expands and moves farther up the tube. Different scales can be used to measure temperature, but scientists usually use the Celsius scale.

Measure the Temperature of a Cold Liquid

1. Half fill a cup with chilled liquid.

2. Hold the thermometer so that the bulb is in the center of the liquid. Be sure that there are no bright lights or direct sunlight shining on the bulb.

3. Wait until you see the liquid in the tube of the thermometer stop moving. Read the scale line that is closest to the top of the liquid in the tube. The thermometer shown reads 21°C (about 70°F).

Using a Balance

A balance is used to measure mass. Mass is the amount of matter in an object. To find the mass of an object, place the object in the left pan of the balance. Place standard masses in the right pan.

Measure the Mass of a Ball

1. Check that the empty pans are balanced, or level with each other. The pointer at the base should be on the middle mark. If it needs to be adjusted, move the slider on the back of the balance a little to the left or right.

2. Place a ball on the left pan. Notice that the pointer moves and that the pans are no longer level with each other. Then add standard masses, one at a time, to the right pan. When the pointer is at the middle mark again, the pans are balanced. Each pan is holding the same amount of matter, and the same mass.

3. Each standard mass is marked to show its number of grams. Add the number of grams marked on the masses in the pan. The total is the mass of the ball in grams.

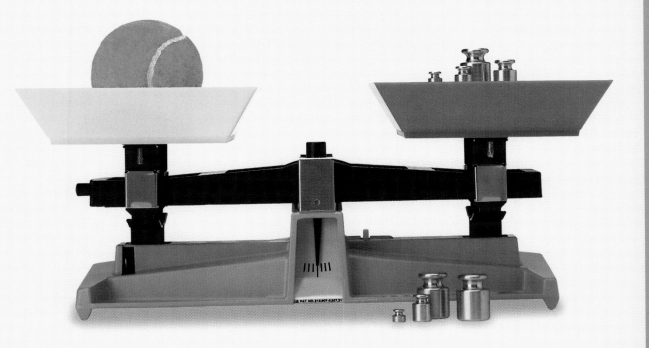

Using an Equation or Formula

Equations and formulas can help you to determine measurements that are not easily made.

Use the Diameter of a Circle to Find Its Circumference

Find the circumference of a circle that has a diameter of 10 cm. To determine the circumference of a circle, use the formula below.

$$C = \pi d$$

$$C = 3.14 \times 10$$

$$C = 31.4 \text{ cm}$$

π is the symbol for pi. Always use 3.14 as the value for π, unless another value for pi is given.

The circumference of this circle is 31.4 cm.

The circumference (C) is a measure of the distance around a circle.

10 cm

The diameter (d) of a circle is a line segment that passes through the center of the circle and connects two points on the circle.

Use Rate and Time to Determine Distance

Suppose an aircraft travels at 772 km/h for 2.5 hours. How many kilometers does the aircraft travel during that time? To determine distance traveled, use the distance formula below.

$$d = rt$$

$$d = 772 \times 2.5$$

$$d = 1,930 \text{ km}$$

d = distance

r = rate, or the speed at which the aircraft is traveling.

t = the length of time traveled

The aircraft travels 1,930 km in 2.5 hours.

Making a Chart to Organize Data

A chart can help you record, compare, or classify information.

Organize Properties of Elements

Suppose you collected the data shown at the right. The data presents properties of silver, gold, lead, and iron.

You could organize this information in a chart by classifying the physical properties of each element.

My Data

Silver (Ag) has a density of 10.5 g/cm³. It melts at 961°C and boils at 2,212°C. It is used in dentistry and to make jewelry and electronic conductors.

Gold melts at 1,064°C and boils at 2,966°C. Its chemical symbol is Au. It has a density of 19.3 g/cm³ and is used for jewelry, in coins, and in dentistry.

The melting point of lead (Pb) is 328°C. The boiling point is 1,740°C. It has a density of 11.3 g/cm³. Some uses for lead are in storage batteries, paints, and dyes.

Iron (Fe) has a density of 7.9 g/cm³. It will melt at 1,535°C and boil at 3,000°C. It is used for building materials, in manufacturing, and as a dietary supplement.

Create categories that describe the information you have found.

Give the chart a title that describes what is listed in it.

Properties of Some Elements

Element	Symbol	Density g/cm³	Melting Point (°C)	Boiling Point (°C)	Some Uses
Silver	Ag	10.5	961	2,212	jewelry, dentistry, electric conductors
Gold	Au	19.3	1,064	2,966	jewelry, dentistry, coins
Lead	Pb	11.3	328	1,740	storage batteries, paints, dyes
Iron	Fe	7.9	1,535	3,000	building materials, manufacturing, dietary supplement

Make sure the information is listed accurately in each column.

Reading a Circle Graph

A circle graph shows the whole divided into parts. You can use a circle graph to compare parts to each other or to compare parts to the whole.

Read a Circle Graph of Land Area

The whole circle represents the approximate land area of all of the continents on Earth. The number on each wedge indicates the land area of each continent. From the graph you can determine that altogether the land area of the continents is 148,000,000 square kilometers.

Together Antarctica and Australia are about equal to the land area of North America.

Africa accounts for more of the Earth's land area than South America.

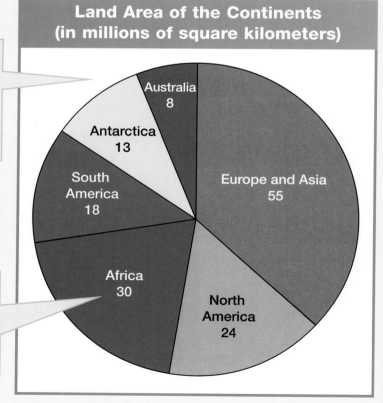

Land Area of the Continents (in millions of square kilometers)

Australia 8
Antarctica 13
South America 18
Europe and Asia 55
Africa 30
North America 24

Making a
Line Graph

A line graph is a way to show continuous change over time. You can use the information from a table to make a line graph.

Dallas–Fort Worth Airport Temperature	
Hour	Temp. (°C)
6 A.M.	22
7 A.M.	24
8 A.M.	25
9 A.M.	26
10 A.M.	27
11 A.M.	29
12 NOON	31
1 P.M.	32
2 P.M.	33
3 P.M.	34
4 P.M.	35
5 P.M.	35
6 P.M.	34

Make a Line Graph of Temperatures

The table shows temperature readings over a 12-hour period at the Dallas–Fort Worth Airport in Texas. This data can also be displayed in a line graph that shows temperature change over time.

1. Choose a title. The title should help a reader understand what your graph describes.

2. Choose a scale and mark equal intervals. The vertical scale should include the least value and the greatest value in the set of data.

3. Label the horizontal axis *Time* and the vertical axis *Temperature (°C)*.

4. Write the hours on the horizontal axis. Space the hours equally.

5. Carefully graph the data. Depending on the interval you choose, some temperatures will be between two numbers.

6. Check each step of your work.

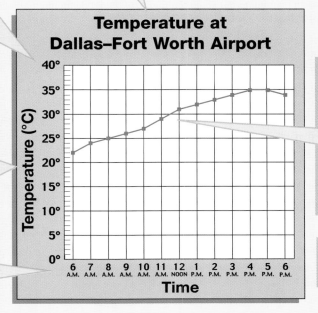

Temperature at Dallas–Fort Worth Airport

Measuring
Elapsed Time

Sometimes you may need to find out how much time has passed, or elapsed. A clock is often used to find elapsed time. You can also change units and add or subtract to find out how much time has passed.

Using a Clock to Find Elapsed Minutes

You need to time an experiment for 20 minutes. It is 1:30.

Minutes

Start at 1:30. Count ahead 20 minutes, by fives to 1:50. Stop the experiment at 1:50.

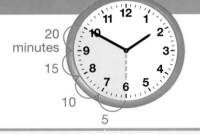

Using a Clock or Stopwatch to Find Elapsed Seconds

You need to time an experiment for 15 seconds. You can use a second hand on a clock. You can also use a stopwatch to figure out elapsed seconds.

60 seconds = 1 minute

Seconds

Wait until the second hand is on a number. Then start the experiment.

Stop the experiment when 15 seconds have passed.

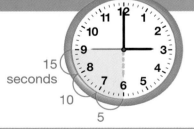

Press the reset button on the stopwatch so you see 0:00oo.

Press the start button to begin.

When you see 0:15oo, press the stop button on the watch.

Changing Units and Then Adding or Subtracting to Find Elapsed Time

If you know how to change units of time, you can use addition and subtraction to find elapsed time.

To change from a larger unit to a smaller unit, multiply.

$$2 \text{ d} = \blacksquare \text{ h}$$
$$2 \times 24 = 48$$
$$2 \text{ d} = 48 \text{ h}$$

Units of Time

60 seconds (s) = 1 minute (min)

60 minutes = 1 hour (h)

24 hours = 1 day (d)

7 days = 1 week (wk)

52 weeks = 1 year (yr)

To change from a smaller unit to a larger unit, divide.

$$78 \text{ wk} = \blacksquare \text{ yr}$$
$$78 \div 52 = 1\tfrac{1}{2}$$
$$78 \text{ wk} = 1\tfrac{1}{2} \text{ yr}$$

Another Example

Suppose it took juice in an ice-pop mold from 6:40 A.M. until 10:15 A.M. to freeze. How long did it take for the juice to freeze? To find out, subtract.

	9 h	75 min
	~~10 h~~	~~15 min~~
−	6 h	40 min
	3 h	35 min

Rename 10 h 15 min as 9 h 75 min, since 1 h = 60 min.

You can also add to find elapsed time.

	3 h	30 min	14 s
+	1 h	40 min	45 s
	4 h	70 min	59 s = 5 h 10 min 59 s

MEASUREMENTS

Volume
1 L of sports drink is a little more than 1 qt.

Area
A basketball court covers about 4,700 ft². It covers about 435 m².

Mass and Weight
A basketball has a mass of about 650 g. It weighs about 1½ lb.

Metric Measures

Temperature
Ice melts at 0 degrees Celsius (°C)

Water freezes at 0°C

Water boils at 100°C

Length and Distance
1,000 meters (m) = 1 kilometer (km)

100 centimeters (cm) = 1 m

10 millimeters (mm) = 1 cm

Force
1 newton (N) =
   1 kilogram x meter/second/second
   (kg x m/s²)

Volume
1 cubic meter (m³) = 1 m x 1 m x 1 m

1 cubic centimeter (cm³) =
   1 cm x 1 cm x 1 cm

1 liter (L) = 1,000 milliliters (mL)

1 cm³ = 1 mL

Area
1 square kilometer (km²) = 1 km x 1 km

1 hectare = 10,000 m²

Mass
1,000 grams (g) = 1 kilogram (kg)

1,000 milligrams (mg) = 1 g

Temperature
The temperature at an indoor basketball game might be 25°C, which is 77°F.

Length/ Distance
A basketball rim is about 10 ft high, or a little more than 3 m from the floor.

Customary Measures

Temperature
Ice melts at 32 degrees Fahrenheit (°F)
Water freezes at 32°F
Water boils at 212°F

Length and Distance
12 inches (in.) = 1 foot (ft)
3 ft = 1 yard (yd)
5,280 ft = 1 mile (mi)

Weight
16 ounces (oz) = 1 pound (lb)
2,000 pounds = 1 ton (T)

Volume of Fluids
8 fluid ounces (fl oz) = 1 cup (c)
2 c = 1 pint (pt)
2 pt = 1 quart (qt)
4 qt = 1 gallon (gal)

Metric and Customary Rates
km/h = kilometers per hour
m/s = meters per second
mph = miles per hour

GLOSSARY

Pronunciation Key

Symbol	Key Words
a	cat
ā	ape
ä	cot, car
e	ten, berry
ē	me
i	fit, here
ī	ice, fire
ō	go
ô	fall, for
oi	oil
oo	look, pull
o͞o	tool, rule
ou	out, crowd
u	up
ʉ	fur, shirt
ə	a in ago
	e in agent
	i in pencil
	o in atom
	u in circus
b	bed
d	dog
f	fall

Symbol	Key Words
g	get
h	help
j	jump
k	kiss, call
l	leg
m	meat
n	nose
p	put
r	red
s	see
t	top
v	vat
w	wish
y	yard
z	zebra
ch	chin, arch
ŋ	ring, drink
sh	she, push
th	thin, truth
th	then, father
zh	measure

A heavy stress mark (′) is placed after a syllable that gets a heavy, or primary, stress, as in **picture** (pik′chər).

A

absolute age (ab′sə lōōt āj) The actual age of an object. (E77) The *absolute age* of this rock is 3,500 years.

absolute magnitude (ab′sə lōōt mag′nə tōōd) The measure of a star's brightness, based on the amount of light it actually gives off. (B61) The Sun's *absolute magnitude* is less than that of many other stars.

adaptation (ad əp tā′shən) A structure or behavior that enables an organism to survive in its environment. (D9) The thick fur of some animals is an *adaptation* to cold environments.

adult (ə dult′) The final stage of an organism's life cycle. (A74) A butterfly is the *adult* form of a caterpillar.

air sacs (er saks) Thin-walled chambers in the lung through which oxygen moves into the blood. (A49) Each lung contains millions of *air sacs.*

alloy (al′oi) A solution of two or more metals, which has properties of its own. (C30) Pewter is an *alloy* of tin and other metals such as copper and lead.

amplitude (am′plə tōōd) The height of a wave from its resting position to its highest or lowest point; a measure of the amount of energy in a sound wave. (F17, F55) The *amplitude* of a loud sound is greater than the amplitude of a soft sound.

anticline (an′ti klīn) An upward fold of rock layers. (E82) Bending layers of rock formed an *anticline.*

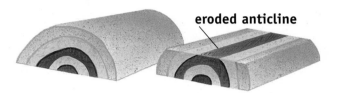

eroded anticline

apparent magnitude (ə per′ənt mag′nə tōōd) The measure of a star's brightness as seen from Earth. (B60) A star's *apparent magnitude* depends on the amount of light it gives off and on its distance from Earth.

arteries (art′ər ēz) Blood vessels that carry blood away from the heart. (A57) *Arteries* have thick, muscular walls.

atom (at′əm) The smallest particle of an element that has the properties of that element. (C22) Water is a combination of one *atom* of oxygen with two of hydrogen.

audiocassette (ô′dē ō kə set) A small container holding magnetic tape that is used for playing or recording sound. (F89) We inserted an *audiocassette* into the tape recorder.

auditory nerve (ô′də tôr ē nʉrv) A nerve in the ear that carries nerve impulses to the brain. (F83) A damaged *auditory nerve* will affect hearing.

axis (ak′sis) The imaginary line on which an object rotates. (B13) Earth's *axis* runs between the North and South Poles.

big-bang theory (big′ baŋ thē′ə rē)
A hypothesis, supported by data, that
describes how the universe began with
a huge explosion. (B39) The *big-bang
theory* holds that everything in the universe was once concentrated at one tiny
point.

biodiversity (bī ō də vʉr′sə tē) The
variety of organisms that live in Earth's
many ecosystems; the variety of plants
and animals that live within a particular
ecosystem. (D56) The *biodiversity* of
an ecosystem quickly changes after a
natural disaster.

biome (bī′ōm) A major land ecosystem having a distinct combination
of plants and animals. (D46) Some
biomes, such as the tundra, do not
easily support human populations.

black dwarf (blak dwarf) The cool,
dark body that is the final stage in the life
cycle of a low-mass star. (B65) When the
Sun dies, it will become a *black dwarf*.

black hole (blak hôl) An extremely
dense, invisible object in space whose
gravity is so great that not even light
can escape it. (B67) Scientists think
that the remains of a very massive star
can collapse following a supernova
explosion to form a *black hole*.

blood (blud) A tissue made up of a
liquid called plasma and several types
of cells. (A56) *Blood* carries oxygen
and nutrients to body cells.

bronchial tubes (brän′kē əl to͞obz)
Tubes that carry air from the trachea to
the lungs. (A48) Air flows to and from
the lungs through the *bronchial tubes*.

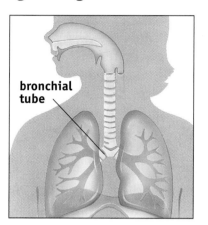

bronchial
tube

capillaries (kap′ə ler ēz) Tiny blood
vessels that connect the smallest arteries with the smallest veins. (A57)
Nutrients pass through the walls of the
capillaries into the cells.

carbon dioxide–oxygen cycle
(kär′bən dī äks′īd äks′i jen sī′kəl)
A natural cycle in which plants and
other producers use carbon dioxide and
produce oxygen, and animals, plants,
and other living things use oxygen and
produce carbon dioxide. (D32) The *carbon dioxide–oxygen cycle* must be
duplicated in space if humans wish to
make long voyages to other planets.

carnivore (kär′nə vôr) A consumer
that eats only other animals. (D16)
Lions are *carnivores* that prey on
zebras and other large plant-eaters.

cell (sel) The basic unit of structure of all living things. (A11) Even though plant *cells* can be different sizes, they still have many of the same structures.

cell membrane (sel mem′brān) A thin layer that surrounds all cells and allows water and dissolved materials to pass into and out of the cell. (A13) In plant cells, the *cell membrane* lies inside the cell wall.

cell respiration (sel res pə rā′shən) The process of using oxygen to release energy from food. (A23, D32) Animals and plants release carbon dioxide as a waste product of *cell respiration.*

cell wall (sel wôl) The tough outer covering of a plant cell that gives the cell its rigid shape. (A13) A *cell wall* is not found in animal cells.

cementation (sē men tā′shən) A process in which minerals, deposited as water evaporates, bind sediments into solid rock. (E44) Sandstone is a sedimentary rock formed by *cementation.*

chemical change (kem′i kəl chānj) A change in which one or more new substances form. (C58) The rusting of an iron nail is an example of a *chemical change.*

chemical formula (kem′i kəl fôr′myo͞o lə) A group of symbols that shows the elements that make up a compound. (C26) The *chemical formula* for water is H_2O.

chemical property (kem′i kəl präp′ər tē) A description of how a kind of matter can change into other kinds of matter. (C14) The ability to burn is a *chemical property* of kerosene.

chemical symbol (kem′i kəl sim′bəl) A shorthand way to represent the name of an element. (C23) The *chemical symbol* for iron is Fe.

chloroplast (klôr′ə plast) A structure in plant cells that captures light energy that is used in the food-making process. (A13) *Chloroplasts* are located within cells in the leaves of a plant.

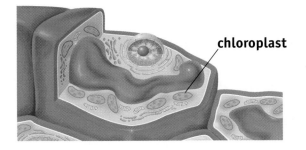

chloroplast

circulatory system (sur′kyo͞o lə tôr ē sis′təm) The transport system of the body that carries oxygen and nutrients to all cells and then removes wastes. (A56) The *circulatory system* brings nutrients and oxygen to the cells.

cleavage (klēv′ij) The tendency of some minerals to split along flat surfaces. (E15) Salt, or halite, shows *cleavage* in three planes.

coastal ocean (kōs′təl ō′shən) A saltwater ecosystem close to the shoreline that supports an abundance of life. (D52) The *coastal ocean* is an ecosystem that lies beyond the shoreline.

comet (käm′it) A small object in space, made of ice, dust, gas, and rock, that orbits a star and that can form a gaseous tail. (B24) A *comet* begins to melt as it approaches the Sun.

commensalism (kə men′səl iz əm) A close relationship between two kinds of organisms that benefits one of the organisms while neither benefiting nor hurting the other. (D20) The way that some insects use their resemblance to plants to hide from predators is an example of *commensalism*.

community (kə myo͞o′nə tē) All the organisms living together in a particular ecosystem. (D8) Raccoons, deer, and trees are part of a forest *community*.

compact disc (käm′pakt disk) A small disk on which sounds are digitally recorded and played back when read by a laser beam. (F90) This *compact disc*, or CD, plays for one hour.

complete metamorphosis (kəm-plēt′ met ə môr′fə sis) The development of an organism through four stages—egg, larva, pupa, and adult. (A74) The life cycle of a butterfly is an example of *complete metamorphosis*.

compound (käm′pound) A substance made up of two or more elements that are chemically joined, or linked. (C26) Water, made of the elements hydrogen and oxygen, is an example of a *compound*.

compound microscope (käm′pound mī′krə skōp) A viewing instrument that uses two lenses to magnify objects many times. (F41) The human hair appeared 1,000 times larger than actual size under the *compound microscope*.

compression (kəm presh′ən) A region in a sound wave where particles have been pushed together. (F55) The *compressions* produced by a vibrating tuning fork are areas of greater-than-normal air pressure.

concave lens (kän′kāv lenz) A lens that is thicker at the edges than it is in the middle and that causes light rays to spread apart. (F32) A *concave lens* is used to correct nearsightedness.

concave mirror (kän′kāv mir′ər) A mirror that curves inward at the middle. (F23) A *concave mirror* is used in a reflecting telescope.

concrete (kän′krēt) A mixture of rock material and cement that is used as a building material. (E24) This sidewalk is made of *concrete*.

condensation (kän dən sā′shən) The process by which a gas changes to a liquid. (C56, D34) *Condensation* can occur on a glass containing ice cubes as the gas water vapor changes to liquid water.

conduction (kən duk′shən) The transfer of heat energy by direct contact between particles. (C40) Heat travels through a metal by *conduction*.

conifer (kän′ə fər) A tree or shrub that bears its seeds in cones. (A91) The cones of each species of *conifer* are distinct and different from each other.

constellation (kän stə lā′shən) A group of stars that form a fixed pattern in the night sky. (B10) The *constellation* known as the Little Dipper contains the North Star.

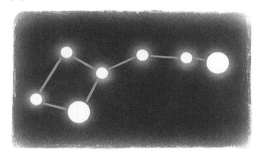

consumer (kən so͞om′ər) A living thing that obtains energy by eating other living things. (D16) Meat eaters and plant eaters are *consumers*.

contact lens (kän′takt lenz) A thin lens worn over the cornea of the eye, usually to correct vision problems. (F35) Some people use *contact lenses* rather than eyeglasses to improve their vision.

controlled experiment (kən trōld′ ek sper′ə mənt) A test of a hypothesis in which the setups are identical in all ways except one. (S7) In the controlled experiment, one beaker of water contained salt.

convection (kən vek′shən) The transfer of heat energy through liquids and gases by moving particles. (C41) When a pot of water is placed on a heat source, the heat is carried throughout the water by *convection*.

convex lens (kän′veks lenz) A lens that is thicker in the middle than at the edges and that brings light rays together. (F32) A *convex lens* is used to correct farsightedness.

convex mirror (kän′veks mir′ər) A mirror that curves outward at the middle. (F23) The side-view mirror of a car is a *convex mirror.*

core (kôr) The innermost layer of Earth, which consists of a molten outer part and a solid inner part. (E69) Temperatures inside the *core* of Earth are nearly as hot as those on the Sun's surface.

crest (krest) The highest point of a wave; in a sound wave, the regions of lower air pressure. (F17, F55) The top of a wave is its *crest*.

crust (krust) The outer layer of Earth. (E68) Earth's *crust* is a thin layer of rock.

cytoplasm (sīt′ō plaz əm) The jelly-like substance that fills much of the cell. (A13) The nucleus, vacuoles, and many other cell structures float in the *cytoplasm.*

decibel (des′ə bəl) A unit used to measure the loudness or intensity of sound. (F77) Sounds that have an intensity greater than 120 *decibels* (db) can hurt your ears.

decomposer (dē kəm pōz′ər) A living thing that breaks down the remains of dead organisms. (D16) *Decomposers*, such as fungi, get their energy from the remains of dead plants they break down.

deciduous forest (dē sij′o͞o əs fôr′ist) A biome that contains many trees and in which rainfall is moderate. (D49) *Deciduous forests* support a great variety of animal life.

desert (dez′ərt) A biome in which plant life is not abundant and rainfall is low. (D48) Plants that live in a *desert* have adaptations to conserve water.

diaphragm (dī′ə fram) The dome-shaped muscle that separates the chest from the stomach area. (A46) When you breathe in, the *diaphragm* moves down, and air rushes into the lungs.

digestive system (di jes′tiv sis′təm) The organ system in which food is broken down into a form that body cells can use. (A38) Many medicines treat disorders of the *digestive system*.

donor (dō′nər) A person who gives blood for a blood transfusion. (A58) Blood banks depend on *donors* to provide blood for transfusions.

ecosystem (ek′ō sis təm) An area in which living and nonliving things interact. (D8) An oak tree and the organisms that inhabit it can be thought of as a small *ecosystem*.

egg (eg) The first stage in an organism's life cycle. (A74) A baby bird hatches from an *egg*.

electromagnetic radiation (ē lektrō mag net′ik rā dē ā′shən) Wave energy given off by the Sun and some other objects. (F8) Visible light is a form of *electromagnetic radiation*.

electron microscope (ē lek′trän mī′krə skōp) A viewing instrument that magnifies objects thousands of times by using a beam of electrons instead of a beam of light. (F42) Doctors studied the virus through an *electron microscope*.

element (el′ə mənt) A basic kind of matter made up of just one kind of atom. (C22) Iron and oxygen are *elements*.

embryo (em′brē ō) An organism in its earliest stages of development; in most plants it is found inside a seed. (A85) When conditions for growth are suitable, the *embryo* inside the seed develops into a young plant.

endangered (en dān′jərd) In danger of becoming extinct. (D59) As the destruction of the Amazon rain forest continues, the number of *endangered* species increases.

energy (en′ər jə) The ability to cause change. (C11, F8) *Energy* from the Sun warms the air.

enzymes (en′zīmz) Chemicals that help break down food. (A39) Digestive *enzymes* in the stomach break down food into smaller particles.

erosion (ē rō′zhən) The breaking down and carrying away of rock and soil caused by such forces as wind and flowing water. (E82) The pounding waves caused *erosion* of the sandy shoreline.

esophagus (i säf′ə gəs) The muscular tube that connects the mouth to the stomach. (A40) After food is swallowed, it travels through the *esophagus* to the stomach.

eustachian tube (yoo stā′kē ən toob) A tube that connects the throat and the middle ear. (F83) The *eustachian tube* equalizes the air pressure on both sides of the eardrum.

evaporation (ē vap ə rā′shən) The process by which liquid water changes to water vapor. (C56, D34) One phase of the water cycle is the *evaporation* of water from lakes, rivers, and oceans.

excretory system (eks′krə tôrē sis′təm) The system for ridding the body of harmful wastes produced by the cells. (A62) The kidneys, lungs, and skin are all organs of the *excretory system*.

extinct (ek stiŋkt′) No longer living as a species. (D59) The passenger pigeon is an *extinct* species.

passenger pigeon

extraterrestrial (eks trə tə res′trē əl) A being from outer space; any object from beyond Earth. (B88) It would be extraordinary for scientists to discover that there is *extraterrestrial* life.

fault (fôlt) A break in rock along which rocks have moved. (E89) Forces within Earth's crust produce *faults*.

fertilization (furt′′l ə zā′shən) The process by which a male sex cell joins with a female sex cell. In flowering plants, fertilization takes place in the pistil. (A85) *Fertilization* occurs after a pollen tube reaches the ovary.

filter (fil′tər) A device that lets certain colors of light pass through while absorbing others. (F47) The stage manager placed a red *filter* over the spotlight.

focal point (fō′kəl point) The point at which light rays passing through a lens come together. (F32) Rays of light meet at the *focal point*.

fold (fōld) A bend in a layer of rock. (E81) Forces within Earth can cause a *fold* to form in rock layers.

food chain (food chān) The path of energy transfer from one living organism to another in an ecosystem. (D27) Energy moves from producers to consumers in a *food chain*.

food web (fŏŏd web) The overlapping food chains that link producers, consumers, and decomposers in an ecosystem. (D28) Some consumers in a *food web* eat both plants and animals.

fossil (fäs′əl) The remains or traces of a living thing from the past, preserved in rock. (E46) *Fossils* can include imprints of animal skeletons pressed into rock.

free fall (frē fôl) The motion of a freely falling object, such as that of a spacecraft in orbit around Earth. (B79) Astronauts experiencing *free fall* in space feel weightless.

frequency (frē′kwən sē) The number of waves produced in a unit of time, such as a second. (F18, F55) The *frequency* of light waves varies with the color of the light.

fruit (frōōt) The enlarged ovary of a flower that protects the developing seeds. (A85) Some *fruits*, such as peaches or mangoes, contain only one seed.

―――――― **G** ――――――

galaxy (gal′ək sē) A vast group of billions of stars that are held together by gravity. (B70) The Milky Way is a typical spiral *galaxy*.

gas (gas) Matter that does not have a definite shape or volume. (C21) Helium is a light *gas* that is sometimes used to fill balloons.

gas giant (gas jī′ənt) A large planet that is made up mostly of gaseous and liquid substances, with little or no solid surface. (B47) Jupiter is a *gas giant*.

geocentric model (jē ō sen′trik mäd′′l) A representation of the universe in which stars and planets revolve around Earth. (B37) Ptolemy proposed a *geocentric model* of the universe.

germination (jʉr mə nā′ shən) The sprouting of a seed. (A86) After *germination*, an acorn begins to form a seedling, or tiny young plant.

grassland (gras′land) A biome containing many grasses but few trees and having low to moderate rainfall. (D48) Taller grasses occur in *grasslands* that have more abundant rainfall.

―――――― ――――――

hardness (härd′nis) A measure of how easily a mineral can be scratched. (E13) The *hardness* of diamond is greater than that of any other mineral.

heart (härt) The pump that pushes blood throughout the entire circulatory system. (A56) The human *heart* normally beats about 70 to 80 times per minute.

heliocentric model (hē lē ō sen′trik mäd′′l) A representation of the relationship between the Sun and planets in which the planets revolve around the Sun. (B37) Copernicus hypothesized a *heliocentric model* of the solar system.

herbivore (hur′bə vôr) A consumer that eats only plants or other producers. (D16) Pandas are *herbivores* that have a very limited diet because they only eat bamboo.

hertz (herts) A unit used to measure wave frequency. (F18, F66) If 100 waves are produced per second, their frequency is 100 *hertz*.

hypothesis (hī päth′ə sis) An idea about or explanation of how or why something happens. (S6) The *hypothesis* about the expanding universe has been supported by evidence gathered by astronomers.

I

igneous rock (ig′nē əs räk) A type of rock that forms from melted rock that cools and hardens. (E40) Obsidian is an *igneous rock* that forms when lava cools quickly.

index fossil (in′deks fäs′əl) A fossil used to determine the relative age of rock. (E76) The remains of a living thing that lived only at a certain time in the past makes a good *index fossil*.

intensity (in ten′sə tē) A measure of the amount of energy in a sound wave. (F76) A sound that has high *intensity* is loud enough to be heard from a distance.

Internet (in′tər net) A system of interconnected computer networks. (F91) Telephone lines link computer users with the *Internet*.

J

joule (jool) The basic unit of energy and of work. (C47) Scientists measure amounts of energy in *joules*.

K

kidneys (kid′nēz) A pair of organs that clean and filter the blood. (A63) The *kidneys* help remove excess water and salts from the blood.

kinetic energy (ki net′ik en′ər jē) The energy that something has because of its motion. (C48) As a boulder rolls down a steep hill, it gains *kinetic energy*.

L

lake (lāk) A freshwater ecosystem characterized by still water. (D51) *Lakes* support fish, birds, algae, and other forms of life.

H27

large intestine (lärj in tes'tən) The organ that absorbs water and salts from undigested material. (A43) The major job of the *large intestine* is to absorb water from wastes and return it to the bloodstream.

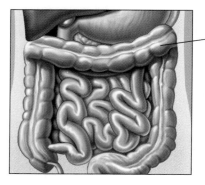

large intestine

larva (lär'və) The wormlike, or grub, stage that follows the egg stage of an insect's life cycle. (A74) The caterpillar is the *larva* stage in the life cycle of a butterfly.

larynx (lar'iŋks) The part of the throat that is used in speaking. (A48) The *larynx* is another name for the voice box.

lava (lä'və) Melted rock material that reaches Earth's surface before it cools and hardens. (E41) A volcano carries *lava* to Earth's surface.

leaf (lēf) A plant part in which photosynthesis takes place. (A19) In a plant such as cabbage, it is the *leaf* that people eat.

lens (lenz) A piece of glass or other transparent material with at least one curved surface that brings together or spreads apart light rays passing through it. (F32) The *lens* in a camera focuses an image on the film.

life processes (līf prä'ses ēz) The functions that a living thing must carry out to stay alive and produce more of its own kind. (A11) Digestion is one of the essential *life processes*.

light-year (līt yir) A unit of measurement representing the distance that light travels in one year. (B61) The distance to stars is measured in *light-years*.

liquid (lik'wid) Matter that has a definite volume but no definite shape. (C21) Water is the most abundant *liquid* on Earth.

luster (lus'tər) The way that the surface of a mineral looks when it reflects light. (E13) Silver and gold have a shiny, metallic *luster*.

magma (mag'mə) Melted rock material that forms deep within Earth. (E40) Some igneous rocks, such as granite, form from *magma*.

mantle (man'təl) A thick layer of rock between the crust and the core of Earth. (E69) The top of the *mantle* is solid rock, but below that is a section of rock that can flow.

mass (mas) A measure of how much matter there is in an object. (C10) A large rock has more *mass* than a pebble.

matter (mat'ər) Anything that has mass and takes up space. (C10) Coal, water, and air are three kinds of *matter*.

melting (melt′iŋ) The change of state from a solid to a liquid. (C56) The process of *melting* changes ice from a solid to liquid water.

metamorphic rock (met ə môr′fik räk) A type of rock that forms from existing rocks because of changes caused by heat, pressure, or chemicals. (E47) Slate is a *metamorphic rock* that forms from the sedimentary rock shale.

meteor (mēt′ē ər) A piece of rock or metal from space that enters Earth's atmosphere. (B25) A *meteor* appears as a streak of light, which is why it is also called a shooting star.

meteorite (mēt′ē ər īt) The remaining material of a meteor that has landed on the ground. (B25) In 1902, scientists were able to examine the largest *meteorite* ever known to land in the United States.

microgravity (mī kro grav′i tē) The condition of very low gravity. (B84) Astronauts experience *microgravity* aboard the space shuttle.

Milky Way Galaxy (milk′ē wā gal′ək sē) A gigantic cluster of billions of stars that is home to our solar system. (B70) The Sun is located in one of the arms of the *Milky Way Galaxy*.

mineral (min′ər əl) A solid element or compound from Earth's crust that has a definite chemical composition and crystal structure. (E12) Quartz is a *mineral*.

mixture (miks′chər) Matter made up of two or more substances. (C27) Air is a *mixture* of many gases, including oxygen, carbon dioxide, and nitrogen.

model (mäd″l) Something used or made to represent an object or an idea. (E68) Layers of clay can be used as a *model* of layers of rock.

molecule (mäl′i kyool) A particle made up of two or more atoms, which may be alike or different. (C57) A *molecule* of water contains two hydrogen atoms and one oxygen atom.

moon (moon) A natural object that revolves around a planet. (B44) The planet Mars has two known *moons*.

mutualism (myoo′choo əl iz əm) A close relationship between two or more organisms in which all organisms ben-efit. (D20) Bees carrying pollen from flower to flower as they obtain nectar is an example of *mutualism*.

natural resource (nach′ər əl rē′sôrs) Any useful material or energy source found in nature. (E31) *Natural resources* include water, minerals, oil, and coal.

nebula (neb′yə lə) A huge cloud of gas and dust found in space. (B64) A *nebula* can form when a supernova explodes.

neutron star (no͞o′trän stär) The remains of a massive star that has exploded in a supernova. (B67) A typical *neutron star* is less than 20 km in diameter.

niche (nich) The role that each species plays in a community. (D9) Bees have an important *niche* in pollinating flowers as they gather nectar to make honey.

nitrogen cycle (nī′trə jən sī′kəl) The cycle through which nitrogen changes into compounds that can be used by living things and then returns to the atmosphere. (D40) The *nitrogen cycle* is important to all life forms because nitrogen is needed to make protein.

noise pollution (noiz pə lo͞o′shən) The occurrence of loud or unpleasant sound in the environment. (F78) The sounds of city traffic are a form of *noise pollution*.

nonrenewable resource (nän ri-no͞o′ ə bəl rē′sôrs) A resource that can't be replaced in nature. (E31) Fossil fuels such as oil and coal are *nonrenewable resources*.

nucleus (no͞o′klē əs) 1. The cell structure that controls all of a cell's activities. (A13) The *nucleus* was clearly visible after the cell was stained. 2. The central part of an atom, made up of protons and neutrons. (C23) The *nucleus* of a helium atom contains two protons and two neutrons.

nutrients (no͞o′trē ənts) Substances that are needed for an organism to live and grow. (A11) Proteins, carbohydrates, and fats are *nutrients* found in food.

octave (äk′tiv) The series of eight notes that makes up a musical scale. (F67) The music student practiced playing *octaves* on the piano.

omnivore (äm′ni vôr) A consumer that eats both plants and animals. (D16) Because they eat both meats and vegetables, many humans are *omnivores*.

opaque (ō pāk′) Not letting light through. (F46) The *opaque* curtains kept out the sunlight.

open ocean (ō′pən ō′shən) The large saltwater ecosystem containing both floating and free-swimming organisms. (D53) The *open ocean* covers much of Earth's surface.

ore (ôr) A mineral or rock that contains enough of a metal to make mining the metal profitable. (E27) Hematite is an *ore* mined for its iron content.

organ (ôr'gən) Different types of tissue working together to perform a certain function. (A12) The heart, skin, and lungs are *organs* of the human body.

organ system (ôr'gən sis'təm) Groups of organs working together. (A12) The digestive system is an *organ system* that includes the stomach, small intestine, and large intestine.

overtone (o'vər tōn) A fainter, higher tone that harmonizes with the main tone produced by a musical instrument or the human voice. (F56) The blending of *overtones* gives the flute its unique sound.

parasitism (par'ə sīt iz əm) A relationship between two organisms in which one organism lives on or in the other, feeds upon it, and usually harms it. (D19) The way in which fleas live on dogs is an example of *parasitism*.

peristalsis (per ə stal'sis) A wavelike motion that moves food through the digestive system. (A41) Swallowed food is moved through the esophagus to the stomach by means of *peristalsis*.

phonograph (fō'nə graf) A device that reproduces sounds recorded on a disk. (F88) We played old records on the *phonograph*.

photosynthesis (fōt ō sin'thə sis) The process by which producers, such as plants, make their own food by using energy from the Sun. (A19, D33) *Photosynthesis* takes place primarily in the leaves of plants.

physical change (fiz'i kəl chānj) A change in which the size, shape, or state of matter changes but no new substances are formed. (C57) Cutting an apple in half and freezing water into ice are examples of *physical change*.

physical property (fiz'i kəl präp'ər tē) A characteristic of matter that can be detected or measured with the senses. (C13) A *physical property* of a ball is its round shape.

pistil (pis' til) The female part of a flower. (A84) Pollen grains stick to the stigma, which is at the tip of the *pistil*.

pitch (pich) The highness or lowness of a sound. (F66) A tuba produces sounds with a low *pitch*.

plane mirror (plān mir'ər) A mirror that has a flat surface. (F22) The mirror over the bathroom sink is a *plane mirror.*

planet (plan'it) A large body in space that orbits a star and does not produce light on its own. (B17) Saturn is one of nine known *planets* that revolve around the Sun.

pollen grain (pal'ən grān) A structure produced in the male part of a flower and which contains the male sex cell. (A85) The *pollen grains* of a flower must be carried from the stamen to the pistil in order for seeds to be formed.

pollination (päl ə nā'shən) The transfer of pollen grains to the pistil of a flower. (A85) Bees often help in the process of *pollination*.

population (päp yo͞o lā'shən) A group of the same kind of organisms that live in an area. (D8) There is a *population* of frogs in that marsh.

potential energy (pō ten'shəl en'ər jē) The energy that an object has because of its position or structure; stored energy. (C46) A coiled spring has *potential energy*.

producer (prō do͞os'ər) An organism that makes its own food through photosynthesis. (D16) Plants and algae are examples of *producers*.

protein (prō'tēn) Organic compounds that form the structure of and control the processes that take place in living things. (D39) *Proteins* provide the body with materials that help cells grow and repair themselves.

protostar (prōt'ō stär) A concentration of matter found in space that is the beginning of a star. (B64) When the temperature inside a *protostar* becomes high enough, nuclear reactions begin and the protostar turns into a star.

pulse (puls) The throbbing caused by blood rushing into the arteries when the lower chambers of the heart contract. (A57) A doctor takes a patient's *pulse* by feeling an artery in the wrist.

pupa (pyo͞o'pə) The stage in a life cycle between the larva and the adult. (A74) The cocoon is the *pupa* stage in the life cycle of a moth.

quarry (kwôr'ē) A mine, usually near or at Earth's surface, from which rock is removed. (E52) Granite, sandstone, limestone, slate, and marble are some rocks that come from a *quarry*.

radiation (rā dē ā'shən) The transfer of energy by waves. (C39) Energy given off by the Sun travels as *radiation* through space.

radioactive element (rā dē ō ak'tiv el'ə mənt) An element that releases energy and tiny particles from the nuclei of its atoms. (C55) Two *radioactive elements* are uranium and plutonium.

radio telescope (rā' dē ō tel'ə skōp) A gigantic antenna on Earth designed to receive radio signals from space. (B90) *Radio telescopes* are important tools for studying distant stars and galaxies.

rarefaction (rer ə fak'shən) A region in a sound wave where there are fewer particles than normal. (F55) The *rarefactions* that a vibrating violin string produces are areas of lower-than-normal air pressure.

recipient (ri sip'ē ənt) A person who receives blood in a blood transfusion. (A58) An accident victim is often the *recipient* of transfused blood.

red giant (red jī'ənt) A very large old reddish star that has greatly expanded and cooled as its fuel has begun to run out. (B65) As the Sun reaches old age, it will turn into a *red giant*.

reflecting telescope (ri flekt'iŋ tel'ə skōp) An instrument for viewing distant objects that uses a curved mirror at the back of its tube to gather light and produce an image. (B22, F39) This observatory uses a *reflecting telescope* to observe faraway galaxies.

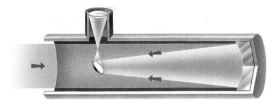

reflection (ri flek'shən) The bouncing of light from a surface. (F22) The *reflection* of sunlight off the snow made us squint.

refracting telescope (ri frakt'iŋ tel'ə skōp) An instrument for viewing distant objects that uses two lenses to gather light and produce an image. (B21, F38) The *refracting telescope* allowed a closer look at the Moon.

refraction (ri frak'shən) The bending of light as it passes from one material into another. (F24) Light traveling from air into water will undergo *refraction*.

relative age (rel'ə tiv āj) The age of an object as compared to that of other objects. (E76) The order of layers of rock shows the *relative ages* of the layers.

renewable resource (ri nōō'ə bəl rē'sôrs) A resource that can be replaced in a fairly short time. (E31) Trees are considered to be *renewable resources*.

respiratory system (res'pər ə tôr ē sis'təm) The body parts that work together to take air into the body and push it back out. (A46) The lungs are the central organs in the *respiratory system*.

retina (ret''n ə) The light-sensitive area at the back of the eye on which an image is formed. (F34) The *retina* contains two kinds of cells.

revolution (rev ə lōō'shən) The movement of an object around another object or point. (B13) It takes about 365 days for Earth to make one *revolution* around the Sun.

river (riv'ər) A freshwater ecosystem characterized by running water. (D50) Salmon are able to swim against the current in a *river*.

rock (räk) A solid material made of minerals that forms Earth's crust. (E40) Earth's crust is made of *rock*.

rock cycle (räk sī'kəl) The continuous series of changes that rocks undergo. (E60) In the *rock cycle*, changes are brought about by factors such as weathering, melting, cooling, or pressure.

root (ro͞ot) The underground part of a plant that anchors the plant and absorbs water and nutrients. (A16) Carrots and turnips have one large *root*.

rotation (rō tā'shən) The spinning motion of an object on its axis. (B13) It takes about 24 hours for Earth to make one complete *rotation*.

saliva (sə lī'və) The watery liquid in the mouth that begins the chemical breakdown of food. (A38) Just the thought of food, as well as its odor and taste, will cause *saliva* to flow into the mouth.

satellite (sat''l īt) A natural or human-built object that revolves around another object in space. (B44) The Moon is a natural *satellite* of Earth.

sediment (sed'ə mənt) Bits of weathered rocks and minerals and pieces of dead plants or animals. (E43) Over time *sediments* can form sedimentary rocks, such as sandstone and limestone.

sedimentary rock (sed ə men'tər ē räk) A type of rock that forms when sediments harden. (E43) Most *sedimentary rocks* form in layers.

semicircular canal (sem i sʉr'kyə lər kə nal') Any of three curved tube-like structures of the inner ear that help the body to maintain balance. (F83) The *semicircular canals* respond to movements of the head.

sexual reproduction (sek'sho͞o əl rē'prə duk'shən) The production of offspring that occurs when a male sex cell joins a female sex cell. (A84) The *sexual reproduction* of flowers is greatly aided by insects.

shoreline (shôr'līn) The ecosystem where land and ocean meet. (D52) Tides affect organisms that live along the *shoreline*.

simple microscope (sim'pəl mī'krə skōp) A microscope that uses a single lens to magnify objects. (F41) A magnifying glass is a *simple microscope*.

small intestine (smôl in tes'tən) The long coiled organ where most digestion takes place. (A42) The *small intestine* is about 6 m (20 ft) long.

smelting (smelt′iŋ) The process of melting ore to remove the metal from it. (E28) Workers obtain iron by *smelting* iron ore in a blast furnace.

solar system (sō′lər sis′təm) The Sun and the planets and other objects that orbit the Sun. Also, any star and the objects that revolve around it. (B34) Our *solar system* consists of the Sun, nine known planets, and many smaller objects.

solid (säl′id) Matter that has a definite shape and a definite volume. (C21) A rock is an example of a *solid*.

solution (sə lōō′shən) A mixture in which the different particles of matter are spread evenly. (C28) A *solution* of salt in water has some properties that are different from those of water alone.

sound (sound) A form of energy that travels through matter as waves. (F54) The *sound* made the floor vibrate.

sound synthesizer (sound sin′thə-sī zər) An electronic device that can produce a wide variety of sounds. (F69) The composer used a *sound synthesizer* to create a new musical composition.

stamen (stā′mən) The male reproductive structure of a flower. (A84) Pollen is produced in the *stamen*.

star (stär) A huge globe of hot gases that shines by its own light. (B17) Many *stars* may have systems of planets.

stem (stem) The part of a plant that supports the leaves and flowers and carries water to those parts. (A18) The trunk of a tree is a *stem*.

stomach (stum′ək) The muscular organ that stores food and helps digest it. (A41) The *stomach* squeezes and churns food into a souplike mixture called chyme.

streak (strēk) The colored powder made by rubbing a mineral against a ceramic surface. (E15) Although pyrite is yellow, it produces a black *streak*.

supernova (sōō′pər nō və) An exploding star. (B66) When a massive red giant star uses up all its fuel, it collapses and explodes in a *supernova*.

sweat glands (swet glandz) Small coiled tubes that end at pores on the skin's surface. (A64) The *sweat glands* help to adjust the temperature of the body.

syncline (sin′klīn) A downward fold of rock layers. (E82) Forces in Earth pushing on rock formed a *syncline*.

taiga (tī′gə) A biome that contains many coniferous trees and in which rainfall is moderate. (D49) The *taiga* is south of the tundra.

terrestrial planet (tə res′trē əl plan′it) An object in space that resembles Earth in size, in density, and in its mainly rocky composition. (B44) Mars is a *terrestrial planet.*

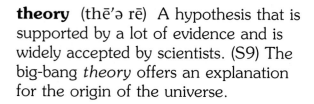

theory (thē′ə rē) A hypothesis that is supported by a lot of evidence and is widely accepted by scientists. (S9) The big-bang *theory* offers an explanation for the origin of the universe.

timbre (tam′bər) The quality of sound that sets one voice or musical instrument apart from another. (F56) The same note played on a violin and on a trumpet differ in *timbre.*

tissue (tish′o͞o) Similar cells working together. (A12) Muscle *tissue* contains cells that contract.

trachea (trā′kē ə) The air tube that joins the throat to the lungs. (A46) Choking occurs when an object becomes stuck in the *trachea.*

translucent (trans lo͞o′sənt) Letting light through but scattering it; objects cannot be clearly seen through translucent material. (F47) The *translucent* lampshade dimmed the room.

transparent (trans per′ənt) Letting light through; objects can be clearly seen through transparent material. (F47) Window glass is usually *transparent* so that people can see through it.

tropical rain forest (träp′i kəl rän fôr′ist) A biome distinguished by lush vegetation, abundant rainfall, and plentiful sunlight. (D48) The *tropical rain forest* supports the greatest variety of life of any biome.

tropism (trō′piz əm) A growth response of a plant to conditions in the environment, such as light or water. (A24) Growing toward a light source is an example of a plant *tropism.*

trough (trôf) The low point of a wave; in a sound wave, the regions of lower air pressure. (F17, F55) A *trough* occurs between two wave crests.

tundra (tun′drə) A biome characterized by cold temperatures and low precipitation. (D49) The *tundra* blooms in summer.

universe (yo͞on′ə vʉrs) The sum of everything that exists. (B38) Our solar system is part of the *universe.*

urine (yoor′in) The yellowish liquid containing wastes and water from the filtering units of the kidneys. (A63) A doctor may test a sample of *urine* to check a patient's health.

vacuole (vak′yo͞o ōl) A cell part that stores water and nutrients. (A13) Some plant cells have large *vacuoles.*

variable (ver′ē ə bəl) The one difference in the setups of a controlled experiment; provides a comparison for testing a hypothesis. (S7) The *variable* in an experiment with plants was the amount of water given each plant.

veins (vānz) Blood vessels that carry blood from the capillaries to the heart. (A57) The walls of *veins* are thinner than those of arteries.

vertebrate (vur′tə brit) An animal with a backbone. (A76) *Vertebrates* are the large group of living things that includes mammals, fish, birds, reptiles, and amphibians.

vibration (vī brā′shən) A back-and-forth movement of matter. (F54) The *vibration* of guitar strings produces sound.

villi (vil′ī) Looplike structures in the wall of the small intestine in which nutrients are passed from the small intestine into the blood. (A43) The *villi* release mucus as well as absorb nutrients in the small intestine.

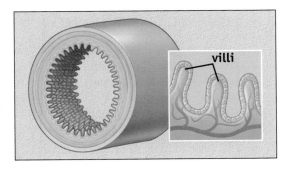

villi

visible light (viz′ə bəl līt) A form of electromagnetic energy that can be seen. (F8) The eye responds to *visible light*.

volume (väl′yo͞om) 1. The amount of space an object takes up. (C10) A great *volume* of snow drifted over the road. 2. The loudness or softness of a sound. (F76) Please turn up the *volume*.

water cycle (wôt′ər sī′kəl) A continuous process in which water moves between the atmosphere and Earth's surface, including the use of water by living things. (D34) The *water cycle* is powered by energy from the Sun.

wave (wāv) A disturbance that carries energy and that travels away from its starting point. (F17) The experiment measured how quickly light *waves* travel.

wavelength (wāv′ləŋkth) The distance between one crest of a wave and the next crest. (F17, F55) Red light has a longer *wavelength* than blue light does.

weathering (weth′ər iŋ) The breaking up of rocks into sediments by such forces as wind, rain, and sunlight. (E62) Through *weathering*, igneous rock can be broken down into sediments.

wetland (wet′land) Any one of three ecosystems—marsh, swamp, or bog—where land and fresh water meet. (D51) *Wetlands* help purify water.

white dwarf (wīt dwarf) A very small dying star that gives off very little light. (B65) When the Sun's fuel runs out, it will collapse into a *white dwarf*.

INDEX

* Activity

CREDITS

ILLUSTRATORS
Cover: Olivia McElroy.

Think Like a Scientist: 3–4: Garry Colby. 14: Laurie Hamilton. *Border:* Olivia McElroy.

Unit A 10–11: Paul Mirocha. 13: Carlyn Iverson. 16–17: Walter Stewart. 18, 20: Steve Buchanan. 22: Carlyn Iverson. 24–25: Patrick Gnan. 28: Carlyn Iverson. 30: Richard LaRocco. 34: Leonard Morgan. 39–43, 46–50, 56–57: Richard LaRocco. 58–59: Albert Lorenz. 62–63: Richard LaRocco. 64, 66: Carlyn Iverson. 72–73: Ilene Robinette. 75: Patrick Gnan. 76: Rob Schuster. 79: Michael Maydak. 84–85: Glory Bechtold. 86–87: Catherine Deeter. 88–89: Eldon Doty. 91–92: Michael Maydak.

Unit B 9: Delores Bego. 10–11: *border* Dale Glasgow. 11: Tom Powers. 13: Jeff Hitch. 14: Michael Carroll. 15: Tony Novak. 17: Robert Schuster. 21: Lane Yerkes. 22: Fred Holz. 24–25: Jim Starr. 27: Tom Powers. 30: Dale Glasgow. 34–35: Dennis Davidson. 36: *b.m.* Dale Glasgow; *m.m.* Verlin Miller; *m.r.* Susan Melrath. 37: *t.l.* Dale Glasgow, Susan Melrath. 38–39: Michael Carroll. 42–43: Dennis Davidson. 44–49: Robert Schuster. 50: *t.r.* Dale Glasgow; *m.l.* Michael Carroll; *m.t.* Robert Schuster. 57: Tom Powers. 60–61: Lu Matthews. 64–65: Joe Spencer. 67: Tom Powers. 70: Michael Carroll. 71: Tom Powers. 72: Joe LeMonnier. 73: Tom Powers. 79: Terry Boles. 80: Stephen Wagner. 82–83: Nina Laden. 91: Andy Myer. 92: Dale Glasgow. 93: Terry Boles.

Unit C 23: Nadine Sokol. 24, 25, 29: Olivia. 31: Nadine Sokol. 40: *t.* Carolyn Bracken; *b.* Ron Fleming. 48–49: David Uhl. 50: *b.* Ka Botzis. 50–51: *t.* Sarah Jane English. 55: Eldon Doty. 56, 57: Ron Fleming. 58: *m.* Stephen Bauer; *b.* Ron Fleming, Joe Spencer. 59: *b.* Ron Fleming, Joe Spencer. 60, 61: Ron Fleming.

Unit D 8–9: Robert Hynes. 10–11: Jim Salvati. 15: Wendy Smith-Griswold. 17: Marcos Montiero. 18: Lori Anzalone. 26: David Barber. 27, 29: Andy Lendway. 32–35: Don Stewart. 36–37: Jim Starr. 39–40: Don Stewart. 41: Andy Lendway. 46–49: Rodica Prato. 50–53: Paul Mirocha. 54: Joe LeMonnier. 57: Carlos Ochagavia.

Unit E 12–16: Lingta King. 20–21: Wendy Smith-Griswold. 28: Jeanette Adams. 30–31: Bill Morse. 40: Brad Gaber. 47: Robert Pasternack. 55: Scot Ritchie. 58–59: Brad Gaber. 60: Michael Sloan. 61–63: Terry Boles. 68–69: Chuck Carter. 70: Scot Ritchie. 71: Chuck Carter. 74: Eldon Doty. 75: Carlyn Iverson. 76: *t.* Susan Melrath; *b.* Carlyn Iverson. 83: *t.* Robert Pasternack; *b.* Joe LeMonnier. 84: Verlin Miller. 85: Jim Starr. 89: Robert Pasternack. 91: Joe LeMonnier.

Unit F 8: *t.* Scot Ritchie. 8–9: *b.* Michael Carroll. 12, 13: Eldon Doty. 16: Jeanette Adams. 17, 18–19: Robert Pasternack. 18, 19: Ron Magnes. 22, 25, 26, 27: Bob Brugger. 32: J.A.K. Graphics. 33: *t., b.* Patrick Gnan, Carlyn Iverson. 34: *b.* J.A.K. Graphics, Carlyn Iverson. 35: Marie Dauenheimer. 36, 37: George Kelvin. 39: *t.* Bob Bredemeier; *b.* Eldon Doty. 43: Andy Miller. 45: Jim Fanning. 46: Len Morgan. 49: Rose Berlin. 54, 55, 57: Dale Glasgow & Assoc. 61: Terry Boles. 64–65: Tom Lochray. 66–67: *t.* Mark Bender. 66, 67: *b.* Roger Chandler. 69–70: Larry Moore. 76: *t.* Marty Bucella; *m.* Ray Vella. 76–77: *b.* Ray Vella. 83: Ellen Going Jacobs. 89, 90: Dale Gustafson. 91: Dale Glasgow & Assoc. 91–92–93: *t.* Dale Glasgow & Assoc. 92: *m.* Tim Blough. 95: Patrick Gnan.

Math and Science Toolbox: *Logos:* Nancy Tobin. 14–15: Andrew Shiff. *Borders:* Olivia McElroy.

Glossary 19: Ellen Going Jacobs. 20: Robert Margulies. 21: Fran Milner. 23: Tom Powers. 26: Carlyn Iverson. 28: Richard Larocca. 29, 31: Robert Pasternack. 33: Gary Torrisi. 37: Robert Margulies.

PHOTOGRAPHS
All photographs by Houghton Mifflin Co. (HMCo.) unless otherwise noted.

Front Cover: *t.* Superstock; *m.l.* G.K. & Vikki Hart/The Image Bank; *m.r.* Runk/Schoenberger/Grant Heilman Photography, Inc.; *b.l.* NASA/Media Services; *b.r.* Superstock.

Think Like a Scientist: 2: *b.* Chip Porter/Tony Stone Images. 3: *t.* Paul Seheult, Eye Ubiquitous/Corbis. 10: *b. bkgd.* PhotoDisc, Inc.

Table of Contents vii: *l.* Anglo-Australian Observatory; *m.l.* © Royal Observatory, Edinburgh/AATB/Science Photo Library/Photo Researchers, Inc.; *m.r.* © Royal Observatory, Edinburgh/AATB/Science Photo Library/Photo Researchers, Inc.; *r.* MGA/Photri, Inc. x: *t.* J.C. Carton/Bruce Coleman Incorporated; *b.* Michael Fogden/Bruce Coleman Incorporated. xi: DN Metalsmith. xii: *inset* E.R. Degginger/Color-Pic, Inc.; *bkgd.* E.R. Degginger/Color-Pic, Inc.; *b.* E.R. Degginger/Color-Pic, Inc.; *r.* Doug Sokell/Tom Stack & Associates. xiv: © Cecil Fox/Science Photo Library/Photo Researchers, Inc.

Unit A 1: Prof. P. Motta/Dept. of Anatomy/University "La Sapienza", Rome/Science Photo Library/Custom Medical Stock Photo, Inc. 2–3: Prof. P. Motta/Dept. of Anatomy/University "La Sapienza", Rome/Science Photo Library/Custom Medical Stock Photo, Inc. 4–5: *bkgd* Ron Garrison/The Zoological Society of San Diego; *inset* Ken Kelley for HMCo. 7: *t.m.* Clive Druett; Papilio/Corbis Corporation; *b.m.* Kim Sayer/Corbis Corporation; *b.r.* Mitchell Gerber/Corbis Corporation; *b.l.* E.R. Degginger/Color-Pic, Inc. 9: Ken Karp for HMCo. 10: *l.* E.R. Degginger/Color-Pic, Inc.; *inset* Don & Pat Valenti/DRK Photo. 12: *t.* © P. Dayanandan/Photo

H46

Krasemann/DRK Photo. 56: *t.l.* J.C. Carton/Bruce Coleman Incorporated; *t.r.* J.C. Carton/Bruce Coleman Incorporated; *m.l.* Michael Fogden/Animals Animals/Earth Scenes; *m.r.* Thomas R. Fletcher/Stock Boston; *b.* Michael Fogden/Bruce Coleman Incorporated. 58: *t.* Michael Fogden/DRK Photo; *b.* Greg Vaughn/Tom Stack & Associates. 59: Mark Carwardine/Still Pictures/Peter Arnold, Inc. 60: *l.* BIOS/Peter Arnold, Inc.; *r.* David Dennis/Tom Stack & Associates. 61: *t.* B. Herrod OSF/Animals Animals/Earth Scenes; *m.l.* Stephen J. Krasemann/Peter Arnold, Inc.; *m.r.* Norbert Wu/Peter Arnold, Inc.; *b.* R. Andrew Odum/Peter Arnold, Inc.

Unit E 1: Joseph Sohm/ChromoSohm Inc./Corbis Corporation. 2–3: Joseph Sohm/ChromoSohm Inc./Corbis Corporation. 4: DN Metalsmith. 4–5: *bkgd.* JLM Visuals; *inset* DN Metalsmith. 5: DN Metalsmith. 6–7: Grant Huntington for HMCo. 8: Grant Huntington for HMCo. 8–9: Grant Huntington for HMCo. 9: *t.* Grant Huntington for HMCo.; *b.* Grant Huntington for HMCo. 10: Grant Huntington for HMCo. 12: *m.l.* Joy Spurr/Bruce Coleman Incorporated; *m.r.* E.R. Degginger/Color-Pic, Inc. 13: *l.* E.R. Degginger/Bruce Coleman Incorporated; *r.* Runk/Schoenberger/Grant Heilman Photography, Inc. 15: *t.* Grant Huntington for HMCo.; *b.l.* Runk/Schoenberger/Grant Heilman Photography, Inc.; *m.b.* E.R. Degginger/Color-Pic, Inc.; *b.r.* Breck P. Kent Photography. 16: *t.* Runk/Schoenberger/Grant Heilman Photography, Inc.; *b.* E.R. Degginger/Color-Pic, Inc. 17: *b.l.* Grant Huntington for HMCo.; *m.b.* Grant Huntington for HMCo.; *b.r.* Grant Huntington for HMCo. 18: *l.* Grant Huntington for HMCo.; *m.* Grant Huntington for HMCo.; *r.* Grant Huntington for HMCo. 21: *l.* Breck P. Kent Photography; *m.* © Bill Bachman/Photo Researchers, Inc.; *r.* © Phillip Hayson/Photo Researchers, Inc. 23: Grant Huntington for HMCo. 24: *l.* Runk/Schoenberger/Grant Heilman Photography, Inc.; *m.l.* I.S. Stepanowicz/Bruce Coleman Incorporated; *m.r.* Doug Sokell/Visuals Unlimited; *r.* © Roberto De Gugliemo/Science Photo Library/Photo Researchers, Inc. 25: *t.l.* E.R. Degginger/Color-Pic, Inc.; *t.r.* Chuck O'Rear/Corbis; *b.* Runk/Schoenberger/Grant Heilman Photography, Inc. 26: *t.m.* Phil Degginger/Color-Pic, Inc.; *t.r.* © 2000 Chuck O'Rear/Woodfin Camp & Associates. 27: *l.* © Gerard Vandystadt/Photo Researchers, Inc.; *m.* © Christian Grzimek/Photo Researchers, Inc.; *r.* © 2000 George Hall/Woodfin Camp & Associates. 29: *t.* © David Guyon/Science Photo Library/Photo Researchers, Inc.; *m.* Chuck O'Rear/Corbis; *b.* © James Holmes/Photo Researchers, Inc. 31: Bruce Forster/Tony Stone Images. 32: Myrleen Ferguson Cate/PhotoEdit. 33: Barry L. Runk/Grant Heilman Photography, Inc. 34–35: *bkgd.* © Chromosohm/Joe Sohm/Photo Researchers, Inc. 36–37: Grant Huntington for HMCo. 37: Grant Huntington for HMCo. 41: *t.* Phil Degginger/Color-Pic, Inc. 42: *l.* E.R. Degginger/Color-Pic, Inc.; *m.* Doug Sokell/Tom Stack & Associates; *r.* E.R. Degginger/Color-Pic, Inc.; *inset* E.R. Degginger/Color-Pic, Inc. 43: *l.* E.R. Degginger/Color-Pic, Inc.; *r.* E.R. Degginger/Color-Pic, Inc.; *inset* E.R. Degginger/Color-Pic, Inc. 44: *t.* E.R. Degginger/Color-Pic, Inc.; *b.* inset E.R. Degginger/Color-Pic, Inc.; *b.r.* Richard Hutchings for HMCo. 46: *t.l.* Tom & Susan Bean, Inc.; *m.t.* © 2000 Gary Braasch/Woodfin Camp & Associates; *m.b.* Doug Sokell/Tom Stack & Associates; *b.* Stephen Trimble Photography. 46–47: E.R. Degginger/Color-Pic, Inc. 48: *l.* E.R. Degginger/Color-Pic, Inc.; *m.* E.R. Degginger/Color-Pic, Inc.; *r.* Breck P. Kent Photography. 49: *inset* Breck P. Kent Photography; *l.* Breck P. Kent Photography; *r.* E.R. Degginger/Color-Pic, Inc. 52: *l.* © Guy Gilette/Photo Researchers, Inc.; *m.* E.R. Degginger/Color-Pic, Inc.; *r.* E.R. Degginger/Color-Pic, Inc. 52–53: Steven Frame/Stock Boston. 54: Reagan Bradshaw/The Image Bank. 55: *t.* Brick Institute of America; *m.* Brick Institute of America; *b.* Brick Institute of America. 56: Grant Huntington for HMCo. 57: Grant Huntington for HMCo. 58: *l.* Breck P. Kent Photography; *r.* Breck P. Kent Photography. 59: *l.* Breck P. Kent Photography; *r.* Breck P. Kent Photography. 62: James Watt/Animals Animals/Earth Scenes. 64: Courtesy, Rufus Catchings. 64–65: *bkgd.* Robert Frerck/Tony Stone Images; *b.* Angie Williams/U.S. Geological Survey. 72: Grant Huntington for HMCo. 73: Grant Huntington for HMCo. 74: *l.* The Granger Collection, New York; *r.* The Natural History Museum, London. 76: Breck P. Kent Photography. 77: Tom Bean/The Stock Market. 78: Grant Huntington for HMCo. 78–79: Grant Huntington for HMCo. 80: *l.* Grant Huntington for HMCo.; *r.* Grant Huntington for HMCo. 81: © Bill Bachman/Photo Researchers, Inc. 82: Grant Huntington for HMCo. 83: Michael P. Gadomski/Bruce Coleman Incorporated. 85: *t.* Lee Foster/Bruce Coleman Incorporated; *b.* Jewel Cave National Monument/US Department of the Interior, National Park Service. 86: Grant Huntington for HMCo. 87: Grant Huntington for HMCo. 88: Trevor Wood/The Image Bank. 89: Tom & Susan Bean, Inc. 90: Myrleen Ferguson Cate/PhotoEdit. 91: Paul X. Scott/Sygma Photo News. 92: Alan Pitcairn/Grant Heilman Photography, Inc.

Unit F 1: © Tom Myers/Photo Researchers, Inc. 2–3: © Tom Myers/Photo Researchers, Inc. 4: Courtesy, Richard Green/Wildfire, Inc. 4–5: *bkgd.* Dan McCoy/Rainbow; *inset* Ian Howarth. 5: Ian Howarth. 9: *l.* Paul Silverman/Fundamental Photographs; *r.* Richard Megna/Fundamental Photographs. 10: *t.* Bob Krist/Tony Stone Images. 11: *l.* Richard Megna/Fundamental Photographs; *m.* Robert Campbell; *r.* J. Pickerell/The Image Works Incorporated. 13: *t.* Stock Montage, Inc.; *b.* Culver Pictures, Inc. 16: Ebet Roberts. 17: James H. Karales/Peter Arnold, Inc. 22: *t.* Richard Hutchings. 23: *l.* Alan Oddie/PhotoEdit; *r.* David Phillips for HMCo. 24: H.R. Bramaz/Peter Arnold, Inc. 26: John M. Dunay/Fundamental Photographs. 34: *l.* Richard Megna/Fundamental Photographs; *r.* Richard Megna/Fundamental Photographs. 38: *l.* Art Resource, NY; *r.* © Dr. Jeremy Burgess/Science Photo Library/Photo Researchers, Inc. 39: *l.* Corbis Corporation; *r.* Corbis Corporation. 40: *l.* FPG International; *r.* William E. Sauro/NYT Pictures. 41: *l.* Image Select; *r.* Image Select. 42: *t.l.* © Dr. Jeremy Burgess/Science Photo Library/Photo Researchers, Inc.; *t.r.* © Cecil Fox/Science Photo Library/Photo Researchers, Inc. 43: *l.* CNRI/Science Photo Library/Custom Medical Stock Photo, Inc.; *r.* Stanley Flegler/Visuals Unlimited. 48: *t.* Diane Schiumo/Fundamental Photographs; *b.* Comstock. 50–51: *bkgd.* Paul Warchol/Sonic Architecture, Bill & Mary Buchen; *inset* Paul Warchol/Sonic Architecture, Bill & Mary Buchen. 55: *l.* Comstock; *r.* James Darell/Tony Stone Images. 57: *l.* Comstock; *r.* Comstock. 60: Stephen Green/Focus On Sports. 64: *r.* S.R.H. Spicer/The Shrine to Music Museum University of South Dakota. 65: *b.l.* S.R.H. Spicer/The Shrine to Music Museum University of South Dakota; *b.r.* S.R.H. Spicer/The Shrine to Music Museum University of South Dakota; *r.* Richard Hutchings. 70: Spencer Grant/Stock Boston. 72: Philips Hearing Instruments. 72–73: *bkgd.* F. Scott Schafer, Photographer; *inset* Philips Hearing Instruments. 78: *t.* Ebet Roberts. 79: *l.* Jeffrey Aaronson/Network Aspen; *r.* Mary Kate Denny/PhotoEdit. 84: Corbis Corporation. 85: *r.* Visuals Unlimited. 88: *t.* Corbis Corporation; *b.* Brown Brothers. 91: Phil Jason/Tony Stone Images.

Science and Math Toolbox 2: *r.* Grant Huntington for HMCo

Glossary 24: S. Nielsen/Imagery. 27: Doug Sokell/Tom Stack & Associates. 30: MGA/Photri, Inc. 32: © Guy Gilette/Photo Researchers, Inc. 34: E.R. Degginger/Color-Pic, Inc. 35: *b.* © James Holmes/Photo Researchers, Inc. 36: USGS, Flagstaff, Arizona/Corbis Corporation.